INSTRUCTIONS & WARNINGS
THE ANNOTATED BIBLIOGRAPHY

INSTRUCTIONS & WARNINGS
THE ANNOTATED BIBLIOGRAPHY

James M. Miller
University of Michigan

Mark R. Lehto
Purdue University

J. Paul Frantz
University of Michigan

Fuller Technical Publications
Ann Arbor, Michigan

Author Contacts:
James M. Miller, P.E., Ph.D.
J. Paul Frantz
Department of Industrial and Operations Engineering
University of Michigan
Box 7995
Ann Arbor, Michigan 48107
(313) 665-1293

Mark R. Lehto, Ph.D.
School of Industrial Engineering
Purdue University
West Lafayette, Indiana 47907
(317) 494-5428

Distribution:
Fuller Technical Publications
2392 Fuller Road
Ann Arbor, Michigan 48105
(313) 662-9953

Other Relevant Publications:
Warnings: Volume I: Fundamentals, Design, and Evaluation Methodologies
Warnings: Volume II: Annotated Bibliography with Topical Index
Instructions and Warnings: Electronic Hypertext Version

Library of Congress Cataloging-in-Publication Data

Miller, James M., 1940-
    Instructions and warnings.

    1. Risk communication—Bibliography.   2. Signs and symbols—Bibliography.   I. Lehto, Mark R., 1956-
II. Frantz, J. P. 1966-   . III. Title.
Z7914.R6M54   1990   [T10.68]   016.3631'072   89-23362
ISBN 0-940537-06-0Fuller Technical Publications, Ann Arbor, Michigan 48105

© 1990 by Fuller Technical Publications
All rights reserved.
Printed in the United States of America
First Printing: February 1990

Contents

Preface vii

PART I. Annotated Bibliography
    Annotations 001-100.. 3
    Annotations 101-200.. 49
    Annotations 201-300.. 91
    Annotations 301-400.. 141
    Annotations 401-500.. 185
    Annotations 501-577.. 247

PART II. Topical Index
    Communication Theory.. 295
    Education/Persuasive Programs.. 295
    Information Theory.. 296
    Instructions... 296
    Labeling and Safety Signage Systems... 298
    Litigation: Warning Related.. 300
    Posters... 302
    Product Information and Warnings.. 302
    Risk Perception.. 302
    Symbol/Message Descriptions... 302
    Symbol/Message Design.. 304
    Symbol/Message Evaluation... 305
    Visual Displays... 312
    Warning Labels.. 312
    Warning Systems... 313

PART III. Author Index.. 317

PART IV. References by Year
    1940-1969... 331
    1970-1974... 332
    1975-1979... 337
    1980... 347
    1981... 350
    1982... 352
    1983... 355
    1984... 356
    1985... 361
    1986... 362
    1987... 364
    1988... 367
    1989... 369

PART V. Key Word Index.. 373

Appendix A: Additional 1989 References from the 33rd Annual Meeting of
    The Human Factors Society... 389

Appendix B: Table of Contents, *Warnings: Volume I: Fundamentals, Design, and
    Evaluation Methodologies* by Mark R. Lehto and James M. Miller.................. 393

Preface

This is the third volume in our safety ergonomics series which addresses the area of warnings, labeling and instructions. Our earlier books, now in their third printing, are *Warnings: Volume I (Fundamentals, Design, and Evaluation Methodologies)* and *Warnings: Volume II (Annotated Bibliography with Topical Index)*. It appears that these works have contributed to the advancement of this field. *Volume I* remains timely for its objectives of documenting the scientific foundations of the field and proposing the new directions that must be pursued if that state-of-the-art is to be advanced. *Volume II* also appears to have been a useful resource; however, several factors inspired us to supersede it with the current work.

First, the area of labeling and warning design has evolved toward an increased interest in *instructions* and *user manuals*, not only labels and warnings. This is an appropriate progression since a large portion of warnings are actually imbedded within instructions. Recognizing the distinction between "warnings" and "instructions" is a positive step in the field. Authors of instruction and user manuals will now be in a better position to decide what product information should be developed along guidelines appropriate for "instructions" and what product information should follow criteria for "warnings." To suggest, however, that consensus exists at this time for either would be misleading.

Second, there has been a growing concern for how instruction-type documents are designed. This concern is evident in the current effort by the American National Standards Institute (ANSI) to establish guidelines for limited aspects of "user instructions" design. This effort does not come under a traditional standards committee designation at this time but resides within an ANSI Consumer Interest Council (CIC) task force, chaired by Mr. Albert S. Dimcoff. Members of the task force represent several distinguished organizations, including Ford Motor Company, Underwriters Laboratory, Black & Decker, General Electric, and the U.S. Consumer Product Safety Commission. The first draft of the committee's report is entitled "An American National Standards Institute Guideline to Assist Writers of User Instructions," dated September 1988. In the introduction the committee states, "...there has not been a single source document to which writers of user instructions could refer easily when seeking ideas for preparing product user instructions and related documents." Among those documents which the task force did locate and considered to be relevant was *Warnings: Volume II: The Annotated Bibliography*. Within *Volume II* were more than thirty references listed under the Topical Index heading of "Instructions." However, as a result of our experiences with instructions over the past few years, we added to this volume approximately one hundred instruction-related references. We hope that these additional references will assist the ANSI task force in progressing efficiently and that our personal involvement with that committee will likewise be beneficial.

A third factor which motivated this volume arose from the legal environment. Providing a compilation of litigation-oriented warnings references was *not* a primary objective of our 1987 bibliography, *Volume II*. Since the publication of *Volume II*, however, it has come to our attention that a number of our readers have an active interest in such warnings. Knowing this, we have extended our coverage under the Topical Index heading "Litigation: Warning Related" from forty articles in the previous volume to over one hundred in the present.

As a side note, legal practitioners have recently shown more concern for the instructions that accompany products. This trend follows a time when "failure to adequately warn" gained considerable popularity as a legal criterion against which to test a manufacturer's negligence. Litigators are now more willing to go beyond the relatively easy-to-present failure to warn allegations into the more complex allegations based on a "failure to provide adequate instructions." Such allegations address the broader, and probably more safety-relevant, issues of product use.

A final reason for publishing this volume stems from our scholarly roots which lead us to serve those in the research community who wish to build upon previous research in the field. Our colleagues have produced quite a number of warning-related articles over the past few years, evidenced by the number of publications which have become available since *Volume II* was published in 1987.

Table 1. Comparison of Titles By Year (1987 v. 1990 edition)

	Warnings: Vol. II Annotated Bibliography (1987)	*Instructions & Warnings* (1990)
1940 - 1969	25	26
1970 - 1979	214	225
1980	41	47
1981	28	33
1982	26	38
1983	20	27
1984	23	48
1985	9	31
1986	12	37
1987	-	30
1988	-	27
1989	-	8
Total Annotated	398	577

Approximately two hundred references were added to the new volume (see Table 1). Note that numerous additional references were found from those years included in the earlier publication. Some references were found when searching sources that are considered outside of the realm of safety. Other sources became available as a result of advanced database systems. Hence, even though one searches electronic and other bibliographical data bases for information published in a particular year, information will be added for possibly five to ten years. Also, some articles are of limited availability and were discovered only by chance when they were referenced by authors who had access to their distribution. Thus, in spite of our diligent efforts to be exhaustive, there will undoubtedly still be references which we have not yet discovered and which will appear in later editions.

In summary, then, the contents of this new volume reflect the above four factors which motivated it. We believe it to be a thorough treatment of the areas of instructions, instruction manuals, warnings, and labeling. In addition, we believe that the organization of the book, as described below, makes it convenient to locate topics and references.

How To Find References From *Volume II*

Users of *Volume II* have indicated a concern about being able to locate in this new version references of interest from the earlier edition. These references are not lost! They are all included in the present edition, revised if needed and renumbered (unfortunately). To find a "favorite" reference from the earlier edition, one has only to seek it alphabetically by its author.

Organization of this Book

Indexes proven useful from our earlier *Annotated Bibliography* have been carried over into this volume, including the Topical Index (Part II), the Author Index (Part III), and References by Year (Part IV). The present edition adds several new features which should further enhance its usefulness. These include:

1) **Key Word** descriptors, which have been added to every reference;
2) a **Key Word Index** (Part V), which accumulates and organizes all key words into an index appearing at the end of the book; and
3) an **Electronic Hypertext Version,** which has been developed in tandem with the hard copy book, and which is available through separate purchase. This is a self-contained Macintosh-formatted set of discs which has the complete contents of the hard copy book, plus indexing and global search extras. These features are described further following the descriptions of the various parts of the book.

Part I. Annotated Bibliography

As seen in Figure 1, the first section of the book includes the reference number, bibliographical citation, key words, and annotation for each reference. These annotations should be considered only as a partial guide to the types of information available in the original source. If a given annotation is not sufficiently detailed to meet the reader's need, the reader is encouraged to study the cited references in their original form.

Figure 1: Organization and Information Retrieval

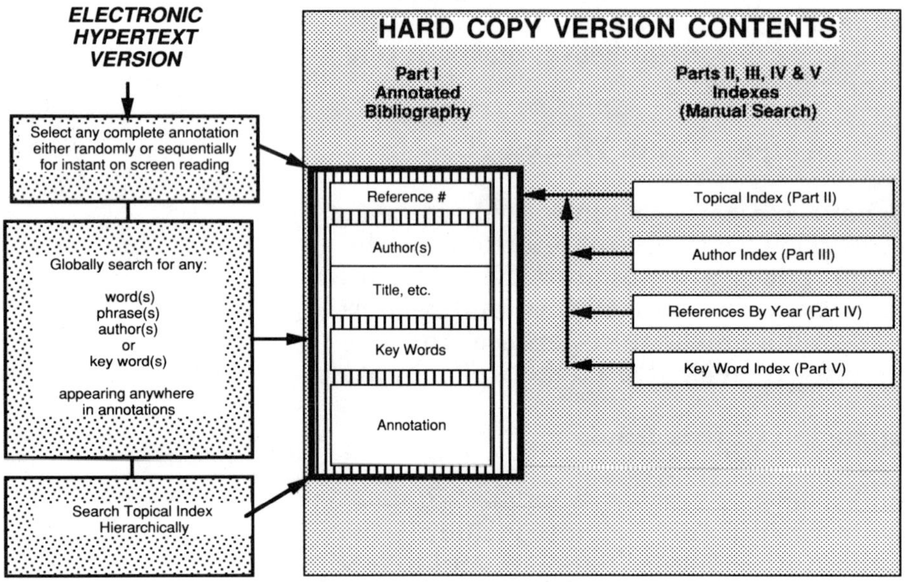

We realize that locating references may be difficult. By way of assistance, we have in our library all of the references annotated in this book. If you are in need of assistance from one of our staff, please use the telephone contact numbers listed on the copyright page.

Part II. Topical Index

The Topical Index is organized in a hierarchy of research topics. These complement the scientific and state-of-the-art treatments we provided in our *Warnings: Volume I: (Fundamentals, Design, and Evaluative Methodologies)*. This index is useful when undertaking research within a general topic area; this research might begin with one of the Topical Index's major headings:

        Communication Theory
        Educational/Persuasive Programs
        Effectiveness
        Information Theory

>   Instructions
>   Labeling and Safety Signage Systems
>   Litigation: Warning Related
>   Product Information and Warnings
>   Symbol/Message Descriptions
>   Symbol/Message Design
>   Symbol/Message Evaluation
>   Visual Displays
>   Warning Labels
>   Warning Systems

These categories have been broken down to an exhaustive level of detail contained in nearly twenty pages of sub-categories. If a given reference is of particular importance to a reader, the reader is encouraged to study that reference in its original form.

Part III. Author Index

This index contains an alphabetical list of primary authors, co-authors, and editors. It provides answers to such questions as, "Was John Smith an author, co-author, or editor for any of the references within this book?" In addition, this index also answers a question that frequently arises in academic and forensic circles: "Who are the individuals with recognized expertise in the area of warnings and instructions?"

Part IV. References by Year

References by Year provides a chronological perspective of warnings and instructions literature. This index identifies the leading titles, publishers, and authors in any given year, and as a whole illustrates the efforts devoted to various research topics over the last fifty years. Distribution of these titles by year was provided in Table 1.

One concern about the use of Part 4 must be mentioned. It has been suggested that one use of such an index might be to determine the date of "availability" of a particular publication. However, the reader is cautioned that the date of publication of a reference is not necessarily synonymous with its "availability" to the practitioner. We make this point because of the tendency within the legal community to place on manufacturers the responsibility of putting into application evolving concepts or findings as soon as such developments are published. However, from the publication date of a reference, it is usually several years before that article or referrals to it appear in locations accessible to the average private industry practitioner. For those practitioners who must rely on a secondary source to learn of such publications (i.e. trade organizations), the first date of availability may be extended by another year. Only the professional researcher or academician has the obvious advantage of discovering such references immediately, since it is the researcher's primary job to be aware of the latest developments in the fields to which he/she contributes. Also, these newer developments are likely to appear first in the less application-oriented publications which are familiar only to the researcher. Even after the original publication of a new development, it may still be several years before there are confirming publications arising from other authors. In total, then, it could be five years for a particular new concept to reach the practicing community and possibly another five years before it is considered to be within the state-of-the-art.

Part V. Key Word Index

The Key Word Index is an alphabetical listing of the key words for all references. This index can be used to locate specific issues of interest and can lead the reader from one reference to others which address similar issues.

Acknowledgements

It was a pleasure in publishing this volume to work with such a talented and dedicated team of people. Dr. Lehto and I gained considerable technical strength with the addition of Paul Frantz as our third author. This is a designation he well deserves for his rapid assimilation of the scientific principles involved and for the significant advancement to the state-of-the-art he has already contributed.

We were also fortunate in having Susan Churinoff agree to be managing editor for this publication and take on the task of trying to satisfy three authors, each of whom added new information or new references almost daily as she frustratingly attempted to finalize, among everything else, the complicated and integrated indexes we insisted on. Susan also was marvelous in collecting and coordinating an excellent staff under her; among them, we particularly thank Christine Deutsch and Angela Carhart.

Our final thanks are extended to our colleagues around the world who have given us the motivation to continue this type of effort by their testimonials as to how useful the material has been to them and to their organizations. They have also helped by continuing to provide us with criticisms as to what in their opinion we have incorrectly included, excluded, or concluded.

James M. Miller

Instructions and Warnings
The Electronic Hypertext Version

A Hypercard electronic version of *Instructions and Warnings* is also available for purchase through Fuller Technical Publications. The program, developed in tandem with this volume, is intended to help both the busy practitioner and the academic researcher as they search through the large list of authors, titles, and annotations found in this volume. The *Instructions and Warnings* hypertext program presents distinct advantages in speed when the goal is to find information on specific topics. Of perhaps even more importance is the ease of browsing between related topics, which quickly assists the reader in becoming knowledgeable on specific subtopics of interest.

The Hypercard version of *Instructions and Warnings* contains everything within the hardcover book—the bibliographical citations, Topical Index, Author Index, Key Word Index and all of the annotations. Several interesting features are added, including unrestricted key word searches and hard copy report generation, complete with automatic bibliographical referencing. The program is entirely menu-driven and easy to use. By selecting a topic in any of the menus, the system user can immediately browse, create a report file, or print all or any part of the references. The program, however, goes far beyond this useful feature. The user can also browse or print any reference within a *related* topic, as well as the annotations for those references. This software program requires a Macintosh computer and Hypercard application. The *Instructions and Warnings* hypertext program was developed by co-author Dr. Mark Lehto, who can be contacted at the address provided on the copyright page for additional technical development details. Since this is a new approach to providing technical information, the following background to its development is provided.

Background—The Hypertext Approach

Growth in the field of warning and instruction-related literature has been explosive. With the increased variety and amount of information available, it has become important to develop a means to filter out the irrelevant and focus on that information of specific interest. Books and well-developed indexes are, of course, the traditional means for accomplishing this goal. Recent advances in computer science, however, have given us some interesting alternatives.

Of particular interest is the emerging technology of hypermedia, first proposed as a means of organizing in readily accessible form all the knowledge of humanity. This ambitious concept has led to the development of several interesting programs which organize complex databases as hypermedia. The central concept of such programs is to allow access in flexible ways to that knowledge in the database which is relevant. Perhaps the easiest way to illustrate this idea is in terms of an electronic book which allows the reader to browse the text in any order he chooses, shifting from general concepts to highly detailed expositions and back again, in a completely flexible manner. All related topics are linked together in a network of information which the reader can follow efficiently in non-linear patterns. Examples of such systems include electronic textbooks for physicians, alternative instruction manuals, or help stacks for computer programs.

One hypermedia approach which offers an exciting potential is called "hypertext." The hypertext approach differs from traditional printed books in that it emphasizes the relationship between concepts. Using such a philosophy, hypertext provides a more flexible method of accessing and storing information in contrast to the traditional book, which emphasizes the arrangement of information in a simple linear sequence.

With recent developments in microcomputer hardware and software, the hypertext approach has become a viable option. Apple Computer is committed to this approach to the extent that it now bundles Hypercard, a hypertext program, free of charge with all its Macintosh computers.

Recognizing the strength of this emerging technology and its potential advantages in organizing and making accessible warning and instruction-related knowledge, we chose to provide a Hypercard electronic version of this volume.

PART I
Annotated Bibliography

Annotations 001-100

Key Words:
Color Coding,
Industrial

001
———, "Color Coding Hazards (Compliance Procedure)," *National Safety News,* April 1976, 54-58.

This paper discusses the use of color coding to: 1) signify hazards in general; 2) indicate hazards via color codes on signs and tags; and 3) indicate hazards presented by piping systems. The colors considered are: red, orange, yellow and combinations of yellow and black, green, blue, purple, black, white, and combinations of black and white.

Key Words:
Biohazard,
Caustic Materials,
Explosives,
Industrial,
Poison,
Review Papers

002
———, "How to Make Signs and Labels for Safety... A Guidepost," *National Safety News,* 125:3, March 1982, 43-44.

The FMC Corporation system for designing warning labels is briefly discussed along with other guidelines for label and sign design.

Key Words:
Color Coding,
Electrical Hazard,
FMC, Hazard/Alert,
Industrial, OSHA,
Posted Feedback,
Signal Words

003
———, "Making Warning Signs Effective," *Best's Safety Directory,* 25th Edition, 1985, 1198-1199.

A general introduction to warning signs is provided and reference is made to the Occupational Safety and Health Administration's (OSHA) color code. Also defined are the signal words DANGER, WARNING, and CAUTION.

Key Words:
Control/Display
  Elements,
Fire,
Industrial,
Industrial Safety,
Safety Information,
Slip/Fall

004
———, "Messages for Men in Motion," *National Safety News,* May 1981, 64-67.

It is claimed here that signs, posters, and displays can effectively convey information, as well as change attitudes and behavior. No supporting data is furnished. The low cost of posters and the importance of changing posters and displays are noted. The article furnishes several examples of National Safety Council (NSC) posters.

Key Words:
Caustic Materials,
Duty/Failure to Warn,
Explosives,
Fire

005
———, *National Commission on Product Safety: Final Report,* Government Printing Office, Washington, D.C., June 1970, 63-79.

This historically significant report led in part to the passage of the Consumer Product Safety Act of 1972. It includes an over-

Annotations (001-100)

Key Words (cont.):
Negligence and
 Warnings,
Poison

view of the problem of product safety along with discussions of consumer injuries and refers to instructions and warnings or their absence as a basis for litigation.

Key Words:
Posters

006
———, "Posters, Bulletin Boards and Safety Displays," *National Safety and Health News*, 134:6, December 1986, 35-42.

The author describes the ingredients that go into an effective safety poster which can stimulate and maintain concern for job safety in particular. A good poster must catch the worker's eye and communicate the benefits of safe behavior. The author gives some very unique recommendations including that safety slogans be printed on paper towels, paper cups and other items in daily use.

Key Words:
Food,
Foreseeability

007
———, "Products Liability: Deceptive Packaging," *Association of Trial Lawyers of America Law Reporter*, 30, February 1987, 15-16.

The manufacturer of an adult food supplement may be liable for instructions which fail to warn that the product is dangerous to infants where a retailer mistakenly stocked the item on its baby product shelf. The trial court ruled that because of the "deceptive packaging" and failure to warn, it was reasonably foreseeable that the product might be mistakenly purchased and fed to infants.

Key Words:
Exclusionary Rule,
Post-injury Warning,
Strict Liability and
 Warnings,
Subsequent Remedial
 Measures

008
———, "Products Liability—Problems of Proof," *Association of Trial Lawyers of America Law Reporter*, 27, April 1984, 104-108.

Evidence of subsequent remedial measures in the form of a post-accident warning was held as being properly admitted. In Schelbauer v. Butler Manufacturing, the court followed the modern trend in some states by holding that the exclusionary rule commonly applied to subsequent remedial measures is inapplicable in strict liability actions.

Key Words:
Children,
Design of: educational/
 persuasive programs,
Effectiveness of:
 educational/persuasive
 programs

009
———, "Signs and Symbols, Trail-Blazing Through a Forest of Hazards," in *National Safety News*, June 1974, 102-104.

This paper briefly outlines some of the signing requirements of the Occupational Safety and Health Act in a simplified form. It

Key Words (cont.):
Formal Teaching/
  Counseling/Education,
Smokers

references the relevant ANSI (American National Standards Institute) standards from which OSHA standards were either derived or to which these standards refer.

Key Words:
ANSI, Biohazard,
Fire, Hazard/Alert,
Industrial,
Industrial Safety,
Introducing New
  Systems,
Moving Vehicle,
Point of Operation
  Guarding,
Radiation, Routing,
Safety Information,
Slip/Fall

010
———, "Warning: Signs are Changing," *National Safety News*, March 1978, 113-114.

ANSI standards for warning signs are briefly discussed in this two page article.

Key Words:
Posters

011
———, "What Makes an Effective Safety Poster?" *National Safety and Health News*, 134:6, December 1986, 32-34.

This article is based on a meeting of international experts held in Belgium in the spring of 1986 to discuss what makes an effective safety poster. They agreed that the message on a poster should be simple and specific. They also agreed that a message should prescribe safe behavior rather than proscribe negative (prohibited) behavior.

Key Words:
Color of Stimulus,
Drivers,
Recognition Time,
Redundancy,
Symbol Legend,
Symbol Shape,
Traffic,
Traffic Settings,
Visual Noise

012
Adams, A.S. and Hsu L., "The Coding of Symbol Signs," *Hazard Prevention*, March/April 1981, 5-7.

The relative importance of color, shape, and legend coding, as they influence recognition time, was evaluated using four common South Wales traffic signs. Four variants of each sign type (STOP, NO ENTRY, GIVE WAY, CROSSING) were presented to subjects for a period of 25 ms. against a distracting background. The standard sign in each sign category was tested against variations of that standard sign. These variants were: one with modified color; one with modified shape; and one with modified legend.

It was found that color changes were most frequently noticed (17.8% to 79.3%), followed by shape changes (10.6% to 57.8%), with legend changes being least noticed (0.0% to 19.4%). A study by Jones (1978) is cited, and the conclusion is drawn that

Annotations (001-100)

color coding may be good for attracting initial attention from experienced drivers, but has little effect when unlimited viewing time is available. The usefulness of redundancy when quick communication is required is also cited. However, the authors fail to mention the important point that multidimensional, rather than unidimensional, redundancy is being referred to here.

Key Words:
Auditory,
Auditory Coding,
Auditory Noise,
Industrial,
Industrial Setting,
Noise,
Reaction Time,
Workers

013
Adams, S.K. and Trucks, L.B., "A Procedure for Evaluating Auditory Warning Signals," *Proceedings of the Human Factors Society - 20th Annual Meeting*, Human Factors Society, Santa Monica, CA, 1976, 166-172.

This document discusses the potential problem caused when industrial noise masks auditory signals. The causes are: 1) the wide diversity of natural industrial sounds as measured in terms of frequency and amplitude; and 2) the limited choices for selecting the auditory characteristics of desired signals.

Eight types of signals were tested: wail (conventional siren); yelp (rapid siren); Hi-Lo (alternating highs and lows); whoop (ascending low to high repeated); yeow (descending high to low repeated); horn (steady horn); beep (60 cycles/min horn); and stutter (140 cycles/min horn). The reaction time of subjects to each of these signals while performing a simulated task with simulated industrial noise was evaluated. Significantly different reaction times were obtained for the different pairings of signals and simulated industrial noise. A methodology for selecting the best signal for a given environment is provided, with the intent being that its use would minimize signal masking.

Key Words:
Biohazard,
Caustic Materials,
DOT,
Explosives,
Hazardous Materials,
Motor Vehicle,
Poison,
Radiation

014
Alff, T.R., "Symbols for Materials Handling," *National Safety News*, July 1974, 76-77.

Some of the Department of Transportation's (DOT) labeling requirements for hazardous materials during transportation are summarized. Particular emphasis is placed on the use of nonverbal symbols.

Key Words:
Drivers,
Separation Between Symbols,
Traffic,
Traffic Settings

015
Anderton, P.J. and Cole, B.L., "Contour Separation and Sign Legibility," *Australian Road Research*, 12:2, June 1982, 103-109.

This article reports on a previous study which showed that a narrow spacing between characters slightly reduced legibility, especially for white characters on a black background. It also investigates the extent to which contours surrounding characters reduce legibility. Three versions of a metric speed regulatory sign (a ring surrounding numbers) were studied: the standard sign; a sign for which the width of the standard ring was increased 1.5 times; and a sign with the ring width narrowed to one-half of the standard ring width. Results indicated that the wide ring obviously reduces digit legibility, whereas the narrow ring has no significant effect.

Key Words:
Drugs,
Duty/Failure to Warn,
Learned Intermediary Rule,
Unavoidably Unsafe Product

016
Ashman, A., "Manufacturer of Dangerous Drug Need Not Warn Consumer," *American Bar Association Journal*, **70, August 1984, 145.**

The Supreme Court of Alabama has held that in order to avoid strict liability, the manufacturer of an unavoidably dangerous drug must warn only physicians, not ultimate consumers, of dangers. As a medical expert, familiar with both the drug and the particular patient, a prescribing physician is then expected to act as a "learned intermediary" between the manufacturer and the consumer.

Key Words:
Color of Stimulus,
Drivers,
Reaction Time,
Slow Moving Vehicle,
Traffic,
Traffic Settings

017
Asper, O., "The Detectability of Two Slow Vehicle Warning Devices," *Journal of Safety Research*, **4:2, June 1972, 85-89.**

This study compares the detectability of two slow moving vehicle warning devices now used in the United States: the red flag and the Slow Moving Vehicle (SMV) emblem (a fluorescent yellow-orange triangle, 14" x 16", with a red reflective border).

This study was motivated by two previous studies which indicated that the red flag was not as easily identified as the SMV emblem. Variables considered included sex, age, and place of residence (rural or urban). The subjects were recruited from a shopping center in Bloomington, Illinois. They each viewed five different scenes in a videotape simulation.

Significant differences in reaction time were found between the two slow moving vehicle warning devices. The mean time in which the SMV emblem was detected was 3.703 seconds less than for the red flag. If a vehicle was traveling at 50 mph, this 3.703 seconds corresponds to approximately 270 feet of additional warning distance. It is noted that the study did not collect and correlate its findings with similar data from the actual road environment.

Key Words:
Conveying Procedures,
Describing Objects,
Design of: instructions,
Development Cycle,
Information Coding,
Ordering of
  Conditions/Actions,
Population Stereotypes,
Prior Knowledge,
Task Analysis,
Understanding of
  Instructions,
User Modeling

018
Baggett, P. and Ehrenfeucht, A., "Conceptualizing in Assembly Tasks," *Human Factors*, 30:3, June 1988, 269-284.

This paper presents an academic approach to describing how people conceptualize complex objects in terms of assemblies and sub-assemblies. The approach is particularly useful as it provides a method for going from an abstract representation of a product in terms of connected components to a best choice procedure for describing how to assemble the product. The paper also presents a method for describing how people conceptualize a product. from the sequences in which they ask for particular parts while assembling it. From these descriptions of peoples' innate conceptualization of the object, it is then possible to develop inferences as to the best procedural description of the assembly.

To explore their theories the authors conducted a series of three experiments. These were directed toward evaluating conceptualizations that different subjects have of a product. Also evaluated was the efficiency of presenting instructions to subjects that either corresponded to natural conceptualizations or to minority conceptualizations. The studies revealed that the conceptualizations of a majority of subjects were highly similar. In fact, 70% of all the conceptualizations were minor variants of one another. The results also indicated that assembly instructions based on a majority conceptualization resulted in better performance than instructions based on a minority conceptualization.

The authors conclude that: 1) they have developed a method for describing a set of instructions based upon its conceptualization by particular subjects; 2) their technique provides a method for describing how people will conceptualize objects; and 3) their technique is useful for determining whether an object has a natural conceptualization. They held their results to support the theory that by applying their methodology, one can determine how assembly instructions should be designed in accordance with natural conceptualization.

In reviewing these results and conclusions, we find them particularly interesting. They support the feasibility of developing a practical methodology for matching instructions to the ways in which people actually conceptualize products. The approach holds the further advantage of being on a firm methodological grounding by making use of data collected from human subjects who, in fact, may be the same people ultimately using the product. This is somewhat novel to the present state of the art where assembly instructions are developed by the same technicians or engineers who designed the product.

Key Words:
Design of: instructions,
Illustrations,
Readability Measures,
Translation of
 Instructions,
Writing Instructions

019
Bailey, R.W., "Chapter 19: Printed Instructions," in *Human Performance Engineering: A Guide for System Designers*, Prentice-Hall, Inc., Englewood Cliffs, 1982, 403-445.

Bailey notes that no matter how well the software or hardware in a system is designed to be friendly, people still may have difficulty efficiently using it without clear, accurate, and complete instructions. To avoid such problems, Bailey notes the importance of: 1) determining the exact information needed for an acceptable performance; 2) determining the best way to store information until it is needed; 3) devising methods of presenting information effectively; and 4) writing for a specific audience.

Also included in Bailey's chapter are discussions on: presenting instructions; formatting procedural instructions; translating foreign instructions; computer-based documentation; and readability measures. We strongly recommend this chapter to those who design instructions and operator manuals for computer software/hardware and for consumer products.

Key Words:
Data Processing Setting,
Separation Between
 Symbols

020
Barnard, P., Wright, P. and Wilcox, P., "The Effects of Spatial Constraints on the Legibility of Handwritten Alphanumeric Codes," *Ergonomics*, 21:1, 1978, 73-78.

Writing legibility on different types of forms is evaluated. The authors conclude that alphanumeric characters are easier to read on forms which have arrays of blank lines than on forms where each character is inserted into a separate box.

Key Words:
Absolute Liability

021
Barry, D.T. and DeVivo, E.C., "The Evolution of Warnings: The Liberal Trend Toward Absolute Product Liability," *The Forum*, 20, 1984-1985, 38-58.

The authors express their concern that the trend toward absolute product liability threatens to eliminate the manufacturer's incentive to invest time and money into product safety because under this doctrine liability is virtually certain no matter what the manufacturer does. The authors believe that the manufacturer, rather than the courts, is in the best position to know a particular product and to market it in the safest manner.

Annotations (001-100)

Key Words:
ANSI,
Duty/Failure to Warn,
FMC,
Instructions in Litigation

022

Bass, L. and Rennert, L., "Chapter 10: Warnings," in *Products Liability: Design and Manufacturing Defects*, Shepard's/McGraw-Hill, Colorado Springs, 1986, 190-222.

This paper provides a general description of warning labels, making use of information found in the FMC Product Safety Sign and Label System, the Westinghouse Product Safety Label Handbook and the ANSI Draft Standard Z535.4: Product Safety Signs. The description is at a level which could be applied by designers, although not at the level of detail of the original sources. The authors also provide a brief introduction to instructions. This includes the duty to provide "adequate" instructions and the use of warnings on the product that refer to information found in the instruction manual. The approach taken is based primarily on presumed legal requirements. The authors occasionally reference the "Human Factors" literature in their discussion.

Key Words:
Duty/Failure to Warn

023

Bates, P., "The Manufacturer's Liability for Failing to Warn of Defective Products," *Advocate's Quarterly*, 5, July 1984, 253-256.

The courts have recognized that there is a duty for a manufacturer to know its own product, keep up to date with technological information affecting it and be aware of any dangers in its use. If the manufacturer learns of defects or dangers associated with its product, it must warn both past and present purchasers of those dangers. In a recent case, the trial court extended the obligations of the manufacturer beyond the duty merely to provide a warning. The manufacturer must also apply its resources and expertise to determine the most effective remedial measures to reduce the hazards inherent to its product, whether by redesign or product instructions.

Key Words:
ANSI,
Application Guidelines,
Design of: instructions,
Development Cycle,
Duty/Failure to Warn,
Instructions in Litigation,
Loss Prevention
  Programs,
Warranties/Disclaimers

024

Bedford, M.S. and Stearns, F.C., "The Technical Writer's Responsibility for Safety," *IEEE Transactions on Professional Communication*, 30:3, September 1987, 127-132.

This article provides a general introduction for technical writers who compose or edit safety information. It is written at a general level, but still provides descriptions of some of the fundamental legal requirements including definitions of a defect, the duty to warn, and the sufficiency of warnings. It provides an introduction to some of the requirements found in safety standards such as the ANSI Z534 series. A brief discussion is given regarding the role of warranties and disclaimers and the need for retaining a library of the information provided to consumers. Finally, the article describes the use of warning signs or warning labels within instructions.

Key Words:
Actual Behavior,
Behavior Factors,
Children,
Design of:
  educational/persuasive programs,
Discrepancy Between
  Self-Reports,
Evaluation Difficulties,
Memory of:
  symbol/message,
Recall,
Recognition,
Traffic

025
Belbin, E., "The Effects of Propaganda on Recall, Recognition and Behaviour: I. The Relationship Between the Different Measures of Propaganda Effectiveness," *British Journal of Psychology,* **47:3, August 1956, 163-174.**

Two experiments designed to evaluate the influence of safety propaganda on safety-related behavior are summarized. The hypothesis in the first experiment was that verbalized behavior given in one social context is not necessarily an accurate predictor of behavior in other contexts; more specifically, tests of recall and recognition might not accurately predict behavioral responses.

The first experiment evaluated the influence of various types of propaganda on children's road crossing behavior. This propaganda included film slides, discussions by a police sergeant, and a cartoon slide. The major finding was that children were able to remember and recall the information, but did not necessarily behave in conformance with it.

In the second experiment, a large group of subjects performed a psychomotor task at either a high or low speed. While past experience suggested that it would be easier to get high scores at a low speed, the propaganda, displayed close to the task, stated that better performance would occur at a high speed. One group of subjects received the propaganda after they had learned to perform the task, while the other received the propaganda throughout the learning period. The experimental measures included the attention that the subjects gave to the displays, the actual behavior (high or low speed), the ability to recall the propaganda on the display, and the ability to explain what the propaganda meant.

The results showed that of the eighteen subjects who originally chose a slow speed, four changed to a fast speed after seeing the propaganda. For the subjects who received the propaganda while learning, two out of seven subjects changed from the slow to the fast rate; three out of seventeen subjects, who received propaganda after learning the task, changed their behavior. Additional analysis showed that there was no relation between attention and the ability to recall the propaganda.

Annotations (001-100)

Key Words:
Actual Behavior,
Behavior Factors,
Drivers,
Evaluation Difficulties,
Forgetting Rate,
Memory of:
  symbol/message,
Message Tone,
Prior Knowledge,
Recall,
Recognition,
Traffic

026
Belbin, E., "The Effects of Propaganda on Recall, Recognition and Behaviour: II. The Conditions Which Determine the Response to Propaganda," *British Journal of Psychology*, **47:4, 1956, 259-270.**

The effects of four types of safety propaganda were tested: pictorial, horror, verbal positive and verbal negative. Subjects were exposed to safety posters as they sat in a waiting room for approximately three minutes. The subjects' ability to locate traffic hazards from photographs similar to those depicted on the posters was then evaluated, and a *Use* score resulted from this analysis. The impact of the propaganda was also measured by the amount of information contained in the posters which could be recalled by the subjects. For control purposes, the posters included a list of photographs which were not related to traffic safety.

The results showed that each type of propaganda had a significant effect on *Use* scores, but there were no differences in effect among the different types of propaganda on either *Use* scores or *Recall* scores. The influence of the posters on *Use* scores was much greater for subjects with driving experience than for those with no driving experience. However, the ability to recall the information was not influenced by driving experience. Also, the older subjects were worse at recalling the propaganda, but had slightly higher mean *Use* scores. The observed decay in *Use* and *Recall* scores as a function of time was also of interest. In particular, scores were evaluated for different groups of subjects, from 0 to 14 days after they were exposed to the posters. Interestingly, *Use* scores dropped at a much slower pace than *Recall* scores. For both *Use* and *Recall* scores, after roughly 1 or 2 days, performance quickly became asymptotic at a low level not greatly different from that of the control group.

To conclude, the results indicate that propaganda is more likely to influence behavior if the individual already has learned the appropriate behavior. Such effects possibly occurred in this experiment, since experienced drivers should have been more capable of relating some of the traffic posters to actual photographs of traffic situations than non-drivers.

Key Words:
Agreement with
  Symbol/Message,
Application Guidelines,
Consumer Surveys,
Consumers

027
Beltramini, R.F., "Perceived Believability of Warning Label Information Presented in Cigarette Advertising," *Journal of Advertising*, **17:1, 1988, 26-32.**

Using young adults as subjects, this study evaluated four new cigarette warning labels developed in 1984 by the Federal

Key Words (cont.):
Existing/Past Behavior Patterns,
Influences of Warning Labels,
Labels,
Perceived Risk,
Prior Knowledge,
Risk Taking,
Smokers,
Smoking,
Smoking Education Act,
Students

Trade Commission which provided more specific information than previous warnings. In justifying this study, the author notes that earlier research on consumer response to product information has yielded mixed results and that many factors related to presentation format can influence consumer response to warning label information.

Reactions to the four recently mandated warning labels and the traditional label were evaluated in a questionnaire administered to two large sections of a class of university business students. The average respondent was 23 years old and 55% were male. Three hypotheses were evaluated; the first of which was that no differences would be found in the perceived believability of the five warning labels, (the four new warning labels and the more traditional label). The second hypothesis was that there would be no differences in the perceived believability of any of the five warning labels as a function of how strongly people felt that cigarette smoking is hazardous to their health. The third hypothesis was that no significant differences would be found in the perceived believability of the five warning labels among smokers versus non-smokers.

The results showed that the perceived believability of the label was somewhat higher when the label described the consequences of smoking rather than simply listing the components of cigarette smoke. It was also found that people who held a strong belief prior to seeing the labels that smoking was hazardous to their health were more likely to perceive the warning information as believable. A third result was that the believability of the labels was no different between smokers and non-smokers. These results suggest that the strength of initial attitudes toward the particular danger warned against has significant influence on the believability of the information which will be presented in a warning label.

028
Berry, E., "How to Get Users to Follow Procedures," in *IEEE Transactions on Professional Communication*, 25:1, March 1982, 22-25.

Key Words:
Amount of Information,
Conveying Procedures,
Design of: instructions,
Prior Knowledge,
Problems in Design,
Understanding of Instructions

The author lists three basic criteria for getting users to follow written procedures: 1) use a format that is appropriate for the procedure; 2) do not assume knowledge that the user does not have; and 3) be "fair" to the user. The author notes that the appropriate format varies with the nature of the procedure being conveyed. The following nine categories of procedure formats are discussed: narrative, step-by-step list, step-by-step list with visual aids, playscript, question list, flowchart, narrative flowchart, decision logic table, and decision tree. The author notes that descriptions of procedures often erroneously assume user knowledge. This can happen because the writers of such material have been following the procedure for a long time or are the same persons who designed the equipment or the system. Finally, the author feels that many procedures fail because they are not "fair" to the user; that is, they are not written with the user's viewpoint and convenience in mind. Suggestions to remedy this are provided.

Key Words:
Agencies,
Amount of Information,
Buying Behavior,
Consumer Labeling and Signage Systems,
Consumers,
Design of: educational/ persuasive programs,
Design of: labeling and safety signage systems,
FDA,
Information Overload,
Introducing New Systems,
Labels,
Radio/TV,
Review Papers

029
Bettman, J.R., "Issues in Designing Consumer Information Environments," *Journal of Consumer Research*, 2, December 1975, 169-177.

The author analyzes a proposal for the provision of nutritional information by the Federal Trade Commission. In doing so, focus is placed on research in human information processing that addresses attention, memory functioning and parameters, and processing of alternatives. Implications for the design of consumer information environments are derived from this effort.

Key Words:
Amount of Information,
Describing Objects,
Design of: instructions,
Information Overload,
Reading of: instructions,
Tables and Flowcharts

030
Bettman, J.R. and Kakkar, P., "Effects of Information Presentation Format on Consumer Information Acquisition Strategies," *Journal of Consumer Research*, 3, March 1977, 233-240.

This article examined the influence of information presentation format on: the way consumers acquired information; the amount of information acquired; and how much time was spent on particular forms of information. The study consisted of displaying particular brands of breakfast cereal and various attributes of these breakfast cereals. The results showed that the format in which information was provided had a large influence on the types of information which were evaluated by consumers. The authors conclude that in presenting information to consumers, focus should be placed not only on the content and quality of the information made available, but also on the format in which the information is structured and presented, since consumers tend to process information in the form in which it is given.

Key Words:
Amount of Information,
Design of: instructions,
Information Overload,
Prior Knowledge,
Tables and Flowcharts

031
Bettman, J.R. and Park, C.W., "Effects of Prior Knowledge and Experience and Phase of the Choice Process on Consumer Decision Processes: A Protocol Analysis," *Journal of Consumer Research*, 7, December 1980, 234-248.

Ninety-nine housewives in a mid-western college community were randomly selected from the telephone directory. Subjects were classified into the categories of low, moderate or high prior knowledge and experience in the use of microwave ovens. They were then asked to select a microwave oven based upon the information contained in a matrix describing nine attributes of fifteen brands of microwave ovens. The primary finding was that the group with a moderate level of knowledge and experience appeared to use more of the provided information and rely less on prior knowledge than did either the high or the low groups. The authors conclude that subjects in the low prior knowledge group may not have possessed the cognitive ability to utilize the information that was provided to them. On the other hand, the group with high knowledge had the ability, but not necessarily the motivation, to utilize as much of the provided information.

Key Words:
Design of: instructions,
Design of: labeling and safety signage systems,
Organizing Information,
Tables and Flowcharts

032
Bettman, J.R., Payne, J.W. and Staelin, R., "Cognitive Considerations in Designing Effective Labels for Presenting Risk Information," *Journal of Public Policy & Marketing*, 5, 1986, 1-28.

The authors provide a brief review of human information processing principles and from this review develop a set of general guidelines for designing instructional labels which include risk information.

They begin their review by discussing some of the limitations people have in thinking about risk. They note problems in risk perception and the difficulty people may have when making choices between risky options which could lead to either a gain or a loss. They also discuss the role of human memory and some of the implications of consumer information processing limitations. In particular they distinguish between the availability versus the processability of information, where processability refers to the ease with which information can be both comprehended and used. They note that instructional information should be formatted and organized so as to reduce the cognitive effort and time needed to locate and process the relevant information.

From their review the authors developed several general guidelines for designing effective instructional labels. The guidelines, if applied, could assist users in efficiently locating and encoding the needed information. These guidelines are: 1) make important information more salient by the choice of color and or type size; 2) use a common organization for information on all labels; 3) design this common organization hierarchically to be compatible with the scheme used by most consumers to store information about the product; 4) use symbols which quickly convey the concept when possible; 5) collect information on benefits in one place on the label; 6) collect information on risks in one place on the label; 7) organize the label so that the descriptions on the risks and benefits are in close proximity; 8) provide information in a relative or comparative format; and 9) consider in-store comparative point of sale lists in addition to the information appearing only on the labels.

The authors conclude that no one mode of information presentation is effective for all types of consumer product knowledge acquisition. The authors then provide an example of a labeling system for products containing toxic chemicals in which they describe the interplay between the various modes of providing product information to consumers. In particular they address advertisements, in-store displays, package labels, package inserts and general consumer education programs. They note that each of these modes is best suited to provide certain types of information but may be ill-suited to others. For example, ads can be effective in conveying general moods and settings, but they are probably not as effective in providing hazard information as are point of purchase displays, labels, or instructional package inserts which are available at time of purchase or use. The authors note that point of purchase displays have been shown to have a strong influence on purchase behavior in situations where comparative product information has value. They recommend that retailers post lists that provide relative hazard levels for all brands that could be used for a particular application. The authors also suggest that labels should be organized to facilitate the processing of needed information. To best attain this objective, they recommend that labels should be designed hierarchically. Along these lines the authors provide a general format for label design. They note that instructional package inserts can be used to provide additional detailed information at the point of usage. They hypothesize that a preferred function of the package insert may be to provide instructional details on how to best gain the benefits of the product while the label information might better provide instructions on how to avoid the risks associated with improper use.

Key Words:
Human Factors

033
Bliss, W.D., "Defective Product Design—Role of Human Factors," *Lawyers Cooperative Publication,* **18 POF 2d, 1979, 117-147.**

The role and use of human factors experts is discussed from an attorney's viewpoint. Particularly important is the interrogation of the expert to discover his qualifications and education. The paper also discusses the importance of task analysis and places emphasis on human behavior.

Key Words:
Agencies,
Consumers,
Effectiveness of:
  educational/persuasive
  programs

034
Bloom, P.N., "How Will Consumer Education Affect Consumer Behavior?" *Proceedings of the Association for Consumer Research - 6th Annual Conference,* **3, 1975, 208-212.**

Bloom notes a rapidly growing interest in consumer education. He briefly summarizes some current consumer education programs associated with federal agencies, such as the Office of Consumer Affairs, the Department of Agriculture, the Consumer Product Safety Commission, and the Federal Trade Commission. He notes that state governments and business firms are getting involved, as are private, non-profit organizations, such as the Consumers Union, the Council of Better Business Bureaus, and the American Council on Consumer Interests. Although many programs have been in existence for quite some time, Bloom is concerned that there has not been any research on how they affect consumer behavior. We are particularly sympathetic to this last concern which addresses the ultimate question of whether a particular education program modifies consumer behavior or not.

A number of hypotheses are given concerning the influences consumer education programs may have on behavior. It is suggested that consumers in the future will: 1) express their wants and needs more explicitly; 2) seek out more information; 3) buy fewer products that are potentially harmful to their own health or to the health of others; 4) more actively seek redress or restitution; and 5) become more active in the legislative process.

Key Words:
Consumers,
Design of:
  educational/persuasive
  programs,
Evaluation Difficulties

035
Bloom, P.N. and Ford, G.T., "Evaluation of Consumer Education Programs," *Journal of Consumer Research,* **6, December 1979, 270-279.**

Developing measures of effectiveness, choosing a research design, and interpreting results are cited as problems in evaluating consumer education programs. The measures of effectiveness discussed in this paper are pen and pencil tests, questionnaires, direct observation of behavior, and use of archival data. It is noted that pen and pencil tests are easy to administer, but may lack validity. Questionnaires have a similar problem, which may be reduced by skilled interviewers. Direct observation of behavior is difficult and expensive, while archival data may be difficult to relate to the education program.

With regard to choosing a research design, the authors note that ideal research designs are randomized and allow for the effects of variables to be independently isolated. However, they emphasize that because such studies are difficult to perform, many investigations of consumer research programs are of the weaker but more "do-able" correlational-type design. Regarding the interpretation of results, the authors note that studies which evaluate educational effects are notorious for finding weak results. This means that in the future evaluators will be faced with distinguishing between statistically and practically significant results.

Key Words:
Color of Stimulus,
Laboratory/Generic Settings,
Predictive User Response Equations,
Search Time,
Visual Displays: miscellaneous

036
Bloomfield, J.R., "Visual Search with Embedded Targets: Color and Texture Differences," *Human Factors*, **21:3, 1979, 317-330.**

Visual search time is predicted for targets embedded within displays. For this study, the background was always yellow. On this yellow background it was found that red targets were the easiest to discriminate, followed in descending order by blue, green, tan, and white targets.

Key Words:
Conspicuity,
Consumer Setting,
Consumers,
Luminance,
Noise,
Probability/Frequency of Presentation,
Routing,
Stimulus Size,
Visual Noise

037
Boersema, T. and Zwaga, H.J.G., "Measuring the Conspicuity of Routing Signs in Public Environments," *Proceedings of the Human Factors Society - 28th Annual Meeting*, **Human Factors Society, Santa Monica, CA, 1984, 822-823.**

Boersema and Zwaga define visual conspicuity as the probability that an object will be noticed by an observer, when it is presented at an unknown location in a stimulus field. They state that the static physical properties of objects and environments (size, color, shape and luminance) have been experimentally shown to influence conspicuity. The authors note that the conspicuity of objects is relatively high when they have a low probability of appearing in a certain environment.

The paper presents a brief summary of an experiment which indicated that the conspicuity of routing signs decreased when advertisements were also presented in the same environment.

Key Words:
Accuracy,
Context,
Control/Display
 Elements,
Conveying Action,
Conveying Conditions,
Conveying Procedures,
Illustrations,
Redundancy,
Response Time,
Task Analysis,
Task Specific Context,
Understanding of
 Instructions,
Verbal vs. Nonverbal
 Symbol/Message

038
Booher, H.R., "Relative Comprehensibility of Pictorial Information and Printed Words in Proceduralized Instructions," *Human Factors,* **17:3, 1975, 266-277.**

This article describes ways that context, focus, and action information can be presented via pictures, words, or a combination of pictures and words. As defined here, context refers to the general surrounding and scope of actions; focus refers to the specific objects attended to and acted upon; and action refers to the specific operational steps to be performed.

Tests were conducted for the following three types of tasks: 1) location; 2) comparison; and 3) recognition. It was found that the most efficient initial understanding of procedural information occurs when pictures are used as the primary channel and printed words are used as a secondary, aiding channel to clarify the pictures. In this situation, performance was quite similar for all three types of tasks. Performance when only printed information was given was more accurate but slower than when only pictorial information was given. The pictorial channel was better for presenting static objects and the print channel was better for presenting action information. Redundancy between channels had little effect. Performance speed was aided by the presence of pictures; accuracy was about the same with or without pictures. These findings seem to be applicable to a wide variety of instructions and operator manuals.

Key Words:
Design of: instructions

039
Booher, H.R., "Job Performance Aids: Research and Technology State-of-the-Art," Navy Personnel Research and Development Center, San Diego, NTIS No. AD AO57562, July 1978, 1-86.

The author describes the state-of-the-art in Job Performance Aid technology. This technology is one that has proved useful to the military services in their goal to provide information which facilitates the attainment of desirable levels of performance in complex systems. The paper provides a systematic review of one hundred job performance aid systems and classifies the systems which have been developed into five major categories: 1) format/content; 2) display media; 3) applied training; 4) peripheral test/diagnostic; and 5) delivery systems.

This paper is of interest to developers of instruction manuals in that it provides an overview of a large variety of tested methods for instructing and improving the performance in complex settings of people at diverse ability levels.

Key Words:
Confusion Matrix,
Control/Display
   Elements,
Military,
Radar

040

Bowen, H.M., Andreassi, J.L., Truax, S. and Orlansky, J., "Optimum Symbols for Radar Displays," *Human Factors*, **February 1960, 28-33.**

This study evaluates the confusions among twenty different symbols for radar displays. The results are summarized in a confusion matrix, thereby providing useful information about the combinations of symbols least likely to be confused. Based on this matrix, a table is presented which lists the optimum combinations of from two to ten symbols.

Key Words:
Active Processing,
Information Coding,
Ordering of Conditions/
   Actions,
Prior Knowledge,
Understanding/
   Perception Models,
User Modeling

041

Bower, G.H., Black, J.B. and Turner, T.J., "Scripts in Memory for Text," *Cognitive Psychology*, **11, 1979, 177-220.**

The authors report on a series of six experiments directed toward specifying how people understand and remember narratives. Their work is inspired by Schank and Abelson (1977), who proposed script theory as a method of describing how people organize knowledge within their memory. The basic idea is that people store and retrieve from memory "scripts" containing stereotypical sequences of actions followed during ordinary activities such as entering and ordering food in a restaurant.

The authors found a large degree of conformity in the actions and events subjects described for five different hypothetical situations that the subjects were likely to experience. These included visiting a doctor, attending a lecture, shopping at a grocery store, eating at a restaurant and getting up in the morning and going to school. The authors also found that the memories of subjects were strongly influenced by the types of scripts they seemed to use to organize their memories. For example, subjects were more likely to remember textual information which was strongly implied by a particular script. Subjects preferred to recall script actions in their familiar order and also tended to read text faster when statements in the text corresponded to one step sequences in the underlying script rather than two or three step sequences.

The results of this work imply that, as an early step in the development of instruction manuals, it might be very useful to document the scripts of the subjects likely to use them. It might then be possible to explicitly increase the correspondence between specific instructions and scripts in subject memory. Improved correct use of the information in such manuals could then be expected. However, before this approach may be applied, we must develop a technology for efficiently eliciting scripts.

Key Words:
Design of: labeling and safety signage systems,
Fall,
Industrial,
Kinesthetic/Tactile,
OSHA,
Population Stereotypes,
Slip/Fall

042
Boydstun, L.E., Stobbe, T.J. and Chaffin, D.B., "OSHA Standards: Human Factors Research Needs for Fall Hazard Warning Systems," *Proceedings of the Human Factors Society - 22nd Annual Meeting*, **Human Factors Society, Santa Monica, CA, 1978, 5-11.**

The authors note that there is no available methodology for estimating the effectiveness of fall hazard warning systems either prior to or after installation. A number of factors are considered related to the design of warning systems and a few general models are summarized, including Lawrence's human error model and Surry's stage-type model.

They also summarize material concerning the design of warning systems and describe sign legibility guidelines. A few general principles concerning floor delineators (used to mark fall hazards, walkways, and storage areas) are noted. They point out, however, that no available research evaluates the effectiveness of delineators. The advantages of using temporary ropes and barriers are given, and the authors stress the importance of placing ropes at appropriate heights.

Key Words:
Design of: instructions,
Development Programs,
Illustrations,
Task Analysis,
Understanding of Instructions

043
Boyer, H., " 'Do-It-Yourself' IBM Products and the Role of the Technical Illustrator in Human Factors Testing," *Proceedings of the Symposium: Human Factors and Industrial Design in Consumer Products*, **Poydar, H.R. (Ed.), Tufts University, Medford, 1980, 342-351.**

The author suggests that: 1) illustrators and writers should participate as test subjects for a product which is being assembled or set up; 2) instructions should be written simply and economically; and 3) line drawings rather than photos should be used. A short case history illustrating how these suggestions were put into practice is also described.

Key Words:
Discrepancy Between Self-Reports,
Reading of: warning labels

044
Bozinoff, L., "A Script Theoretic Approach to Information Processing: An Energy Conservation Application," in *Advances in Consumer Research*, **9, Mitchell, A.A. (Ed.), 1981, 481-486.**

In this study the author examines the usefulness of Script Theory to explain why the many attempts to reduce consumers' energy consumption have failed. The author postulates that the act of consuming energy (such as by driving, operating appliances, etc.) has become so routine that it is seldom consciously considered. As a result, the use of energy has become a part of many well established scripts. To advance this proposal an overview of Script Theory is provided. Essentially, a "script is a knowledge structure stored in long term memory which contains a sequential ordering." Examples of common scripts such as going to a restaurant and visiting the dentist are discussed.

In this study, forty-three undergraduates were asked to generate a list of actions (a script) associated with three different situations: getting up in the morning, preparing a Thanksgiving dinner, and spending a day at the office. The subjects were also queried on their attitudes toward energy conservation and ecological issues.

The results showed that subjects were able to generate scripts for all three situations and that there was a reasonably high degree of reliability associated with the specific events mentioned in the scripts. With regards to an individual's attitude concerning energy consumption, the results showed that the extent to which a respondent claimed to be interested in energy conservation did not significantly influence the likelihood that energy related activities would be reported in a script. That is, in general, individuals more concerned with the energy conservation were not more likely to incorporate specific energy related activities in their script reports. An exception, however, occurred with the "day at the office" scenario. In this case, subjects more concerned with energy issues were significantly more likely to specifically report driving their car to work and using an elevator than those less concerned with energy issues.

The author points out that a potential advantage of studying scripts rather than self-reported behaviors is associated with the tendency for subjects to be more inclined to report "socially acceptable" behaviors rather than their actual behavior. Script methods help control this problem by virtue of the fact that the goal of script research is not readily apparent to the respondent. This could be especially important when probing consumers about their safety habits, since they may perceive "safer" behaviors as being more "acceptable" than their actual behavior.

We find that this research methodology has interesting implications for those interested in what consumers do with products or equipment after purchasing an item. For example, the absence of critical precautionary behavior in a consumer's script is obviously of interest to those responsible for warnings, labels, and instructions. If important safety behaviors are not a part of a user's/consumer's script, then methods of introducing such actions into their scripts should be explored. In addition, the impact of pre-purchase information on the development of a consumer's script(s) should be considered during the design of instructional information.

045

Brainard, R.W., Campbell, R.J. and Elkin, E.H., "Design and Interpretability of Road Signs," *Journal of Applied Psychology,* **45:2, 1961, 130-136.**

Key Words:
Abstractness,
Accuracy,
Introducing New Systems,
Learning Nonverbal Symbols,
Motor Vehicle,
Population Stereotypes,
Prior Knowledge,
Production Method,
Students,
Symbol Generation,
Traffic

This five phase study evaluated the interpretability of thirty European road signs. The subjects were psychology students at Ohio State University. In the first phase, the thirty signs were shown to the subjects for thirty seconds; for each sign the subjects wrote down what they thought the meaning should be. In phase 2, the subjects were shown the same thirty signs from phase 1; however, they were given an answer sheet containing potential sign meanings. The subjects chose the one meaning from the list which best matched the sign being shown. In phase 3, the experimenter explicitly told the subjects the meaning of the signs, then the method in phase 1 was repeated. In phase 4, the subjects' task was to draw, within a two minute interval, a sign which they felt would convey a desired meaning. In phase 5, ten signs were made from the drawings of phase 4. Twenty-nine different subjects then evaluated the new signs following the procedure from phase 1.

The results indicated that signs employing pictorial representations, and signs having direct counterparts in existing American signs, were most likely to be recognized. Interestingly, once the subjects were told the meaning of the signs (phase 3 completed), the interpretability increased from 85% to 100%. In phase 1, the signs which received low scores used abstract coding dimensions such as circles or slashes to denote prohibitive actions. The phase 5 results indicated a generally high level of performance for many of the signs generated on the basis of the gathered population stereotypes (phase 4). However, a sizeable percentage of the subjects were unable to identify such signs correctly, demonstrating that the stereotypes were not universal.

046

Bresnahan, T., "The Hazard Association Value of Safety Signs," *Professional Safety,* **30:7, July 1985, 26-31.**

Key Words:
ANSI,
Association Rankings/ Indexes,
Color Coding,
Color/Hazard,
ISO, Industrial
Industrial Safety,
Prohibition,
Safety Information,
Shape Coding,
Shape/Hazard,
Workers

The author examines the proposed International Standards Organization standard for safety signs and colors (Draft Recommendation for Safety Signs and Colors, Technical Committee #80). In doing so, he reviews the classification of signs in the ISO Draft Recommendation; these include the regulatory sign, prohibition sign, cautionary warning sign, and two information signs. Associated with each class of sign are particular features (e.g. geometric form, symbols, color) which are intended to convey particular pieces of information to the viewer.

An experiment was conducted in which the effect of the color, the symbol, and the geometric shape of the signs were evaluated for an industrial population in the United States. It was hypothesized that geometric forms would have significantly different hazard association values which would decrease in the following order: circle with a slash or circle without a slash, triangle, and square or rectangle. The second hypothesis stated that colors have significantly different hazard association values which decrease in the following order: red, yellow, and green.

These hypotheses were not shown to be statistically significant, but some potential trends could be inferred by graphically describing the data. The circle with a slash was somewhat associated with a higher degree of hazard, particularly when it was red rather than black and white. The data also suggest the possibility that different shapes may be associated with different levels of hazard, depending on color. In the black and white scenario, there appeared to be no significant difference in the hazard association value of the different shapes. When color was included as a variable, the red circle alone and the red circle with a slash had a high hazard association value. Of these two the slashed circle had a slightly higher value. Yellow and black triangles were at an intermediate level, while green rectangles were at the lowest level. With regard to the symbols within the signs, the results indicate that higher hazard association values accompany more graphic and definitive symbols.

Based on the results of the experiment, Bresnahan concludes that the ISO provisions cannot be accepted or incorporated into ANSI standards without further research.

047
Bresnahan, T.F. and Bryk, J., "The Hazard Association Values of Accident-Prevention Signs," *Professional Safety*, **January 1975, 17-25.**

The responses to ANSI Z35.1 accident signs by 65 subjects from two plants (food processing and light manufacturing) were evaluated. Six sign types were considered: danger, caution, caution X, safety instruction, safety instruction X, and informational.

It was found that sign type was significantly related to hazard perception. The danger sign type had the highest degree of hazard association, followed in descending order by caution, safety instruction, and informational signs. The colors red and yellow were associated with higher hazard perceptions than green and blue. The signal words associated with danger signs elicited a higher hazard association value than those associated

Key Words:
ANSI,
Association Rankings/ Indexes,
Color Coding,
Color/Hazard,
Hazard/Alert,
Industrial,
Industrial Safety,
Safety Information,
Shape Coding,
Shape/Hazard,
Signal Words,
Signal Words/Hazard,
Workers

with caution signs, which in turn had a higher value than those associated with all other signs.

Key Words:
Consumer Expectation, Marketplace Honesty Policy

048

Britain, J.E., "Product Honesty is the Best Policy: A Comparison of Doctors' and Manufacturers' Duty to Disclose Drug Risks and the Importance of Consumer Expectations in Determining Product Defect," *Northwestern University Law Review*, 79:2, 1984, 342-422.

The author is concerned that product information stressing a "marketplace honesty policy" is being inappropriately subordinated to concerns for injury prevention. He recommends that those aspects of a product that raise prevention concerns be evaluated with a risk/benefit analysis, while concerns regarding market honesty be tested against the consumer expectation standard.

Key Words:
Design of: instructions, Message Tone
Ordering of Conditions/ Actions,
Understanding of Instructions,
Writing Instructions

049

Broadbent, D.E., "Language and Ergonomics," *Applied Ergonomics*, 8:1, March 1977, 15-18.

Several experimental findings related to the wording found in instructions are summarized. Some examples of miswordings and the influence of translations are cited. Based on these findings and examples, the author initially recommends that instructions be written in simple affirmative sentences in active voice, since the use of passive or negative forms may cause problems. Passive or negative phrases may be incorrectly remembered when changed to an active or positive form, and it is easier to remember actively worded phrases. However, in some situations it may be better to use passive or negative forms. If a question is negative or passive, the reply should be in the same form. Passive constructions may be needed for sentence sequence to correspond to action sequence, but negative phrases should be used to challenge false suppositions.

The author concludes that blanket rules are not adequate. Special cases must be considered, and experimental investigations are likely to be necessary to address the specific requirements needed in various applications.

Key Words:
Design of: labeling and safety signage systems

050

Bruening, E.B., "Signs and Symbols for Safety," *National Safety News*, January 1972, 59-63.

The author distinguishes between abstract and realistic symbols and provides simple guidelines for symbol design. Supporting evidence favoring these guidelines is not given.

Annotations (001-100)

Key Words:
Control/Display Elements,
Visual Displays: miscellaneous

051
Buck, J.R., "Chapter 7: Visual Displays," in *Human Factors: Understanding People-System Relationships*, Kantowitz, B.H. and Sorkin, R.D. (Eds.), John Wiley & Sons, New York, 1983, 195-231.

This chapter describes visual displays as being an essential element of the communication process. It provides a number of general design principles useful during the development of effective displays. It also emphasizes the importance of task analysis to a designer and notes the major influence of individual specific factors on users' responses.

Key Words:
Drugs,
Duty/Failure to Warn,
Strict Liability and Warnings

052
Bukstein, Y., "Drug Products Liability: Duty to Warn," *University of Pittsburgh Law Review*, 49:1, Fall 1987, 283-306.

The author believes that a duty to warn consumers of adverse reactions to prescription drugs should be imposed on pharmacies and pharmacists because a consumer's right to self-determination includes the right to be informed of the benefits and risks associated with prescription drugs. This article outlines a proposal to impose this duty. A breach of this duty would result in strict liability. It is asserted that imposition of this duty will be the best means of ensuring that consumers will be supplied with necessary drug information and warnings.

Key Words:
Tables and Flowcharts

053
Burnhill, P., Hartley, J. and Young, M., "Tables in Text," *Applied Ergonomics*, 7:1, March 1976, 13-18.

The authors found that when tables were placed in text, a group of 340 secondary school pupils preferred single column format to double column layout and also scanned it significantly faster. It appears that these results could be explained by greater interference between tables and multi-column text than between tables and single column text. The implication of these results is that tabular information in multi-column text should be confined to a single column rather than being allowed to extend across columns.

Key Words:
Negligence and
   Warnings,
Strict Liability and
   Warnings

054

Bussain, J.A., "Using Negligence Analysis to Win 'Strict Liability' Failure to Warn Cases," *For the Defense,* **April 1987, 6-8.**

Until the courts abolish strict liability in failure to warn cases, the author advocates a negligence-based defense which involves using expert testimony to establish that the instruction or warning was adequate in content and method of conveyance. Content is governed by a reasonableness standard, requiring that known hazards be described and instructions for safe use be given. The method of conveyance requirement may be satisfied by communication to a "learned intermediary" if the product is industrial, the intermediary is knowledgeable, the manufacturer's warning is adequate, and the manufacturer has "reasonable assurance" that the warnings will be communicated through such learned intermediary users.

Key Words:
Abstractness,
Accuracy,
Control/Display
   Elements,
Conveying Action,
Describing Objects,
Heavy Equipment
   Controls,
Industrial,
Message Complexity,
Motor Vehicle,
Prior Knowledge,
Students,
Training

055

Cahill, M.C., "Design Features of Graphic Symbols Varying in Interpretability," *Perceptual and Motor Skills,* **42:2, April 1976, 647-653.**

Cahill notes that the interpretability of graphic symbols is influenced by both the context in which they are presented and the relevant prior experience of the observer. To test these influences, an experiment was performed in which thirty male college seniors in mechanical engineering were randomly divided into context and no-context groups, which were then classified as either experienced or inexperienced. Context subjects were given a drawing of a typical machine's cab interior (Kolb, 1967), the assumption being that a drawing of this type would provide contextual information normally given by the machinery itself. The symbols used in the study were designed by Henry Dreyfus Associates for use on Deere and Company farm and industrial machinery.

It was found that certain symbols benefitted more than others from the addition of context. So influenced symbols were those denoting "Transmission" and "Choke." Symbols representing verbs, or actions (e.g. "engage"), were less effective in conveying their message than those representing nouns (e.g. "horn"). No relationship was found between the accuracy of identification and the location of the symbol inside the cab.

Annotations (001-100)

Key Words:
Abstractness,
Accuracy,
Control/Display
  Elements,
Heavy Equipment
  Controls,
Industrial,
Message Complexity,
Motor Vehicle,
Prior Knowledge,
Students,
User Group

056
Cahill, M.C., "Interpretability of Graphic Symbols as a Function of Context and Experience Factors," *Journal of Applied Psychology*, **60:3, 1975, 376-380.**

Cahill states that given the serious limitations of pictographic symbols as a language form (Easterby, 1967; Kolers, 1969), a machine's "visual voice" should carry only the simplest labels and instructions. To test the effectiveness of this visual voice, an experiment was performed wherein symbols were presented in context and in isolation to subjects with varied experience. Henry Dreyfus Associates designed the symbols for Deere and Company equipment; they had been used in a University of Michigan conference on Human Factors Engineering.

The subjects were randomly divided into context and no-context groups and shown ten labeling symbols. Context subjects were given a drawing of the interior of a machine's cab in which these symbols were said to be used. Subjects' responses were recorded as correct or incorrect. The context group had an overall score of 62% correct; the no-context group scored 44% correct. Subjects' experience made some difference. Experienced subjects in the context group scored 27.73% higher than those with no experience; for the no-context group, experienced subjects scored 13.3% higher than inexperienced ones. The interaction of experience and context was not statistically significant.

Cahill notes that the influence of context on symbol interpretation has profound design implications. Symbols are not encoded within themselves; information gained from symbols is an interactive process involving the observer's memory. Symbol designers should address the middle range of user experience since highly experienced operators will find the symbol superfluous and inexperienced subjects will find the symbol insufficient. It is not evident that symbols should be designed to stand alone to convey a message to a wide range of persons. We find this type of study to be what, in the future, may be considered "reasonable" efforts to determine the user's understanding of instructive product information. In conducting such a study Deere and Company was certainly well ahead of the state-of-the-art.

Key Words:
Abstractness,
Accuracy, Biohazard,
Caustic Materials,
Consumers,
Cultural Factors,
Electrical Hazard

057
Cairney, P. and Sless, D., "Communication Effectiveness of Symbolic Safety Signs with Different User Groups," *Applied Ergonomics*, **13:2, June 1982, 91-97.**

A set of occupational safety symbols, intended to convey messages of mandatory action, prohibition, warning, and emer-

Key Words (cont.):
Explosives,
Fire,
Hazard/Alert,
Industrial,
Industrial Safety,
Ingress/Egress,
Learning Nonverbal
   Symbols,
Memory of:
   symbol/message,
Message Complexity,
Multiple Referents,
Personal Protective
   Equipment,
Prior Knowledge,
Prohibition,
Public Information,
Radiation,
Recall,
Safety Information,
Workers

gency, was presented to a group of subjects. After one week, respondents were re-tested with the same signs in a different random order. The testing consisted of a simple recognition task in which each subject assigned meanings to the symbols. Overall, performance improved from the initial test to the re-test. The subjects consisted of: migrants of European origin; Vietnamese new to Australia; and native-born Australians. All were attending literacy courses.

It was evident 1) that the different groups differed in their recognition task performance, and 2) that differing degrees of learning occurred as a result of initial exposure. A finding of major importance was that subjects had difficulty comprehending symbols with multiple referents. The authors concluded that the psychological processes of encoding and decoding by users must be explored to determine what makes symbols effective.

Key Words:
Abstractness,
Accuracy,
Drivers,
Memory of:
   symbol/message,
Message Complexity,
Motor Vehicle,
Recall, Traffic

058
Cairney, P.T. and Sless, D., "Evaluating the Understanding of Symbolic Roadside Information Signs," *Australian Road Research*, **12:2, June 1982, 97-102.**

A recognition and a recall test were used to evaluate a set of roadside symbolic signs proposed for inclusion in Australian Standard AS1742. Five groups of respondents were tested. The results for each group showed that performance varied considerably depending on the particular sign.

Key Words:
Data Processing Setting,
Justification of Text,
Reading Speed

059
Campbell, A.J., Marchetti, F.M. and Mewhort, D.J.K., "Reading Speed and Text Production: A Note on Right-Justification Techniques," *Ergonomics*, **24:8, 1981, 633-640.**

Two experiments were conducted to assess the reading efficiency associated with justified versus unjustified text and fixed- versus variable-character spacing.

A total of 156 introductory psychology students (57 in the first experiment and 99 in the second) read ten paragraphs of text presented in one of three forms: unjustified right margin, justified right margin with fixed-character spacing, and justified right margin with variable-character spacing. The experimenters informed the subjects that they were interested in both reading speed and accuracy. After reading the passages, subjects completed a questionnaire to assess their comprehension.

Annotations (001-100)

The results showed that reading time was significantly faster for the variable-space right-justified text than for the other two conditions. Also, there was no difference in reading speed for the unjustified text and the right-justified fixed-character spacing. The comprehension scores for the different conditions revealed that the decrease in reading time for the variable-space right-justified text was not a speed/accuracy trade-off; the variable-space right-justified text produced faster reading times without sacrificing accuracy when compared to the other text formats.

Key Words:
Design of: labeling and safety signage systems,
Prior Knowledge,
Routing,
Task Analysis

060
Canter, D., "Chapter 13: Way-finding and Signposting: Penance or Prosthesis?" in *Information Design: The Design and Evaluation of Signs and Printed Material*, Easterby, R.S. and Zwaga, H.J.G. (Eds.), John Wiley & Sons, New York, 1984, 245-264.

Canter notes that when analyzing those cognitive processes involved in orienting, way-finding, and locating-identifying, it is necessary to consider: 1) the existing knowledge of the individual; 2) the fact that the world is frequently represented through signs and simulations; 3) the environmental roles and conceptual systems that influence the processes of utilizing public information systems; and 4) the strengths and weaknesses of information and sign systems. The author discusses each topic as it relates to the design of signs and printed material.

Key Words:
Buying Behavior,
Consumer Labeling and Signage Systems,
Consumer Preferences,
Consumers,
Design of:
   educational/persuasive programs,
Effectiveness of:
   educational/persuasive programs,
FDA,
Government Involvement
Governmental Labeling and Signage Systems,
Information Overload,
Labels,
Level of Detail,
Location

061
Capon, N. and Lutz, R.J., "A Model and Methodology for the Development of Consumer Information Programs," *Journal of Marketing*, 43, January 1979, 58-67.

The author advocates a marketing framework for the provision of information to consumers by policy makers involved in development of information programs. This approach emphasizes the need to identify consumer market segments and their information needs and information processing abilities and then serving these segments with information defined in terms of the marketing mix variables of product, distribution, promotion and price. The product is defined as information which varies in its type and source. Distribution refers to the manner in which the information reaches consumers. Price refers to the monetary and non-monetary price which consumers must pay for this information. This includes time, thinking and annoyance. In addition to distribution, the information must be promoted. That is, the consumer must be made aware of the information's availability and persuaded to purchase (i.e. use) it.

Key Words (cont.):
Personal Presentations,
Review Papers

A methodology is proposed which describes the development of an action matrix for the policy maker. This action matrix arrays the information combinations actually used by the consumer in making a purchase decision, the information combinations which are perceived to be available, the information combinations actually available and, lastly, the information combinations which the consumer desires. These combinations are interpreted and used to develop a best policy.

Key Words:
Basic Associations,
Public Information,
Semantic Differential

062
Caron, J.P., Jamieson, D.G. and Dewar, R.E., "Evaluating Pictographs Using Semantic Differential and Classification Techniques," *Ergonomics*, **23:2, 1980, 137-146.**

This article describes the development of a procedure for evaluating people's reactions to pictographs using a type of factor analysis. By this methodology the meaning of symbols was rigorously evaluated in terms of three primary dimensions. These dimensions were: 1) evaluative (good/bad, fair/unfair); 2) potency (strong/weak, large/small); and 3) activity (active/passive, fast/slow). Experiments describing how the basic classification technique was developed are outlined.

Key Words:
Color of Background,
Color of Stimulus,
Information Coding,
Laboratory/Generic
 Settings,
Predictive User Response
 Equations,
Search Time,
Visual Displays:
 miscellaneous

063
Carter, R.C. and Cahill, M.C., "Regression Models of Search Time for Color-Coded Information Displays," *Human Factors*, **21:3, 1979, 293-302.**

Visual search times for color-coded displays are predicted using regression.

Key Words:
Basic Associations,
Control/Display
 Elements,
Military,
Radar,
Reaction Time

064
Carter, R.J., "Standardization of Geometric Radar Symbology: Stereotyped Meanings and Paper-and-Pencil Testing," *Proceedings of the Human Factors Society - 23rd Annual Meeting*, **Human Factors Society, Santa Monica, CA, 1979, 443-447.**

To establish a standard symbology for use by military personnel, Carter first evaluated the correlation between various shapes and certain meaning categories, namely, "friendly," "hostile," and "unknown." He also evaluated the discriminability of these symbols. The results of phase one indicated that: 1) the circle, 5-sided star, flag, and heart are seen as friendly signs; 2) the swastika, collapsed square, and X are seen as hostile signs; and 3) the three-sided U, six-sided U, and question mark are seen as unknown signs.

In phase two, several symbol combinations were evaluated in more detail. It was found that certain symbol combinations were distinguished more easily and reacted to more quickly than others.

Key Words:
Duty/Failure to Warn,
Hazard Communication Rule,
Misuse

065
Centner, T.J., "OSHA's Hazard Communication Rule and State Right to Know Laws," *Georgia State Bar Journal*, **21:4, May 1985, 172-174.**

The Occupational Health and Safety Administration's hazard communication rule requires that employers using hazardous chemicals make a good faith effort to communicate these hazards to employees in a manner that can be understood by each employee. If an employee does not understand the hazards, the statutory duty to warn has been breached. A breach of this kind can result in liability for an employee's injuries resulting from use or misuse of a hazardous chemical. We note that what is not addressed is the role, if any, that the suppliers and manufacturers play. Their roles may depend on whether the criteria is the administrative OSHA rule or the common law theories of duty.

Key Words:
Abstractness,
Auditory,
Auditory vs. Visual Messages,
Message Complexity,
Message Modality,
Understanding of Instructions

066
Chaiken, S. and Eagly, A.H., "Communication Modality as a Determinant of Message Persuasiveness and Message Comprehensibility," *Journal of Personality and Social Psychology*, **34:4, 1976, 605-614.**

Easy versus difficult-to-understand persuasive messages were presented to the subjects by written, audiotaped, or videotaped media. For easy messages, the persuasive effect was greatest for videotaped and least for written messages, while comprehension was equivalent for all media. For difficult messages, persuasion and comprehension were highest for the written media. We would be interested in how pictographic presentations which could be used in instruction manuals would rate in this type of study. One would suspect that they also would be efficient in achieving persuasion and comprehension goals for moderately difficult parts of instruction manuals. Also, while probably premature to this article, the issue of using a symbol versus a few words to convey simple information is inherent to the areas addressed in it.

Key Words:
Design of: instructions,
Problems in Design,
Task Analysis,
Translation of Instructions,
Understanding of Instructions,
Writing Instructions

067
Chapanis, A., "Words, Words, Words," *Human Factors*, 7, February 1965, 1-17.

The author argues that more attention should be paid by human factors professionals to the wording which is associated with machines. Several examples of misleading wording are presented. The author also outlines a basic program of language research which calls for: 1) language quality control in documents; 2) critical-incident studies of language difficulties; 3) use of intelligibility criteria; 4) application of task analysis to writing instructions; 5) rules for structuring short sentences; 6) the experimental validation of principles; 7) checklists for evaluating manuals; 8) evaluation of verbal versus non-verbal communication; 9) special word lists for specialized fields; and 10) consideration of the problems caused by the multiplicity of human languages. We note this article as one of the classics by the author who will continue to be immortal to the human factors discipline.

Key Words:
Illustrations,
Page Layout

068
Cheickna, S., Drury, C.G. and Babu, A.J.G., "A Human Factors Design Investigation of a Computerized Layout System of Text-Graphic Technical Materials," *Human Factors*, 30:3, June 1988, 347-358.

A questionnaire was administered to fourteen human factors experts in an attempt to develop or describe rules for page splitting and page layout. From the rules derived from these human factors experts, an algorithm was then devised and implemented on a computer page layout system to automate page splitting. A second algorithm was then devised to organize the graphics and labels of the individual pages. The algorithm used in the computerized layout system closely matched human page splitting in the results. The system is currently in use at the Naval Training System Center.

Key Words:
Illustrations,
Information Coding,
Message Modality,
Verbal vs. Nonverbal Symbol/Message,
Visual vs. Verbal Symbol/Message

069
Childers, T.L., Heckler, S.E. and Houston, M.J., "Memory for the Visual and Verbal Components of Print Advertisements," *Psychology & Marketing*, 3, Fall 1986, 137-150.

The authors begin their paper by stating that a pervasive and consistent finding within the literature is that the pictorial element of a printed ad results in better recall of message-related attributes than does the verbal message part of an ad. On the other hand, results comparing the relative effectiveness of pictorial and verbal information have been less clear when the dependent variable has been the influence on attitudes and persuasion. The authors discuss methods of explaining these effects on the basis of information processing theory.

They conclude that information stored in a pictorial form may be processed differently and may also be processed to a different level than that which is verbal. In an experiment with a subject pool of 56 undergraduate students the authors evaluated the influence of pictorial and verbal information within a single advertisement. Notably, it was discovered that subjects were five times more likely to recall information that was provided pictorially than when information was presented verbally. There also was a tendency toward fewer memory errors for visually encoded information. The authors conclude that the visual pictorial component of a printed ad is both more elaborately and more distinctively encoded than is the verbal component. We again find in this article the implication that pictorial information is likely to play a vital role in the ultimate usefulness and effectiveness of instructional publications.

Key Words:
Illustrations,
Information Coding,
Message Modality,
Visual vs. Verbal
    Symbol/Message

070
Childers, T.L. and Houston, M.J., "Conditions for a Picture-Superiority Effect on Consumer Memory," *Journal of Consumer Research*, **11, September 1984, 643-654.**

The authors note that most findings in psychological literature show that pictorially represented information is remembered better than that which is verbally-encoded. The authors therefore set out to more precisely describe when this advantage for visually-encoded information is likely to be present. They hypothesized that this effect is less likely to be present when the information is processed heavily at a semantic level. A subject pool of 271 undergraduate subjects was used.

The authors found that for stimulus material selected from the yellow pages of the metropolitan telephone directories, under immediate recall conditions in heavy semantic processing, there was no advantage in recall for information presented visually. On the other hand, there continued to be an advantage for the pictorially presented information when the recall was delayed and when subjects were asked to concentrate on the sensory aspects of the advertisement. The authors conclude that a verbally based message is probably most appropriate under conditions where the audience is motivated and capable of processing the semantic content of the message. On the other hand, visually oriented messages seem particularly appropriate under conditions where audiences are less motivated or less capable of semantic processing. Since the criterion for evaluation is incidental learning and subsequent memory, no attempt was made in this study to consider the situation where the criteria is attitude change or persuasive effects of the ad.

071

Childers, T.L., Houston, M.J. and Heckler, S.E., "Measurement of Individual Differences in Visual versus Verbal Information Processing," *Journal of Consumer Research,* **12, September 1985, 125-134.**

Key Words:
Information Coding,
Message Modality,
User Modeling

The authors report on a study evaluating methods of describing or assessing individual differences in visual versus verbal information processing. If such tools are indeed effective, they could be employed to identify those groups of subjects to whom visual rather than verbal information should be provided, and vice versa. The best results were obtained for a Style of Processing (SOP) scale developed by the authors, as it showed better discrimination and criterion validity. The SOP scale was also significantly correlated with the recall and recognition of advertisement components.

072

Christ, R.E., "Color Research for Visual Displays," *Proceedings of the Human Factors Society - 18th Annual Meeting,* **Human Factors Society, Santa Monica, CA, 1974, 542-546.**

Key Words:
Color of Background,
Color of Stimulus,
Information Coding,
Laboratory/Generic Settings,
Predictive User Response Equations,
Recognition Time,
Search Time,
Visual Displays: miscellaneous

The literature on the relative efficiency of color coding versus other coding schemes is summarized (43 studies between 1952 and 1973). The findings are presented in a table. Color codes appear to be quite efficient for both identification and search tasks. In particular, if the target color is known in advance and the color is unique to that target, color coding does aid both identification and search tasks. In certain situations, however, non-chromatic coding methods (e.g., alphanumeric methods) are superior.

073

Christensen, J.M., "Human Factors Considerations in Lawsuits," in *Safety Law: A Legal Reference for the Safety Professional,* **Peters, G.A. (Ed.), American Society of Safety Engineers, Park Ridge, 1983, 5-7.**

Key Words:
Adequacy of Warnings,
Application Guidelines,
Design of: labeling and safety signage systems,
Development Programs,
Durability,
Hazard Prevention/ Analysis Models,
Human Factors

A simple model for reducing hazards is suggested. The five elements in the model are: 1) design; 2) remove; 3) guard; 4) warn; and 5) train. Also, a set of idealistic rules is proposed for the design of warning labels: 1) don't try to correct poor design with warnings; 2) explain the nature of the hazard and what to do about it; 3) be clear, comprehensive and complete for all potential users, regardless of their degree of literacy or their native language; 4) warn against hazards of both use and foreseeable misuse; 5) make the labels conspicuous, attention-demanding, urgent, and emphatic; 6) make the labels durable and legible, and affix them to the product, as well as to the case or container; 7) conform to standards, but consider standards to be minimum requirements; 8) use pictures, symbols and diagrams if they will be universally understood and adequate; 9) reflect latest design and user experience; 10) use redundancy; and 11) test effectiveness on a representative sample of potential users.

The author also notes that perception does not necessarily imply action, and that complex interactions make testing under representative conditions important. We find significant merit in the points made by Dr. Christensen as reasonable goals for the practitioner, but feel obligated to point out that sophisticated methodologies will be required to implement his rules completely. Such sophistication probably exceeds the state-of-the-art approaches applied by most hardware or information designers. An obvious though not explicit parallel goal is to make available to designers in-house or out-of-house the human factors expertise required to implement these suggested guidelines.

Key Words:
Application Guidelines,
Design of: labeling and safety signage systems,
Hazard Prevention/ Analysis Models,
Human Factors

074
Christensen, J.M., "Human Factors in Hazard/Risk Evaluation," *Proceedings of the Symposium: Human Factors and Industrial Design in Consumer Products*, Poydar, H.R. (Ed.), Tufts University, Medford, 1980, 442-477.

Christensen provides a wide-ranging survey of human factors in relation to safety, beginning with basic definitions of hazard, risk, and danger. He follows with a discussion of several models and approaches. These include: 1) a simple man-machine model; 2) Ramsey's information processing model; 3) task analysis (behavior classification); 4) use of checklists; 5) the critical incident technique; 6) accident review teams; 7) failure modes and effects analysis (fault tree analysis); 8) human reliability data; 9) K. U. Smith's hazard control postulates; and 10) G. L. Smith's method for quantifying hazard. After introducing these approaches, Christensen traces the logic of Ramsey's model - moving from perception to response - in a more detailed discussion. He also provides tables which summarize guidelines for warning devices and rules for warning labels.

Key Words:
ANSI,
Advantages of Nonverbal Symbols,
Color Coding,
Comprehension of: warning labels

075
Clark, D.R., "Model for the Analysis, Representation, and Synthesis of Hazard Warning Communication," Ph.D. Dissertation, Department of Industrial and Operations Engineering, University of Michigan, December 1988.

The research focuses on: 1) past and present use of hazard warning signs and labels as indicated by the U.S. Code of

Key Words (cont.):
Consumer Labeling and Signage Systems,
Design Consistency,
Design of: instructions,
Design of: labeling and safety signage systems,
Development Programs,
Elemental Breakdowns,
Elemental Synthesis,
FMC,
Governmental Labeling and Signage Systems,
Hazard Prevention/ Analysis Models,
Hazard/Alert,
Industrial,
OSHA,
Organizing Information,
Prohibition,
Signal Words,
Symbol Generation,
Symbol Taxonomies

Federal Regulations (CFR) and the American National Standards Institute (ANSI), and 2) the modeling of warnings as a way to improve their design and application.

The findings of the analysis of almost 500 warning regulations in the CFR relate differences found in specific warning component requirements to the contexts in which they are to be used. A model is developed that considers the contextual elements of human exposure to hazards (using concepts of Hazard Envelope and Hazard Modules), and the physical (Syntax) and communication components (Semantics) of warnings. This recursive, layered model is used to analyze and represent the ANSI Z535 and Z129 warning label systems for occupational, environmental, chemical, and consumer product hazards. A pilot computer program, HazComCAD™, based on the model was written and is reviewed. It assists inexperienced designers in producing facsimiles of existing warnings and synthesizing new warnings that are more consistent with people's expectations for hazards in a given context.

Guidelines are given for warning design that focus on how to reconcile requirement differences between regulations and/or standards to synthesize a composite warning that preserves the functional intent of each. A proposed design template for visual warnings is presented. It is suggested that these results can be applied to types of warnings other than visual signs and labels, as well as to other product information such as instruction manuals, for which the author gives preliminary design guidelines.

076
Clark, W.C., "Witches, Floods, and Wonder Drugs: Historical Perspectives on Risk Management," in *Societal Risk Assessment*, Schwing, R.C. and Albers, W.A. (Eds.), Plenum Press, New York, 1980, 287-318.

Key Words:
Acceptability

The author reports on a retrospective study of societal risk, in an attempt to clarify the issues within the contemporary risk debate. It is suggested that the debates about risk assessment are currently based on personal faith rather than skeptical, open inquiry, and that these debates do not yet recognize the essentially meaningless forms which unstructured "facts" may take. Clark compares the present risk assessment movement to the "Inquisition" (which occurred during the European witch craze). This is because it possesses an element of opportunistic careerism that has the potential to bring an entire profession into disrepute, as well as to do harm to that part of the society which the profession is ideally meant to protect.

Annotations (001-100)

Clark also cites several examples demonstrating the apparent futility of many attempts to control risk, where these projects often achieve their short-term goals; however, expensive and unanticipated long-term consequences are also incurred. Man's efforts to control human disease are considered as illustrative problems, as seemingly straightforward efforts which often result in unanticipated complications. In addition, abandoning an initially successful risk-reduction plan is noted to be delicate and expensive. He concludes that fear of the unknown may be better replaced by respect and appreciation for it. Mistakes must be recognized, learned from, and utilized appropriately to modify future plans. Such an approach is essential to modern risk-assessment policy formulations.

077
Clarke, M.M. and Carroll, L., "Human Factors Guidelines for Writers of User Manuals," *Proceedings of the Human Factors Society - 27th Annual Meeting,* **Human Factors Society, Santa Monica, CA, 1983, 496-500.**

Key Words:
Writing Instruction Guidelines

The authors summarize their experiences in teaching basic writing guidelines to writers of various instruction and user manuals and provide an outline of the material covered. They found that manuals produced by participants prior to taking the course were poorly written and, the participants had little understanding of human factors.

The participants could be contrasted in distinct categories, such as supervisors versus writers, and young versus older engineers. Since most of the participants were unfamiliar with human factors, the course had a heavy emphasis on the basics of this area. It was particularly significant that most participants were not enthusiastic about taking the course, and evaluations indicated that the participants did not feel that knowing about human factors would be particularly useful in their jobs.

We find these results somewhat explanatory of why such a large proportion of instructive information designed is ineffective and not understandable. The writers apparently don't even realize that better designs are possible if the newer disciplines within human factors engineering are applied.

Key Words:
Design of: instructions,
Design of: labeling and safety signage systems,
Duty/Failure to Warn,
Instructions in Litigation

078
Clement, D.E., "Human Factors, Instructions and Warnings, and Products Liability," *IEEE Transactions on Professional Communication,* **30:3, September 1987, 149-155.**

In a general overview paper the author introduces the science of human factors in the context of developing instructions, operator manuals and warnings by technical writers. Topics addressed include specific factors which affect human performance, the prediction and modification of behavior, and individual subject differences. The author also notes the need for information gathering and pilot testing of products and instructions, a need which we are particularly sympathetic to and supportive of. Likewise we are in strong agreement with the author's position of considering both the benefits and costs of warnings placed within instruction manuals or on labels as opposed to an approach of proliferating warnings on products and within instruction manuals for all conceivable potential hazards.

079
Close, D.B., "The Risk Manager's Role in Preventing Product Liability Claims," *Risk Management,* **May 1987, 36-40.**

Key Words:
Advertising,
Development Cycle,
Warranties/Disclaimers

The author provides an introductory paper describing some of the areas of involvement that Risk Managers should be concerned with. These include advertising, packaging, instructions, warranties and quality control.

080
Coates, F.D., "Human Factors and the Consumer: The Aesthetic Factor," *Proceedings of the Human Factors Society - 17th Annual Meeting,* **Human Factors Society, Santa Monica, CA, 1973, 440-443.**

Key Words:
Aesthetics,
Consumer Setting

Coates argues that aesthetic factors play a major role in consumer behavior. These aesthetic factors may conflict with functional factors (the product chosen may look good but not function well). Coates then attempts to provide a theory by which aesthetics can be defined. This theory emphasizes the effects of deviation from certain adaptation levels. Large deviations result in high arousal levels and are considered unpleasant, while small deviations cause a smaller change in arousal levels and are considered pleasant. The relation between arousal and attractiveness is an inverted "U". Many factors will influence the extent of deviation, including harmony, rate of change of stimuli, and stimulus strength.

081
Cochran, D.J., Riley, M.W. and Douglass, E.I., "An Investigation of Shapes for Warning Labels," *Proceedings of the Human Factors Society - 25th Annual Meeting,* **Human Factors Society, Santa Monica, CA, 1981, 395-399.**

Key Words:
Comprehension of:
  warning labels,
Consumers,
Elderly,
Shape Coding,
Shape/Hazard,
Students

Nineteen different warning label shapes (or symbols within warning labels) were investigated in a paired comparison type experiment. Sixty-six college students were used as subjects. A triangle pointing downward was found to be most associated with hazard, followed by a square on a point and other regular shapes on a point. Simple rounded shapes and polygons on a base were least associated with hazard.

082
Cole, B.L. and Jacobs, R.J., "A Comparison of Alternative Symbolic Warning Signs for Railway Level Crossings," *Australian Road Research*, **11:4, December 1981, 37-45.**

Key Words:
Drivers,
Legibility Distance,
Motor Vehicle,
Population Stereotypes,
Railroad Crossing,
Railroad Settings,
Traffic

Warning signs are stated to be the only justifiable protection for level railway crossings with light traffic and good accident records. In an attempt to guide the development of effective signs, two Australian Standard railway warning signs were compared, one consisting of a single steam train symbol and the other of two diesel trains. Interpretability and legibility distance were the two evaluation criteria. Consideration was also given to population stereotypes regarding railway warning signs.

083
Collins, B.L., "Evaluation of Mine-Safety Symbols," *Proceedings of the Human Factors Society - 27th Annual Meeting*, **Human Factors Society, Santa Monica, CA, 1983, 947-949.**

Key Words:
Accuracy,
Age,
Association
  Rankings/Indexes,
Biohazard,
Color Coding,
Color/Hazard,
Contrast,
Durability,
Illumination Level,
Industrial,
Industrial Safety,
Industrial Setting,
Message Complexity,
Mine Safety,
OSHA,
Prior Knowledge,
Shape Coding,
Shape/Hazard,
Workers

A three-phase evaluation of mine safety symbols was performed. Phase 1 used 72 symbols which expressed a total of 40 messages. These were presented to a sample of 267 miners at 10 different mine sites, and the degree of comprehension was evaluated. Significant variation in the comprehension of different symbols referring to the same message was found 72% of the time. There were also significantly variant levels of comprehension among miners of different age groups and among miners at different sites. Of the 40 messages, 34 were correctly interpreted by 85% or more of the subjects. Symbols which miners had trouble identifying were highly abstract or referred to unfamiliar topics.

In Phase 2, the hazard association value of various shapes that surrounded symbols were evaluated. The diamond and octagon shapes were judged to be more indicative of hazard than circles or squares, and the colors red, yellow, and orange were selected as the most appropriate colors for indicating hazard.

In Phase 3, the effectiveness of a subset of 20 symbols was evaluated in an on-site investigation. Effectiveness was judged by further assessment of ease of comprehension, as well as evaluation of contrast, luminance, and durability. The comprehension results did not differ substantially from those in phase 2, and the researchers concluded that further research on symbol legibility under field conditions should be performed.

Key Words:
Accuracy,
Age,
Biohazard,
Consumer Labeling and Signage Systems,
Consumers,
Fire,
Fire Safety Signs,
ISO,
Ingress/Egress,
Prohibition,
Routing

084
Collins, B.L. and Lerner, N.D., "Assessment of Fire-Safety Symbols," *Human Factors*, 24:1, 1982, 75-84.

Twenty fire-safety signs proposed by the ISO, and five other international fire-safety signs, were investigated, using 91 U.S. subjects. The investigators used three modes of presentation (slides, placards, and booklets) and the participants used one of two response methods (definition or multiple choice). The mode of presentation had no significant effect, while the answers were similar for both response methods. Comprehension of the 25 symbols ranged from near zero to near 100%. In particular, subjects had problems comprehending several of the exit and no-exit type symbols. A significant correlation (R=-.3) between age and symbol comprehension was found. The researchers concluded that this wide variation in comprehension demonstrates the need to test symbols before implementing them.

Key Words:
Accuracy,
Biohazard,
Caustic Materials,
Electrical Hazard,
Explosives,
Fire,
Hazard/Alert,
Industrial,
Ingress/Egress,
Message Complexity,
Moving Vehicle,
Personal Protective Equipment,
Poison,
Prior Knowledge,
Prohibition,
Readability Measures,
Routing,
Safety Information,
Simple Comprehension of: verbal symbols,
Slip/Fall,
Workers

085
Collins, B.L., Lerner, N.D. and Pierman, B.C., "Symbols for Industrial Safety," National Bureau of Standards, Washington, D.C., NBSIR 82-2485, June 1982, 1-102.

This comprehensive document consists of a literature review combined with a summary of a four-phase evaluation of selected workplace symbols. The literature review summarizes highway, automotive and machinery, public information, product labeling, and safety symbols. In Phase 1 of the evaluation, site visits, sign catalogues, publications and manufacturers, and symbol standards were used to classify and select thirty-three safety messages. These messages related to five basic areas: 1) hazards; 2) protective gear; 3) first aid and emergency equipment; 4) prohibited actions; and 5) egress. In Phase 2, two to forty symbols for each of the selected thirty-three messages were rank ordered by safety oriented participants, and a subset was specified for further evaluation. In Phase 3, 222 employees provided short definitions for each of these symbols. In Phase 4, all of the symbols for each message were provided along with the message, and the subjects selected the symbol which they felt best communicated the given message.

The results of this study showed much variation in symbol comprehension. Abstract symbols indicating biohazard, radiation, and lasers were poorly understood, even though these symbols have been in use for some time. More concrete symbols

Annotations (001-100)

signifying first aid, emergency equipment, or protective gear were better understood. All symbols for radiation, lasers, biohazard, general warning, poison, combustibility, eyewash, exit, no entrance, and no exit were perceived correctly less than 85% of the time. The first four of these symbols were poorly perceived by both informed and naive participants.

Key Words:
Sources of Bias

086
Combs, B. and Slovic, P., "Newspaper Coverage of Causes of Death," *Journalism Quarterly,* **Winter 1979, 837-843, 849.**

Hazards compete with one another for public attention. There is evidence that peoples' perceptions of risk are subject to large and systematic biases. These biases may misdirect the actions of the government and public interest groups, resulting in inadequate control of risk. Experience with adversity comes through various forms of the media; if the media is biased, our experience will be also. In the pursuit of that theme, this study examined the newspaper coverage of various causes of death; the amount of coverage is compared to the frequencies of these causes.

A previous study provided data on judged frequencies of various causes of death. These causes were assigned to one or more categories. Computed were: the number of deaths reported, number of occurrences of the event, number of articles published, and other measures. The correlations show high agreement between newspapers. Frequent causes like emphysema, diabetes, and various forms of cancer were rarely reported. Overall, the amount of coverage designated to a specific cause is not closely related to its frequency of occurrence. Catastrophic or violent events are over-reported, while all forms of disease are greatly under-reported. Homicides are over-reported most, and homicide articles tend to be twice as long as those for either disease or accident-related deaths. The media biases observed are widespread and correspond closely to the biases in judged frequencies found in previous studies. However, the determinants of these biases have not been identified; the media may influence judgment, or judgment may influence media coverage.

Key Words:
Biohazard,
Color Coding,
Consumer Labeling and Signage Systems,
Design Consistency,
Electrical Hazard,
Fire,
Ingress/Egress

087
Committee on Consumer Policy, "Compulsory Labeling of Packaged Consumer Products," Organization for Economic Cooperation and Development, Paris, France, 1974, 5-42.

This document reviews and evaluates various countries' national labeling regulations concerning the nature, composition, and quantity content of prepackaged consumer products

Key Words (cont.):
International Labeling and Signage Systems
Moving Vehicle,
Point of Operation Guarding,
Radiation,
Routing,
Safety Information,
Signal Words,
Slip/Fall

(household cleaning products). While the document is primarily concerned with consumer economic interests, some attention is given to product-related hazards.

The countries addressed include Austria, Belgium, Canada, Denmark, Finland, France, Germany, Ireland, Japan, Luxembourg, the Netherlands, Norway, Portugal, Spain, Sweden, Switzerland, the United Kingdom, and the United States. Canada had the most elaborate system of warning labels for hazardous household cleaning products in their Hazardous Products Act of 1970. These labels indicate both the nature of the hazard (signified by a simple symbol) and the degree of the hazard (signified by the shape surrounding the symbol).

The need for developing international consistency in warning label design is noted. It is suggested that member countries require some or all of the following items on warning labels: 1) symbols indicating the nature and degree of the hazard; 2) color coding that emphasizes danger; 3) names of hazardous ingredients; 4) precautionary wording; 5) instructions for emergency treatment in case of accidents; and 6) instructions for storage and use.

088
Connolley, D., "AUDISAFE: A General Accident-Preventive Device," *Ergonomics,* **22:2, 1979, 199-210.**

Key Words:
Road Side Radio Transmitter

The author describes an audio transmitter/receiver. When this device was installed in automobiles, and at appropriate roadside locations, it had the capability of warning or providing other kinds of information to drivers. Several examples are given of how accidents might be prevented using this device.

089
Conrads, J.A., " 'Illustruction': Increasing Safety and Reducing Liability Exposure," *IEEE Transactions on Professional Communication,* **30:3, September 1987, 133-135.**

Key Words:
Design of: instructions,
Development Cycle,
Illustrations,
Understanding of Instructions

The author describes a style of documentation developed by Deere and Company that is intended to increase the effectiveness of operator/owner manuals and simultaneously decrease liability exposure. The author coins the term "illustruction," which is a contraction of the words illustration and instruction. The theory driving this approach is that most instruction is achieved through illustration, not through the text. Examples are presented of the application of this approach although not in a highly detailed form. We find that approaches such as this

Annotations (001-100)

for designing instructions are particularly worthy of more formal evaluation to determine the specific circumstances for which they may be superior.

Key Words:
Design of: labeling and safety signage systems,
Public Information,
Routing,
Task Analysis

090
Cook, T.R. and Smith, D.B., "Communications—Complex Problem Solving: Design and Development of a Signage System for the Columbus International Airport in Columbus, Ohio," *Proceedings of the Symposium: Human Factors and Industrial Design in Consumer Products*, Poydar, H.R. (Ed.), Tufts University, Medford, 1980, 329-341.

The authors applied an interdisciplinary approach to design a sign system for the Columbus airport expansion program. They first performed a passenger and vehicular traffic flow analysis in an attempt to determine the major decision points in the roadway and terminal system. Next, objectives were developed for the signage system. With these objectives in mind, members of the design team performed simulations during which each member assumed the role of one of several different user types and simulated activities throughout seven domestic airports. This activity was documented with photographs and audiotape. The data from this procedure were used to investigate the signage requirements in terms of the traffic patterns within the proposed terminal.

Key Words:
FDA,
Supremacy Clause

091
Cooper, R.M., "Drug Labeling and Products Liability: The Role of the Food and Drug Administration," *Food Drug Cosmetic Law Journal*, 41:3, July 1986, 233-240.

The author suggests that the role of a regulatory agency such as the Food and Drug Administration (FDA) should be one of neutrality with respect to private civil litigation. In keeping with this principle, some courts have held that approval of a warning by the FDA is not necessarily conclusive evidence of its adequacy. Others have argued that this decision violates the Supremacy Clause of the U.S. Constitution.

Key Words:
Absolute Liability,
Bankruptcy

092
Cooter, R.D., "Defective Warnings, Remote Causes, and Bankruptcy: Comment on Schwartz," *The Journal of Legal Studies*, 14:3, December 1985, 737-750.

The author discusses the application of warnings to inherently dangerous products from an economic and legal standpoint. He first describes his conception of the relationship between the "dangerousness" of a product and the strength of its accompanying warning. Without empirical evidence he states that "a stronger warning causes fewer consumers to buy the product, and those who do take more precautions. . . ." The result of this assumption is the theory that accident costs are a function of warning strength.

Cooter proposes a legal rule whereby the manufacturer is held liable for the harm caused by inadequate warnings (a warning is considered inadequate if it is too lax). For accidents associated with such warnings, the manufacturer is responsible for damages. By applying this theory, the author proposes that the optimal strength of a warning can be derived through economic analyses (accident costs versus profits).

The author also introduces the idea of "efficient warnings." Such warnings take into account the immediate profit and liability associated with the product. This "efficient liability rule" attempts to balance the social benefits of the product with the social costs of accidents. Theoretically, this balancing act would dictate the strength of the warning. The author concludes with a discussion of insurance strategies for firms exposed to tort claims.

093
Coskuntuna, S. and Mauro, C., "Instruction Manuals: A Component of a Product's 'Teaching Package,'" *Proceedings of the Symposium: Human Factors and Industrial Design in Consumer Products,* **Poydar, H.R. (Ed.), Tufts University, Medford, 1980, 300-313.**

Key Words:
Conveying Procedures,
Design of: instructions,
Illustrations,
Problems in Design,
Writing Instructions

The authors note that although products are becoming too complex to be used without accompanying documentation, such documentation is frequently inadequate. Some common failings are: 1) operational sequences are interrupted with "hype" or other extraneous material; 2) operational information is buried; 3) warning material is separated from operational material describing where the hazard might occur; 4) jargon is used unnecessarily; 5) the instructions are beyond the users' level of comprehension; 6) the correlation between graphics and written material is poor; and 7) too much of the information is conveyed through diagrams.

The following rules of thumb are provided: 1) avoid informational overload; 2) use only concrete information; 3) concentrate on the "how's rather than the "why's; 4) remember that learning comes from doing; and 5) avoid hype. The authors emphasize the need for empirical testing of instructions. Other considerations include the need for task analysis and the need to identify and accommodate the least competent potential user. They also discuss the application of a general design model to the design of instruction that incorporates a planning stage, a design stage, a development stage, and an evaluation stage. We find this to be an excellent paper which realistically addresses the problems found in current instruction manual design and in the approaches necessary to upgrade the present state-of-the-art.

Key Words:
Drugs,
Duty/Failure to Warn

094
Cox, S.N., "The Drug Manufacturer's Duty to Warn and the Alabama Extended Manufacturer's Liability Doctrine," *Alabama Law Review*, **37:3, Spring 1986, 681-698.**

This article stresses the importance of the language contained in Alabama's Extended Manufacturer's Liability Doctrine (AEMLD). Under AEMLD, the drug manufacturer's duty to warn will proceed from the manufacturer's reasonable ability to discover the drug's risks before and after production. Thus, the doctrine protects consumers from unreasonable risk while maintaining that liability can stem from the manufacturer's failure to make reasonable discovery efforts to determine such hazards inherent to their product's use or foreseeable misuse.

Key Words:
Children,
Consumers,
Credibility of Source,
Source

095
Craig, C.S. and McCann, J.M., "Assessing Communication Effects on Energy Conservation," *Journal of Consumer Research*, **5, September 1978, 82-88.**

One thousand heavy users of electricity received messages which described ways of saving money by reducing their consumption of electricity for air conditioning. The messages were sent from either the Manager of Consumer Affairs at Consolidated Edison or from the Chairman of the New York State Public Service Commission. The recipients were asked to return a postcard request to receive more information. Approximately 18% of the users who received the messages from the Public Service Commission returned the card, as compared to a 10% return rate from the users who received the Con Edison messages. During the two month period after the messages were sent, individuals who had received a message from the Public Service Commission consumed significantly less electricity (approximately $4.25 worth) than those who had received a message from Con Edison. Repetition of messages did not have a significant effect.

These results were held to support the theory that the credibility of a source of information is directly related to the likelihood that the information will be heeded. We find similar findings from other authors' results. The general issue of interest is the determination of why warnings or instructions which are completely understood and remembered are heeded in some contexts and not heeded in others. All other things being equal, the source is apparently quite important in partially explaining this type of behavior.

Key Words:
Adequacy of Warnings,
Application Guidelines,
Design of: labeling and safety signage systems,
Human Factors

096
Cunitz, R.J., "Psychologically Effective Warnings," *Hazard Prevention*, **17:3, May/June 1981, 5-7.**

The author defines psychologically effective warnings using the following criteria: 1) they are present when needed; 2) they are present where needed, 3) they attract attention; 4) they motivate behavioral change; 5) they tell how to avoid harm; 6) they provide first aid instruction; and 7) they address certain other human factors. The need for efficiency testing, evaluation of readability, and standardization is also mentioned.

Key Words:
Design of: instructions,
Illustrations,
Problems in Design,
Readability Measures,
Understanding of Instructions

097
Curran, T.E., "Survey of Technical Manual Readability and Comprehensibility," Navy Personnel Research and Development Center, San Diego, NTIS No. AD AO42335, June 1977.

The author notes that the volume of technical manual materials in current use by the Navy is estimated to be in excess of seventy million pages. This material is used by approximately one million personnel with reading abilities extending from perhaps a fourth or fifth grade level to that of a graduate engineer. For these reasons the readability of technical manuals has become a major concern of Navy personnel. The author surveys a wide variety of techniques for predicting the difficulty of reading different forms of writing, methods of producing readable and comprehensible writing, and the role of graphic and pictorial illustration. The author provides conclusions and recommendations in a fairly substantial annotated bibliography of articles examining comprehension. In addition, this article has an appendix which describes several systems for evaluating technical documentation, many of which are computerized.

Key Words:
Alcohol,
Duty/Failure to Warn,
Statute of Limitations

098
D'Amico, D., "A Spirited Call to Require Alcohol Manufacturers to Warn of the Dangerous Propensities of Their Products," *Nova Law Review*, **11:4, Summer 1987, 1611-1629.**

The author states that although the public generally knows that alcohol abuse is harmful, the public is not sufficiently aware of the specific health risks of alcohol consumption. For this reason, the author advocates imposing civil liability on the alcohol industry for damage caused by its products in the absence of a warning. This may force the industry to voluntarily provide warning labels on its products. D'Amico notes that past efforts by Congress to mandate warning labels on alcoholic beverages have been defeated by the strong alcohol lobby in Washington. The author also discusses some obstacles that have faced plaintiffs in lawsuits against the alcohol industry including statutes of limitations and the charge that the dangers of alcohol are so obvious that no warning is needed.

Key Words:
Drivers,
Illumination Level,
Legibility Distance,
Luminance,
Stimulus Size,
Symbol Size,
Traffic,
Traffic Settings,
Viewing Distance

099
Dahlstedt, S. and Svenson, O., "Detection and Reading Distances of Retroreflective Road Signs During Night Driving," *Applied Ergonomics*, **8:1, March 1977, 7-14.**

The detectability and legibility of road signs with different reflective intensities were studied under night driving conditions. The results indicated that to obtain optimal detectability and legibility distances, the reflective intensity of a new road sign should be in the range of 4 to 10 mcd/lux cm^2. For signs in this range, doubling the area of a sign was shown to increase detection distance of about 600 m by about 150-200 m. Opposing headlights decreased detection distances of 500-900 m by about 100 m. Finally, it was found that standard signs, with a text 170 mm high, could be read from a distance of about 115 m.

Key Words:
FDA

100
Dallas, H. and Enlow, M., "Read Your Labels," Institute for Consumer Education, Columbia, MO, 1943, 1-31.

The authors provide a classic and very readable introduction to the Food, Drug and Cosmetics Act. They discuss some of the Act's background and briefly explain many of its provisions.

ANNOTATIONS 101-200

Key Words:
Duty/Failure to Warn,
Foreseeability,
Misuse

101
Darden, T.M., "Products Liability in Minnesota: the Manufacturer's Duty to Warn of Foreseeable Misuse," *William Mitchell Law Review*, 13:4, 1987, 1011-1030.

The Minnesota Supreme Court recently held that a manufacturer has a duty not only to warn of risks arising from any foreseeable use of its products, but also of risks arising from foreseeable misuse of the product. Such misuse may include the user's failure to properly maintain safety devices provided by the manufacturer. The general rule is that the duty to warn rests heavily on the question of foreseeability.

Key Words:
Chemicals,
Proximate Cause

102
Davé, N., "Hazard Communication Standard Guidelines," *Professional Safety*, 33:1, January 1988, 21-24.

The author discusses OSHA's hazard communication standard, 29 CFR 1910.1200, and its application to the hazardous chemicals industry. Davé provides a step-by-step approach to implementing the standard which would be helpful to anyone developing a compliance program for the first time, or for those who wish to review and upgrade existing programs.

Key Words:
Consumers,
Print Size,
Reading of: warning labels,
Smokers,
Smoking,
Smoking Education Act,
Stimulus Size,
Symbol Size,
Traffic Settings,
Viewing Distance

103
Davis, R.M. and Kendrick, J.S., "The Surgeon General's Warnings in Outdoor Cigarette Advertising: Are They Readable?" *The Journal of the American Medical Association*, 261:1, January 1989, 90-94.

The authors discuss an experimental evaluation of the readability of cigarette advertisements in two outdoor media: billboards and taxicab advertisements. Under simulated driving conditions on city streets, observers were able to read the entire health warning on eighteen of the thirty-nine billboards studied; for highway driving conditions only two of thirty-nine highway billboards had readable health warnings. In a similar study of cigarette advertisements placed on taxicabs in New York City, observers were unable to read the health warning for any of the advertisements. For both the taxicab and the billboard advertisements, the observers were able to identify the brand name, other wording and noticeable imagery over 95% of the time. The authors conclude that for the majority of billboard and taxicab advertisements, the Surgeon General's warning is not readable in its current form.

Annotations (101-200)

Key Words:
Duty/Failure to Warn,
Strict Liability and
Warnings

104
DeMarco, M.M., "Products Liability—Strict Liability in Tort—Manufacturer's Duty to Warn Not Extinguished by User's Actual Knowledge of Danger," *Seton Hall Law Review*, 15, 1984-1985, 714-716.

The New Jersey Supreme Court has held that the plaintiff's actual knowledge of product hazards is not relevant to the issue of the defendant's duty to warn, but it is relevant to the question of whether the absence of a warning was the proximate cause of the injury. In addition, the court advocates the use of pictorial warnings in order to reach illiterate and non-English speaking individuals who may use the product.

Key Words:
Industrial,
OSHA

105
Denny, D., "Labeling Standard May Re-define Health and Safety Responsibilities," *Occupational Health and Safety*, January 1984, 30-32.

Some of the effects of the OSHA hazard communication standard on health professionals are discussed. It is predicted that implementation of the standard will result in more private sector employment for health and safety professionals.

Key Words:
Consumers,
Effectiveness of:
   educational/persuasive
   programs,
Parents,
Personal Presentations

106
Dershewitz, R.A. and Williamson, J.W., "Prevention of Childhood Household Injuries: A Controlled Clinical Trial," *American Journal of Public Health*, 67:12, December 1977, 1148-1153.

In this study the authors evaluate the impact of an educational program aimed at reducing childhood injuries in the home. Over two hundred mothers were randomly assigned to either an experimental or a control group. The experimental group participated in a personalized health education program that was meant to reduce household hazards. The program included discussions and readings about household risks and injuries to children.

A month after the program concluded, both groups received an unannounced household hazard assessment and survey questionnaire by a "blind" home visitor. The two groups were compared with regard to their knowledge, attitudes, and behavior regarding household hazards. Eleven potential hazards, each covered in the program readings, were selected for evaluation. Each of these eleven hazards was evaluated during the home visits and a composite score reflecting overall household safety was obtained.

The health education program apparently failed. There was no difference between the experimental and control groups for the final scores on any of the eleven individual hazards or the cumulative safety index score. Interestingly, individuals who participated in the education program *thought* that their homes were safer as a result of their participation in the study. The authors speculate that the failure of the program may have been due to the lack of a well-defined target population and the attempt to modify more than one behavior. The authors conclude that attempts at changing human behavior may be less effective than passive measures of injury control such as product safety regulations.

Key Words:
Brochures/Flyers,
Consumers,
Effectiveness of:
    educational/persuasive
    programs,
Parents,
Personal Presentations

107
Dershewitz, R.A., "Will Mothers Use Free Household Safety Devices?" *American Journal of Diseases of Children*, 133, January 1979, 61-64.

Two groups were studied to determine if mothers would use free safety devices to safety-proof their homes. The experimental group consisted of 101 families receiving health information on home safety-proofing. The control group consisted of 104 families. Each of the 205 families were given Kindergards (plastic locking devices for cupboards and cabinets) and electric outlet covers. All families received identical instruction on the uses of these devices. Both groups showed a significant increase in the use of the outlet covers, with the experimental group showing the greater increase. There was no significant increase in the use of the Kindergards by either group.

Key Words:
Familiarity with Product,
Perceived Risk,
Sources of Bias

108
Desaulniers, D.R., "Consumer Products Hazards: What Will We Think of Next?" *Proceedings of INTERFACE '89 - The Sixth Symposium on Human Factors and Industrial Design in Consumer Products*, Human Factors Society, Santa Monica, CA, 1989, 115-120.

This study was directed toward determining how individuals' perceptions of product hazardousness and their willingness to take precautions is affected by their perception of the probability and severity of product related accidents, their perception of accident controllability, and their familiarity with the product.

In the first experiment, seventy undergraduates were given a list of eighteen consumer products and asked to rate the degree of precaution they would take when using each product. They were also instructed to "Imagine using each product. What accidents involving each product would you fear occurring?" The subjects recorded the first three accidents that came to mind. They were next asked to rate the severity of injuries involved in each of these accidents, the likelihood of each accident occurring during their next use, and the hazardousness of each product. The results indicated that the best predictor of perceived hazardousness was the severity rating of the first accident scenario that came to mind. Also of interest was that the correlation between product hazardousness and the probability of accident occurrence increased from .03 for the first accident scenario to .15 for the second scenario and then to .61 for the third accident scenario that came to mind. According to the authors, these data suggest that the focus of hazard judgments switches from primarily attending to the severity of the most likely scenario for low hazard products, to the severity of the most severe scenario for high hazard products. With regard to the individual's intent to engage in precautionary behavior, a significant relationship (r =.97) was found between the mean rating of hazardousness and the intended level of precautionary behavior.

In the second experiment, seventy undergraduates were given a deck of eighteen cards, each displaying the name of a consumer product, and asked to rank the cards according to 1) perceived hazardousness, 2) likelihood of causing a minor injury, 3) likelihood of causing a severe accident, 4) extent to which likelihood of accidents involving the product were controllable, 5) extent to which severity of accidents involving the product was controllable, and 6) the frequency with which the subject used the product. As in the first experiment, a high correlation was found between ratings of product hazardousness and the likelihood of severe accidents. Interestingly enough, the rankings of the likelihood of minor accidents were not related to product hazards (r =.00). The results also showed that products used more frequently were judged to be less hazardous. In terms of accident controllability, products in which the likelihood of accidents was judged to be controllable were judged to be less hazardous.

As a result of this research, the authors indicate that manufacturers and safety professionals should be concerned with the types of accident scenarios the product immediately brings to mind.

Key Words:
Layout,
Organizing Information

109
Desaulniers, D.R., "Layout, Organization, and the Effectiveness of Consumer Product Warnings," *Proceedings of the Human Factors Society - 31st Annual Meeting,* **Human Factors Society, Santa Monica, CA, 1987, 56-60.**

The term "layout" refers to the spatial structure of a warning and the term "organization" refers to the semantic structure. According to Desaulniers, these two features are likely to influence an individual's propensity to read and remember warning information. The author conducted three preliminary experiments to evaluate this conjecture. He concluded that outline layout is preferable to paragraph layout and that the most effective type of organization is hierarchical. We would expect that these findings could also be applied to instruction manual design.

Key Words:
Process Charts/
Sequences,
Structured Text,
Understanding of
Instructions

110
Desaulniers, D.R., Gillan, D.J. and Rudisill, M., "The Effects of Format in Computer-Based Procedure Displays," *Proceedings of the Human Factors Society - 32nd Annual Meeting*, **Human Factors Society, Santa Monica, CA, 1988, 291-295.**

The authors investigated three possible formats for displaying procedural information on computer displays, such as those used for diagnosis. These formats were: flow chart, text, and extended text (a structured prose format which presents information less densely than the text format). For the nine subjects in this experiment (employees of Lockheed Engineering and Management Services Inc. and the NASA Johnson Space Center), it was found that the flow chart format resulted in a lower error rate than either text format. However, overall completion times for the various procedures did not vary significantly across the three formats.

Key Words:
Conveying Procedures,
Memory of:
   symbol/message,
Memory of: warning
   labels,
Recall,
Students

111
deTurck, M.A. and Goldhaber, G.M., "Consumers' Information Processing Objectives and Effects of Product Warnings," *Proceedings of the Human Factors Society - 32nd Annual Meeting*, **Human Factors Society, Santa Monica, CA, 1988, 445-449.**

The authors cite research indicating that a person's information processing objective determines how much information he or she can recall as well as the attitudes or judgements formed from the information. A study examining this issue was conducted involving forty-two subjects from an introductory communication class at the State University of New York at Buffalo. The subjects were instructed either to memorize the labels or simply form an impression of a product; the authors felt that these two conditions corresponded to different information-processing objectives.

Subjects who were instructed to memorize as much information as possible from product labels were found to spend more time examining or reading labels; they retained more, and they were about twice as likely to follow the behavior recommendation on the label than those who only formed impressions of the product. However, the authors note that subjects are more likely to form an impression of a product than to memorize its label. This behavior is logical for practical reasons, since it takes much more effort to memorize all product related information than it does to simply form an impression.

Key Words:
Adequacy of Warnings,
Warning Process Models

112
Deutsch, S., "Product Design and Consumer Safety: An Informational Approach," in *CP News*, 5:2, Consumer Products Technical Group, The Human Factors Society, August 1980, 3-4.

Deutsch states that to be effective, safety labels must: 1) be detected; 2) be recognized; 3) be read; 4) be understood; and 5) motivate appropriate behavior.

Key Words:
Consumers,
Degradation/Noise,
Glance Legibility,
Prohibition,
Prohibitive Slash,
Traffic,
Traffic Settings

113
Dewar, R.E., "The Slash Obscures the Symbol on Prohibitive Traffic Signs," *Human Factors*, 18:3, 1976, 253-258.

Two experiments were performed to evaluate the glance legibility of prohibitive symbols. The symbol variants were: slash over symbol; slash under symbol; partial slash; and no slash. The first experiment involved 1/25 secs viewing times under optimum viewing conditions, the second involved 1/10 secs viewing times under degraded viewing conditions. In both experiments, subjects were better able to identify symbols accurately when no slash was present. We note that the experiment did not determine whether the prohibitive information conveyed by a slash could be conveyed efficiently by other means.

Key Words:
Glance Legibility,
Prior Knowledge,
Semantic Differential,
Traffic,
Traffic Settings

114
Dewar, R.E. and Ells, J.G., "The Semantic Differential as an Index of Traffic Sign Perception and Comprehension," *Human Factors*, 19:2, 1977, 183-189.

The authors used factor analysis to investigate the meanings associated with various traffic signs. The factors considered were evaluative, potency, activity, and understandability. The resulting semantic differential scores were highly correlated with comprehension, but were unrelated to glance legibility; however, evaluative and understandability factors were correlated with glance legibility. The advantages of this procedure are: 1) the ability to precisely measure meaning; 2) the ability to separate meaning from simple preference, which may simply correspond to familiarity; and 3) the increased likelihood that more careful responses are elicited from subjects.

Key Words:
Design of: instructions,
Reading of: instructions,
Task Analysis,
Task Specific Context

115
Diehl, W. and Mikulecky, L., "Making Written Information Fit Workers' Purposes," *IEEE Transactions on Professional Communication*, 24:1, March 1981, 5-9.

The authors reference recent research suggesting that workers' purposes for using instructional materials may strongly influence their willingness and ability to use those materials. In "reading-to-do" tasks, the material serves only as a reference; in "reading-to-learn" tasks, the material is read more thoroughly and usually is read away from the job-related task it concerns; in "reading-to-assess" tasks, material is only skimmed to evaluate its usefulness for a future task or for another person. On-the-job reading tasks tend to be highly repetitive and integrated with other tasks. Also, written information is used as an aid in completing tasks.

The authors conclude that the design of instructional materials should vary with the purpose. The estimated readability of most material is not as important as the extent to which the material can quickly be used for particular tasks. It is noted that written material is often viewed as only one of the multiple sources for specific information.

Key Words:
Drivers,
Seat Belt Reminder,
Task Analysis

116
Dillon, J. and Galer, I.A.R., "Car Starting Sequence and Seat Belt Reminders," *Applied Ergonomics*, 6:4, 1975, 221-223.

The authors report on a study investigating the sequence of actions carried out by drivers when starting a car. This provided data relevant to the design of seat belt reminder systems. The actions, in sequence, were: OPEN DOOR, SIT IN SEAT, SHUT DOOR, START ENGINE, PUT CAR IN GEAR, RELEASE HANDBRAKE, MOVE AWAY. Ninety percent of the subjects followed this procedure. One hundred subjects (half of them male), representing the driving population, participated in the study. Seventy-five percent of the subjects tested were between the ages of twenty-one and fifty.

Theoretically, a seat belt reminder signal could be provided at any time. However, the authors concluded that it seems most advantageous to associate the signal onset both with the engagement of the gear box (most specifically, the forward gears) and with engagement of the ignition switch. This conclusion was justified by the finding that one in seven persons puts on his seat belt after starting the engine. We point out that these findings reinforce the importance of performing task analysis when deciding whether, when or how to provide warning information.

Annotations (101-200)

Key Words:
Biohazard,
Explosives,
Fire,
Hazard/Alert,
Industrial,
Ingress/Egress,
Moving Vehicle,
OSHA,
Personal Protective
  Equipment,
Point of Operation
  Guarding,
Prohibition,
Radiation,
Safety Information

117
Dionne, E.D., "Effective Safety Signs and Posters," *National Safety News*, **October 1979, 48-52.**

This paper very briefly describes the Occupational Safety and Health Act's warning requirements. The changes resulting from the most current set of deletions to 29 CFR Part 1910 General Industry Safety and Health Standards are pointed out.

As a side note we point out that the objective of this project was to remove from the OSHA safety and health standards those provisions which did not relate to true occupational safety matters. These included "requirements" which related more to convenience, public health, and product manufacturing specifications not falling under the employer's control. Our familiarity with this report stems from the fact that one of the authors (Miller) was responsible for the project during the time he was serving within the OSHA organization.

Key Words:
Conveying Action,
Conveying Conditions,
Conveying Procedures,
Design of: instructions,
Ordering of
  Conditions/Actions,
Writing Instructions

118
Dixon, P., "Plans and Written Directions for Complex Tasks," *Journal of Verbal Learning and Verbal Behavior,* **21, 1982, 70-84.**

The author notes that operating complex equipment, performing periodic maintenance, and following a recipe all require the efficient and accurate use of language to specify the necessary procedures. It was also noted that indirect requests take longer to respond to than direct ones, and that presenting instructions in the order of use (the "use-order" principle) makes sentences easier to understand and increases comprehension. In regard to the "use-order" effects, the author emphasizes a distinction between the action and condition clauses found in instructions, and performed a study in which they compared the effectiveness of instructions which provided either actions or conditions at the start of each sentence.

In this study, subjects were shown a video display and then told that it represented an electronic device that they would have to operate. Immediate trials and recall trials measured reading time, which, for immediate trials, was defined as the time from the onset of the sentence display to the first movement of the indicated knob or button. For recall trials, reading time was measured from the sentence display to the onset of the next foot press. It was found that sentences were generally read faster when the action information came before the condiion information. This effect was present when the condition information was a consequent of the action, when the action was in the main clause, and when the action was performed immediately or from memory.

However, the opposite trend appeared when conditions were used to specify which of many possible actions should be performed. The author feels it is unlikely that information-order effects merely reflect linguistic convention. Instead, he feels the information-order effect should be considered as an interaction with the various other sources of information available in most applications of written materials. Further studies should be performed to precisely describe this interaction and its impact on the effectiveness of different information orderings.

Key Words:
Design of: instructions,
Task Specific Context,
Understanding of Instructions,
Understanding/ Perception Models,
User Modeling

119
Dixon, P., "The Structure of Mental Plans for Following Directions," *Journal of Experimental Psychology: Learning, Memory, and Cognition*, 13:1, 1987, 18-26.

The author proposes a framework for how directions or instructions are used to construct mental plans. The model assumes that a plan can be described as a hierarchy of schemata in which a general description of the action to be performed is given at the top level, and then lower levels describe the action in greater detail. It is also assumed that this hierarchy is formed while a person reads the instructions which he is going to follow.

In accordance with this model, it would be reasonable to design instructions that allow the plan hierarchy to be developed effectively from the top down. Predictions of performance times made on the basis of this model were confirmed in a series of three experiments.

Key Words:
Design of: instructions,
Development Cycle,
Instructions in Litigation,
Problems in Design,
Understanding of Instructions

120
Dobrin, D., "Do Not Grind Armadillo Armor in This Mill," *IEEE Transactions on Professional Communication*, 28:4, December 1985, 30-37.

The author presents an interesting critique of many forms of instructions included with common consumer products. He cites the current trend of providing information solely for the purpose of avoiding liability which often results in nonsensical instructions or those that are unlikely to be read. After presenting examples of such instructions he develops an alternative set of instructions for a coffee mill. He notes that developing more effective instructions, which are not necessarily traditional, may pose difficulties with those who are traditionally minded.

Annotations (101-200)

Key Words:
Overapplication of Warnings

121
Dodds, T., "On the Lighter Side," *Family Safety & Health,* **44:2, Summer 1985, 11.**

F.M. Armbrecht of Wilmington, Delaware, discusses a sign on the hand dryers in the men's rooms at the Kansas City airport that reads, "Danger - Electric Shock Hazard - Do Not Operate with Wet Hands." (To paraphrase the old saying: One example is worth a thousand words. Hopefully, this sign is not typical of warning labels in the future.)

Key Words:
Cueing

122
Donner, K.A. and Brelsford, J.W., "Cuing Hazard Information for Consumer Products," *Proceedings of the Human Factors Society - 32nd Annual Meeting,* **Human Factors Society, Santa Monica, CA, 1988, 532-535.**

In a study involving fifty-four college students, the authors examined the effect of product attribute lists on the recall of hazard knowledge. The subjects participated in one of two conditions. In the first, they were presented a product alone; in the second, they were presented a product along with a list of attributes. Both groups of subjects were asked to generate as many hazards as they could for each product.

The surprising result was that the number of generated accident scenarios did not significantly differ between the two groups. There also were no reliable differences between the two groups in: the degree of precaution they said they would take; their self-reported likelihood of reading an accompanying warning; their rating of hazardousness; their rating of the severity of potential injury, or their perception of the likelihood of injury.

The authors concluded that providing lists of product attributes had little or no impact on these particular subjects. In reviewing this study, we were unable to conclude whether it suggested that attribute information provided with a product is only redundant or whether these particular results were unique to the subjects, products, and product attributes involved; a distinction for further study, indeed.

Annotations (101-200)

Key Words:
Amount of Information,
Information Overload,
Laboratory/Generic Settings,
Level of Detail,
Overapplication of warnings

123
Dorris, A.L., Connolly, T., Sadosky, T.L. and Burroughs, M., "More Information or More Data?: Some Experimental Findings," *Proceedings of the Human Factors Society - 21st Annual Meeting*, Human Factors Society, Santa Monica, CA, 1977, 25-28.

This paper surveys literature on how the amount of available information influences the quality of decision making. A clear distinction is made between data and information; information is defined as the useable portion of data. The authors note that providing irrelevant data (data bearing little or no information) has been shown to reduce performance in certain contexts.

Key Words:
Consumer Setting,
Filtering,
Human Factors,
Reading Measures,
Reading of: warning labels,
Students,
Warnings: evaluating effects on behavior

124
Dorris, A.L. and Purswell, J.L., "Warnings and Human Behavior: Implications for the Design of Product Warnings," *Journal of Products Liability*, 1, 1977, 255-263.

This paper discusses the warning process, warning design, and requirements for further research on these topics. It is stated that a warning must be received, understood, and acted upon accordingly. A well-controlled study is described in which one hundred high school and college students were asked to perform a simple task using a hammer that had one of three different types of warning labels attached; none of the subjects said they noticed the warning labels. A general discussion is given regarding human capacity to understand warnings, and the weak correlation between CPSC accident data and hazard perceptions is noted. General design concepts, such as those found in the classical Van Cott and Kincade or the McCormick books, are described.

Key Words:
Adequacy of Warnings,
Durability,
False Alarms,
Human Factors

125
Dorris, A.L. and Purswell, J.L., "Human Factors in the Design of Effective Product Warnings," *Proceedings of the Human Factors Society - 22nd Annual Meeting*, Human Factors Society, Santa Monica, CA, 1978, 343-346.

In this paper, the authors provide a short, general introduction to the role of human factors in warnings design. They state that warnings are necessary because people are unable to accurately estimate risk. References are given documenting this inability. Issues associated with effective warnings are listed and include: 1) the duty to warn; 2) warnings versus instructions; 3) understandability; and 4) durability.

The paper concludes by introducing several topics for future research and development. These are: 1) development of design criteria; 2) research on the optimum amount of information to be presented; 3) clarification of symbolic versus verbal warning issues; 4) development of an appropriate methodology for studying behavior; and 5) investigation of factors that influence responses, since for natural hazard warnings, individuals are unlikely to heed warnings when repeated false alarms occur. The authors point out that the lack of large scale federal funding may be impeding academic research, and that the current situation encourages the proliferation of consulting firms, which often must work for their clients in an environment of confidentiality.

Key Words:
Frequency Estimates,
Severity Estimates

126
Dorris, A.L. and Tabrizi, M.F., "An Empirical Investigation of Consumer Perception of Product Safety," *Journal of Products Liability*, **2, 1978, 155-163.**

The hazardousness of sixteen products was estimated by two hundred middle to upper middle class respondents. Each product is included in one of the following general categories of the NEISS product index: 1) space heating, cooling, and ventilating appliances; 2) kitchen appliances; 3) home workshop appliances; and 4) child nursery equipment. The rank ordered hazard ratings were then compared to NEISS injury frequency data and AFSI ratings. Nonsignificant correlations were obtained with both injury frequencies and AFSI ratings.

Both sex differences and age differences were minor. The perceived hazardousness of products with cutting edges was generally too high. Such a result may correspond to those predicted by the availability heuristic discussed by Kahneman. (NEISS is the National Electronic Injury Surveillance System of the Consumer Product Safety Commission. AFSI is the Adjusted Frequency Severity Index given to each product category on the basis of the collected data.)

Key Words:
State of the Art Defense,
Strict Liability and
 Warnings

127
Dossick, R., "The State of the Art Defense and Time Rule in Design and Warning Defect Strict Products Liability Cases," *Rutgers Law Review*, **38:3, Spring 1986, 505-537.**

In a warning defect case, state-of-the-art evidence refers to the available scientific knowledge of the risks associated with the product at the time of design, manufacture and sale. Dossick proposes that the state-of-the-art defense should be redefined to include knowledge and feasibility up to the time of product consumption or use. We add that some jurisdictions have favored these viewpoints in their recent decisions, a controversial finding of great concern to manufacturers and sellers of products.

Key Words:
Duty/Failure to Warn,
Negligence and
 Warnings,
Sophisticated User
 Defense,
Strict Liability and
 Warnings

128
Downs, C.P., "Duty to Warn and the Sophisticated User Defense in Products Liability Cases," *University of Baltimore Law Review*, **15:2, Winter 1986, 276-309.**

The sophisticated user defense asserts that if the user had the knowledge to understand the risks associated with the use of a product, then the manufacturer was reasonable to sell the product without a warning. This defense may be used only in negligence actions, not strict liability. The author proposes the elimination of strict liability failure to warn as a cause of action so that the sophisticated user defense may be used in all failure to warn cases.

Key Words:
Consumers,
Industrial,
Military,
Symbol Taxonomies,
Traffic

129
Dreyfuss, H., *Symbol Sourcebook*, **McGraw-Hill, New York, 1972.**

This reference book provides an exhaustive collection of existing symbols in a well organized, professional form. No attempt is made to evaluate the effectiveness of these symbols. Nevertheless, this book continues to be the classic references in the field of symbol design.

Key Words:
Advantages of Nonverbal
 Symbols,
Consumers,
Control/Display
 Elements,
Design Consistency,
Design of: labeling and
 safety signage systems,
Development Programs,
Industrial,
Moving Vehicle,
Multiple Referents,
Poison,
Radiation,
Routing,
Safety Information,
Symbol Generation,
Symbol Taxonomies,
Traffic,
User Group,
Verbal vs. Nonverbal
 Symbol/Message

130
Dreyfuss, H., "Visual Communication: A Study of Symbols," Society of Automotive Engineers, SAE 700103, 1970, 1-7.

The author presents an excellent introduction to graphic, nonverbal symbols. He notes that symbols have traditionally been designed for controlled conditions and select audiences, and that there is a potential for confusion when different symbols are used to convey the same meaning. The challenge is to make universally acceptable symbols. He summarizes the theoretical advantages of symbols over verbal signs, which include: 1) safety (symbols generate a quicker response and have more impact); 2) efficiency (symbols require much less area); and 3) economy (symbols do not need to be linguistically translated, so they can easily be universally used and interchanged). Symbol development is discussed in terms of content (e.g., pictographs versus abstract symbols), form (the actual appearance of symbol, e.g., line width), and symbol relations (the individual symbol in relation to the context of the system to which it belongs). Several interesting examples relevant to both development and testing are given.

General conclusions drawn from a 1969 survey of symbols are: 1) perspective drawings are not recommended; 2) figurative symbols are preferable to abstract ones; and 3) multiple element symbols are more difficult to understand than single element symbols.

Key Words:
Advantages of Nonverbal Symbols,
Consumers,
Control/Display Elements
Design Consistency,
Design of: labeling and safety signage systems,
Development Programs,
Industrial,
Introducing New Systems,
Moving Vehicle,
Poison,
Radiation

131
Dreyfuss, H. and Clifton, P., "Visual Communication: A Study of Symbols," *Graphic Science*, **April 1970, 21-26.**

This paper discusses the "new" symbol systems that are being designed to communicate a variety of messages to practically everyone. These symbols, the parameters of their development, graphic design and application, and the problem of their integration within current communication channels are considered. When shared terminology was translated into symbols, different graphic representations were frequently adopted by different groups. Confusion was added when new groups developed a new set of symbols for their own purposes.

Safety, efficiency, and economic advantages of utilizing symbols are noted, as are issues related to symbol design, testing, and coordination. The authors emphasize that properly designed and applied symbols can significantly enhance the exchange of information via visual communication. Such a proposition presumes the demonstrated correct meaning of those symbols to the intended target user population.

Key Words:
Application Guidelines,
Development Cycle,
Overapplication of warnings,
Warning Process Models

132
Driver, R.W., "A Communication Model for Determining the Appropriateness of On-Product Warnings," *IEEE Transactions on Professional Communication*, **30:3, September 1987, 157-163.**

Driver begins with the statement, "We are rapidly approaching the point of over-use of on-product warnings (OPWs) in the United States—if, indeed, we have not already reached it." To help sensitize readers to this point, he provides a qualitative communication model which gives insight into determining the most effective way of communicating product safety and use information. He also discusses potential problems with on-product warnings and emphasizes the negative effects of overwarning and the use of potentially ineffective and impractical warnings. We find this article interesting, as it points out the other side of the OPW issue: Have we exceeded the saturation point by providing too much information on product labels, and is it now time to conduct investigations which will lead to a rational alternative?

Annotations (101-200)

Key Words:
Accuracy,
Age,
Drivers,
Hand Signals,
Motor Vehicle,
Traffic,
Traffic Settings

133
Drury, C.G. and Pietraszewski, P., "The Motorists' Perception of the Bicyclists' Hand Signals," *Ergonomics*, **22:9, 1979, 1045-1057.**

Twenty-seven male and female graduate students and faculty viewed slides of a bicyclist approaching an intersection. They were asked to interpret the intended action of the bicyclist and to rate their confidence in their response. The results clearly demonstrated that the subjects obtained considerable information from the rider's position and informal body signals. Hand signals were interpreted with an accuracy of 80% for straight-arm signals and 65% for bent-arm signals.

In 1978, Drury found that, on a pencil-and-paper test, rules of the road knowledge declined with age. The same was found in this study; people most likely to be driving automobiles (people over 40 years of age) had very high error rates. A communication problem exists between bicyclists and motorists when judging each others' intentions. A strong case can be made for the use of hand signals based on logical and empirical arguments.

Key Words:
Conveying Action,
Decision Tables,
Description/Modeling,
Illustrations,
Process Charts/
 Sequences,
Tables and Flowcharts,
Verbal vs. Nonverbal
 Symbol/Message

134
Duchastel, P. and Waller, R., "Pictorial Illustration in Instructional Texts," in *The Technology of Text*, **19:11, Educational Technology Publications, Inc., Englewood Cliffs, 1979, 20-25.**

The authors introduce a function-based taxonomy of illustrations. They distinguish seven functions of explicative illustrations: 1) descriptive, 2) expressive, 3) logico-mathematical, 4) functional, 5) constructional, 6) algorithmic, and 7) data-display. For each function particular methods of display are more likely to work well.

Key Words:
Illustrations,
Organizing Information,
Page Layout,
Tables and Flowcharts,
Underlining/Highlighting

135
Duchastel, P.C., "Chapter 8: Textual Display Techniques," in *The Technology of Text*, **Jonassen, D.H. (Ed.), Educational Technology Publications, Inc., Englewood Cliffs, 1982, 167-191.**

This chapter from Jonassen's book addresses the broad issue of how textual display techniques, as a whole, fit into text design. It begins by introducing the nature of text in text processing. The author then moves on to some of the difficulties encountered in text processing and the problem of "focus" which addresses the need to somehow make it easy to select important information from the text. Display techniques to aid text processing are also summarized, including the use of labeling, highlighting, and illustrating. We believe the issues addressed in this article have significant relevance to the design of information for instructive purposes.

136
Duchon, J.C and Laage, L.W., "The Consideration of Human Factors in the Design of a Backing-Up Warning System," *Proceedings of the Human Factors Society - 30th Annual Meeting*, **Human Factors Society, Santa Monica, CA, 1986, 261-264.**

Key Words:
Back-Up Signals,
False Alarms,
Filtering,
Industrial Setting,
Probability/Frequency of Presentation,
Warnings: evaluating effects on behavior

This general paper discusses the role of audible back-up warning signals used on large vehicles. It notes that backing-up collisions have continued to be a problem even after the warnings were put into use. The warnings may have failed to solve the problem because workers become habituated to the signals as a result of continual exposure. One possible solution, which the author feels is feasible and deserves further study, is to only emit the warning signal when obstacles are present behind the vehicle. Such a system would require the use of advanced technology.

We have reviewed the circumstances surrounding numerous injuries to persons hit by vehicles backing up. It is often alleged that if an audible warning, mirrors, or other systems were present, these accidents would probably have been prevented. Before such a conclusion can be drawn, a thorough analysis must be made of the interactions between driver, vehicle, pedestrian and the environment in which all performing their respective roles. Often it is the case that the addition of such back-up safety systems does not make it "more likely that not" that a particular accident would have been prevented. Of course, this does not mean that the devices should not be provided. The focus of the present paper, in our opinion, is to point out that research must be done to determine which safety system design can enhance the likelihood of preventing back-up collision and injuries.

137
Duffy, T.M., "Chapter 6: Readability Formulas: What's the Use?" in *Designing Usable Texts*, **Duffy, T.M. and Waller, R. (Eds.), Academic Press, Inc., Orlando, 1985, 113-140.**

Key Words:
Readability Measures,
Understanding of Instructions

This chapter examines the logic and research support for primary applications of readability formulas in evaluating and producing texts (including the text within instructions and warnings). The author discusses the role of readability formulas as a means of predicting how easily certain texts can be comprehended. He further notes that over one hundred of these formulas have been developed, indicating a need for specialized readability formulas in certain contexts during the military services where certain technical terms, difficult for the general population, are well understood. This need to consider contextual factors has often been misunderstood or ignored (such as in the design of instructions). This paper also addresses various alternatives to readability formulas which might be used as predictors of comprehension.

Key Words:
Development Programs,
Readability Measures,
Understanding of
   Instructions,
Writing Instructions

138
Duffy, T.M. and Kabance, P., "Testing a Readable Writing Approach to Text Revision," *Journal of Educational Psychology*, **74:5, 1982, 733-748.**

A troublesome issue in the development of text is that faced when the available textual material is written at a level well beyond that for which the consumers of that information are able to comprehend. The question becomes one of determining how to best revise the text so that it has a readability for a larger population, or a population that is at a lower reading level. Past efforts to revise text by simplifying vocabulary and syntax have not always been successful.

In the research discussed in this paper, the authors sought to determine the effectiveness of current guidelines for readable writing as a means of revising text to increase comprehensibility. In this multi-stage experiment, involving several hundred Naval recruits (who typically are subjected to quantities of instructional and procedural type manuals), it was surprisingly found that simplifying vocabulary and sentences did not seem to be an effective method of facilitating comprehension.

The authors conclude that the practical implication of these findings is that a readability formula is not an effective production criterion. They note that comprehensibility might be better controlled through the use of what they have called the "transformer concept." The transformer is a group or individual who is competent in the subject area and who acts as an expert spokesman for the reader. Such an approach reflects the need to more explicitly consider the knowledge of the user of the technical information and the specific form in which this user organizes his knowledge.

Key Words:
Frequency Estimates

139
Dunn, J.G., "Subjective and Objective Risk Distribution," *Occupational Psychology*, **46, 1972, 183-187.**

Several interesting findings are summarized on risk perception regarding group effects, perceived risk, and accidents. A study is presented in which twenty-five experienced chain-saw operators were asked to rank the likelihood of injuring their various body parts. These answers were compared to accident reports for 250 chain-saw related accidents. No significant correlations were found between the subjective rankings and the objective data, which suggests that operators incorrectly perceive the level of hazard present for this type of work. On the other hand, increased precautions by operators under perceived conditions of high risk may alter accident rates, which would, of course, reduce the correlation between subjective rankings and incidence of injury.

140
Dupuy, R.K., "Torts—in Iowa, Warning of Foreseeable Material Risk Must be Specific and is Not Encompassed by a General Description of Greater Peril, Must Extend to the Ultimate User of an Unavoidably Unsafe Product, and If Inadequate, Raises a Rebuttable Presumption of Causation in a Mass Utilization of 'Hardsell' Advertising Context," *Drake Law Review*, 34:4, 1985-1986, 1091-1108.

Key Words:
Duty/Failure to Warn,
Foreseeability,
Immunizations,
Learned Intermediary Rule,
Unavoidably Unsafe Product

In Iowa, the duty to warn is imposed upon the manufacturer of an unavoidably unsafe product. In a mass immunization context where there is no learned intermediary, the duty extends to the ultimate recipient. The warning must specifically mention and describe all foreseeable, material risks.

141
Easterby, R.S., "Perceptual Organization in Static Displays for Man/Machine Systems," *Ergonomics*, 10:2, 1967, 195-205.

Key Words:
Context,
Control/Display Elements,
Description/Modeling,
Understanding/Perception Models,
Visual Displays: miscellaneous

This article provides a theoretical discussion of displays and the ways they are perceived. Its interesting aspects include: 1) a treatment of the human mind as a model information processor; 2) a classification of display types (on-line vs. off-line, with further subdivisions); 3) a focus on meaning and significance (e.g., whether symbols should be based on geographical, operational, or functional criteria); 4) specification of symbolic verbs, nouns, and adjectives; 5) application of the Gestalt figure/ground ideas (e.g., stability, continuity, unity and closure, symmetry, simplicity, and line and contrast boundaries); 6) the role of internal and external structure; and 7) the presentation of displays as a form of language that follows the three principles of language design. This latter includes: pragmatics (rules between signs and things, and the inference that there is a context in which the signs are applicable); semantics (relations between signs and referent objects, ideas, actions or qualities); and syntactics (relationships between signs).

Key Words:
Point of Operation
 Guarding,
Understanding/
 Perception Models

142
Easterby, R.S., "The Perception of Symbols for Machine Displays," *Ergonomics*, **13:1, 1970, 149-158.**

The author discusses the role of pattern perception theory based on the Gestalt view of perception as it applies to the practical design of symbols for machine displays. Several Gestalt principles and their applicability to symbol design are presented. These principles include: figure/ground, figure boundary, geometrical forms, closure, continuity, simplicity, and symmetry. The author provides an overview of experimental studies pertaining to the discriminability of symbols as well as studies that address the comprehension of symbols.

Key Words:
Accuracy,
Age,
Caustic Materials,
Consumer Labeling and
 Signage Systems,
Consumer Surveys,
Consumers,
Elderly,
Electrical Hazard,
Fire,
Fire Safety Signs,
Hazard,
Hazard/Alert,
Hazardous Materials,
Housewives,
Message Complexity,
Poison,
Prior Knowledge

143
Easterby, R.S. and Hakiel, S.R., "Field Testing of Consumer Safety Signs: The Comprehension of Pictorially Presented Messages," *Applied Ergonomics*, **12:3, 1981, 143-152.**

All known symbols pertaining to fire, poison, caustic, electrical, and general hazards were surveyed, and a subset was selected for further analysis. This subset (which consisted of symbols that were fairly abstract, as opposed to being pictographs) was incorporated into a set of sign variants. The variants were tested using a structured random national sample of 4000 British residents. The highest comprehension of any sign was only 20% when comprehension criteria were rigid, and ranged to 50% with less rigid criteria. Some of the poorer signs were comprehended at rates of 5% or less, even with less rigid comprehension criteria. Prior experience with the symbol increased comprehension by a factor of 1.5 to 2; housewives and older individuals had more difficulty comprehending the symbols.

With its extensive number of symbols and large sample size, this is obviously a very significant study in our opinion. Since the study focused only on residents of Great Britain, caution must be used in extending its results to other populations and other symbol sets. However, its findings seem generalizable in concluding that literacy for symbols is on the average quite low.

Key Words:
Caustic Materials,
Color Coding,
Color/Hazard,
Consumers,
Design Consistency,
Design of: labeling and
 safety signage systems

144
Easterby, R.S. and Hakiel, S.R., "Safety Labelling of Consumer Products: Shape and Colour Code Stereotypes in the Design of Signs," University of Aston in Birmingham, AP Report No. 75, December 1977.

This study investigated whether stereotypes exist for shape and color coding of safety signs. The British subjects were provided with materials of different shapes and colors, and then asked to

Annotations (101-200)

Key Words (cont.):
Elemental Breakdowns,
Fire,
Hazard/Alert,
Poison,
Population Stereotypes,
Production Method,
Shape Coding,
Shape/Hazard,
Symbol Generation,
Symbol Taxonomies

use them to make up descriptive, prescriptive, and proscriptive signs for caustic, inflammable, and poisonous products. Subjects had some problem distinguishing between descriptive, prescriptive and proscriptive messages, so no conclusions were drawn regarding stereotyping and these types of messages. Certain stereotypes were found, but a large degree of variation was present.

This paper also presents an interesting discussion of the structural elements of non-verbal signs. These elements include: 1) the color of the image; 2) the color of the image's background; 3) the use of a shaped enclosure; 4) the color of such an enclosure; 5) the use of a surrounding shape on which the sign is mounted; and 6) the color of the surrounding shape. The researchers also state that safety signs should assist in: 1) discriminating products from one another; 2) identifying products; 3) attending (highlighting a product's distinctive characteristics); 4) searching (locating a particular product among a selection of products); 5) classifying and categorizing; and 6) comprehending (understanding a course of action, as well as recognizing the sign).

145
Easterby, R.S. and Zwaga, H.J.G., "Evaluation of Public Information Symbols, ISO Tests: 1975 Series," AP Report No. 60, March 1976.

Key Words:
Accuracy,
Consumer Labeling and Signage Systems,
Consumer Surveys,
Consumers,
Cultural Factors,
Design Consistency,
ISO,
Public Information

The researchers studied symbols for: 1) stairs; 2) waiting rooms; 3) drinking water; 4) taxis; 5) information; and 6) toilets. Subjects from Australia, Canada, Spain, Argentina, India, the Netherlands, and the U.K. were used for testing. A wide degree of variation in understandability was found for the symbol variants, but there was no interaction between country and symbols (poorer symbols tended to be universally misunderstood). From these results, the researchers developed methodological conclusions related to cross cultural testing. In particular, they conclude that matching-type tests measure dependencies between symbol variants, while recognition-type tests provide measures for specific symbols which are independent of other symbols.

146
Eaton, J.T., "The Manufacturer's Duty to Warn Consumers of Possible Side Effects of Prescription Drugs," *Illinois Bar Journal*, 74:8, April 1986, 376-380.

Key Words:
Contraceptives,
Drugs,
Duty/Failure to Warn,
Immunizations,
Learned Intermediary Rule

As a general rule, the prescription drug manufacturer has no duty to warn ultimate consumers of product hazards since there is a physician acting as a "learned intermediary." There is a concern that without this rule, the patient may receive too much information and suffer from "sensory overload." There are two exceptions to this rule, mass immunizations and oral contraceptives, where the consumer has less contact with the prescribing physician and greater freedom of choice in the decision to take the drug.

Key Words:
Illustrations,
Information Coding,
Understanding/
 Perception Models,
User Modeling,
Verbal vs. Nonverbal
 Symbol/Message

147
Edell, J.A. and Staelin, R., "The Information Processing of Pictures in Print Advertisements," *Journal of Consumer Research*, **10, June 1983, 45-61.**

The authors note that previous research has consistently shown that advertisements which include pictures are more easily recalled than those which contain text alone. They performed specific research directed toward determining a model of the process by which a viewer evaluates, encodes and stores information found in such ads.

For a set of 27 subjects between the ages of 20 and 28, it was found that significant influences on their information processing activity could be attributed to: whether the message was conveyed pictorially or verbally; whether the picture itself was framed (with a verbal message of some type), or unframed; and whether the type of claim made in the advertisement was either objective, subjective, or a characterization. Information provided in pictures was more apt to be recalled and this tendency increased when the picture was framed with a verbal message. In addition, brand evaluative thoughts were more likely to be elicited when the picture was framed. Interestingly, the verbal or framed picture diagram was better for describing objective rather than subjective information. Consistently, the unframed picture seemed to be the best for providing subjective information.

Key Words:
Drivers,
Effectiveness of:
 educational/persuasive
 programs,
Existing/Past Behavior
 Patterns,
Formal Teaching/
 Counseling/Education

148
Edwards, M.L. and Ellis, N.C., "An Evaluation of the Texas Driver Improvement Training Program," *Human Factors*, **18:4, August 1976, 327-334.**

The purpose of this major research effort was to evaluate the effects of the driver improvement training program of the Texas Department of Public Safety on driving records and to design a method for predicting the frequencies of violations and accidents for the twelve months following training. Between November 1, 1972 and August 31, 1973, about 2350 drivers took part in the program (with a control group of 1666 drivers). Data collected for twelve months prior to program participation and for twelve months following were studied. The number of accidents, the number of violations, and the sum of accidents and violations were the measures of driver performance.

The following experimental groups showed greater improvement in the number of violations than the control group: males 25-34, accident category; males and females 17-24, violation category; males and females, total entry category; and males 35 or older, total entry category. Note that only one group (males 25-34) experienced a reduction in accidents following the program. Finally, males 17-24 experienced an improvement in driving attitude and significant improvements in driving-related knowledge.

149
Ellington, D., "The Smokeless Tobacco Industry's Failure to Warn," *Journal of Legal Medicine,* **6:4, December 1985, 489-507.**

Key Words:
Individual Autonomy,
Informed Consumer,
Smokeless Tobacco

Existing products liability law suggests that some tobacco suppliers could be held liable for failure to warn of the dangers of smokeless tobacco. Studies show a causal link between use of the product and health disorders. However, many users believe the product is innocuous. The author feels that this situation can be resolved by requiring the smokeless tobacco industry to warn consumers. By providing a warning, companies may avoid tort claims and at the same time recognize the right of individuals to choose for themselves whether to confront certain risks.

150
Ells, J.G. and Dewar, R.E., "Rapid Comprehension of Verbal and Symbolic Traffic Sign Messages," *Human Factors,* **21:2, 1979, 161-168.**

Key Words:
Drivers,
Motor Vehicle,
Reaction Time,
Traffic,
Traffic Settings,
Verbal vs. Nonverbal
  Symbol/Message

This paper summarizes two experiments where verbal and symbolic traffic signs were compared on the basis of reaction times (time needed to comprehend and begin stating whether the sign was of a given type). In general, such reaction times were lower for symbolic signs. This effect was even greater when the signs were degraded (i.e. visual noise). For a few sign variants, however, reaction time was higher for symbolic signs, suggesting the necessity of considering a specific symbol in the context of where it will appear and what its intended function is to be. We caution that without such studies, generalization could lead to an incorrect conclusion about a specific sign.

Key Words:
Accuracy,
Color of Stimulus,
Drivers,
Legibility Distance,
Motor Vehicle,
Railroad Crossing,
Railroad Settings,
Reaction Time,
Recognition Time,
Traffic

151
Ells, J.G., Dewar, R.E. and Milloy, D.G., "An Evaluation of Six Configurations of the Railway Crossbuck Sign," *Ergonomics,* **23:4, 1980, 359-367.**

At the request of Transport Canada, a federal government agency, six variations of the railway crossbuck sign were evaluated. The following response variables were used to evaluate each version: speed of message comprehension; accuracy of identification for short exposure durations; maximal identification distance; and degree to which new versions of the sign were initially comprehensible to subjects. The subjects were male and female university students between the ages of eighteen and thirty. The results indicated that the existing Canadian version of the crossbuck sign was inferior to two of the experimental versions, a white sign with a red border, and a yellow sign with a black border. Between these two versions, either no difference was found or the red and white version was more effective, depending on the particular response variable.

Key Words:
Drivers,
Effectiveness of:
  educational/persuasive
  programs,
Feedback,
Incentives,
Seat Belt Nonusers

152
Elman, D. and Killebrew, T.J., "Incentives and Seat Belts: Changing a Resistant Behavior Through Extrinsic Motivation," *Journal of Applied Psychology,* **8:1, 1978, 72-83.**

In justifying this study, the authors note that there is a common assumption that simply providing seat belts and then advising the public of the value of seat belt use will be sufficient to induce drivers to "buckle up." This assumption is a significant mistake, since less than one in four drivers wears a seat belt at any given time. As an alternative approach, they hypothesized that offering tangible, positive incentives would increase seat belt use.

A specific study was performed that tested the immediate behavioral effects of offering drivers monetary rewards contingent on the wearing of seat belts. The subjects were 1026 female and 1646 male drivers of noncommercial, passenger automobiles. The maximum usage rate by the experimental group increased significantly to about 40%. Another interesting finding was that a safety message which did not mention seat belts tended to decrease seat belt use. The strength of the latter finding was, however, questionable, since such effects occurred only in one phase of their experiment. We expect that the findings of this study regarding the value of positive incentives will continue to be valid. However, since so many states now have mandatory seat belt laws, their usage rate findings may no longer be valid.

Annotations (101-200)

Key Words:
Children,
Consumers,
Effectiveness of:
  educational/persuasive
  programs,
Formal Teaching/
  Counseling/Education,
Parents

153
Embry, D.D. and Malfetta, J.L., "Reducing the Risk of Pedestrian Accidents to Preschoolers by Parent Training and Symbolic Modeling for Children: An Experimental Analysis in the Natural Environment," *Research Report 2,* **1978, 1-78.**

In a surprisingly successful experiment with a group of thirteen children, the effects of a parental workshop and a specially designed children's storybook were evaluated. The dependent variables were 1) the rate of entries into the street, and 2) parental reinforcement of safe play. After intervention, street entries by children were reduced by a factor of twelve. The results also indicate that the program caused parents to provide positive reinforcement for safe behavior. The program was credited with reducing children's daily exposure to vehicular traffic from sixteen occasions to one occasion per twenty-four hours of outdoor play.

Key Words:
CPSA,
Disclosure Rule

154
Epstein, J.M., "Failure to Warn," *Trial,* **22, April 1986, 67-68.**

The Consumer Product Safety Act provides that an individual who sustains an injury by reason of a manufacturer's "knowing" violation of a consumer product safety rule or the disclosure rule, may sue in federal court to recover damages, costs and attorney fees. The disclosure rule requires that the Commission be notified of any products that fail to comply with existing product safety standards. We point out that such provisions of course do not preclude the normal rights of litigation under tort law for product related injuries.

Key Words:
Risk Compensation

155
Evans, L., Wasielewski, P. and Von Buseck, C.R., "Compulsory Seat Belt Usage and Driver Risk-Taking Behavior," *Human Factors,* **24:1, February 1982, 41-48.**

The authors describe the "danger compensation principle," which suggests that the potential safety advantages of seat belts may be decreased or neutralized by an increase in driver risk taking. In support of this theory, studies are cited showing that seat belt use has generally increased after the passage of mandatory seat belt use laws, but often without equivalent reductions in occupant deaths. The authors cite Conybeare (1980) who, using a regression model, demonstrated that pedestrian injuries and deaths increased well beyond their predicted values after the passage of mandatory use laws, while deaths and injuries of vehicle occupants decreased. (We suggest that this may be an indication of driver behavior which is more risky or reckless.)

To evaluate the extent to which the danger compensation principle holds for automobile drivers, a study was performed that compared the car-following distances chosen by drivers who were wearing seat belts versus those who were not. Of the 4812 cars and light-duty trucks observed driving in the study in the State of Michigan, 2446 were driven by seat belt users and 2366 were driven by non-users. Since users of seat belts did not appear to follow at riskier distances than nonusers, no evidence was found for the difference in risk acceptance of users compared to nonusers—as predicted by the danger compensation principle. However, since use of seat belts was not mandatory, it is quite possible that the belt users were simply more safety conscious to begin with. Consequently, the results of this study clearly do not rule out the possibility of risk compensation.

Key Words:
Actual Behavior,
Behavior Factors,
Children,
Discrepancy Between Self-Reports,
Effectiveness of: educational/persuasive programs,
Message Tone

156
Evans, R.I., Rozelle, R., Lasater, T.M., Dembroski, T.M. and Allen, B.P., "Fear, Arousal, Persuasion, and Actual vs Implied Behavioral Change: New Perspective Utilizing a Real-Life Dental Hygiene Program," *Journal of Personality and Social Psychology*, 16:2, 1970, 220-227.

Differing types of information were given to junior high students in an attempt to influence tooth brushing behavior. The provided forms of information were respectively described as: high fear arousal; moderate fear arousal; positive appeal; elaborated recommendations only; and brief recommendations only. Among these, high fear induced the largest change in reported behavior followed by recommendations only. Actual behavior was changed the most by elaborated instructions, followed by positive appeals.

Key Words:
Cigarettes,
Preemption,
Smoking Education Act

157
Ewell, T.A., "Preemption of Recovery in Cigarette Litigation: Can Manufacturers Be Sued for Failure to Warn Even Though They Have Complied with Federal Warning Requirements?" *Loyola of Los Angeles Law Review*, 20:3, April 1987, 867-919.

The author analyzed the purpose, the language and the debates associated with the passage of the comprehensive Smoking Education Act of 1984. The author concludes that Congress did not intend to preempt common law causes of action against the tobacco industry using a failure to warn theory. Congress only intended to preempt the "requirements" and "prohibitions" of federal and state regulatory agencies with respect to labeling and advertising.

Annotations (101-200)

Key Words:
Chemicals,
Sophisticated User
 Defense

158
Faulk, R.O., "Product Liability and the Chemical Manufacture: Limitations on the Duty to Warn," *Oklahoma Law Review*, 38:2, Summer 1985, 233-234.

Unlike most products, generic chemicals are typically marketed to sophisticated industrial distributors and users. These customers generally are fully aware of product dangers and have a greater opportunity to prevent injuries than a remote manufacturer. In circumstances involving bulk sales, the manufacturer's connection becomes even more remote. Since distributor storage, barrelling and sales are beyond the scope of a manufacturer's control, an adequate warning to the distributor may discharge the manufacturer's liability.

Key Words:
Advantages of Nonverbal
 Symbols,
Public Information,
Symbol Taxonomies

159
Feinstein, R.A., "Symbolically Speaking," *Bell Telephone Magazine*, 50:4, November/December 1971, 10-14.

This paper summarizes many of the principles and findings discussed in Dreyfuss (1972).

Key Words:
Effectiveness of:
 educational/persuasive
 programs,
Feedback,
Workers

160
Fellner, D.J. and Sulzer-Azaroff, B., "Increasing Industrial Safety Practices and Conditions through Posted Feedback," *Journal of Safety Research*, 15:1, Spring 1984, 7-21.

This study was conducted in a 500-employee paper mill. Weekly surveys of the mill were taken with respect to 31 practices and conditions. The results of the surveys were posted weekly in conspicuous locations. Safe practices and conditions increased significantly during the study, and injury rates were decreased by 50% (p <.1). However, the program did not equally affect the behavior of all employee groups: while nine of the 17 groups improved, six stayed the same and one became worse. Further work on determining why these differences occurred is recommended by the authors.

Key Words:
Drugs,
FDA,
Preemption,
Punitive Damages

161
Fern, F.H and Sichel, W.M., "Failure to Warn in Drug Cases: Are Punitive Damages Justifiable?," *For the Defense*, 27, June 1985, 12-20.

Generally, courts will award punitive damages if the defendant's conduct is found to be malicious, willful, wanton or in conscious disregard for the consequences. The authors argue that the recent trend of awarding punitive damages in products liability cases should not spill over to drug product liability

Annotations (101-200)

failure to warn cases because the FDA's extensive and exclusive regulation of product labeling preempts state legislative and judicial action in this field.

Key Words:
Conflicting Objectives

162
Fhaner, G. and Hane, M., "Seat Belts: Relations between Beliefs, Attitude, and Use," *Journal of Applied Psychology*, 59:4, 1974, 472-482.

Questionnaires regarding seat belts were mailed to car owners; a total of 368 responded. Factor analysis and regression analysis revealed that two factors, perceived effectiveness and discomfort, were the best predictors of reported use of seat belts (r = .52). Discomfort was the best single predictor of seat belt use. We point out that since the time of this study, both the designs and knowledge of effectiveness have changed. Seat belt designs have attempted to reduce discomfort; perhaps at the expense of effectivenes. Such trade-offs appear to be an inherent aspect of safety engineering.

Key Words:
Auditory,
Auditory Coding,
Drivers,
Emergency Vehicles,
Reaction Time,
Symbol Generation,
Traffic Settings

163
Fidell, S., "Effectiveness of Audible Warning Signals for Emergency Vehicles," *Human Factors*, 20:1, 1978, 19-26.

Twenty-four subjects performed a simulated driving task in which they were asked to respond to warning signals by stepping on the brakes. Six different types of auditory signals, corresponding to four standard emergency signals and two modified signals, were developed. Each of the signals was electronically processed to ensure that all the signals would be of approximately equal perceptibility. Reaction times to these signals were approximately equivalent.

Key Words:
Attention Measures,
Children,
Effectiveness of:
  educational/persuasive programs,
Labels,
Location,
Memory of:
  symbol/message,
Reading of:
  warning labels,
Recognition,
Smoking,
Education Act,
Warnings: evaluating effects on behavior

164
Fischer, P.M., Richards, J.W., Berman, E.J. and Krugman, D.M., "Recall and Eye Tracking Study of Adolescents Viewing Tobacco Advertisements," *The Journal of the American Medical Association*, 251:1, January 1989, 84-89.

The researchers examined the viewing of tobacco advertisements by sixty-one adolescents. They found that the average viewing time of warning information amounted to only 8% of the total advertisement viewing time. In 43.6% of the cases the warning was not viewed at all. Following the study of viewing behavior, the participants were asked to identify the previously displayed warnings within a list that included other simulated warnings. Subjects did only slightly better than random guessing in this recognition test. Based on these results, the authors conclude that the federally mandated warning against smoking appears to be an ineffective public health message in so far as adolescents are concerned.

Key Words:
Acceptability,
Frequency Estimates,
Perceived Risk,
Sources of Bias

165
Fischhoff, B., "Cognitive Liabilities and Product Liability," *Journal of Products Liability*, **1, 1977, 207-219.**

This paper provides a very readable introduction to risk perception. It implies that although risk perception may seem to be irrational, it has a definable methodology. In other words, the discrepancies between objective measures of risk and subjective estimates can be explained in some cases by the way people process risk information, the way risk information is presented, and by various characteristics of the risk itself.

Fischoff summarizes several studies, demonstrating the following sources of bias and attributes of risk perception: 1) the use of the availability heuristic; 2) the tendency to overestimate the risk factors of unlikely but sensational causes of death and to underestimate likely but "quiet" causes of death; 3) the difficulty of including all relevant information in fault trees and the effect of fault trees on risk perception; 4) the effect of providing sets of problems together rather than separately; 5) the tendency toward excessive confidence in risk estimates and in one's knowledge in general; 6) excessive confidence in one's ability to avoid accidents; 7) the difficulty of combining information from many sources in a way that is consistent with rational decision-making principles; 8) the effects of problem phrasing; 9) bias due to the so-called "wisdom" of hindsight; 10) differences between the acceptable levels of voluntary and involuntary risk; and 11) the relationship between benefits and risk acceptance.

Key Words:
Acceptability,
Effectiveness of:
  educational/persuasive
  programs

166
Fischhoff, B., Slovic, P., Lichtenstein, S., Read, S. and Combs, B., "How Safe Is Safe Enough? A Psychometric Study of Attitudes Towards Technological Risks and Benefits," *Policy Sciences*, **9:2, April 1978, 127-152.**

This study examined the "expressed preferences" approach of measuring public attitudes toward risks and benefits. Using a questionnaire, the subjects evaluated thirty different activities and technologies in terms of their perceived benefit to society, their perceived risk, the acceptability of their current risk level, and their position on nine different risk dimensions. Members of the Eugene, Oregon League of Women Voters participated.

The nine risk dimensions were: voluntariness of risk; immediacy of effect; relevant knowledge of persons exposed to the risk; knowledge possessed by science; control over risk; newness of risk; type of risk (chronic or catastrophic); people's feeling about the risk ("common-dread"); and severity of consequences. The activities and technologies varied broadly in the quality and quantity of their respective risks and benefits.

Both tangible and intangible benefits were estimated by participants. Other subjects were told to consider the risk of dying as a consequence of the activity or technology. After rating the risks, the subjects judged the acceptability of the current level of risk of each activity or technology in terms of whether it was acceptable or too risky.

Perceived risk declined slightly with benefit, and people thought that most items ought to be made safer, despite the fact that this would require serious societal action. None of the risk characteristics were significantly correlated with perceived benefit, but perceived risk correlated with dread and severity. Ratings of the nine dimensions were highly intercorrelated; two factors (severity and technological risk) seemed to account for these intercorrelations.

Key Words:
Frequency Estimates,
Sources of Bias

167
Fischhoff, B., Slovic, P. and Lichtenstein, S., "Fault Trees: Sensitivity of Estimated Failure Probabilities to Problem Representation," *Journal of Experimental Psychology: Human Perception and Performance,* **4:2, 1978, 330-344.**

This study investigated the effects of varying different aspects of fault tree structure. The subjects were presented fault trees describing why a car fails to start. The trees used in the study had four to eight branches. The results showed that the subjects were insensitive to omitted information. Also, slight perception-related effects resulted from increasing the amount of detail in the whole tree or in some of the branches. By presenting a branch in pieces, its perceived importance was increased.

Key Words:
Contraceptives,
Drugs,
Duty/Failure to Warn,
Immunizations,
Learned Intermediary
  Rule

168
Flannagan, B.P., "Products Liability: The Continued Viability of the Learned Intermediary Rule as it Applies to Product Warnings for Prescription Drugs," *University of Richmond Law Review,* **20:2, Winter 1986, 405-423.**

The author surveys the development of and the rationale behind the learned intermediary rule which states that drug manufacturers only have a duty to warn physicians of dangers associated with prescription drugs, not ultimate consumers. She also discusses several exceptions to this rule, including mass immunizations and oral contraceptives. The author advocates requiring drug manufacturers to warn consumers when a warning can be conveyed in lay person's language. In situations involving medical complexities, she believes the physician has the duty to warn the patient.

Key Words:
Drivers,
Effectiveness of:
  educational/persuasive
    programs

169
Fleischer, G.A., "An Experiment in the Use of Broadcast Media in Highway Safety: Systematic Analysis of the Effect of Mass Media Communication in Highway Safety," National Highway Traffic Safety Administration, Washington, D.C., DOT HS-800 629, December 1971, 1-131.

In the spring of 1971, public service announcements promoting the use of seat belts were distributed to radio and TV stations. The impact of these announcements was evaluated in two demographically-matched communities in California (Modesto and Salinas). Observations of seat belt use were taken for the two weeks prior to the broadcast, for the five week period of the campaign, and for the four weeks following the campaign. Over 22,000 vehicles and 28,000 occupants were observed, and 2,000 telephone interviews were conducted to collect data. No significant effect on safety belt use or related attitudes was found to be connected to the communication campaign.

Key Words:
Case of Text,
Laboratory/Generic
  Settings,
Legibility Distance,
Perception of
  Symbol/Message

170
Foster, J.J. and Bruce, M., "Reading Upper and Lower Case on Viewdata," *Applied Ergonomics*, 13:2, June 1982, 145-149.

The authors argue that letter size is usually a confounding variable when case is varied. They report that in comparisons of print of the same nominal size, upper case letters were identified at greater distances than lower case letters. Comparisons also showed that lower case letters were read more rapidly. For Viewdata, upper case text did not seem to be less legible than lower case. The authors conclude that the Prestel page designer probably does not impair reading efficiency.

Key Words:
Adequacy of Warnings,
Application Guidelines,
Design of: labeling and
  safety signage systems,
Duty/Failure to Warn,
Negligence and
  Warnings,
Strict Liability and
  Warnings

171
Fowler, F.D., "Failure to Warn: A Product Design Problem," *Proceedings of the Symposium: Human Factors and Industrial Design in Consumer Products*, Poydar, H.R. (Ed.), Tufts University, Medford, 1980, 241-250.

This paper provides a very general introduction to the issue of warnings and product design. Anecdotal examples are given, as well as a short, simple summary of the designer's responsibility under product liability law. Basic requirements of adequate warnings and instructions and general guidelines to be applied during warning design are listed.

Key Words:
Drivers,
Effectiveness of:
  educational/persuasive
  programs,
Formal Teaching/
  Counseling/ Education

172
Fuchs, C., "Wisconsin Driver Improvement Program: A Treatment-Control Evaluation," *Journal of Safety Research*, 12:3, Fall 1980, 107-114.

In introducing this extremely large study, Fuchs notes that only a few driver improvement programs have been evaluated in terms of their ability to affect the subsequent driving of program participants. To remedy such problems, this study was performed. It was restricted to the individual counseling element of the Wisconsin Driver Improvement program. The subjects were habitual violators, drivers with 7-11 points in a one-year period or drivers about to have their licenses reinstated after revocation/suspension. A control group was created by randomly selecting 10% of this group; members of this group were not notified to attend counseling. During the year following the counseling, 84,300 drivers were in the experimental group and the control group consisted of nearly 11,000 drivers. The Wisconsin program was not shown to be effective in reducing traffic incidents, as counseling was not found to be beneficial for any subgroup of driver violators in the study.

Key Words:
Accuracy,
Agencies,
Comprehension of:
  warning labels,
Consumers,
Effectiveness of:
  educational/persuasive
  programs,
Governmental Labeling
  and Signage Systems,
Labels,
Memory of:
  symbol/message,
Message Tone,
Recognition

173
Funkhouser, G.R., "An Empirical Study of Consumers' Sensitivity to the Wording of Affirmative Disclosure Messages," *Journal of Public Policy and Marketing*, 3, 1984, 26-37.

The Federal Trade Commission (FTC) requires so called affirmative disclosure messages for particular product categories where consumers may have been mislead by product claims or other industry produced information. This paper presents a field-experimental study directed toward evaluating consumer comprehension of three versions of such affirmative disclosure messages. In this case, the affirmative disclosure statements were health warnings pertaining to a dried protein food supplement. The warnings differed in relatively slight and subtle ways but resulted in certain significant differences in comprehension by the subjects. Relatively minor changes in wording of the messages was shown to result, in certain cases, in very dramatic differences in comprehension. The author therefore concludes that there is a strong need for empirical testing of any such messages that are intended to effect consumer beliefs or behavior.

Annotations (101-200)

Key Words:
State of the Art Defense, Strict Liability and Warnings

174

Funston, C.E., "The 'Failure to Warn' Defect in Strict Products Liability: A Paradigmatic Approach to 'State of the Art' Evidence and 'Scientific Knowability'," *Insurance Counsel Journal*, 51, January 1984, 39-54.

This article examines the issue of whether state-of-the-art evidence is relevant to the defense of a failure to warn strict products liability case. Some courts have held that state-of-the-art evidence is irrelevant since in strict products liability, knowledge of the product hazard is imputed to the defendant. Other courts have held that strict liability will not apply until state-of-the-art evidence is offered to prove that the defendant knew or should have known about the danger. The author suggests a two-step approach regarding the application of state-of-the-art evidence in failure to warn cases. First, determine whether or not there was a technical capacity to discover the danger. If there was, the second step is to determine whether or not the suggestion of danger or the use of a particualr testing method would have been warranted at the time of manufacture.

Key Words:
Accuracy,
Auditory,
Drivers,
Kinesthetic/Tactile,
Motor Vehicle,
Task Specific Context,
Traffic

175

Galer, M., "An Ergonomics Approach to the Problem of High Vehicles Striking Low Bridges," *Applied Ergonomics*, 11:1, March 1980, 43-46.

The East Midlands and Southampton were the sites for interview surveys of 497 drivers of tall trucks. The survey dealt with three major topics: drivers' knowledge of their vehicle heights; understanding of the low bridge warning signs; and opinions of accident prevention methods. Of the 497 drivers, only 12% correctly estimated their vehicle height; 25% of the incorrect estimates were too low.

Drivers were shown illustrations of road signs both in and out of context. Context was provided by a photograph that showed the sign mounted on a low bridge. Almost three-fourths of the drivers were acceptably or completely correct in their understanding of the sign, "Headroom at Hazard Ahead." However, the sign, "Available Width of Headroom at Hazard" was understood by only 36% of the drivers; 37% of the drivers who did not originally understand the "Headroom at Hazard Ahead" sign understood the sign after context was provided.

The author also discusses a number of novel warnings, such as suspending bells across the road at a safe height in advance of the bridge, or installing rumble strips at advance approaches to low bridges. Galer emphasized that drivers followed warning systems which gave them relevant information.

Key Words:
Assumption of Risk,
Contributory Negligence,
Drugs,
Misuse,
Negligence and
 Warnings,
State of the Art Defense,
Strict Liability and
 Warnings,
Warranties/Disclaimers

176
Gallagher, J., "Rise of the Phoenix—Feldman v. Lederle Laboratories: From the Remnants of State of the Art Evidence Comes a New Standard for Design Defect-Failure to Warn Cases," *The University of Toledo Law Review*, **16:4, Summer 1985, 1053-1098.**

The author provides a concise survey of theories of recovery, including warranty, negligence and strict liability. The defenses include contributory negligence, assumption of risk and misuse of the product. She discusses the application of these principles to failure to warn and design defect cases. She then focuses on a New Jersey case, Feldman v. Lederle Laboratories, involving a drug manufacturer's failure to warn of dangers associated with the use of its product.

Key Words:
Control/Display
 Elements,
Description/Modeling,
Elemental Breakdowns,
Elemental Synthesis,
Predictive User Response
 Equations,
Symbol Taxonomies

177
Geiselman, R.E., Landee, B.M. and Christen, F.G., "Perceptual Discriminability as a Basis for Selecting Graphic Symbols," *Human Factors*, **24:3, 1982, 329-337.**

Subjects rated the similarity of twenty different symbol types. These symbols were then analyzed to determine their primitive attributes (e.g., number of lines and number of arcs) and their configural symbol attributes such as a V or a triangle. One-fourth of the rate variance could be explained by a regression equation using primitive attributes, while 67% of the variance was explained by a regression equation using configural symbol attributes. The researchers conclude that such regression equations can be used to choose from among alternative candidate symbols.

Key Words:
Duty/Failure to Warn,
Negligence and
 Warnings,
Strict Liability and
 Warnings

178
Gershonowitz, A., "The Strict Liability Duty to Warn," *Washington and Lee Law Review*, **44:1, Winter 1987, 71-107.**

Most courts decide warnings cases by applying a standard of reasonableness in the context of what was technically and scientifically known or feasible at the time of manufacture. The author feels this gives manufacturers an incentive to deny the existence of danger until a court or legislature compels a warning. The author therefore advocates a strict liability duty to warn instead of the reasonableness test. As information about a product danger becomes known earlier, the duty to warn will also arise earlier than under the negligence duty to warn.

Annotations (101-200)

Key Words:
Drugs,
Duty/Failure to Warn,
Learned Intermediary Rule

179
Gilhooley, M., "Learned Intermediaries, Prescription Drugs, and Patient Information," *Saint Louis University Law Journal; Health Law Symposium*, 30:3, 1986, 633-702.

This article examines the drug manufacturer's duty to warn, including the "learned intermediary" rule and its exceptions. The author recommends imposing a duty on drug manufacturers to warn the ultimate consumer of product hazards, not just the physician or learned intermediary, because patients should have a legal right to make the decision to use a drug on an informed basis, and the law should ensure that this right is realized in practice.

Key Words:
Color Coding,
Labels

180
Gill, R.T., Barbera, C. and Precht, T., "A Comparative Evaluation of Warning Label Designs," *Proceedings of the Human Factors Society - 31st Annual Meeting*, Human Factors Society, Santa Monica, CA, 1987, 476-478.

The authors conducted an experiment to compare the effectiveness of three different warning label designs: 1) traditional, 2) color-coded "ski pass," and 3) color-coded interactive. They found that the interactive label, which requires the user to interact with the label in order to use the equipment, was the most effective in attracting the user's attention. The labels were equally effective in influencing behavior.

Key Words:
Design of: instructions

181
Gleason, J.P. and Wackerman, J.P., "Manual Dexterity– What Makes Instruction Manuals Usable," *IEEE Transactions on Professional Communication*, 27:2, 1984, 59-61.

The authors provide tips for writers of instruction manuals for home computers, office systems, and word processing equipment. The article addresses various factors thought to influence the effectiveness of manuals. Such factors include the organization of information, the content of the manual, the physical appearance of the manual, and the characteristics of the language used in conveying technical information.

Key Words:
Consumer Setting,
Filtering,
Perceived Risk,
Reading of: instructions,

182
Godfrey, S.S., Allender, L., Laughery, K.R. and Smith, V.L., "Warning Messages: Will the Consumer Bother to Look?" *Proceedings of the Human Factors Society - 27th Annual Meeting*, Human Factors Society, Santa Monica, CA, 1983, 950-954.

In the first of two experiment described in this article, thirty-two undergraduates were asked to numerically rate thirty-two products on perceived hazardousness, likelihood of warning label perusal, and familiarity with the product. A correlation of .53 was found between perceived hazardousness and perusal of the warning label. An interaction between perceived hazard and familiarity was also found. For products perceived as being hazardous, familiarity had no influence on the likelihood of looking at the label, while for products with low hazard ratings, low familiarity increased the tendency to look at the warning. It was also found that females were more likely to look at warnings than males. In the second experiment a larger sample of undergraduates evaluated forty products. Perceived hazard ratings increased for: unfamiliar brands; products used infrequently; and products not recently used.

Key Words:
Color of Stimulus,
Conflicting Objectives,
Consumer Setting,
Consumers,
Filtering,
Hazardous Materials,
Housewives,
Industrial,
Labels,
Prior Knowledge,
Reading Measures,
Reading of: warning labels,
Stimulus Size

183
Godfrey, S.S. and Laughery, K.R., "The Biasing Effects of Product Familiarity on Consumers' Awareness of Hazard," *Proceedings of the Human Factors Society - 28th Annual Meeting*, **Human Factors Society, Santa Monica, CA, 1984, 483-486.**

The authors report on a survey designed to measure women's perception of hazards presented by tampon use, their awareness of related warnings, and their knowledge of toxic shock syndrome (TSS). The survey was administered to 110 women. Of the 96 women who reported using tampons, 73% noticed a warning on the package. However, only 42% noticed the warning when changing from one brand to another. The authors conclude that these data support the hypothesis that people are less likely to look at warnings when they are familiar with the product on which the warning is placed. They note that this tendency might create a serious problem for women who switch to high absorbancy tampons after using the older models.

Key Words:
Behavior Factors,
Reading of: warning labels,
Students,
Warnings: evaluating effects on behavior

184
Godfrey, S.S., Rothstein, P.R. and Laughery, K.R., "Warnings: Do They Make a Difference?," *Proceedings of the Human Factors Society - 29th Annual Meeting*, **Human Factors Society, Santa Monica, CA, 1985, 669-673.**

The authors conducted four experiments aimed at determining when warnings are likely to be effective. In the first two experiments, warnings placed on a copy machine and telephone, respectively, effectively reduced use of the two products. These warnings both stated that the products were out-of-order and described potential problems. The warning on the phone stated that money would be lost while that on the copy machine stated that a delay was likely. As might be expected, the warning on the phone had a slightly greater effect on behavior.

In the third experiment, a warning of contamination was placed near a water fountain. The use of a large very noticeable and explicit sign was found to change behavior to a much greater extent than a small sign.

In the fourth and final experiment, a sign was placed on a door. The warning said that it was broken and that another exit should be used. Results demonstrated that people were much more willing to follow the warning when the cost of compliance was low. Specifically, only 3 out of 51 people followed a sign telling them to use an alternate exit fifty feet away. None followed a sign telling them to turn around and return down the hall. In another experiment involving a set of double doors, only 4 out of 64 people failed to follow a warning which said to use the right instead of left door.

185
Goldhaber, G.M. and deTurck, M.A., "Effectiveness of Warning Signs: Familiarity Effects," Department of Communication, State University of New York, Buffalo, Report 14260, 1988.

Key Words:
Behavior Factors,
Children,
Consumers,
Existing/Past Behavior Patterns,
Gender,
Memory of: symbol/message,
Memory of: warning labels,
Prior Knowledge,
Reading Measures,
Students,
Swimming Pool,
Warnings: evaluating effects on behavior

The authors discuss a study in which three warning signs telling people not to dive into shallow water were affixed for a period of one month next to a middle school swimming pool. A questionnaire was then administered to more than five hundred students who participated in the study. The questionnaire was directed toward determining whether the students had seen and were able to recall the signs or the presence of the signs. Questions were also directed toward ascertaining students knowledge of the hazards associated with diving into shallow water. In addition, questions were directed toward their stated behavior whether or not they would dive into shallow water in swimming pools.

The results showed that approximately 60% of the students were uncertain as to whether any signs were posted. When they were specifically asked whether a sign stating "no diving" was present, roughly 40% reported having seen the sign. When knowledge of the consequences of diving into shallow water was evaluated, the authors found no difference between students in the school where the "no diving" sign was present and those in a controlled condition who had not been exposed to the "no diving" sign. It was also found that the presence of the "no diving" sign did not significantly influence self reports of the likelihood of diving into shallow water in the future or the perceived danger associated with diving into the shallow end of their school's swimming pool.

On the other hand, it was found that past behavior patterns such as previous experience with diving into the shallow end of a pool or past experience with diving into above ground pools or participating on a swim team tended to result in higher self reported likelihood of diving into shallow water pools and a lower perceived danger of such diving. The authors argue that these findings indicate that warning signs against diving are unlikely to be effective. As an alternative strategy, the authors recommend that the owners of such pools actively engage in preventing such activity through other controls.

186
Goldhaber, G.M. and deTurck, M.A., "Effects of Consumers' Familiarity with a Product on Attention to and Compliance with Warnings," *Journal of Products Liability,* **11:1, 1988, 29-37.**

Key Words:
Effectiveness of: educational/persuasive programs,
Familiarity with Product,
Swimming Pool

The authors conducted a study using an above-ground pool with a warning not to dive. The study allegedly demonstrated that a warning label is not likely to be noticed by consumers who are reasonably familiar with a product. It was suggested that one way to make sure a warning will be processed by consumers is to communicate the message orally and then ask if the individual understood how to use the product safely. Because written warnings do not afford the consumer an opportunity to indicate his or her uncertainty about product safety, it may be necessary to re-think the modality of communicating product warnings.

187
Goldhaber, G.M. and deTurck, M.A., "Effectiveness of Warning Signs: Gender and Familiarity Effects," Department of Communication, State University of New York, Buffalo, 1988, 14-260.

Key Words:
Behavior Factors,
Children,
Consumers,
Existing/Past Behavior Patterns,
Gender,
Memory of: symbol/message,
Memory of: warning labels,
Prior Knowledge,
Reading Measures,
Students,
Swimming Pool,
Warnings: evaluating effects on behavior

In a study related to an earlier Goldhaber and deTurck article (1988), the authors evaluated the effects of placing three "no diving" signs in conspicuous locations by a swimming pool in a Buffalo suburban high school. The experimental group consisted of students at the high school in which the three "no diving" signs were placed near the pool. Students at a nearby high school served as controls. The total group of 328 subjects were then administered a questionnaire after a one month period during which the three swimming pool warning signs were continually present. The questionnaire was designed to measure recall of the presence of the warning sign, the perceived danger of diving into a shallow above ground pool and the self-reported likelihood of diving into such a pool.

Results showed that males were more likely to recall seeing the warning sign than were females. However, their self-reports of the likelihood of diving were significantly higher than those of females. Strangely, this effect was more pronounced when the sign was present than when it was absent. Results also showed that students with a history of diving into shallow water gave self-reports of the likelihood of diving that were higher than those given by students who did not have such a history. Conclusions are given by the author which are similar to those given in the earlier Goldhaber and deTurck article (1988).

188

Key Words:
Duty/Failure to Warn,
Patent Danger

Golia, S., "Products Liability—Manufacturers Not Liable for Failure to Warn Where the Danger is Obvious, Well-Known and Avoidable by the Exercise of Common Sense," *Seton Hall Law Review*, 14, 1983-1984, 821-822.

Campos v. Firestone Tire & Rubber Co. held that a manufacturer has no duty to warn where the risk of danger is well-known and the hazard could be avoided by the exercise of common sense drawn from the experience of a skilled worker. The intent of the Court was to avoid the application of rules of law which would result in the manufacturer becoming the insurer for every product it distributes.

189

Key Words:
Behavior Factors,
Belief in Danger,
Conduct of
  Consumer/User,
Effectiveness of: warning
  related litigation,
Industrial Safety,
Warnings: evaluating
  effects on behavior,
Workers

Gomer, F.E., "Evaluating the Effectiveness of Warnings Under Prevailing Working Conditions," *Proceedings of the Human Factors Society - 30th Annual Meeting*, Human Factors Society, Santa Monica, CA, 1986, 712-715.

The author presents the results of a field study, conducted in the context of litigation, that was directed toward measuring the effectiveness of a label which warned about the risk of delayed lung disease. The study attempted to reconstruct the conditions and labeling requirements corresponding to the state-of-art in the mid-1960s. Administrative and production controls of limestone dust levels were intentionally removed, resulting in an extremely dusty environment. The seventeen subjects (actual employees) handled bags of limestone in this environment over a period of two days.

On the second day, strong warnings of the hazard of limestone dust were placed on the bags. One recommendation in the warning was that respirators be worn. Only three subjects requested and then wore respirator masks after seeing the warning. Before seeing the warning, three other subjects had requested respirators, meaning that a total of eleven subjects voluntarily went without the protection recommended by the warning. It should be noted that all of the workers reported that they had seen the warning on the second day.

190
Gordon, D.A., "The Assessment of Guide Sign Informational Load," *Human Factors*, **23:4, 1981, 453-466.**

Key Words:
Drivers,
Information Overload,
Reaction Time,
Routing,
Traffic,
Traffic Settings,
Visual Noise

This study evaluated the effects of increasing the amount of instructions on highway guide signs. Including additional non-guidance information on the signs did not increase average reaction time. Increasing the number of signs did increase reaction times, but these times appeared to be well within required limits. Of particular significance was the finding that when navigational information was missing, the subjects were forced to make navigational decisions without specific instructions, and their reaction times became significantly longer.

191
Green, D.A., "Emergency Vehicle Warning Systems and Identification," PND80019, N.S.W. Department of Public Works, New South Wales, May 1978, 1-24.

Key Words:
Emergency Vehicles

A number of general concerns related to the safe and unimpeded travel of emergency vehicles are discussed. These include the need to communicate an emergency vehicle's nature, motion and resting states, location, volume and shape, and direction of movement. These factors must be considered both during day and night, whether under artificial illumination or not. Also, the existing environment's illuminated signs and signals must not confuse or reduce the effectiveness of special lights on emergency vehicles; the luminance of high intensity warning lights might have to be reduced to avoid disabling glare and discomfort. Four emphasized elements included the use of: audible alarms; vehicle color and color schemes; special light systems; and signs and symbols.

192
Green, P., "Development of Pictograph Symbols for Vehicle Controls and Displays," Society of Automotive Engineers, SAE 790383, 1979, 1-31.

Key Words:
Automobile Controls,
Consumers,
Control/Display
  Elements,
Drivers,
Production Method,
Symbol Generation

Green notes that the designers of pictograph symbols use three development approaches: 1) they use symbols that appear in the *Symbol Sourcebook*, Dreyfuss (1972); 2) they create their own unique symbol designs; or 3) they use suggestions collected from a sample population. Green summarizes an experiment in which the latter approach is applied. Forty-three drivers drew pictures that they thought were appropriate symbols for the items in question. Comprehension of the intended meaning of the pictures was evaluated by presenting them to a separate set of sixty-two drivers. The results showed substantial variation in comprehension, demonstrating the need for testing such pictograph symbols among the ultimate users.

Annotations (101-200)

Key Words:
Accuracy,
Association
  Rankings/Indexes,
Automobile Controls,
Confusion Matrix,
Consumers
Control/Display
  Elements,
Learning Nonverbal
  Symbols,
Legibility,
Prior Knowledge,
Reaction Time,
Training

193
Green, P. and Pew, R.W., "Evaluating Pictographic Symbols: An Automotive Application," *Human Factors*, 20:1, 1978, 103-114.

In the first phase of the experiment described by the authors, a group of fifty subjects viewed nineteen automotive pictographs. Each symbol was evaluated using indexes for communicative ratings, associations, reaction time, and confusions. Only six of the pictographs met a criterion of 75% recognition and 5% confusion. Gender and technical background had an interactive effect on recognition ability: technically trained females had lower accuracy scores than non-technically trained females. Conversely, technically trained males scored higher than non-technically trained males.

In the second phase, subjects continued to learn symbol meanings in a paired associate learning task. Reaction time and association strength were not strongly correlated here (r=-.482). The communicative rating was correlated with both the reaction time (r=-.521) and association strength (r=.727), leading the authors to conclude that this rating is useful. It was also noted that reaction times decreased during the course of the learning process, and that ease of learning was independent of the other measures.

Key Words:
Conveying Action,
Conveying Procedures,
Description/Modeling,
Process Charts/
  Sequences,
Symbol Taxonomies

194
Green, T.R.G., "Pictures of Programs and Other Processes, or How to Do Things with Lines," *Behaviour and Information Technology*, 1:1, 1982, 3-36.

This paper describes, but does not evaluate, a number of flow charting methods. Flowcharts have been used primarily for documenting computer programs. However, they also are potentially useful for a wide variety of consumer products. This has become especially true in recent years due to the increasing complexity of many modern products.

Key Words:
Drugs,
Duty/Failure to Warn,
Learned Intermediary
  Rule

195
Gregory, D.R., "Physician's Duty to Warn," *Legal Aspects of Medical Practice*, 12:4, April 1984, 6-7.

Once the physician is warned by the drug manufacturer of possible side effects of a prescription drug, it is his duty to choose the treatment and explain the risk to the patient. The rationale behind this rule is that the physician is in the best position to evaluate the patient's needs, assess the risks and benefits of a particular therapy and supervise its use.

Key Words:
Symbol Taxonomies,
Understanding/
 Perception Models

196
Gregory, K., "Determining the 'Consumer Object,'" *Applied Ergonomics*, **13:1, March 1982, 11-13.**

The author defines products as collections of meanings and their "personalities" as sets of complex attributes. Gregory notes that the most commonly used technique to measure product images is the Semantic Differential, described in Osgood, et al. (1957).

Key Words:
Understanding/
 Perception Models

197
Gregory, R.L., "On How Little Information Controls So Much Behaviour," *Ergonomics*, **13:1, 1970, 25-35.**

Perception is described as a process of selecting "internal models." The models shape decisions and behavior on the basis of incoming data. Selection of an appropriate internal model is held to be critical to performance, as the outputs of the internal models can vary dramatically for the same incoming data. The advantages and disadvantages of this type of neurological system are outlined. Perceptual illusions are used to illustrate how these internal models operate; illusions occur due to incorrect models or errors in scaling. It is suggested that the bizarre imagery of dreams can be understood as the random creation of models in the absence of sensory input. It is also stated that these models resemble analogue rather than digital computers.

Key Words:
CPSA,
Consumer Labeling and
 Signage Systems,
Design Consistency,
FDA,
Industrial,
Introducing New
 Systems,
OSHA,
Organizing Information,
Risk Hazard Scales

198
Hadden, S.G., *Read the Label*, **Westview Press, Boulder, CO, 1986.**

This book presents a thorough review of labeling systems with an emphasis on the evolution, implementation, and evaluation of labeling policies. The author draws heavily upon the fields of quantitative risk analysis, psychology, and economics. She presents three major topics: 1) Labeling via regulation (a history of labeling in the United States and the theoretical basis for using labeling as a means of risk control are discussed); 2) Products and agencies that have and are using labels as a primary means of risk regulation (the author specifically examines the success of labeling systems for products such as drugs, pesticides, consumer products, and food); 3) Labeling as a risk control policy (the author critiques current labeling systems and some of the underlying assumptions of such systems).

In addition, she provides suggestions for new labeling systems which would include, among other things, the use of consistent symbology, hierarchically ordered information, increased specificity of information, risk information presented on some type of meaningful scale, and the provision of consistent risk information. We find this to be a very useful book and recommend that it be read.

Key Words:
Contrast,
Drivers,
Durability,
Illumination Level,
Luminance,
Routing
Stimulus Size,
Subjective Ratings,
Symbol Legend,
Traffic Settings,
Visual Noise

199
Hahn, K.C., McNaught, E.D. and Bryden, J.E., "Nighttime Legibility of Guide Signs," New York State Department of Transportation, Albany, Research Report 50, August 1977.

Throughout New York State, the nighttime legibility of 120 large guide signs was evaluated by measuring the brightness of their legend, panel, and surroundings. Sign age, material type, and sign position were recorded. Panel and legend condition, background brightness, and sign legibility were then subjectively rated. The authors found that sign brightness was highly variable, and usually less than sufficient for optimum legibility. The physical measurements also indicated that many signs do not provide adequate nighttime legibility, especially in areas of high ambient illumination. The subjective ratings further confirmed these conclusions.

Key Words:
Design Consistency,
Design of: labeling and safety signage systems,
Development Programs

200
Hakiel, S.R. and Easterby, R.S., "Chapter 22: Issues in the Design of Safety Sign Systems," in *Information Design: The Design and Evaluation of Signs and Printed Material*, Easterby, R.S. and Zwaga, H.J.G. (Eds.), John Wiley & Sons, New York, 1984, 419-448.

This chapter provides a review of conceptual and methodological issues in the design of safety signage systems. The authors functionally define a sign as a message intended to convey information or knowledge. Three types of messages are defined: descriptive, prescriptive and proscriptive. The authors also define four basic structural components of signs: image, background, enclosure, and surround. The process of mapping a message onto a sign and seeing a message within a sign is investigated. Various methodological issues in sign design are then discussed. These include: image appropriateness, configural attributes, visibility, and comprehensibility.

ANNOTATIONS 201-300

Key Words:
Adequacy of Warnings,
Duty/Failure to Warn

201
Hall, G., *The Failure to Warn Handbook*, Hanrow Press, Columbia, MD, 1986.

This is one of the first books dedicated to litigation based on the "failure to warn" theory. The handbook includes : traditional legal theories, some human factors guidelines, and several OSHA and CPSC warnings or labeling standards. The appendices have thirty-eight illustrated pages of example warning signs, a section listing state and federal warnings related cases, and a one page list of model plaintiff pleadings.

Key Words:
Aircraft,
Aircraft Setting,
Control/Display
 Elements,
Pilots,
Visual Displays:
 miscellaneous

202
Hart, S.G. and Loomis, L.L., "Evaluation of the Potential Format and Content of a Cockpit Display of Traffic Information," *Human Factors*, 22:5, 1980, 591-604.

Aviation pilots and instrument-related general aviation (GA) pilots viewed more than one hundred display options and were solicited for their opinions concerning display format, information content, and symbology. Several graphic and symbolic display formats were then evaluated in simulated encounters between aircraft. This evaluation of symbolic displays should be of particular interest because it effectively focuses on the *relevant* user population.

Key Words:
Design of: instructions,
Illustrations,
Laboratory/Generic
 Settings,
Problems in Design,
Typeface/Font,
Writing Instructions

203
Hartley, J., *Designing Instructional Text*, Nichols Publishing Company, New York, 1978.

This book summarizes many general principles in the design of instructional text. Topics considered are described by the following chapter titles: Page-size; Basic Planning Decisions; Typesize and Spacing; Typefaces; Theory Into Practice; The Role of Illustrations; Tables, Graphs, Diagrams and Symbols; Prose and Some Alternatives; Programmed Textbooks; Lecture Handouts, Worksheets and Writing Books; Forms and Questionnaires; Listed Information; The Layout of Bibliographies, Indexes and References; and Evaluating Instructional Text. This early book is obviously very much on point to those readers with instruction manual responsibilities or interests. It of course does not include the research findings of the last ten years or the litigation consequences which have altered some philosophies on that topic.

Annotations (201-300)

Key Words:
Design of: instructions,
Illustrations,
Laboratory/Generic
  Settings,
Problems in Design,
Typeface/Font,
Writing Instructions

204
Hartley, J., "Eighty Ways of Improving Instructional Text," *IEEE Transactions on Professional Communication*, 24:1, March 1981, 17-27.

This paper suggests eighty ways to improve instructional text based on a review of research findings. These suggestions are presented under three main headings: prose materials; graphic materials; and typographic considerations. In so doing, the author provides useful guidelines for developing instructional material. However, it must be recognized that many of these suggestions are generalizations drawn from a small number of particular studies: their application should be supplemented with additional study.

Key Words:
Accuracy,
Active Processing,
Children,
Laboratory/Generic
  Settings,
Memory of:
  symbol/message,
Recall,
Underlining/Highlighting

205
Hartley, J., Bartlett, S. and Branthwaite, A., "Underlining Can Make a Difference—Sometimes," *The Journal of Educational Research*, 73:4, March/April 1980, 218-224.

This paper summarizes a number of studies which evaluated how underlining portions of text influenced elements of behavior, primarily retention. Most of these studies show that underlining can result in increased performance, although some show the opposite. The authors performed an experiment using a group of sixth grade students. The student subjects read a passage which included underlined words, and were then tested on their recall of those underlined words, as well as other words in the passage which were not underlined. Results clearly showed that underlined words were more likely to be recalled. The "close procedure" was used to test recall; this consisted of presenting text with missing words which had to be filled in.

Key Words:
Behavior Factors,
Brochures/Flyers,
Design of:
  educational/persuasive
  programs,
Effectiveness of:
  educational/persuasive
  programs,
Evaluation Difficulties,
Formal Teaching/
  Counseling/Education,
Letters,
Posters,
Radio/TV

206
Haskins, J.B., "Effects of Safety Communication Campaigns: A Review of the Research Evidence," *Journal of Safety Research*, 1:2, June 1969, 58-66.

This paper summarizes the literature related to the effects of mass communication on drinking/driving in particular and safety in general. Several safety campaigns are summarized and critiqued. The conclusions drawn from this survey include: 1) many safety campaigns are performed without measuring their effectiveness; 2) the research designs of those few studies of effectiveness tend to be inadequate; and 3) few communication campaigns have conclusively demonstrated their effectiveness.

Key Words:
Behavior Factors,
Brochures/Flyers,
Design of:
  educational/persuasive
  programs,
Effectiveness of:
  educational/persuasive
  programs,
Evaluation Difficulties,
Formal Teaching/
  Counseling/Education,
Letters,
Posters,
Radio/TV,
Review Papers

207
Haskins, J.B., "Evaluative Research on the Effects of Mass Communication Safety Campaigns: A Methodological Critique," *Journal of Safety Research*, 2:2, June 1970, 86-96.

This paper critiques the validity of methodologies which have been used to measure the effects of safety campaigns on behavior. The following four points were deemed essential to the evaluation process: 1) naturalistic communication conditions should prevail during research; 2) the cause-effect relation should be clearly explained; 3) measurement should be both unobtrusive and valid; and 4) the total communications and research design should be accurately executed. Examples are given of safety campaigns which to varying degrees fulfill these requirements.

Key Words:
Prior Knowledge,
Problems in Design,
Reading of: instructions,
Understanding of
  Instructions,
Writing Instruction
  Guidelines

208
Henk, W.A. and Helfeldt, J.P., "How to Develop Independence in Following Written Directions," *Journal of Reading*, April 1987, 602-607.

The authors seek to explain why seemingly simple instructions can present so much of a problem to even capable readers of narrative text. They hold that this effect may be due to the fact that schools center on teaching reading-to-learn rather than reading-to-do. Because reading strategies associated with these two types of activity are significantly different, they feel it is not surprising there is little or no immediate transfer from academic to real world settings. As a means to help reduce such problems, the authors briefly describe an instructional program they have developed. The authors also note the need for the traditional educational curriculum to incorporate reading-to-do type instruction.

Key Words:
Consensual Labeling and
  Signage Systems,
Fire,
OSHA,
Poison,
Radiation

209
Henning, J.C., "Labeling Hazardous Materials Can Be Complex—A Practical Approach," *Professional Safety*, November 1975, 36-40.

NIOSH recommendations for hazard identification are discussed. The National Fire Protection Association (NFPA) and the Manufacturing Chemists Association (MCA) system criteria are listed. Several references to older standards are also provided.

Key Words:
Individual Autonomy,
Informed Consumer,
Polio Vaccine

210
Hensely, D.R., "Polio Vaccine Warnings—A Crippling Blow to Individual Autonomy," *Journal of Products Liability*, **11:1, 1988, 39-54.**

The goal of an adequate warning is to protect the informed consumer and allow individual autonomy in decision-making. Contributing to this goal, warnings should be required to disclose available alternatives and their risks. They must also accurately, clearly, and strongly state the risk and must convey information on risks, benefits and contraindication of the product. In Johnson v. American Cyanamid Company, the plaintiff accused the defendant of watering down its warning and not stating alternatives. Courts have held manufacturers liable for watered-down warnings because they give a false assurance of safety. In Johnson, the Kansas Supreme Court found the polio vaccine warning adequate as a matter of law. The author laments the impact of this decision on freedom of choice and on society's need to spread the cost of injuries among purchasers of the product by holding defendants liable.

Key Words:
Alcohol,
Drivers,
Legibility Distance,
Luminance,
Traffic,
Traffic Settings,
Visual Acuity

211
Hicks, J.A., "An Evaluation of the Effect of Sign Brightness on the Sign-Reading Behavior of Alcohol-Impaired Drivers," *Human Factors*, **18:1, February 1976, 45-52.**

The author notes that past research on the visibility and legibility of non-illuminated highway signs has not considered the alcohol-impaired driver. A study was consequently performed to evaluate the effects of increasing the standard brightness level of signs on the sign-reading performance of intoxicated drivers.

Fourteen subjects, ranging in age from 21 to 53 years old, participated in the study. Testing with a Snellen eye chart determined that all but one of the subjects had at least 20/20 vision, the exception had 20/40 vision. The dependent measure of correct sign reading distance was collected under actual driving conditions at night. Three blood alcohol content levels (BAC) were considered: 0.00% (sober), 0.08%, and 0.15%. As BAC increased, sign-reading distances decreased significantly. The mean reading distances were: 168.55m for 0.00%, 166.12m for 0.08%, and 146.91m for 0.15%. Low reflectance signs had significantly shorter reading distances than high reflectance signs, 153.6m as compared to 170.99m for high reflectance signs. For all BAC conditions, increased sign reflectance was correlated with improvements in performance. Hicks concludes that brighter signs can increase sign-reading distances of both sober and alcohol-impaired drivers.

212

Hicks, L.E., *Coping with Packaging Laws: An AMA Management Briefing*, AMACOM, New York, 1972.

This document outlines the packaging requirements of the Food, Drug and Cosmetic Act of 1938, the Federal Hazardous Substances Act of 1960, the Federal Cigarette Labeling and Advertising Act of 1965, the Child Protection Act of 1966, the Child Protection Act and Toy Safety Act of 1969, the Fair Packaging and Labeling Act of 1968, and the Poison Prevention Act of 1970.

Key Words:
Consumer Labeling and Signage Systems,
FDA,
Governmental Labeling and Signage Systems

213

Hicks, L.E., *Product Labeling and the Law: An AMA Management Briefing*, AMACOM, New York, 1974

This document outlines the labeling requirements of the Food, Drug and Cosmetic Act of 1938, the Federal Hazardous Substances Act of 1960, the Federal Cigarette Labeling and Advertising Act of 1965, the Child Protection Act of 1966, the Child Protection Act and Toy Safety Act of 1969, the Fair Packaging and Labeling Act of 1968, the Poison Prevention Act of 1970, the Flammable Fabrics Act of 1958, and the Consumer Product Safety Act of 1972.

Key Words:
Consumer Labeling and Signage Systems,
Governmental Labeling and Signage Systems

214

Hill, P.S. and Jamieson, B.D., "Driving Offenders and the Defensive Driving Course—An Archival Study," *The Journal of Psychology*, 98, 1978, 117-127.

Six post-treatment driving measures were used to compare 275 drivers who had been ordered by the court to take part in a Defensive Driving Course (DDC) with 275 drivers who had also appeared in court but had not been required to take the course. The experimental group showed greater reductions in serious and accident-promoting convictions, but did not show a reduction in accidents when compared with the control group.

Key Words:
Drivers,
Effectiveness of: educational/persuasive programs,
Formal Teaching/ Counseling/Education

215

Hind, P.R., Tritt, B.H. and Hoffmann, E.R., "Effects of Level of Illumination, Strokewidth, Visual Angle and Contrast on the Legibility of Numerals of Various Fonts," *Session 25: 8th Australian Road Research Board Proceedings*, Perth, Australia, 1976, 46-55.

This paper summarizes a number of useful findings regarding: levels of luminance; viewing distances; interactions between the various aspects of font design; and interactions between fonts and contrast.

Key Words:
Contrast,
Drivers,
Luminance,
Strokewidth,
Traffic Settings,
Typeface/Font,
Visual Angle

Annotations (201-300)

Key Words:
Case of Text,
Confusion Matrix,
Industrial Setting,
Stimulus Size,
Students,
Symbol Size

216
Hodge, D.C., "Legibility of a Uniform-Strokewidth Alphabet: I. Relative Legibility of Upper and Lower Case Letters," *Journal of Engineering Psychology*, 1:1, January 1962, 34-46.

This study was meant to provide a starting point for a set of studies investigating the relative legibility of upper and lower case letters of uniform strokewidth. Legibility is defined here as the greatest viewing distance at which the entire alphabet can be identified. Four male and eleven female subjects, ranging in age from 16 to 44 years old, participated in the experiment. The subjects were all enrolled in an introductory psychology course and all had 20/20 vision, as determined by a Snellen chart.

Upper case letters were correctly identified at significantly greater distances than were lower case letters; this agrees with previous research. The critical detail for lower case letters was, on the average, smaller than that for upper case ones. However, the results did not suggest that lower case letters should be avoided for displays and labeling purposes on instrument panels, because lower case letters may be preferable for reasons not related to legibility.

Key Words:
Task Analysis

217
Hodgkinson, G.P. and Crawshaw, C.M., "Hierarchical Task Analysis for Ergonomics Research," *Applied Ergonomics*, 16:4, December 1985, 289-299.

The Hierarchical Task Analysis (HTA) was originally developed by Annett and Duncan (1967). This paper describes the use of this technique to identify the various human factors issues that must be considered in the design and evaluation of sound mixing consoles. The focus of the research was on comparing the effectiveness of various methods for grouping controls.

To test the hypothesis that the functional grouping of control knobs (increased spacing between functional groups compared to spacing within functional groups) is superior to functional grouping, a comparative simulation study was conducted. Forty male and sixteen female subjects, ranging in age from eighteen to forty-five, participated in the simulation. The subjects were ordinary members of the public, not experienced sound engineers. Data on reaction time strongly supported the functional grouping hypothesis. The authors conclude that arranging control panels so that the components are of equidistant or quasi-equidistant spacing, regardless of their function, is detrimental to operator performance.

The authors discuss the role and significance of task analysis in human factors research. They claim that because the methodology facilitates a systematic identification of ergonomics problems, hierarchical task analysis is a useful investigative technique. We consider such task analysis approaches a prerequisite to designing instructions.

Key Words:
Design of: instructions,
Development Cycle,
Illustrations

218
Hodgkinson, R. and Hughes, J., "Developing Wordless Instructions: A Case History," *IEEE Transactions on Professional Communication,* **25:2, June 1982, 74-79.**

The authors describe the development of unpacking and set-up instructions for the IBM Selectric II Typewriter which was marketed in Europe. It was essential that these instructions be easily comprehended by users in different countries who would be speaking different languages. The article concisely describes the development of these instructions over a period of several years.

Of particular interest is their discussion of cycles of development which were driven by intermittent testing of the instructions with users from the expected consumer population. Specific changes in design inspired by test results are clearly presented, as are examples illustrating the progression of graphic design concepts.

The authors conclude that efficient interaction between the graphic designer and a human factors engineer during testing of the instructional material is very desirable. They also discuss some general advantages of drawings over photographs and provide other practical design recommendations. The apparent success of these authors' approach in the difficult setting of multi-lingual communication suggests that a similar approach would be useful when consumers speak a single language. An interesting research study could be devoted to comparing the "wordless" instructions generated by this approach to those which use a combination of graphics and more extensive narrative.

Key Words:
Abstractness,
Illustrations

219
Hoecker, D.G., "Some Performance Correlates of Technical Illustration Level," *Proceedings of the Human Factors Society - 26th Annual Meeting,* **Human Factors Society, Santa Monica, CA, 1982, 88-92.**

Fifteen undergraduates, all inexperienced with oscilloscopes, used an oscilloscope and a volt-ohmmeter to perform three similar tasks. The tasks involved troubleshooting the printed circuit board of an electronically-triggered oscilloscope camera to identify component faults (e.g., resistor capacitor diode). For each of the tasks a different level of illustration detail was provided in the enclosed instructional material to help users identify the different components of the oscilloscope. On the first task, illustrations with a medium or high level of detail aided performance, while performance stayed constant regardless of illustration level on the second and third tasks.

The investigator concluded that the illustration level was most important while learning how to use the oscilloscope. High detail illustrations may provide irrelevant information, but are economical since they are applicable to many different problems; many versions of medium detail drawings must be made since they only list components that are needed for the task at hand. Subject preference was about equally divided between medium and high detail illustrations. We find this study to be interesting because it is one of the few that has addressed the level of illustration. It is an important consideration which any designer of instructions should address carefully.

Key Words:
Advertising,
Product Literature

220
Hoenig, M., "The Influence of Advertising in Products Liability Litigation," *Journal of Products Liability*, **5, 1982, 321-340.**

The author examines the role of advertising in product liability litigation. He lists the following legal doctrines as potentially relevant to advertising issues: 1) ordinary negligence; 2) deceit and fraudulent concealment; 3) negligent misrepresentation; 4) strict liability for misrepresentation; 5) express warranties (other than those implied); 6) implied warranties (those concerned with "merchantability" and fitness for a particular use); 7) strict liability in tort (consumer expectation theory). Several case histories are cited as examples.

Key Words:
Drivers,
Memory Capacity,
Memory of:
 symbol/message,
Recall,
Traffic,
Verbal vs. Nonverbal
 Symbol/Message

221
Hoffman, E.R. and MacDonald, W.A., "Short-Term Retention of Traffic Turn Restriction Signs," *Human Factors*, **22:2, 1980, 241-251.**

Short-term retention of traffic sign material was evaluated in two laboratory experiments. The retention of material from symbolic signs was more adversely affected by symbolic interference than by interfering material presented in verbal signs, and vice versa. However, the researchers conclude that these effects are not practically significant.

Key Words:
Industrial Setting,
Noise,
Visual Noise

222
Holahan, C.J., "Relationship Between Roadside Signs and Traffic Accidents: A Field Investigation," Austin, Texas Council for Advanced Transportation Studies, Austin, Research Report 54, November 1977, 1-14.

The author notes the lack of research concerning the relationship between visual distractors in the roadside environment and traffic safety. This particular study investigated the relationship between signs located near urban traffic intersections and the number of traffic accidents at those intersections. For the year 1975, the number of at-fault accidents attributed to drivers approaching the intersection was computed. Accidents seemingly not related to distraction, and accidents occurring at night when signs were not plainly visible, were excluded from the computations.

The results were: 1) no distractor dimensions were significantly related to at-fault accidents for traffic signal approaches; however, 2) total signs, large signs, and non-red signs were positively correlated with at-fault accidents for stop sign intersections. We point out that such a study suggests that there are clearly factors which enhance the likelihood that instructions and warnings will be noticed and responded to. Extension of the findings outside this traffic environment would probably not be justified without specific studies of the particular application.

Key Words:
Design of: instructions,
Organizing Information,
Structured Text,
Tables and Flowcharts

223
Horn, R.E., "Chapter 16: Structured Writing and Text Design," in *The Technology of Text*, Jonassen, D.H. (Ed.), Educational Technology Publications, Inc., Englewood Cliffs, 1982, 341-367.

The author provides an overview of structured writing, which is a technique that has seen increasing application in the development of instructions, training manuals, reference manuals, computer documentation, and other applications. The author describes structured writing as a process that has: 1) a specific set of methods for analysis of the subject matter content within different kinds of documents; 2) a specific set of principles and criteria to guide major writing and graphic choices; 3) labeled blocks, (each with their own standards) to chunk information into organizable modular units; 4) groups of blocks that form maps (each with its own standards), which are aggregated hierarchically into documents.

When documents are described as hierarchically organized groups of blocks, they can be used to develop text which is compatible with similar hierarchical models of human knowledge such as that proposed by Baggett and Ehrenfeucht in 1988.

Annotations (201-300)

Theoretically, structured text could be designed to match a particular mental model that individuals may have. By combining 1) methods of describing mental models and 2) methods of generating structural texts and graphics compatible with mental models, we believe that one would have a highly useful tool applicable to the technology of instructional text development.

224
Horst, D.P., McCarthy, G.E., Robinson, J.N., McCarthy, R.L. and Krumm-Scott, S., "Safety Information Presentation: Factors Influencing the Potential for Changing Behavior," *Proceedings of the Human Factors Society - 30th Annual Meeting*, Human Factors Society, Santa Monica, CA, 1986, 111-115.

Key Words:
Actual Behavior,
Agreement with Symbol/Message,
Application Guidelines,
Behavior Factors,
Belief in Danger,
Effectiveness of: educational/persuasive programs,
Effectiveness of: warning related litigation,
Existing/Past Behavior Patterns,
Overapplication of warnings,
Reading of: instructions,
Reading of: warning labels

This review paper is aimed at determining where the literature has shown warnings to be respectively effective or ineffective. Emphasis was placed on evaluating quantitative findings in realistic settings. Several studies in varied settings showed few behavioral effects attributable to labels, signs, communication campaigns and other forms of warnings. Several examples involved handtools, automobiles, seat belts, cigarettes, poisons, soft drinks and lawnmowers. Also presented were anecdotal examples of effective warnings, such as stop signs, railroad crossing signs, and rest room signs. The obtained conclusions were summarized in a table which matched product, hazard, human, and warning related factors to the probability of changing human behavior.

225
Houston, M.J., Childers, T.L. and Heckler, S.E., "Picture-Word Consistency and the Elaborative Processing of Advertisements," *Journal of Marketing Research*, 24, November 1987, 359-369.

Key Words:
Active Processing,
Amount of Information,
Illustrations,
Information Overload,
Visual vs. Verbal Symbol/Message

The authors present a rather technical paper directed toward describing why people show varying degrees of recall for information presented in advertisements which contain both pictorial and textual information. They show that the total amount of information recalled by subjects exposed to such advertisements varies in a way which can be explained by the degree to which the picture and the text convey discrepant information and by the degree to which the picture and the brand name are interactively linked. The total recall was somewhat higher when the picture and the copy conveyed discrepant information and the picture and brand name were interactively linked. However, the specific item which was discrepant between the two forms of information was generally not recalled as well as consistent items.

The authors feel that these effects can be explained by the elaborated processing that takes place when discrepant information is present. Further support for this hypothesis was given by a diminished superiority in recall under the conditions where discrepant information was provided and consumers were given a shorter time to process the ad.

Key Words:
Auditory vs. Visual Messages,
Confusion Matrix,
Information Coding,
Laboratory/Generic Settings

226
Hull, A.J., "Reducing Sources of Human Error in Transmission of Alphanumeric Codes," *Applied Ergonomics*, **7:2, June 1976, 75-78.**

Methods of reducing errors during the transmission of information to humans are considered. It is noted that errors can be caused by: 1) visual or shape confusions; 2) auditory confusions; and 3) acoustic confusions. An auditory matrix is presented which documents confusion among alphanumeric symbols when spoken using conventional English pronunciations. The auditory matrix indicates that there are fewer confusions within digits than within letters, and that there are a considerable number of confusions between letters and digits. The matrix provides a useful tool for predicting the likelihood of particular confusions that may arise from auditory transmission of alphanumeric strings.

Key Words:
Information Coding

227
Hull, A.J., "Nine Codes: A Comparative Evaluation of Human Performance with Some Numeric, Alpha and Alpha-Numeric Coding Systems," *Ergonomics*, **18:5, 1975, 567-576.**

The relative performance of similar groups of subjects with different types of alpha, numeric, or alpha-numeric coding systems was examined using short-term memory techniques. Coding systems of equivalent informational value but of varying length and code content were not psychologically equivalent for the human operator. The results showed that the codes that were processed the best were either those that were very short, with not more than six items per code recalled, or, if longer, those arranged in pronounceable units.

Key Words:
Drivers,
Legibility Distance,
Motor Vehicle,
Railroad Crossing,
Signal Words,
Stimulus Size,
Symbol Shape

228
Jacobs, R.J., Johnston, A.W. and Cole, B.L., "The Visibility of Alphabetic and Symbolic Traffic Signs," *Australian Road Research*, **5:7, May 1975, 68-86.**

Sixteen regulatory and warning road sign messages were evaluated in both alphabetic and symbolic form. The signs were familiar ones intended to convey messages like, NO ENTRY, SLIPPERY WHEN WET, or RAILWAY CROSSING. Observers

Annotations (201-300)

Key Words (cont.):
Symbol Size,
Traffic,
Traffic Settings,
Visual Acuity

with visual acuities from normal to as low as 6/21 participated. Ten subjects participated in the first phase of the study, five subjects took part in the second phase. Probit analysis was used to calculate threshold visibility for individual signs and for groups of signs.

For symbolic signs, the average 50% threshold legibility distance was about twice that for alphabetic signs. Including shape coding on the signs (i.e., placing borders around the sign) had no effect on the legibility of either of the alphabetic or symbolic signs. In order to achieve 95% probability of correct identification, the size of the sign needed to be about 1.7 times that required to achieve a 50% probability. Reducing visual acuity from 6/6 to 6/12 had a predictable (halved) effect on the 50% threshold legibility distance. The authors conclude that the use of symbolic sign messages and larger alphabetic sign messages is necessary in traffic sign design. We note that the methodology used in this study could yield useful results if applied to product labels, pedestrian signs and other types of user information.

229
Jacoby, J., "Information Load and Decision Quality: Some Contested Issues," *Journal of Marketing Research*, 14, November 1977, 569-573.

Key Words:
Amount of Information,
Buying Behavior,
Information Overload

Jacoby notes that human beings are limited in their ability to assimilate and process information at any given time; information overload results when too much information is provided. Based on several studies surveyed, the author concludes that although certain aspects of this phenomenon remain debatable, it cannot be denied that many consumers in decision-making contexts are subject to information overload.

230
Jacoby, J., Speller, D.E. and Berning, C.K., "Brand Choice Behavior as a Function of Information Load: Replication and Extension," *Journal of Consumer Research*, 1, June 1974, 33-42.

Key Words:
Amount of Information,
Buying Behavior,
Information Overload

A package is emphasized as being the manufacturer's final opportunity to persuade and inform the consumer at point of purchase. Studies are summarized showing a curvilinear relationship existing between the amount of information and the "correctness" of purchase decisions. Within these studies, at both low and high levels of information load, the ability to correctly select the "best" brand was impaired.

An experiment was performed, in an attempt to replicate these earlier findings with different subjects, different products, and improved research methods. The subjects consisted of a sociodemographically heterogeneous sample (in terms of age, education, and family composition) of 192 paid housewife volunteers. Performance accuracies on buying decisions were considered separately for "Most Preferred Brand" (MPB) and "Rank Order." When the data were plotted in terms of total amount-of-information, MPB accuracy initially increased, then tended to decrease. The authors conclude the paper by posing several questions that need to be answered if policy makers are to know how much information, and what type, to make available to consumers. These questions are: Is there an optimal information load? Does this optimal load vary with different consumer populations? Which kinds of information should be provided? How should information be organized?

231
Johansson, G. and Backlund, F., "Drivers and Road Signs," *Ergonomics*, **13:6, 1970, 749-759.**

Key Words:
Active Processing,
Drivers,
Memory of:
  symbol/message,
Recall,
Traffic

Drivers were stopped 710 meters after passing five different types of road signs. Sign recall levels varied from 21% up to 79%, depending upon the content of the signs. The best recall was for signs indicating speed limits and police control, followed by those alerting the driver to wild animals, general danger, and pedestrian crossings. Environmental factors did not have a significant effect. Professional drivers and drivers highly familiar with the road were less apt to recall signs correctly. The authors conclude that these results indicate that the road sign system does not achieve its purpose. We suggest that analyses of results using modern information processing models would reveal that the types of signs users cognitively process may be more related to a driver's personal informational needs than to the specific design features of the signs.

232
Johnson, D.A., "The Design of Effective Safety Information Displays," *Proceedings of the Symposium: Human Factors and Industrial Design in Consumer Products*, **Poydar, H.R. (Ed.), Tufts University, Medford, 1980, 314-328.**

Key Words:
Abstractness,
Aircraft,
Aircraft Setting,
Conveying Action,
Conveying Conditions,
Conveying Procedures,
Describing Objects,
Design of: instructions,
Elemental Synthesis,
Illustrations,
Message Complexity,
Process Charts/
  Sequences,
Symbol Generation,

This paper summarizes an approach used by the Interaction Research Company to design emergency instructions for aircraft passengers and crew. Research indicated that pictorial safety cards are preferable to verbal presentations. The author notes that a lack of grammatical rules for pictures is problematic for designers. A distinction is drawn between presenting simple versus complex concepts and concrete versus abstract concepts. Johnson observes that it is difficult to represent complex, abstract concepts with pictographs.

Key Words (cont.):
Task Analysis
Verbal vs. Nonverbal
 Symbol/Message

A method of display development is presented that recommends: 1) analyzing equipment and procedures to determine what information should be given; 2) recording specific equipment locations and operations; 3) developing pictograms (initial and final views of each subset, with no more than two subsets shown in a single picture); 4) balancing prescriptive information, proscriptive information, and rationale in pictogram design; 5) selecting the proper mode of presentation (drawings are preferable to photographs, since, with drawings, unnecessary information can be eliminated, important material can be emphasized, and modification can be done easily); 6) adding indications of time and motion requirements where necessary; and 7) evaluating the display by testing naive subjects, using behavioral or conceptual tests. We note this as one of the more thorough outlines for developing instructions. Although presented in the aircraft passenger context, it would seem to have applicability elsewhere.

233
Johnson, E.J. and Russo, J.E., "Product Familiarity and Learning New Information," in *Advances in Consumer Research*, 8, Monroe, K.E. (Ed.), 1980.

Key Words:
Buying Behavior,
Consumers,
Familiarity with Product,
Memory of:
 symbol/message,
Prior Knowledge

This study was directed toward determining the relationship between consumers' familiarity with a product and their ability to learn new information about it. Two specific hypotheses were examined: the "enrichment hypothesis" and the "inverted U" hypothesis.

The "enrichment hypothesis" claims that a consumer's prior knowledge of a product provides a means whereby new information can be easily encoded into memory and recalled at a later time. Thus, the more familiar a person is with a product the easier it is to learn more about the product from new information. Bettman and Park (1980), however, propose that the "inverted U hypothesis" describes how product familiarity is related to the learning of new information. This hypothesis claims that inexperienced consumers will search less for information because they have difficulty understanding the information that they encounter. Consumers who are moderately familiar with a product are most likely to encode new information because they not only have the capacity to understand the new information but they also benefit from it. Finally, those consumers who are extremely familiar with a product tend to limit their search for new information because they perceive little need for it.

To test these hypotheses, fifty-four graduate students, who differed in their familiarity with cars, were asked to evaluate information about new sub-compact cars. Half of the subjects were asked to choose which of eight automobiles they preferred the most. The other half were asked to rate each of the cars on a seven-point scale by using just the information provided and not their prior knowledge of sub-compact cars. The subjects were then asked to recall as much as they possibly could including information they may have inferred. Interestingly the results supported both hypotheses to some extent.

The results showed that the inverted U effect was present when subjects were asked to choose the car they most preferred; that is, the subjects with moderate familiarity with cars recalled more information than those subjects with low or high degrees of familiarity. On the other hand, the enrichment hypothesis was supported when subjects were asked to evaluate each car separately; the more familiar the subject was with cars, the more new information they were able to recall. The fact that both hypotheses were supported indicates that the selection of one product among many (choice task) and the evaluation of individual products (judgment task) involve different information acquisition strategies or processes. The authors conclude that these results support the idea that information search and use is stratified according to the consumer's level of familiarity with the product. They also feel that for individuals who are not familiar with a product: "Simply posting information is probably ineffectual, especially for technically sophisticated products and attributes. To help these consumers make better decisions, information about the attributes, their importance, and their relationship to quality must be provided."

This research strongly implies that the developers of product safety-related information should take into account the user's level of familiarity with the product when deciding upon what information to provide. This conclusion follows from the impact of product familiarity on the search for and use of information demonstrated herein.

Key Words:
Agencies,
Brochures/Flyers,
Effectiveness of:
educational/persuasive programs,
Medical Patients,
Patient Package Inserts (PPI),
Understanding of Instructions

234
Johnson, M. W., Mitch, W.E., Sherwood, J., Lopes, L., Schmidt, A. and Hartley, H., "The Impact of a Drug Information Sheet on the Understanding and Attitude of Patients About Drugs," *Journal of the American Medical Association*, **256:19, November 1986, 2722-2724.**

The authors discuss a study evaluating the educational impact of providing written drug information to potential prescription drug users. The authors note the importance of patient education by citing previous research that indicates as many as one-third of patients make potentially serious errors in taking their medications, and such errors are often due to some misunderstanding of drug information.

Annotations (201-300)

In light of this error-prone background, they conducted a study in which one page medication sheets were provided to the subjects. These sheets were designed to describe the principal organ affected by a drug, the drug's primary effects, the dosing regimen, and common side effects and toxicity. The instruction sheets were provided to out-patients and in-patients who received the drugs. Seventy-one patients were evaluated. Testing of the patients prior to provision of the information sheets revealed that patient understanding of basic information regarding commonly used drugs was quite limited. Provision of the information sheets did result in modest improvement which continued to be exemplified one month after provision of the information sheet.

Key Words:
Understanding/
  Perception Models,
User Modeling

235
Johnson-Laird, P.N., "Mental Models in Cognitive Science," *Cognitive Science,* **4, 1980, 71-115.**

The author describes mental models as internal descriptions of the world which people use during problem solving, decision making, or other common forms of mental activity. The role of mental models as a means of explaining inference is explored, as is the relationship between meaning or semantics and mental models.

The paper also addresses the role of imagery and propositional representations in mental models. It is noted that there is a general movement in psychology for researchers to implement their conceptions of mental models in computer programs. Typically such programs are often similar to efforts in the field of artificial intelligence. The author also notes that the methodological synthesis of experimental psychology and artificial intelligence may play an important role in the development of cognitive science. Similar synthesis may eventually lead to a true technology for the development of instructions, warnings, and operator manuals.

Key Words:
Abstractness,
Accuracy,
Basic Associations,
Conveying Action,
Elemental Breakdowns,
Prohibition,
Students,
Traffic

236
Jones, S., "Symbolic Representation of Abstract Concepts," *Ergonomics,* **21:7, 1978, 573-577.**

This experiment tested the hypothesis that the type of message conveyed by road signs could be identified in the absence of the usual color cues. Twenty-two male and twenty-six female university students verbally interpreted fifteen signs and their responses were categorized in terms of message type and sign shape. All subjects had passed their driving test and driving experience ranged from six months to three years. Performance was measured by comparing the subjects' interpretations to the Highway Code definitions of the signs.

Removing the usual red color cue did not affect performance for circle-shaped or triangle-shaped signs, but when the usual blue color cue for rectangle-shaped signs was absent, performance suffered. This could have been due to the ambiguity of rectangle-shaped signs, since rectangular signs are used for many different functions. The slash, used with the ring, was the most significant feature for eliciting prohibitive messages. In the concrete version of signs, the effect of the slash as a prohibitive signal was more prominent than in the abstract case. Prohibitive "no" responses were elicited 89.9% of the time in the former condition and only 50.0% of the time in the latter case.

Key Words:
ANSI,
Hazardous Materials,
Industrial

237
Jones, W.H., "ANSI Standard: Simple, Direct, Flexible," *Occupational Health & Safety*, **47:2, March/April 1978, 29-30.**

This article provides a general introductory paper to ANSI Z 129.1 which provides guidelines for labeling hazardous materials.

Key Words:
Drivers,
Effectiveness of:
  educational/persuasive programs,
Message Tone

238
Kaestner, N., Warmoth, E.J. and Syring, E.M., "Oregon Study of Advisory Letters: The Effectiveness of Warning Letters in Driver Improvement," *Traffic Safety Research Review*, **11:3, September 1967, 67-72.**

This study investigated the the impact of sending letters to problem drivers who persistently violated traffic rules: it was found that drivers receiving a standard, photocopied form letter subsequently had driving records remarkably similar to the driving records of problem drivers who did not receive a letter. However, relative to matched controls, recipients of personalized letters of warning showed a significant improvement in their driving records. The degree of improvement further increased when the personalized letter was less threatening and more encouraging.

Key Words:
Auditory,
Auditory Signal Strength,
Awakening,
Consumer Setting,
Consumers
Effectiveness of: warning related litigation,
Filtering,
Fire,
Olfactory

239
Kahn, M.J., "Human Awakening and Subsequent Identification of Fire-Related Cues," *Proceedings of the Human Factors Society - 27th Annual Meeting*, **Human Factors Society, Santa Monica, CA, 1983, 806-810.**

Twenty-four college age males were each tested for one night to determine their ability to both awaken in response to fire cues (smoke alarms, smoke odor, a sudden increase in room temperature) and correctly identify the cues as being indicative of a fire. Twelve of the subjects were exposed to three intensities of smoke alarm warning signals while the remaining twelve were

Key Words (cont.):
Students,
Temperature

exposed to smoke odor, heat presentation, and a single alarm. Subjects were, in all cases, awakened by alarms that reached their ears at signal/noise ratios of 34 dB. They were considerably less likely to be awakened by heat, smoke odor, and alarms that reached their ears at signal/noise ratios of 10 dB or less. Few of the subjects were able to identify temperature increases and smoke alarm warnings as fire cues.

240
Kammann, R., "The Comprehensibility of Printed Instructions and the Flowchart Alternative," *Human Factors*, **17:8, 1975, 183-191.**

Key Words:
Accuracy,
Consumers,
Logic Trees,
Process Charts/
 Sequences,
Response Time,
Verbal vs. Nonverbal
 Symbol/Message,
Workers

The researcher summarizes several studies that indicated printed instructions would be understood by their intended readers only two-thirds of the time. This estimate is believed to be a minimum level of information loss. The researcher then supplies evidence that flowchart presentations of instructions (e.g., decision trees and hierarchies of yes/no questions) have been shown to be effective in other research.

An experiment is summarized in which ninety Bell scientists and engineers and ninety housewives performed a series of dialing tasks. The subjects received either a standard directory or one of two flowcharts to help them complete the task. The housewives who used the flowcharts attained dramatically better scores for both comprehension, accuracy and speed, and the use of flowcharts resulted in better accuracy scores for engineers and scientists. In a subsequent field study, it was found that employees using the directory alone had a 65% comprehension rate, while employees using flowcharts had 80% to 85% comprehension rates. Performance times were significantly lower only for employees who used the second flowchart. We note that even in this early study, there are suggestions that providing instructional information in non-traditional forms shows advantages.

241
Kann, H.R., "Symbololatry: ICAO's Information Symbols for Airports Heighten the Confusion of International Communications Creating a Modern Tower of Babble," *Industrial Design*, **17:8, October 1970, 56-57.**

Key Words:
Design Consistency,
International Labeling
 and Signage Systems,
Introducing New
 Systems,
Public Information,
Routing

The author notes that the International Civil Aviation Organization (ICAO) has developed its own set of symbols. The defined symbols are claimed to be arbitrary in nature. It is also claimed that they were developed with inadequate research, thereby creating problems.

Key Words:
Amount of Information,
Design of: instructions,
Information Overload,
Message Tone,
Prior Knowledge,
Problems in Design,
Writing Instructions

242
Kanouse, D.E. and Hayes-Roth, B., "Cognitive Considerations in the Design of Product Warnings," in *Product Labeling and Health Risks*, Morris, L.A., Mazis, M.B. and Barofsky, I. (Eds.), Cold Spring Harbor Laboratory, Banbury Report 6, 1980, 147-163.

This very important paper presents a selective review of the psychological literature pertaining to the design of effective health warnings. The paper focuses on warning-type information that is embedded within extended text. More specifically, the authors examine the potential impact of the following four aspects of product warnings: message length, information organization, message tone, and writing style.

The first aspect, message length, poses one major problem: the need to find the proper balance between information overload and insufficient information. The authors provide the following conclusions on this topic: 1) behavioral instructions should be detailed enough for the user to infer other associations if general instructions are insufficient to cover all potentially hazardous situations; 2) specific action-oriented or explicit instructions are often more effective than general and abstract instructions; 3) elaboration of messages by the inclusion of explanations can sometimes reduce memory lapses and misconceptions; 4) however, elaboration can make messages too long, reducing the amount read by poor readers and decreasing retention; and 5) providing both a core message and an elaborated message may reduce problems, since short messages seem to be better for transmitting simple information, while long messages seem better for complex information.

Information organization is the second aspect addressed. The organization of information on health warnings is likely to impact message comprehension, memory of facts needed on a continuing basis, and the memory of facts needed on a contingent basis. The authors recommend incorporating a hierarchical structure in the presentation of facts and conclusions. This structure organizes information for each topic by presenting general information first and then moving to the more specific. The authors cite research literature indicating that a hierarchical structure facilitates identification and recollection of important facts.

The authors make the following observations about message tone: 1) the number of hazards mentioned (independent of probability) has a large effect on perceived risk; 2) emphasis placed on risk can affect recall and actions; 3) general tone (frank or elaborated statements) can effect the memory of facts presented in a document; and 4) detailed description may either reduce or increase perceived risk.

The authors address the last aspect, writing style, by providing rules for clear writing. Their list includes the following: 1) use active verbs; 2) use the active voice; 3) use concrete rather than abstract words and sentences; and 4) use numbers or bullets to present facts in a paragraph.

Key Words:
Adequacy of Warnings,
Duty/Failure to Warn,
Human Factors,
Overapplication of warnings

243
Kantowitz, B.H. and Sorkin, R.D., "Chapter 7: Visual Displays," in *Human Factors: Understanding People-System Relationships*, Kantowitz, B.H. and Sorkin, R.D., (Eds.), John Wiley & Sons, New York, 1983, 272-305.

This chapter describes visual displays as being an essential element of the communication process. It also provides a number of general design principles useful during the development of effective displays, and emphasizes the importance of task analysis and individual specific factors. See below for other chapters from Kantowitz's and Sorkin's informative book.

Key Words:
Auditory,
Kinesthetic/Tactile

244
Kantowitz, B.H. and Sorkin, R.D., "Chapter 8: Auditory and Tactile Displays," in *Human Factors: Understanding People-System Relationships*, Kantowitz, B.H. and Sorkin, R.D. (Eds.), John Wiley & Sons, New York, 1983, 232-271.

Kantowitz's and Sorkin's book is one of the more recent well-done texts in applied human factors engineering. The noted chapter on auditory and tactile displays is of particular interest because of its attention to aircraft cockpit aural alerts, synthesized speech, the vibrotactile sensitivities of various parts of the human body, ANSI alarm signals to emergencies, and tactile (stick-shaker) warnings—the only tactile warning system used in commercial vehicles.

Key Words:
Human Factors,
Overapplication of Warnings,
Negligence and Warnings,
Strict Liability and Warnings,
Warranties/Disclaimers

245
Kantowitz, B.H. and Sorkin, R.D., "Chapter 20: Legal Aspects of Human Factors," in *Human Factors: Understanding People-System Relationships*, Kantowitz, B.H. and Sorkin, R.D. (Eds.), John Wiley & Sons, New York, 1983, 629-644.

The authors introduce a number of legal issues that the human factors specialist must be aware of. These issues include products liability and its relevant legal theories, such as negligence, strict liability, and warranties. Case histories are given illustrating the problems human factors specialists may face when acting as "experts." The authors also place special emphasis on describing the general position of the courts regarding the use of warning labels. It is noted that "from a human factors perspective, excessive warnings are as bad as insufficient warnings," and several illustrative examples of irrational legally required warnings are given. Finally, the authors suggest that, "Eventually, the legal community will take the utility of a warning into account."

Key Words:
ATV (All Terrain Vehicles),
Consumer Setting,
Detection/Perception Measures,
Perceptual Skills,
Workload/Task

246
Karnes, E.W., Leonard, S.D. and Newbold, H.C., "Safety Perceptions and Information Sources for ATVs," *Proceedings of the Human Factors Society - 32nd Annual Meeting*, **Human Factors Society, Santa Monica, CA, 1988, 938-942.**

The authors begin with a general review of potential safety problems associated with the use of ATVs. They then discuss an experiment directed toward determining how well drivers of ATVs can judge the speed at which they are operated. Fifteen college students were paid to participate in an experiment in which they rode two different ATV models at varying speeds. The participants in the experiment were asked to ride the ATV at a randomly selected speed. At the same time the speed was measured and made available to the experimenter. The operators were asked to ride the ATVs at eight different speeds ranging between 5 and 40 mph in increments of 5 mph.

Subjects tended to underestimate their speed when they were traveling less than 15 mph and overestimate their speed when they were traveling greater than 15 mph. The authors suggest , among other things, that speedometers be added to ATVs.

Key Words:
ATV (All Terrain Vehicles),
Existing/Past Behavior Patterns,
Hazard,
Influences of Warning Labels,
Labels,
Level of Detail,
Prior Knowledge,
Severity Estimates,
Students,
Training

247
Karnes, E.W., Leonard, S.D. and Rachwal, G., "Effects of Benign Experiences on the Perception of Risk," *Proceedings of the Human Factors Society - 30th Annual Meeting*, **Human Factors Society, Santa Monica, CA, 1986, 121-125.**

The authors hypothesize based on simple reinforcement theory that repeated benign experience with potentially dangerous events will lead to a lower degree of perceived risk. Two experiments were performed to test the hypothesis. In both, the subjects were shown a videotape of "safe" versus "unsafe" ATV driving. The presence of a warning was found to increase the mean ratings of risk for subjects without experience with ATVs, but had little influence on those subjects who had been either a driver or passenger. The few subjects who had been injured by ATVs were also found to give relatively high risk ratings.

Annotations (201-300)

Key Words:
Perceived Risk,
Sources of Bias

248
Kasper, R.G., "Perceptions of Risk and Their Effects on Decision Making," in *Societal Risk Assessment*, Schwing, R.C., & Albers, W.A. (Eds.), Plenum Press, NY, 1980, 71-84.

Kasper considers two broad categories of risk assessment and their impact on decision makers. The first type of risk assessment may be categorized as "objective." This assessment uses analytical calculations, experimental evidence, or long-term experience, and often results in probability estimates of events. The second type of assessment may be termed "subjective." In this case, risk is assessed by individuals who rely upon their perceptions about a given event or situation. Kasper points out that there are often large discrepancies between these two types of assessment and concludes with a discussion of the governmental and social problems created by such discrepancies. (Also see Slovic, 1979).

Key Words:
Post-injury Warning,
Strict Liability and
  Warnings,
Subsequent Remedial
  Measures

249
Keating, F.J., "Evidence—Products Liability—Evidence of Manufacturer's Post-injury Product Warning is Admissible in Strict Liability Action," *University of Detroit Law Review*, 62:1, Fall 1984, 133-143.

In Schelbauer v. Butler Manufacturing Co., the Supreme Court of California held that evidence of post-injury product warnings is admissible in strict liability actions. Keating feels that the holding is part of a continuing trend in California case law to relieve injured plaintiffs of the onerous evidentiary burdens inherent in product liability actions.

Key Words:
Duty/Failure to Warn,
Negligence and
  Warnings,
Product Literature,
Strict Liability and
  Warnings

250
Keeton, W.P., "Products Liability—Inadequacy of Information," *Texas Law Review*, 48, 1970, 398-415.

This is one of the earliest papers to recommend that the failure to warn issue be subject to the theory of strict liability in tort, rather than to the theory of negligence.

Key Words:
Consumer Labeling and
  Signage Systems,
Consumers,
Development Programs,
Fire, Hazard/Alert,
Ingress/Egress,
Public Information,
Routing,
Students

251
Kegerreis, R.J. and Spiegel, A.P., "A Supplementary Emergency Signage System," *National Safety News*, November 1977, 81-82.

This paper briefly discusses the development of an emergency egress/ingress sign system at Wright State University. Since existing legal sign standards were judged to be inadequate, a system was developed to meet the particular needs of WSU's student body.

Key Words:
Accuracy, Biohazard,
Caustic Materials,
Consumers,
Control/Display
 Elements,
Conveying Procedures,
Electrical Hazard,
Explosives, Fire,
Fire Safety Signs,
Hazard/Alert,
Housewives, Industrial,
Ingress/Egress,
Moving Vehicle,
Personal Protective
 Equipment,
Point of Operation
 Guarding, Poison,
Public Information,
Radiation,
Safety Information,
Students, Traffic,
Understanding of
 Instructions,
User Group

252
Keller, A.D., "Evaluation of Graphic Symbols for Safety and Warning Signs," Master's Thesis, Department of Psychology, University of South Dakota, August 1972.

The recognizability to university students of three symbol variants in ten different categories was evaluated. Well-established symbols were frequently found to be rated low on recognizability. This finding was particularly prevalent for abstract protection symbol (38%), and the biohazard symbol (58%). No significant statistics were computed, and the researcher's use of arbitrary multiple choice questions to establish recognition could be questioned. The findings are also somewhat outdated. As one of the earliest systematic evaluations of symbolic comprehension, this study is, however, historically relevant.

Key Words:
Amount of Information,
Task Analysis,
User Modeling

253
Kern, R.P., "Chapter 13: Modeling Users and Their Use of Technical Manuals," in *Designing Usable Texts*, Duffy, T.M. and Waller, R. (Eds.), Academic Press, Inc., Orlando, 1985, 341-375.

The author contends that a good model of the user is a necessary, if not a sufficient, condition for producing a good job-related manual. The author also presents analytic techniques for developing or determining the task-oriented content of instruction manuals. He notes that this approach is highly dependent on modeling the task which is to be performed and that readability indexes have been extensively applied. He feels that there have been several problems associated with traditional methods for the development of manuals. These include the assumption, by many manual developers, that the manual is the only source of job information. He also feels there has not been enough attention to the variables which affect the use of manuals in the job setting.

Research is presented on the actual use of information by mechanics. The types of information used were subdivided into extrinsic information sources such as manuals and intrinsic sources such as signals emitted by tools or knowledge that the person contains within their memory. A strong correlation was found between the experience of mechanics and the types of information they sought. Highly experienced mechanics obtained far less information from extrinsic sources such as manuals than did the less experienced. Experienced mechanics were also more dependent on intrinsic sources. These results supported the potential value of user modeling during manual development. The demands for specific types of information can be used to determine how the manual should be designed for particular users.

254
Kern, R.P., Sticht, T.G., Welty, D. and Hauke, R.N., "Guidebook for the Development of Army Training Literature," Human Resources Research Organization, Alexandria, NTIS No. AD AO33 935, November 1975.

Key Words:
Conveying Procedures,
Development Cycle,
Illustrations

This guidebook is directed toward assisting writers of narrative training literature. It primarily addresses performance-oriented writing, as opposed to topic-oriented writing, because much of the narrative training literature is designed to help individuals perform job related tasks. The authors provide step-by-step instructions for developing operator and maintenance manuals and other specialized texts. The guidebook provides numerous "before" and "after" examples of graphic illustrations as well as written text. The authors discuss the difference between topic-oriented and performance-oriented writing, various information presentation techniques, and information retrieval aids for users of the literature. Also included is a list of references pertaining to the various aspects of technical writing.

255
Kieras, D.E., "The Role of Prior Knowledge in Operating Equipment from Written Instructions," Report No. 19 (FR-85/ONR-19), University of Michigan, Ann Arbor February 1985.

Key Words:
Design of: instructions,
Prior Knowledge,
Task Analysis,
Understanding/
  Perception Models

This report is a summary of results concerning the role of prior knowledge in how people operate electronic equipment from written instructions. Two situations are addressed: 1) subjects possessed the knowledge prior to the experiment; and 2) the knowledge was provided as part of the experimental training. Non-expert subjects consisted of ordinary undergraduate and graduate students with no special background. Expert subjects were individuals with years of experience in electronics; many had military experience as electronics technicians. The studies reported here included studies of comprehension, memory, descriptive expertise, and knowledge of how a system operates.

Conclusions stated by the author include: 1) readers have specialized methodologies for dealing with unfamiliar material; and 2) careful attention must be paid to the relationship between the knowledge being supplied to the participant and the tasks that the participant is expected to perform. It is also stated that the results of these investigations support the class of theories described in Anderson's book, *The Architecture of Cognition* (1983). The author recommends further research in order to fully explore the significance of the results found.

Key Words:
Writing Instructions

256
Kieras, D.E. and Dechert, C., "Rules for Comprehensible Technical Prose: A Survey of the Psycholinguistic Literature," Technical Report No. 21 (TR-85/ONR-21), June 1985.

As part of a larger study directed toward developing a computerized system for evaluating technical prose, the authors present a set of rules for comprehensible writing. The authors emphasize that these rules are aimed at evaluating what they called the "shallow semantics" of text, rather than the text's deep underlying meaning. To develop this set of rules, approximately 170 papers were examined and summarized. Fifty-nine rules for comprehensible writing are proposed. Since the rules were developed from such an exhaustive foundation of literature, we find them particularly notable.

Key Words:
Development Cycle

257
Killingsworth, M.J. and Eiland, K., "Managing the Production of Technical Manuals: Recent Trends," *IEEE Transactions on Professional Communication*, 29:2, June 1986, 23-26.

The authors developed a questionnaire asking professionals to comment on how they plan and produce product manuals. The questionnaire was sent to eighty-two companies (most were computer-oriented). Based on the survey results, the authors provide the following conclusions: 1) three divisions of an organization usually participate in the production of manuals: product development, communication, and marketing; 2) the influence of communication and marketing specialists has increased; 3) audience analysis is performed primarily by marketing research; 4) manuals are generally tested for effectiveness beginning with in-house tests and ending with tests involving volunteers or target consumers; 5) in addition to traditional management techniques, companies are resorting to automation to control cost in product manual development; and 6) automation has been useful in updating and revising manuals. We note that this is one of the few studies which has probed industry practices with respect to manual writing and design. However, because it focuses on computer-oriented companies, it may not reflect practice in other types of industries.

Annotations (201-300)

Key Words:
Accuracy,
Advantages of Nonverbal Symbols,
Drivers,
Glance Legibility,
Motor Vehicle,
Noise,
Traffic,
Traffic Settings,
Verbal vs. Nonverbal Symbol/Message,
Viewing Time,
Visual Noise

258
King, L.E., "Recognition of Symbol and Word Traffic Signs," *Journal of Safety Research,* **7:2, June 1975, 80-84.**

Twenty-six subjects viewed tachistoscopic images of verbal and symbolic signs. In one condition, the images were displayed for 1/3 second, while in the other condition they were displayed for 1/18 second No differences were observed between the recognizability of verbal versus symbolic signs for the 1/3 second condition. For the 1/18 second condition, the percentage of correct responses was slightly but significantly lower for the verbal signs. This discrepancy was increased by presenting a 10 second reading-interference type task between the time of the image viewing and the image matching. The researcher failed to note that a verbal interference task is more likely to interfere with verbal than with symbolic tasks.

Key Words:
Accuracy,
Drivers,
Glance Legibility,
Motor Vehicle,
Traffic,
Traffic Settings,
Verbal vs. Nonverbal Symbol/Message,
Viewing Time,
Visual Noise

259
King, L.E. and Tierney, W.J., "Glance Legibility – Symbol versus Word Highway Signs," *Proceedings of the Human Factors Society,* **Human Factors Society, Santa Monica, CA, 1970, 1-14.**

A set of symbolic and verbal traffic signs was selected for investigation. The ability of subjects to identify symbols was generally poor but varied; the percentage of correct responses ranged from 26% to 92%, with a mode of about 50%. The glance legibility portion of the experiment showed that subjects were able to more accurately match symbolic test signs than verbal ones against other similar signs, particularly when viewing times were only about 1/18 of a second. For 1/3 second viewing times, however, the number of correct matches was essentially equivalent for both verbal and symbolic signs. Based on the results under the 1/18 second viewing condition, the researchers concluded that symbolic signs are more effective (which we believe is a debatable inference).

Key Words:
Design of: instructions,
Readability Measures,
Understanding of Instructions

260
Klare, G.R., "Chapter 25: Readability and Comprehension," in *Information Design: The Design and Evaluation of Signs and Printed Material,* **Easterby, R.S. and Zwaga, H.J.G. (Eds.), John Wiley & Sons, New York, 1984, 479-495.**

Readability indices and the intervening variables relating readability to comprehension are explored in this chapter. The author characterizes the purposes of readability research as: 1) the prediction of readable writing, as exemplified by the development of readability formulas; and 2) the production of readable writing, as exemplified by the development of manuals for that purpose. A model of the relationship of readability to comprehension is diagrammed and discussed. These factors pertain to the content of material and reader motivation. The results of matching tests were interpreted to show that there are many different definitions of comprehension, and that since there is so little agreement, definers make their definitions fit rather than attempting to find "common ground."

Key Words:
Readability Measures,
Understanding of Instructions

261
Klare, G.R., "Assessing Readability," *Reading Research Quarterly*, **10:1, 1974-1975, 62-102.**

This article summarizes a variety of readability formulas. Readability formulas are often helpful because they can be used to estimate the difficulty of the text without requiring the reader to do so. In order to provide an index of probable difficulty, it uses counts of language variables in the writing sample. The readability formulas and other devices summarized in these pages are grouped as follows: A) recalculations and revisions of existing formulas; B) new formulas; C) application aids; and D) predicting readability for foreign languages.

The Lorge formula, the Flesch formulas, the Dale-Chall formula, the Farr-Jenkins-Paterson formula, the Fog Index, and the Spache formula measure recalculations and revisions (A). The Devereaux formula, the Jacobson formulae, the Botel formula, the Rogers formula, the Danielson-Bryan formula, the readability graph, the Coleman formulas, the Easy Listening formula, the Shaw formula, the Elley formula, the SMOG grading, the Bormuth formulas, the Aquino formulae, the Mugfor Readability Chart, the Boeing readability profile, the Henshall formula, the Syntactic Complexity formula, the FORCAST readability formula, the Lensear Write formula, the Clear River Test, the Damerst Clear Index, the RIDE scale, and the Harris-Jacobson Primary readability formula evaluate new formula (B). To examine application aids (C) the Lorge formula, the Flesch Reading Ease formula, the Farr-Jenkins-Paterson formula, and others were utilized. To predict readability for foreign languages (D), Chinese, Dutch, English, German, Hebrew, Hindi, Russian, and Spanish were considered.

Key Words:
Accuracy,
Association Rankings/
    Indexes,
Elemental Breakdowns,
Military,
Symbol Taxonomies

262
Knapp, B.G., "Scaling Military Symbols: A Comparison of Techniques to Derive Associative Meaning," *Proceedings of the Human Factors Society - 28th Annual Meeting*, **Human Factors Society, Santa Monica, CA, 1984, 309-313.**

This paper addresses symbolic representations of concepts with respect to their inherent, associative meaning. The associative meanings of symbols were assessed by two methods, a rating scale and paired-comparison. One hundred and three entry-level military personnel participated in the paired comparison portion and 130 beginning course military personnel participated in the rating scale task. None of the subjects had previous experience with the symbols. Seven symbol populations (helicopter, missile, radar, nuclear event, fence obstacle, biochemical event, and chemical unit) were included. Five different symbols were presented for each of the symbol populations.

The results indicate that symbols which contain abstract shape have the highest associative value to the concept they represent. The authors note that, although the paired-comparison technique and the rating scale method produce similar results, paired-comparison was superior for practical reasons.

263
Knapp, B.G., Peters, J.I. and Gordon, D.A., "Human Factor Review of Traffic Control and Diversion Projects," Federal Highway Administration, Washington, D.C., FHWA-RD-74-22, July 1973.

Key Words:
Motor Vehicle,
Routing

This paper reviews the design of diversion signs intended to encourage drivers to shift from congested to less congested routes. Reviewed studies of driver behavior include origin-destination studies, economic studies of the dollar value of time, and studies of drivers' attitudes toward route diversion.

264
Komaki, J., Barwick, K.D. and Scott, L.R., "A Behavioral Approach to Occupational Safety: Pinpointing and Reinforcing Safe Performance in a Food Manufacturing Plant," *Journal of Applied Psychology,* **63:4, 1978, 434-445.**

Key Words:
Effectiveness of:
    educational/persuasive
    programs,
Feedback,
Personal Presentations,
Posted Feedback

This article discusses a behavioral modification program designed to increase the prevalence of safe behavior in a food manufacturing plant. The program provided an explanation and visual presentation of the desired behaviors, and emphasized the provision of frequent, low-cost reinforcement through feedback. The two participating bakery departments improved their respective safety performance from 70% and 78% to 96% and 99%. Employees in the "makeup" department (nine males and seven females) and the "wrapping" department (seven males and fifteen females) composed the subject group. Performance returned to baseline during the reversal phase, when feedback was no longer provided. The program, particularly the feedback, was effective in improving safety performance. Employees reacted favorably to the program, and the company subsequently maintained it with a continued decline in the injury frequency rate.

Key Words:
Effectiveness of:
　educational/persuasive
　　programs,
Feedback,
Formal Teaching/
　Counseling/Education,
Posted Feedback

265
Komaki, J., Heinzmann, A.T. and Lawson, L., "Effect of Training and Feedback: Component Analysis of a Behavioral Safety Program," *Journal of Applied Psychology*, **65:3, 1980, 261-270.**

One hundred and sixty-five observations of safety performance were recorded for a city's vehicle maintenance division over a period of forty-five weeks. The observations were organized into four different sections: 1) the proper use of equipment and tools; 2) the use of safety equipment; 3) housekeeping; and 4) general Safety Procedures. These observations were used to assess the impact of training and feedback on safety-related behavior.

The training consisted of a 30 to 45 minute session that required employees to evaluate a series of transparencies in which an unsafe action or condition was depicted; safety rules were also reviewed at this time. Feedback was provided by posting a graph that plotted the results of a random daily safety observation conducted by a supervisor in the maintenance division. The results of the study showed no significant difference in the "mean safety level" between the baseline condition and the training-only phase. However, the training and feedback phase resulted in a significant improvement in mean safety level for three out of four sections in the vehicle maintenance division. The authors concluded that training alone is insufficient as a means of improving and maintaining safety performance. It is proposed that feedback is also necessary to achieve a significant improvement in performance.

Key Words:
Aesthetics,
Consumer Setting,
Perception of
　Symbol/Message

266
Konz, S., Chawla, S., Sathaye, S. and Shah, P., "Attractiveness and Legibility of Various Colours When Printed on Cardboard," *Ergonomics*, **15:2, 1972, 189-194.**

In the first experiment discussed, blue, black, green, purple, red, orange, and yellow letters were tested for legibility and attractivenes when presented on brown and gray cardboard. Legibility and attractiveness were positively correlated. In the second experiment light, medium, and dark shades of blue, black, green, and red letters were studied further using a brown cardboard surface. Legibility and attractiveness again were positively correlated. Light black and red had poor legibility; medium green and black had high legibility. Blue was the color voted the most attractive.

Annotations (201-300)

Key Words:
Accuracy,
Summaries,
Titles,
Underlining/
 Highlighting,
Understanding of
 Instructions,
User Modeling

267
Kozminsky, E., "Altering Comprehension: The Effect of Biasing Titles on Text Comprehension," *Memory & Cognition*, **5:4, 1977, 482-490.**

Previous research is cited indicating that titles can alter the way people comprehend text. The authors describe a propositional theory of text comprehension which postulates that comprehension activity involves the development of an ordered list of semantic units or propositions within memory. If the presence of a title influences the way these propositions are organized within memory, it may be concluded that the title will have a significant influence on what information is comprehended and remembered.

An experiment involving forty-five undergraduate students was performed which was directed toward determining how a title influences the comprehension and memory of text. It was found that slightly more information within text was remembered when the information was consistent with the title than when the information was inconsistent with the title. The author discusses how the comprehension process may be guided by the title in a way that is consistent with this model. We note that within warnings and instructions, the choice of sub-headings may be influential to the text which follows, if the findings from the present study hold.

Key Words:
Development Programs,
Electrical Hazard,
Fire,
Ingress/Egress,
Production Method,
Public Information,
Routing,
Safety Information,
Symbol Generation

268
Krampen, M., "The Production Method in Sign Design Research," *Print*, **November/December 1969, 59-63.**

Much of the work described in this article comes from the ICOGRADA/UIm Project, which was conceived as a practical contribution to the current search for internationally meaningful symbols. The study utilized the Production Method, which involves asking participants to produce drawings of the presented concepts. Krampen states that the value of the Production Method is its ability to convey the sign repertoire of any population to the investigator. Krampen summarizes other studies that incorporate the Production Method and states that it is a useful method for generating iconic signs.

Key Words:
Description/Modeling,
Development Programs,
Illustrations,
Public Information,
Traffic

269
Krampen, M., "Signs and Symbols in Graphic Communication," *Design Quarterly*, **62, 1965, 3-31.**

Krampen notes that past experiments have examined the relative legibility of typefaces and the reader's comprehension of graphs and tables, but almost nothing is known about the effectiveness of a layout. Krampen then presents an illustrated discussion of theoretical and experimental work in graphic communication. The presented topics include: graphic communication and perception; graphic communication and semantics; signs, symbols and surrogates in graphic communication; graphic communication and "pictic" analysis; communication with audiences of low literacy; communication with sophisticated audiences; communication with many language groups simultaneously; and a section on conventionalized picture languages.

Key Words:
Drivers,
Effectiveness of:
educational/persuasive programs

270
Kraus, J.F., Riggins, R.S. and Franti, C.E., "Some Epidemiologic Features of Motorcycle Collision Injuries: I. Introduction, Methods and Factors Associated with Incidence," *American Journal of Epidemiology*, 102:1, 1975, 74-98.

This paper reports on an epidemiologic investigation of motorcycle injuries in Sacramento County, California. Nearly 1,300 individuals with confirmed medically treated motorcycle injuries were studied. The most significant result noted is that the observed statistical risk of injury was higher for riders with training than for those riders who had no training or who operated their motorcycles frequently.

Key Words:
Brochures/Flyers,
Effectiveness of:
educational/persuasive programs,
Letters,
Parents,
Personal Presentations

271
Kravitz, H. and Grove, M., "Prevention of Accidental Falls in Infancy by Counseling Mothers," *Illinois Medical Journal*, 144, December 1973, 570-573.

This article describes a two-year study, conducted in a private suburban pediatric practice, of the falls of infants from elevated surfaces. The control group consisted of 336 infants whose parents received no special safety instructions on prevention of falls in infancy. The parents of the 320 infants in the experimental group were given specific verbal and written instructions on the dangers of falls in infancy. Falls in the counseled and uncounseled groups were categorized as either prospective or retrospective. In the prospective category, the uncounseled group had 17.2% incidence rate of falls, compared to 10.35% in the counseled group.

Annotations (201-300)

Key Words:
Design of: labeling and safety signage systems,
Development Programs,
Fuzzy Set Membership,
Information Coding,
Simple Comprehension of: verbal symbols,
Symbol Generation,
Understanding/ Perception Models,
User Modeling

272
Kreifeldt, J.C. and Rao, K.V.N., "Fuzzy Sets: An Application to Warnings and Instructions," *Proceedings of the Human Factors Society - 30th Annual Meeting*, Human Factors Society, Santa Monica, CA, 1986, 1192-1196.

The authors note that although the terms used in instructions and warnings are defined in the qualitative terms of common discourse, they are often expected to convey precise concepts. Fuzzy set theory is presented as a means of formally describing the meanings which might be inferred from such terminology. Several "fuzzy" terms were obtained by reviewing the instructions and labels on several different products. Membership functions were then experimentally developed for the terms "(about) one inch," "squeeze (hard)," "squeeze (gently)," and "squeeze (firmly)." Interestingly, different membership functions were developed for "(about) one inch," depending upon whether they were developed by estimation, rating, or production.

Key Words:
Problems in Design,
Readability Measures

273
Kreindler, R.J. and Luchsinger, V.P., "How Readable Are Your Safety Publications?" *Professional Safety*, September 1978, 40-42.

The authors provide a very readable introduction to the topic of misreading. In particular, the FORCAST and Flesch readability formulas are summarized at a basic level.

Key Words:
Development Programs,
Emergency Warning Systems: general,
Task Analysis

274
Kroemer, K.H.E. and Marras, W.S., "Ergonomics of Visual Emergency Signals," *Applied Ergonomics*, 11:3, September 1980, 137-144.

The objective of the described research was to determine if visual emergency signalling (VES) devices could be designed for safer and more efficient use by untrained persons under adverse operating conditions. To achieve this objective, the authors felt that ergonomics and human factors information should be intensively employed.

Research was performed to assess the compliance with human engineering principles of existing VES devices. A field study was conducted in which the VES devices were categorized and critical ergonomic aspects were established and compiled. Laboratory tests were performed that indicated the effects of selected Human Engineering design features on locating, unpacking, and operating of VES devices. Finally, the research results were validated in realistically simulated emergencies. Those research findings demonstrated the potential for human factors engineering to reduce the time needed for the successful use of the VES devices by up to 80%.

Key Words:
Contraceptives,
Drugs,
Duty/Failure to Warn

275
Kurtz, J., "A Duty to Warn, a Right to Know: Odgers v. Ortho Pharmaceutical Corporation," *Detroit College of Law Review,* **1, 1986, 163-181.**

This article examines the question whether, under Michigan law, the manufacturer of oral contraceptives has a duty to warn the ultimate consumer of risks and side effects. In Odgers v. Ortho Pharmaceutical Corp., the Michigan Supreme Court discussed but did not decide this issue, leaving the law in a "state" of confusion.

Key Words:
Actual Behavior,
Agreement with
  Symbol/Message,
Behavior Factors,
Existing/Past Behavior
  Patterns,
Industrial,
Industrial Safety,
Perceived Risk,
Warnings: evaluating
  effects on behavior,
Workers

276
Laner, S. and Sell, R.G., "An Experiment on the Effects of Specially Designed Safety Posters," *Occupational Psychology,* **34:3, July 1960, 153-169.**

The authors state that safety posters may provide useful reinforcement of other teaching methods by acting as a reminder of what has been taught. To evaluate this issue, the authors conducted an experiment testing the effectiveness of safety posters that reminded steel workers to hook slings to cranes when the slings were not being used. The study focused on observing behaviors in a realistic setting, because previous research (i.e., Belbin, 1956) indicated that measures of recall and preference were not adequate indicators of effectiveness.

The presence of the posters corresponded to an overall 7.8% increase in the target behavior. In low-roofed shops, where Laner and Sell assume that the necessity of hooking slings is more easily perceived, the presence of the posters corresponded to a 13.5% increase in sling hooking. When a follow-up survey was taken six weeks after the experiment, it was found that sling hooking in general had increased by an additional 4.5%. In the low-roofed shops, the additional increment was 6.3%, resulting in a total change in behavior over the testing period of 19.8%. Another interesting trend was that the amount of behavior change was lowest in shops where hook-slinging behavior prior to the introduction of the sign was either very high or very low. Based on the latter finding, Laner and Sell conclude that the perceived relevance of the safety message is directly correlated to its effect on behavior.

Key Words:
Accuracy,
Biohazard,
Caustic Materials,
Conveying Action,
Electrical Hazard,
Explosives,
Fire,
Fire Safety Signs,
Hazard,
Personal Protective
 Equipment,
Pictographs,
Point of Operation
 Guarding,
Poison,
Radiation,
Students

277
Laux, L., Mayer, D.L. and Thompson, N.B., "Usefulness of Symbols and Pictorials to Communicate Hazard Information," *Proceedings of INTERFACE '89 - The Sixth Symposium on Human Factors and Industrial Design in Consumer Products*, **Human Factors Society, Santa Monica, CA, 1989, 79-83.**

This study was aimed at determining the extent to which people recognize and understand safety related symbols, which are defined by the authors to be abstract graphics whose meanings must be learned. In part one of the study, 108 students from the University of Houston each viewed the sixteen symbols and pictorials from the Westinghouse Product Safety Label Handbook (1981) and were asked to describe the hazard for which a symbol would be used.

The results showed the Flammability and Corrosive pictograms to be most recognizable with nearly 100% and 94% correct responses, respectively. Pictorials for protective equipment resulted in 81% recognition for ear protection and 91% for eye protection. The Moving Gears pictogram was recognized by 85% of the subjects and the Rollers pictogram by only 73%. For the Fumes pictogram, only 50% of the subjects indicated a hazard including the words "gas" and "fumes." The Falling Objects, Biohazard, Laser, and Radiation pictograms were also poorly recognized.

In part two of the study, eighty subjects were shown three pictograms from the Westinghouse Product Safety Label Handbook (1981): Electric Shock (wire shocking hand), Poison (skull-and-crossbones), and Flammability (flames). Half of the subjects were given a checklist of nineteen precautionary behaviors and asked to select the behaviors they would observe if preparing to use a product displaying such a symbol. The other half of the subjects were asked to list four possible hazards associated with the symbol and four precautions they would take if they were preparing to use a product displaying that particular symbol. A particularly interesting result was the finding that the Poison symbol seemed to convey different information depending on the gender of the subject. That is, more males mentioned inhalation as a possible mode of injury than did females. It was also found that only a few subjects mentioned the possibility of flammable vapors as a mode of injury.

The authors conclude that a user's recognition of a pictogram's meaning does not necessarily imply that the user has knowledge that is specific enough to avoid the hazards which the symbol is meant to convey. We note that a next step to this type of study is to test subjects with the same symbols but in specific products, environments, or use contexts.

Key Words:
Familiarity with Product,
Perceived Risk,
Sources of Bias

278
Laux, L. and Brelsford, J.W., "Locus of Control, Risk Perception, and Precautionary Behavior," *Proceedings of INTERFACE '89 - The Sixth Symposium on Human Factors and Industrial Design in Consumer Products,* **Human Factors Society, Santa Monica, CA, 1989, 121-124.**

Locus of control (LOC) refers to the extent to which individuals believe that what happens to them is under their control. Individuals with external LOC, for example, believe that outcomes are controlled by chance or some other source or power. Individuals with internal LOC, on the other hand, believe that they are capable of controlling outcomes by their own actions. In this study, the authors examined the correlation between an individual's LOC for consumer product related accidents and the degree to which users understand product hazards, seek safety related information, and engage in safety oriented behaviors.

Twenty-two statements regarding the controllability of accidents during consumer product use were presented to 58 female and 46 male undergraduates. Using a Likert-type response scale and factor analysis techniques, the authors found that the willingness to engage in precautionary behaviors was substantially influenced by the user's beliefs about how much risk the use of a product involves, whether they can prevent accidents, and who has responsibility for safety. In general, the authors' product safety locus of control (PSLOC) scales indicated that: a) subjects believe precautionary behavior to be an effective means of reducing accidents; b) that government and manufacturers should be responsible for consumer safety; and c) that the risk associated with using consumer products is low. The authors feel that these research results indicate that, for increased warnings and instructions compliance, information should be made available to the consumer about the extent to which engaging in precautionary behaviors will be effective in achieving safe use of a consumer product.

Key Words:
Effectiveness of: warning
 related litigation,
Warning Process Models,
Warnings: evaluating
 effects on behavior

279
Lawrence, A.C., "Human Error as a Cause of Accidents in Gold Mining," *Journal of Safety Research,* **6:2, June 1974, 78-88.**

Lawrence presents an innovative and intuitively appealing human error accident model which combines several interesting aspects of Wiggleworth's, Surry's, and Goeller's models. Specifically, the model outlines a complex flowchart which includes sequential information-processing stages of warning information, the relation of these stages to human errors, and the relation of human errors to feasible combinations of accident, danger, and injury. If primary warnings are given, the warning related material is sequentially processed, and a failure at any point in this sequence results in an error. Given certain chance factors, this error may cause an accident; given other chance factors and the presence of danger, the accident may result in injury.

A questionnaire was developed from this model and several hundred accident reports were analyzed using that questionnaire. Nearly 800 human errors were isolated: 36% of the errors involved failure to perceive a warning, 4.2% involved failure to recognize a warning, 24.7% involved underestimation of a hazard, 17.5% involved failure to respond to a recognized warning, 13.7% involved ineffective response to a warning, and 3.9% involved an inappropriate secondary warning. The probability of a perceptual error was highest when the warning was a composite one rather than a single auditory or visual stimulus, when the participant was a supervisory-level staff member, and when underground tramming operations were involved.

280
Lehto, M.R. and Foley, J., "The Influence of Regulation, Training, and Product Information on Use of Helmets by ATV Operators: A Field Study," *Proceedings of INTERFACE 1989 - The Sixth Symposium on Human Factors and Industrial Design in Consumer Products,* **Human Factors Society, Santa Monica, CA, 1989, 107-113.**

Key Words:
ATV (All Terrain Vehicles),
Effectiveness of: educational/persuasive programs,
Existing/Past Behavior Patterns,
Labels,
Reading of: instructions,
Warnings: evaluating effects on behavior

Convincing consumers to follow safety precautions when using all terrain vehicles (ATVs) has posed problems similar to those of convincing people to use seat belts in automobiles or wear helmets on motorcycles. The provision of training programs and product information has been advocated as a means of attaining this goal. An alternative approach, less under the control of product designers, has been to mandate safe behavior through regulations and law. The research discussed in this paper compares the effectiveness of these approaches.

A field study of ATV operator behavior was conducted in three states over the summer of 1988. For a sample of 136 operators, the use of helmets and other personal protective equipment was observed. Also recorded in the context of each observation were: 1) the presence and enforcement of state regulations governing ATV use; 2) whether operator training courses had been taken; 3) the presence of warning labels and self-reported reading of owner's manuals; and 4) attitudes of operators. Enforced regulations were found to have a large effect on observed behavior. Claimed completion of a training program and reading of an ATV manual did appear to be related to a greater propensity to use a helmet, but may in fact reflect a tendency for subjects concerned with safety to seek out such information. The use of helmets when riding motorcycles and perceived comfort also appeared to be related to helmet use. No positive relation was found between the provision of warning labels and behavior.

281
Lehto, M.R and Miller, J.M., *Warnings Volume I: Fundamentals, Design, and Evaluation Methodologies*, **Fuller Technical Publications, Ann Arbor, 1986.**

This is the first volume in a series that focuses on warning labels and other product and situation-related characteristics that serve warning purposes. The development of the volume was inspired by the increased importance of warning-related issues to both human factors and product design engineering fields, and the limited degree to which these issues have been addressed within other disciplines.

The book contains four major sections. The first section consists of Chapter 1: Important Issues Related to Warnings; and Chapter 2: Definitions and Modeling Techniques. Together, the two chapters indicate the complexity of the warning issue and explore its relationship to human information processing. Important subtopics introduced in Chapter 1 include the shortcoming of "common sense" as a means of analysis of this issue, as well as the roles of the various factions and litigation. In Chapter 2, early emphasis is placed on defining important terminology and laying out a conceptual modeling framework. It is emphasized that much confusion can be traced to the failure to distinguish between the term "warning" and terms such as "educating," "persuading," or "informing." A review is given of communication theory, information processing psychology, and other basic aspects of modeling human performance. The objective of this chapter was to provide an organized description of the warning issue. In later chapters, this organized description was extended and applied to specific questions, such as warning effectiveness, design, and modeling.

The second section consists of Chapters 3 through 6, and evaluates the effectiveness of warnings. These chapters are of topical interest to many professionals, including lawyers, psychologists and engineers. Chapter 3 discusses the difficulties in evaluating effectiveness and provides a general approach for such evaluation. The developed approach and several simple examples illustrated the criticality of the weakest links in the warning process. The next three chapters consider issues related to effectiveness: Chapter 4 - the ability of warnings to attract attention, Chapter 5 - the comprehension of warnings, and Chapter 6 - the effects of warnings on memory, decisions, and actual behavior. In Chapter 4, it was clearly apparent that people are likely to filter out warning information in many sit-

Key Words:
(See Key Word Index and Refs. 283 - 284 Key Words)
Note:
Our *Warnings:Volume I* book, described in the adjacent annotation ,was developed from hundreds of the references listed in this present book, *Instructions and Warnings*.
Consequently, the list of key words which could be included in this column would encompass most of the other key words used throughout the book.
The adjacent annotation should be sufficiently detailed for the reader to assess the usefulness of this book as a reference. Beyond reading the accompanying annotation, we advise the reader to refer directly to the *Key Word Index* and *Topical Index* herein if references dealing with a specific topic are being researched.
Also, two articles which were derived from the adjacent book are listed as Refs. 283 and 284 which follow. The Key Words for these, therefore, provide a listing of a subset of the topics which appear within the Warnings book described in the adjacent column.

uations. Much attention was also given to determining possible determinants of filtering, such as risk perception, information overload, noise, conspicuity, and message tone. The Chapter 5 materials showed that problems are often found in the comprehension of both verbal and nonverbal symbols. Within the chapter, a distinction was drawn between semantic, syntactic, and contextual meaning. Problems in comprehension of both semantic and syntactic meaning were often found for both verbal and nonverbal symbols. It was noted, however, that existing studies have failed to emphasize the context within which symbols occur. The latter point implies that comprehension measures may be artificially low. The Chapter 6 review found few studies documenting the effects of warnings on memory, decisions, and responses. With regard to memory, recall levels were found to be quite low. Also noted were the influence of factors such as active and deep processing, memory reconstruction, and repression. With regard to decisions, consideration was given to the influences of knowledge, risk perception, education, and persuasion. A general conclusion was that people often make decisions that are inconsistent with their safety knowledge, and that the influence of education and persuasion programs was often low. With regard to actual behavioral effects, a large number of studies were found demonstrating the difficulty of modifying behavior in order to increase safety. It was concluded that dynamic warnings are the most likely to effectively influence behavior, but only when they provide feedback defining when unsafe conditions or behaviors are present.

The third section contains Chapters 7 through 10, and addresses several design issues, making it of interest to those professionals who apply, design, and recommend warnings. Chapter 7 provides an initial structure by classifying different types of warnings and applications. Many of the principles and much of the terminology of this chapter are based on material first introduced in Chapter 2. The developed classifications are described as being a useful means of documenting the type of warning and the scenario in which it appears. Chapter 8 introduces an approach for initially screening out inappropriate warning applications. The rationale for screening is that ineffective applications are not desirable. Several guidelines abstracted from the review of warning effectiveness given in Section 3 are used to develop a decision tree. Also described are means of performing the required cost benefit analysis associated with such decisions. Chapter 9 summarizes and critiques the design guidelines available in safety standards and human factors handbooks. Notably, it was concluded that much more research and development is needed before the guidelines become of real value. Chapter 10 provides a multistage description of a warning design process. Emphasized is the use of task analysis and criticality analysis, among other evaluation methodologies. This multistage process consists of: 1) specifying the general flow of information; 2) isolating the critical flows; 3) describing the critical flows in detail; and 4) evaluating the critical flows.

The fourth section, Chapters 11 and 12, addresses the potential of knowledge-based analysis during warning design and evaluation. Chapter 11 considers a knowledge-based way of modeling human performance. A production system model of elemental tasks is considered in relation to traditional safety techniques such as Failure Modes and Effects Analysis (FMEA), and Fault Tree Analysis (FTA). Chapter 12 takes a more fundamental approach; it presents several new methodologies for modeling tasks and products.

Key Words:
Application Guidelines,
Effectiveness of: warning related litigation,
Human Factors,
Laboratory/Generic Settings,
Reading Measures,
Warning Process Models

282
Lehto, M.R., "Ergonomic Considerations in the Evaluation, Design, and Application of Product Warnings," Seminar, University of Michigan, September 1984.

This seminar presented discussions of: the current emphasis on warnings in litigation, various definitions of "warning," current warning issues, research and design of warnings, and conceptual warning models. The author concluded that for many products the presence of a warning label is unlikely to result in a decreased probability of product related injuries. Lehto also concluded that: more research needs to be performed before the effect of specific warning-product-hazard combinations can be predicted a priori; existing research in the area of warnings suffers from several shortcomings; and, existing warning standards and approaches toward warnings are prone to many problems and misconceptions. The problems and misconceptions related to warnings were outlined.

Key Words:
References 283-284
Actual Behavior,
Adequacy of Warnings,
Advantages of Nonverbal Symbols,
Agreement with Symbol/Message,
Amount of Information,
Application Guidelines,
Behavior Factors,
Belief in Danger,
Children,
Comprehension of: warning labels,
Conflicting Objectives,
Credibility of Source

283
Lehto, M.R. and Miller, J.M., "The Effectiveness of Warning Labels," in *Personal Injury Review - 1988*, Denkensohn, B.D. and Fliss, A.A. (Eds.), Matthew Bender & Co., Inc., New York, 1988, 468-524.

The duty to warn has been heavily emphasized in litigation regarding product liability. However, clear, academically-based criteria that would guide the courts in evaluating the costs and benefits of particular warning labels have not been made available to the legal community. Warning-related legal decisions are frequently based upon intuitive rather than scientific grounds; hence, many decisions have long-term counterproductive implications to safety. This article addresses these difficulties by suggesting an initial set of guidelines which can be used by the courts and the legal community in judging the effectiveness of warning labels.

Key Words (cont.):
Design of: instructions,
Discrepancy Between
   Self-Reports,
Duty/Failure to Warn,
Effectiveness of:
   educational/persuasive
   programs, warning
   related litigation,
Evaluation Difficulties,
Existing/Past Behavior
   Patterns, Filtering,
Human Factors,
Incentives, Influences of
   Warning Labels,
Information Overload,
Informed Choice,
Location, Memory of:
   warning labels,
Message Tone,
Overapplication of
   Warnings,
Perceived Risk,
Posters,
Prior Knowledge,
Probability of
   Presentation,
Product Literature,
Reading of: instructions,
   warning labels,
Reading Measures,
Recall,
Review Papers,
Risk Compensation,
Risk Coping Style,
Risk Taking,
Signal Words,
Source,
Understanding/
   Perception Models,
Verbal vs. Nonverbal
   Symbol/Message,
Visual Noise,
Warning Process Models,
Warnings: evaluating
   effects on behavior,
Workload/Task

284
Lehto, M.R. and Miller, J.M., "The Effectiveness of Warning Labels," *Journal of Products Liability*, 11, 1988, 225-270.

This article is a revised and expanded version of the previous article under the same title. The authors note the proliferating attention to warnings effectiveness related issues in products liability and other litigation. The fact that there is a high cost involved with over-warning implies that consideration should be given to providing warnings in an efficient manner. The authors define warning effectiveness as the probability of attaining the goal of an adequate response given that the warning label is present. Efficiency, on the other hand, is described as the change in the probability of the safe response induced by the presence of the label. In other words, efficiency requires consideration of the prior incident rate of the desired response, as well as the behavior after the warning is presented.

The authors review a large body of literature pertaining to the effectiveness and efficiency of warning labels. The review is guided by a sequential model of the warning process which begins with exposure to the warning and ends with performance of the desired response. For any given step of the sequence, and collectively, the authors found that warning labels usually will not have a significant influence on human behavior unless carefully designed and tested with target users. On the other hand, there will be labels which, by chance, will be effective; such labels can be shown after the fact to be of good design.

Key Words:
State of the Art Defense, Strict Liability and Warnings

285
Leibman, J.H., "The Manufacturer's Responsibility to Warn Product Users of Unknowable Dangers," *American Business Law Journal*, **21, 1983-1984, 403-438.**

This article examines state of the art defenses in strict products liability cases. In Beshada v. Johns Manville Corp., the New Jersey Supreme Court completely rejected the state of the art defense, meaning that proof of what was technologically feasible at the time the product was sold would not be accepted as evidentiary proof which would be relevant. Not all other courts will follow the New Jersey precedent, it is suggested, but it demonstrates forcefully the importance of our commitment as a society to distributing risks and losses.

Key Words:
Color Coding, Print Size

286
Leonard, S.D. and Matthews, D., "How Does the Population Interpret Warnings Signals?" *Proceedings of the Human Factors Society - 30th Annual Meeting*, **Human Factors Society, Santa Monica, CA, 1986, 116-120.**

The authors conducted an experiment to determine how the population at large interprets warnings. In particular, they sought to determine whether different signal words produce different perceptions of risk.

Three hundred and sixty-eight undergraduate students viewed warning signs which varied according to the signal word (*caution*, *warning* or *danger*), signal word color (red or black), signal word size, and information pertaining to the consequences of disregarding the warning (consequence versus no consequence). Subjects were told where the signs might be located and were provided with scenarios in which the warning sign might have relevance. Respondents rated the perceived risk associated with each sign and the likelihood that they would obey the sign displayed in the scenarios provided.

The results show that there was no difference in perceived risk associated with the various signal words. Neither the size of the signal word nor the color significantly affected the perception of risk. The perception of risk seemed to be predicated on the information content of the sign. The presence of consequences on the warning sign did influence the rated perception of risk. The authors conclude that information about consequences, if different from prior perception, could raise the average perception of risk.

Annotations (201-300)

Key Words:
Basic Associations,
Consumer Labeling and Signage Systems,
Consumers,
Conveying Action,
Elemental Breakdowns,
Industrial,
Ingress/Egress,
Population Stereotypes,
Symbol Taxonomies

287
Lerner, N.D., "Experimental Evaluation of Exit Directional Indicators," *Proceedings of the Human Factors Society - 25th Annual Meeting*, Human Factors Society, Santa Monica, CA, 1981, 193-197.

The researcher initially notes that there is no standard population stereotype for the message "exit." Arrows are the closest approximation to a stereotype; an arrow by itself, however, is ambiguous. An experiment was designed and carried out in an attempt to select a type of arrow that would be appropriate for indicating exits. The results showed that one specific type of arrow (an inverted V-shaped head with a shaft composed of three smaller inverted V-shapes pointed in the same direction as the head) was more recognizable than the other variables tested.

Key Words:
Abstractness,
Accuracy,
Age,
Consumer Labeling and Signage Systems,
Consumers,
Degradation/Noise,
Design Consistency,
Development Programs,
Elderly,
Fire,
Fire Safety Signs,
Industrial,
Ingress/Egress,
Production Method,
Prohibition,
Public Information,
Symbol Generation,
Visual Noise

288
Lerner, N.D. and Collins, B.L., "The Assessment of Safety Symbol Understandability by Different Testing Methods," National Bureau of Standards, Washington, D.C., PB81-185647, August 1980.

An experiment evaluating the understandability of pictorial safety symbols for fire-safety alerting is reported. Thirty-three men and fifty-eight women, were paid to participate in the study. Subjects ranged in age from 18 to 72 and had no visual problems; though some wore corrective lenses.

In the first phase of the study, symbols were presented in the form of slides, booklets, or placards. The respondents indicated their interpretation of the meaning of each symbol by either writing down a brief definition or by choosing the correct answer from a set of four alternatives. All subjects rated their confidence in the correctness of their responses. Definitions were scored as correct, incorrect, or "no answer." Three different judges scored each answer and total consensus was achieved on 99.6% of the responses. In the second phase of the study the participants were asked to draw a symbol for each of fifteen different messages. The primary result was that the symbol presentation had no effect on understandability. Multiple choice procedures and definition writing tasks confirmed this conclusion. It should be noted that the understandability of the 25 symbols ranged from nearly zero to almost total comprehension. With regards to the drawings produced by the subjects, the authors conclude that the drawings were most likely to be different in image from symbols proposed by the International Standards Organization (ISO) for those particular symbols which are poorly understood. The authors conclude that

Key Words:
Active Processing,
Ingress/Egress

prior to standardizing a set of safety symbols, its understandability must be determined.

289
Lerner, N.D. and Collins, B.L., "Symbol Sign Understandability When Visibility Is Poor," *Proceedings of the Human Factors Society - 27th Annual Meeting*, **1983, Human Factors Society, Santa Monica, CA, 944-946.**

Subjects viewed eighteen exit symbols on slides which were degraded to simulate smoke damage. Certain symbols were more seriously affected by degradation than others. The results suggest that: filled figures are more recognizable than outline figures; the direction of figure, and background contrast (black on white or white on black) had little effect on recognizability; figures with circular surroundings were less reliably identified than those with rectangular or square surroundings; and both simplification of the interaction between graphic elements and background, and reduction in the number of symbol elements, appear to be beneficial. The abstract DOT "no entry" figure was frequently interpreted as an exit figure, as were many "no exit" signs and signs which showed a full human figure instead of a head or torso.

Key Words:
Behavior Factors,
Consumers,
Effectiveness of:
 educational/persuasive
 programs,
Message Tone

290
Leventhal, H. and Singer, R.P., "Affect Arousal and Positioning of Recommendations in Persuasive Communications," *Journal of Personality and Social Psychology*, **4:2, 1966, 137-146.**

Visitors to a state exposition were exposed to high, medium, and low fear communications related to dental hygiene. Visitors exposed to high fear communications expressed a greater intention to follow recommended dental practices than those exposed to low fear communications.

Key Words:
Air Traffic Control,
Aircraft,
Aircraft Setting,
Pilots,
Probability/Frequency of
 Presentation,
Workload/Task

291
Lewis, M.F., "Frequency of Anti-Collision Observing Responses by Solo Pilots as a Function of Traffic Density, ATC Traffic Warnings, and Competing Behavior," *Aerospace Medicine*, **44:9, September 1973, 1048-1050.**

Eighteen instrument-rated pilots completed 2-hour simulated solo missions during which the traffic frequency, Air Traffic Control (ATC) warnings, and ATC clearances were varied. The effects of target noticeability was not of interest in this particular study; therefore, the visibility of air traffic was held constant at 100%. In order to look for traffic, the pilot was required to make a simple, overt observing response which consisted of pressing a button on his control wheel. Observing response rate was affected by the frequency with which the pilot received the traffic warnings and by the amount of competing behavior the flying task imposed on the pilot's work load. The results imply that when the competing behavior was prepotent and the traffic density was low, the consequent decrease in traffic warnings yielded a diminution in vigilance.

292
Ley, P., "Memory for Medical Information," *British Journal of Social and Clinical Psychology,* **18:2, June 1979, 245-255.**

Key Words:
Active Processing,
Consumers,
Forgetting Rate,
Memory of:
  symbol/message,
Recall,
Redundancy

In his review of past research, Ley concludes that medical knowledge was consistently correlated with the ability to recall medical information. However, neither age nor intelligence showed any consistent significant relationship with recall. The studies on the correlation between medical knowledge and recall received additional support from the excellent performance of qualified nurses in recall of fictitious medical information. For samples of patients, the linear regression equation used to predict forgetting was: $y = 0.56x - 0.94$ (where y represented the number of statements forgotten by the patient and x was the number of statements made by the doctor). This regression equation was fit using scores obtained 10-80 minutes after consultation.

Diagnostic statements tended to be recalled best and statements regarding instructions and advice tended to be recalled worst (Spelman, 1965). The poorer recall of instructions and advice was confirmed by Ley et al. (1976b), but not by Ley et al. (1973). The differences in recall were apparently due to a primacy and/or an "importance" effect. Given that the patients were given more information than they could recall, they would best recall what they thought was most important. The use of shorter words and sentences, explicit categorization, repetition, and concrete-specific statements increased total recall. Prior research showed that the use of explicit categorization often led to increased recall of medical information. Ley et al. (1973b) found that no better recall occurred after two or three repetitions than after one. Other investigations showed that anxiety was related to recall in a curvilinear fashion.

We find this study applicable to instructions and warnings design in that medical information is certainly considered more important to subjects than many other types of hazards. One would expect, therefore, good guidelines for the design of instructions and warnings can be derived from this work.

Key Words:
Informed Choice

293
Liccardo, S.A., "Consumer's Right to Know: A New Horizon in Drug Product Liability," *Journal of Products Liability*, **1, 1978, 165-170.**

The article is primarily concerned with the interplay between warnings and the consumer's right to know. An example is given addressing the labeling of birth control pills as seen from a plaintiff attorney's point of view.

Key Words:
Frequency Estimates,
Sources of Bias

294
Lichtenstein, S., Slovic, P., Fischhoff, B., Layman, M. and Combs, B., "Judged Frequency of Lethal Events," *Journal of Experimental Psychology: Human Learning and Memory*, **4:6, November 1978, 551-578.**

The experiments reported here studied how people judge the frequency of death from various causes. Two groups of subjects participated. The first group consisted of fifty-one male and sixty female college students. The second group consisted of seventy-seven female members of the Eugene, Oregon Chapter of the League of Women Voters.

Two biases were identified: a tendency to overestimate small frequencies and underestimate larger ones; and, a tendency to exaggerate the frequency of some specific causes and to underestimate the frequency of others. Several possible reasons for these biases were identified, including: disproportionate exposure; memorability; or imaginability of various events. Even when they were specifically instructed to avoid these sources of bias, subjects were unable to correct for them. From these findings we would infer that simple instructions will not in themselves eliminate biases (and ultimately their unsafe behavior); other more pointed experiences or concrete types of information may be necessary.

Key Words:
Acceptability,
Buying Behavior,
Consumer Preferences,
Consumers,
Credibility of Source,
Familiarity with Product,
Prior Knowledge,
Risk Coping Style,
Sources of Bias

295
Locander, W.B. and Hermann, P.W., "The Effect of Self-Confidence and Anxiety on Information Seeking in Consumer Risk Reduction," *Journal of Marketing Research*, **16, May 1979, 268-274.**

This study examines the impact of anxiety and self-confidence on consumers' propensity to seek information sources as a means of reducing purchasing uncertainty. A sample of 365 respondents from a suburb of Houston, Texas completed a self-administered questionnaire pertaining to their projected information search patterns for five different products: after shave, paper towels, cologne, toaster, lawn mower and stereo. Six sources of information were evaluated: 1) what was called an impersonal advocate (such as advertisements); 2) what was labeled impersonal independent (such as a technical report); 3) what was labeled a personal advocate (which would correspond to a sales clerk or store manager); 4) what was labeled personal independent (which corresponded to items such as remembering what brand a friend or neighbor uses); 5) what was labeled as direct observation experience; and 6) what was labeled as pick a brand (which simply corresponded to selecting a brand without actually asking an outside information source.

It was found that the self-confidence of subjects associated with a particular product (i.e. specific self-confidence) had a significant impact on the information seeking behavior. Specific self-confidence refers to the subjects' confidence as rated on a seven point scale for the specific decision at hand. Therefore, it may be stated that those with high degrees of specific self-confidence were less likely to seek certain types of information. This trend did not hold, however, for all the different types of information for all the different products. Little effect could be attributed to the general trait variables of confidence and anxiety. The results also indicate that, as the total risk of a person's situation increases, the favored source of information is a person's observation and experience.

Key Words:
Hazard/Alert,
Poison

296
Loewenthal, A. and Riley, M.W., "The Effectiveness of Warning Labels," *Proceedings of the Human Factors Society - 24th Annual Meeting*, **Human Factors Society, Santa Monica, CA, 1980, 389-391.**

The authors conducted a stimulus identification experiment in which symbols and words were projected onto a screen; one half of the stimuli (symbols and words) were warnings, the other half were neutral. Six subjects viewed sixteen stimuli, which were each presented in one of four colors (red, amber, white, or green). The dependent measure of stimulus effectiveness was taken to be the time required by the subjects to identify the stimulus as a warning or non-warning. It was found that, in general, the color of the label did not significantly impact the response time. It was also found that the message associated with the stimulus had a significant effect on identification time. This paper offers no practical conclusions, and lacks the experimental rigor necessary to rely upon the results presented.

Key Words:
Belief in Danger,
Consumers,
Credibility of Source,
Effectiveness of:
　educational/persuasive
　programs,
Habituation,
Influences of Warning
　Labels,
Introducing New
　Systems,
Level of Detail,
Memory of:
　symbol/message,
Memory of: warning
　labels,
Message Tone,
Personal Presentations,
Recall,
Recognition,
Smokers,
Smoking,
Smoking Education Act,
Students

297
Loken, B. and Howard-Pitney, B., "Effectiveness of Cigarette Advertisements on Women: An Experimental Study," *Journal of Applied Psychology,* **73:3, 1988, 378-382.**

This study examined the influence of several factors on subjects' perceptions of cigarette advertisements. Two hundred fifteen college women viewed eight different cigarette advertisements for one and a half minutes each. The ads varied according to the presence of a model in the ad and according to the specificity of the warning label content. Half of the ads displayed a healthy, attractive woman smoker and the other half displayed a picture of a cigarette package with no person or scenic background. For the warning content factor, half of the subjects viewed ads which displayed the general message: "Warning: The Surgeon General has determined that cigarette smoking is dangerous to your health," while the other half viewed ads with messages that described more specific negative consequences of smoking.

Other factors considered in the study were the subject's smoking status and whether or not the subject was pretested on their beliefs about the hazards of smoking. After viewing each ad, subjects rated them according to their persuasiveness, attractiveness, and credibility. After viewing all eight of the ads the subjects were asked to recall and then recognize any of the warning messages they had seen in the ads. Finally each subject was asked to complete a smoking beliefs posttest which was identical to the pretest administered to half of the subjects.

The results showed that ads displaying attractive models were found to be significantly more attractive and persuasive but less credible than the non-model ads. Furthermore, the ads with specific warning messages were rated as less attractive and less persuasive than ads with the general warning statement. It was also found that smokers, more so than nonsmokers, rated the specific warnings ads lower on attractiveness and credibility than the general warning ads. In terms of the smoking beliefs pretest variable, it was found that those subjects not pretested rated ads as more attractive and persuasive than those who were pretested. Additional results indicated that the presence of a model did not significantly influence recall or recognition of the warning messages. However, the subjects who had been pretested recognized more warnings than those not pretested. It was also found that nonsmokers were no more likely to recognize warning information than smokers, despite the commonly held selective exposure hypothesis. With regards to beliefs pertaining to the hazards of smoking, this study found that smokers were less inclined to believe that smoking was harmful. In addition, smokers tended to be more resistant than nonsmokers to changes in belief between the pretest and posttest.

In conclusion, the authors note that, while the specificity of the warning message had a significant effect on the evaluation of the ads, the appeal of attractive models had a substantially greater countering effect.

Key Words:
Perceptual Skills,
Personality Factors,
Reaction Time,
Traffic Settings,
Verbal vs. Nonverbal Symbol/Message,
Visual Noise

298
Loo, R., "Individual Differences and the Perception of Traffic Signs," *Human Factors,* **20:1, 1978, 65-74.**

The researchers note that many traffic accidents involve acts such as driving the wrong way on one-way streets and failing to stop or yield right-of-way. Consequently, they were interested in evaluating ways by which the perceptual ability of subjects might be estimated.

In their reported experiment, scores on the Embedded Figures Test were used to classify 28 subjects into four quartiles. The subjects also completed a perceptual traffic sign task, the Eysenck Personality Inventory, and a driving experience questionnaire. Field independent subjects had shorter reaction times to embedded traffic signs ($r = -.54$) and had fewer reported traffic accidents ($r = -.42$) than did field dependent subjects. It was also found that extraverts had longer reaction times to embedded traffic signs ($r = .35$), more reported accidents ($r = .42$), and more traffic convictions ($r = .39$) than introverts. Neuroticism was not found to be correlated with reported accidents. It was also found that reaction times were higher for symbolic than verbal signs, and that this discrepancy became greater when the signs were embedded.

Key Words:
Aircraft,
Aircraft Setting,
False Alarms

299
Loomis, J.P. and Porter, R.F., "The Performance of Warning Systems in Avoiding Controlled-Flight-Into-Terrain (CFIT) Accidents," *Aviation, Space, and Environmental Medicine,* **53:11, November 1982, 1085-1090.**

Accidents in which airliners flew into the ground during controlled flights were a leading cause of accidents prior to 1975. In response to this problem, Ground Proximity Warning Systems (GPWS) were mandated in 1975. According to paragraph 121.360 of the Federal Aviation Regulations, GPWS were to provide for the following four warning modes: 1) excessive sink rate close to terrain; 2) excessive closure rate close to terrain; 3) negative climb after takeoff; and 4) descending into terrain with gear or flaps up.

After GPWS were mandated, questions were raised regarding both the need for and the effectiveness of such systems, based on the argument that the systems may be effective because they couldn't be ignored and turned off. To measure the impact of GPWS on CFIT accidents, National Transportation Safety Board accident data for 1971-1980 were studied by the authors. This entailed a comparison of accident rates prior to and after GPWS were mandated.

During the post-GPWS period of 1976-1980, significantly fewer accidents occurred than during the pre-GPWS period of 1971-1975. Since aviation activity had not decreased in the second period, the authors concluded that the installed GPWS and Minimum Safe Altitude Warning (MSAW) systems were effective. Of the two accidents that occurred in the second period, one was due to an inoperative cockpit voice recorder that did not determine the GPWS alert and the other was due to the fact that the GPWS alert was ignored and the flight engineer later shut off the system without the pilot's knowledge. One example of how a GPWS can save a flight occurred in February, 1977, at Hill Air Force Base. The 11,000 ft. altitude that was assigned was considered normal. However, due to a deep low pressure trough, the aircraft was probably about 1,400 ft. lower than its altimeter read.

The authors also noted that false or nuisance alarms were of concern to pilots because of the following potential hazards: encountering a midair collision while performing a mandatory pull-up; losing control of the aircraft while distracted by an alarm; ignoring a valid alarm because of system credibility problems; and ignoring a valid alarm due to a misunderstanding of what triggered it. A pull-up is a mandatory required response to a GPWS alarm and, since it is a risky maneuver, pilots wondered if the cure wasn't worse than the disease. The authors caution that false alarms have hurt the credibility of the system and may lead to ignoring valid alarms. However, no evidence of nuisance or false alarms causing accidents is presented.

We point out two aspects not directly addressed by its authors. First, a significant factor in complying with an instruction or warning is the believability of the presented information. Higher reliability apparently leads to higher believability. Second, the costs of complying with an instruction or warning in contrast to the benefits (given a false versus non-false alarm) may be more consciously considered than some authors have presumed.

Key Words:
Swimming Pool

**300
Loring, B.A. and Wiklund, M.E., "Improving Swimming Pool Warning Signs,"** *Proceedings of the Human Factors Society - 32nd Annual Meeting*, **Human Factors Society, Santa Monica, CA, 1988, 910-914.**

The authors report on a study sponsored by the Consumer Product Safety Commission (CPSC) in conjunction with the National Swimming Pool and Spa Association. The study was directed toward evaluating existing swimming pool warning signs. Twenty-two existing signs were evaluated. Following the evaluation, a new sign was developed and recommended for adoption.

ANNOTATIONS 301-400

Key Words:
Frequency Estimates,
Severity Estimates,
Sources of Bias

301
Lowrance, W.W., "The Nature of Risk," in *Societal Risk Assessment,* **Schwing, R.C. and Albers, W.A. (Eds.), Plenum Press, New York, 1980, 5-17.**

In this paper risk is defined as a compound measure of the probability and magnitude of adverse effects. Although both of these components of risk are well defined, the author concludes that all estimates of risk contain elements of subjectivity. He also reports that risk estimates become especially difficult to formulate and interpret when the events of interest are infrequent or unusual.

The author also presents a classification of hazards with six categories: 1) infectious and degenerative diseases; 2) natural catastrophes; 3) failure of large technological systems; 4) discrete, small-scale accidents; 5) low-level, delayed-effect hazards; and 6) socio-political disruptions. Choices between risky alternatives involving such hazards becomes difficult because of the limitations which are inherent in quantitative risk management. In particular, social value appraisal is difficult as is the assignment of risks and responsibilities to the influenced parties.

Key Words:
Chemicals,
Consensual Labeling and
  Signage Systems,
Design of:
  educational/persuasive
  programs,
Design of: labeling and
  safety signage systems,
Duty/Failure to Warn,
Formal Teaching/
  Counseling/Education,
Hazard Communication
  Rule,
Hazardous Materials,
Industrial,
Labels,
Loss Prevention
  Programs,
OSHA,
Workers

302
Lowry, G.G. and Lowry, R.C., *Handbook of Hazard Communication and OSHA Requirements,* **Lewis Publishers, Inc., Chelsea, MI, 1985.**

The objective of this book is to help companies comply with the new OSHA Hazard Communication Standard. It accomplishes this by describing the various components of the hazard communication process and by outlining the responsibilities of the manufacturer, distributor, and consumer of hazardous industrial chemicals.

Topics covered in the book include: 1) the legal responsibilities and ramifications of the standard; 2) the process of hazard identification; 3) the characterization of physical and health hazards; 4) the design of labels and material safety data sheets; 5) employee training; and 6) the development of a written hazard communication program. Discussion of these topics is supplemented with the entire text of the Hazard Communication Standard, example Material Safety Data Sheets, and a listing of more detailed information sources on topics such as label design and the identification of physical hazards.

Key Words:
Design of: labeling and safety signage systems

303
Lozano, R.D., "The Visibility, Colour and Measuring Requirements of Road Signs," *Lighting Research & Technology*, **12:4, 1980, 206-212.**

The "correct" design of road signs is reported on in this study. The paper deals mainly with the specifications of the sign's physical attributes that best convey the message to the driver.

Key Words:
Recall,
Recognition,
Understanding/
 Perception Models,
User Modeling

304
Lynch, J.G. and Srull, T.K., "Memory and Attentional Factors in Consumer Choice: Concepts and Research Methods," *Journal of Consumer Research*, **9, June 1982, 18-37.**

The authors describe methods developed within the field of cognitive psychology which can be used to describe memory and attentional processes that occur below the level of consciousness. Topics addressed include memory based versus stimulus based judgments, methods for studying retrieval processes (including a comparison of recall and recognition), applications of the Sternberg paradigm and the use of verbal protocols. The authors also address inference and the role of attentional processes and capacity in decision making. They conclude that these approaches based on cognitive psychology can, potentially, play an important role in consumer research.

Key Words:
Legibility

305
Macdonald-Ross, M. and Waller, R., "Criticism, Alternatives and Tests: A Conceptual Framework for Improving Typography," *Programmed Learning and Educational Technology*, **12:2, March 1975, 75-83.**

The authors note a tendency for typographers to go about their work without consulting academic research on the practice of typography. Part of the reason for this tendency, the authors suggest, may be that much of the classical research in typography has been directed toward experiments which have little relevance to day to day problems. The academic research has also placed little emphasis on developing methods for applying such results.

Furthermore, the authors claim that previous research has not been updated to reflect new developments in typography and is often flawed by the use of highly motivated subjects under conditions that have little relevance to those of the real world. The authors do note a consensus between researchers and typographers toward a more practical orientation in research. Such an orientation is given by a three-part cyclical model, which consists of criticism, generation of alternatives, and tests. Ideally,

Key Words:
Children,
Consumers,
Effectiveness of:
  educational/persuasive
  programs,
Formal Teaching/
  Counseling/Education,
Parents,
Radio/TV

the proposed model allows a practitioner or researcher to begin with a practical problem and end with a justifiable decision.

306
MacKay, A.M. and Rothman, K.J., "The Incidence and Severity of Burn Injuries Following Project Burn Prevention," *American Journal of Public Health*, **72:3, March 1982, 248-252.**

From October of 1977 through May of 1978, in an effort to reduce the incidence and severity of burn injuries, Project Burn Prevention was implemented in the Greater Boston area. The program included three elements: a media campaign; a school-initiated intervention; and a community-initiated intervention. For four years before the installation of the program, for the eight months of the program, and for the twelve months following the program, estimates of burn incidence and severity were recorded for hospital patients. The measures were based on incidents and injuries due to scald, flame, electrical or contact burns, or smoke inhalation.

The analysis of burn incidence during and after the school-initiated intervention showed that the intervention did not reduce the incidence or the severity of burn injuries. A moderate, temporary decline in the rate of burn injuries may have resulted from the community intervention. Random variation appears to be the most feasible explanation for the increase in burn incidence observed for the media campaign. We infer from this that reaching the public and causing behavior changes will only occur slowly, even through intense campaigning. In this case, eight months was not apparently long enough to effect such change.

Key Words:
Abstractness,
Advantages of Nonverbal
  Symbols,
Consumer Setting,
Consumers,
Design of: labeling and
  safety signage systems,
Glance Legibility,
Legibility Distance,
Public Information,
Semantic Differential,
Subjective Ratings

307
Mackett-Stout, J. and Dewar, R.E., "Evaluation of Symbolic Public Information Signs," *Human Factors*, **23:2, 1981, 139-151.**

The authors note a trend in North America toward replacing verbal messages with symbolic signs, while at the same time there is a lack of research directed toward development and evaluation of symbolic signs. Earlier studies which indicate that reaction time is an index of traffic sign perception and that semantic differential ratings are valid measures of symbol comprehension are cited. The authors report an experiment in which four different symbols for each of eight symbol referents were evaluated using the criteria of glance legibility, legibility distance, comprehension, and preference.

Key Words:
ATV (All Terrain
  Vehicles),
Acceptability, Agencies,
Behavior Factors,
Brochures/Flyers,
Buying Behavior,
CPSA, Cleansers,
Comprehension of:
  warning labels,
Consumer Labeling and
  Signage Systems,
Consumers,
Effectiveness of:
  educational/persuasive
  programs,
FDA,
Familiarity with Product,
Habituation, Influences
  of Warning Labels,
Information Overload,
Introducing New
  Systems,
Labels, Level of Detail,
Medical Patients,
Memory of:
  symbol/message,
Message Tone,
Patient Package Inserts
  (PPI), Perceived Risk,
Psychosocial Influences,
Radio/TV, Reading of:
  warning labels,
Review Papers,
Severity Estimates,
Signal Words, Smoking,
Smoking Education Act,
Sources of Bias,
Warnings: evaluating
  effects on behavior

Preference was significantly correlated with comprehension (r=.76) and legibility distance (r=.53); comprehension was significantly correlated with legibility distance (r=.40); and glance legibility was not significantly correlated with any measures. An index comprised of z-scores on each measure was proposed as a measure of symbol utility. The general conclusions drawn from this study by its authors are: 1) abstract symbols are more difficult to comprehend than pictographs; 2) multiple measures are useful in evaluating messages; and 3) the relative importance of different measures is problem specific.

308
Macro Systems, Inc., *Legislative Background Paper on the Issue of Alcohol Warning Labels*; Prepared for Office of Policy Analysis, National Institute of Alcohol Abuse and Alcoholism, January 1987.

This review consists of three major sections. The section first summarizes principal findings of the research on product labeling and its effects. Included here are several summaries studies specifically oriented toward evaluating tobacco, food, drug, consumer product, and chemical labeling. Also provided is a review of general studies of consumer information processing and risk perception. The second major section of this review discusses the research literature on labeling and its effects. For each of the four categories referred to earlier, existing labeling studies are compared in terms of their impact on reported or observed changes in awareness, knowledge, attitudes and behavior of consumers. These findings are summarized in a useful table. Specific implications pertaining to alcohol warnings labels are discussed. Serious concerns are raised regarding the proposed alcohol warning labels in the current House and Senate bills.

The last section of the review summarizes position statements of organizations regarding alcohol warning labels. Organizations supporting warning labels on alcoholic beverages include: the American Academy of Pediatrics, the American Medical Association, the American Medical Society on Alcoholism and Other Drug Dependencies, Inc., the American Council on Alcohol Problems, American Public Health Association, Center for Science in the Public Interest, March of Dimes Birth Defects Foundation, Medical and Public Health School Deans, Mothers Against Drunk Driving, National Association of Alcohol and Drug Abuse Directors, Inc., National Council on Alcoholism, National Parinatal Association, Parent Teachers Association, and Remove Intoxicated Drivers. Organizations against the use of warning labels on alcoholic beverages include: the Health Education Foundation, Inc. and the American Council on Alcoholism, Inc.

309

Key Words:
Duty/Failure to Warn

Madden, M.S., "The Duty to Warn in Products Liability: Contours and Criticism," *West Virginia Law Review*, 89:2, Winter 1987, 221-333.

This article contains an extensive detailed discussion of the duty to warn in products liability law. The author concludes that product sellers must clearly state to product users and consumers germane product safety related information which is known to such sellers but which such sellers have no reason to believe is known to those who will encounter the product. The duty to warn attaches, therefore, "whenever a reasonable man would want to be informed of the risk in order to decide whether to expose himself to it."

310

Key Words:
Insurance, Negligence and Warnings

Madden, M.S., "The 'Products' and 'Completed Operations' Exclusions and the Allegation of Failure to Warn," *Journal of Products Liability*, 7:3, 1984, 205-13.

Comprehensive general liability insurance policies for manufacturers usually cover both 1) the "product hazards" incurred after the product is completed and moved away from the premises of the manufacturer, and 2) the "completed operations hazards" to protect the person who performs a service on the premises of another after such work is completed. The authors discuss the problem presented when the language used in such policies does not cover being negligent because of failing to warn about the dangers of the product.

311

Key Words:
Industrial

Mader, D.A., "Impact...With Pictographs," *National Safety News*, 128:1, July 1983, 62-63.

This article provides a general and easily understood discussion of words, pictures, symbols, and pictographs, along with definitions.

312

Key Words:
Amount of Information, Information Overload

Malhotra, N.K., "Information Load and Consumer Decision Making," *Journal of Consumer Research*, 8, March 1982, 419-430.

The author cites past research showing that information overload can result in poor consumer decisions. To study such effects, the author varied the number of alternative brands a consumer could choose and the number of attributes upon which brands could be evaluated. The effects of this manipulation were tested during personal interviews of three hundred male and female heads of households in a major metropolitan area. Both the number of attributes and the number of alternatives were varied from 5 to 25 in steps of 5.

It was found that the quality of decisions made by the subjects deteriorated when they were provided with 10 or more alternative brands in the choice set or when information was presented on 15 or more attributes. These results were held to be consistent with other findings which have shown that the quality of decision making increases up to a point where the amount of information is optimal. Information provided beyond this point results in degraded decision making.

Key Words:
Duty/Failure to Warn,
Instructions in Litigation

313
Manley, M., "Product Liability: You're More Exposed Than You Think," *Harvard Business Review*, 5, September/October 1987, 28-35.

The author provides a general summary of the increased exposure of companies to products liability lawsuits. Several examples of litigation are provided and attention is given to current issues such as the legal need to provide adequate product warnings, labels, and instruction manuals.

Key Words:
Consumer Surveys,
Drivers,
Illustrations,
Pedestrians,
Symbol Generation,
Traffic

314
Manstead, A.S.R. and Lee, J.S., "The Effectiveness of Two Types of Witness Appeal Sign," *Ergonomics*, 22:10, 1979, 1125-1140.

This paper reports a study that was designed to evaluate the effectiveness of two kinds of signs intended to solicit cooperation from witnesses of serious traffic accidents. The old sign presented verbal information on a single sign. The new sign presented a combination of verbal and pictorial information in a series of three signs. Roadside interviews conducted after drivers and pedestrians passed one of the two sign variants provided data on the noticing, description, and interpretation of the signs.

Results showed that the sequence of three component signs was more effective than the single sign in communicating the message to drivers, probably because it was much more likely to be noticed. For pedestrians, the old sign was more effective. Differences due to sex, age, and familiarity with the test site were also found. Finally, the paper presents recommendations for the design of future witness appeal signs.

315
Manta, J.G., "Proximate Causation in Failure to Warn Cases: The Plaintiff's Achilles Heel," *For the Defense,* **26, October 1984, 10-14.**

Key Words:
Proximate Cause

The author contends that many plaintiff and defense attorneys overlook the issue of proximate causation in failure to warn cases. He explains that in order to win, the plaintiff must prove that the injury would have been prevented if an adequate warning had been present. If the plaintiff would have failed to read or heed the warning, then the absence or inadequacy of a warning was not the proximate cause of his injuries. Also, a failure to warn allegation will fail if the plaintiff already knew of the danger about which the defendant failed to warn.

We would add that these are the precise issues that must be addressed by the engineering experts. Often, studies may be necessary in order for an expert to develop a foundation for his opinions as to whether lack of a warning or instruction was proximate to the accident.

316
Marcel, T. and Barnard, P., "Paragraphs of Pictographs: The Use of Non-verbal Instructions for Equipment," in *Processing of Visible Language,* **1, Kolers, P.A., Wrolstad, M.E. and Bouma, H. (Eds.), Plenum Press, New York, 1979, 501-518.**

Key Words:
Conveying Action,
Conveying Conditions,
Conveying Procedures,
Describing Objects,
Description/Modeling,
Elemental Breakdowns,
Elemental Synthesis,
Illustrations,
Ordering of Conditions/
 Actions,
Process Charts/
 Sequences,
Symbol Taxonomies,
Understanding/
 Perception Models

The authors note that the use of discrete graphic symbols has been the topic of some human factors research. Their function, however, has been limited to denotational reference or single unconditional commands. Sequences of pictures present the problem of logical and semantic links between the individual pictures. The objectives of the research reported here were to find parallels of linguistic variables among and between individual frames of a picture sequence, and to investigate the effects of graphic symbols. The intention was to make available an approach to rules for picture sequences which are much like those of sentence and text grammar. A special concern for pictorial rendering of "if..., then..." relationships between actions and states was reflected. In the first study, only the desired sequences of actions and outcomes were depicted. Eight pictographic sequences were designed; they differed in representation of the equipment and in organization of the sequence of frames.

Concerning the effects of type of instruction on success rate, the authors emphasize these two points: 1) representing the entire equipment fascia in each frame resulted in greater success than showing only the currently relevant parts; and 2) action-state ordering of segments was not consistently better than state-action ordering.

The results support the suggestion that people tend to parse pictorial instructions as cause and effect. The results also indicated that it is invalid to assess the intelligibility of instructions out of the appropriate context since the comprehension of surface messages is a context-dependent, inferential process. The authors note that people often prefer to interact with equipment in a problem-solving manner, especially when using the equipment for the first time, and to interpret instructions in light of their interactions. In approaching instruction design, it is recommended that the designer consider whether there is a set of questions that users tend to have for particular purposes rather than for specific pieces of equipment. Also, the authors observe that the design of pictorial instructions must reflect user knowledge of the task; and, when users have no existing knowledge of the task, it must be provided for them.

Key Words:
Age,
Children,
Hazard/Alert,
Sources of Bias

317
Martin, G.L. and Heimstra, N.W., "The Perception of Hazard by Children," *Journal of Safety Research*, 5:4, December 1973, 238-246.

Male and female subjects in the first, third, and fifth grades evaluated a hazard presented in ten scenes, each of which showed a male or female model performing some potentially dangerous task. Expert ratings for each scene were also developed. Significant differences associated with the sex, age, geographical location, and socioeconomic status of the subjects were found. Subjects tended to provide higher hazard estimates than those given by the experts, and the sex of the model and nature of the hazard scene also affected ratings.

Key Words:
Design of: labeling and safety signage systems,
Understanding/ Perception Models

318
Mashour, M., "On Designing Signals and Their Meanings," *Ergonomics*, 20:6, 1977, 659-664.

Signaling systems are defined as a set of signals $S=(S_1, S_2,...S_i)$ and a corresponding set of meanings or information items $I=(I_1, I_2,...I_i)$. Three types of human transmission errors (errors in detection, perception, and recall) are considered. This framework is used to evaluate the presentation of speed-related information to train operators via signs. Conclusions regarding the amount and coding of information are made and tested.

Key Words:
Behavior Factors,
Motor Vehicle,
Traffic

319
May, K.A. and Wooller, J., "A Review of Non-Regulatory Signs in Relation to Road Safety," *Australian Government Printing Office, Canberra, Australia,* **September 1973, 1-33.**

This paper reviews Australian and international literature covering the effect of road signs and markings on safety. Positive conclusions were drawn regarding: 1) advisory speed signs on curves on rural roads; 2) painted edge lines on rural roads; 3) painted lines across minor roads at junctions with major roads; 4) painted medians and channelization on urban roads; 5) post-mounted, reflectorized delineators on rural roads; and 6) flashing warning devices at rural intersections.

These results clearly support the effectiveness of providing safety information and/or warnings in an appropriate context.

Key Words:
Chemicals,
Duty/Failure to Warn,
Learned Intermediary Rule,
Strict Liability and Warnings

320
Maynard, R.C., "The Duty to Warn: Toxic Tort Litigation," *Cleveland State Law Review,* **33, 1984-85, 69-91.**

This article discusses the responsible intermediary doctrine in hazardous chemical substance cases, including such issues as the manner of shipment, the manufacturer's ability to reach the ultimate user, types of ultimate users and the reliability of the intermediary. The author concludes that the application of strict liability to chemical manufacturers is an unreasonable burden and is not required by policy considerations.

Key Words:
Agencies,
Amount of Information,
Brochures/Flyers,
Consumers,
Effectiveness of: educational/persuasive programs,
Level of Detail,
Patient Package Inserts (PPI),
Reading of: instructions

321
Mazis, M., Morris, L.A. and Gordon, E., "Patient Attitudes About Two Forms of Printed Oral Contraceptive Information," *Medical Care,* **16:12, December 1978, 1045-1054.**

A nationwide survey was conducted of 1720 current users of oral contraceptives. The women were asked their preferences regarding two forms of oral contraceptive information: a short insert commonly included with dispensed drugs and a longer brochure provided by the physician upon patient request.

Longer and more detailed information, especially concerning drug dangers and directions for use, were strongly preferred. This effect was more pronounced for younger and more educated women. This latter segment of the population was also more likely to indicate they had received the oral contraceptive brochure prior to the date of the survey. The authors note that these findings have had an impact on public policy decision making. Notably, the FDA proposed changes in the style and method of delivery of oral contraceptive information in 1976.

Specifically it was proposed that both the insert and the brochure be lengthened to include more details on risks and effectiveness of the pill.

322
McCarthy, J.V. and Hoffmann, E.R., "The Difficulty that Traffic Signs Present to Poor Readers," Department of Transport, Commonwealth of Australia, December 1977, 1-201.

Key Words:
Readability Measures,
Simple Comprehension of: verbal symbols,
Traffic,
User Group

This paper presents a review of the literature describing the difficulties poor readers have in comprehending traffic signs. Several experiments are discussed that address the performance of poor readers in tasks involving legibility, interpretability and short-term retention of traffic signs by these same readers. The results suggest that replacement of some verbal signs by symbolic signs is appropriate in certain locations.

Their research also suggests that, in applicable situations, signs should display either permissive information or a combination of permissive and prohibitive information as opposed to only prohibitive information.

323
McCarthy, R.L, Robinson, J.N., Finnegan, J.P. and Taylor, R.K., "Warnings on Consumer Products: Objective Criteria for Their Use," *Proceedings of the Human Factors Society - 26th Annual Meeting*, Human Factors Society, Santa Monica, CA, 1982, 98-102.

Key Words:
Application Guidelines,
Overapplication of warnings,
Patent Danger

The authors have provided a well thought out and unbiased set of objective warning criteria. They first state that the use of warning labels to reduce risk is based on two assumptions: 1) human behavior is important in controlling the frequency and severity of consumer product related accidents; and 2) such behavior can be modified by the presence of warning labels to reduce the frequency and severity of accidents.

The researchers accept the first point, but dispute the second since it requires that: 1) users notice and read warning labels; 2) users understand warning labels; 3) information in warning labels be useful in preventing accidents or mitigating their severity; and 4) users act appropriately on the information contained in warning labels. The proposal is made that warning labels be considered for common products when the product contributes at least 1% of the total risk associated with home activities and when the risk from the particular accident mode considered for a warning contributes at least 10% of the total risk associated with the product.

The following reasons for limiting the use of warnings are cited: 1) warning against low level risks may distract attention from higher risks; 2) warning against low level risks will lead to a very large number of warnings in the home (17 different injury modes associated with glass soft drink bottles are cited); and 3) warnings for rare or non-obvious events are unlikely to be heeded. A set of contra-indications for warning applications are given: 1) the danger is open and obvious; 2) the danger would result from unreasonable misuse; 3) the danger cannot reasonably be foreseen by the manufacturer; 4) no precautions can be given which will enable the user to anticipate or avoid danger; and 5) the use of warnings is impractical.

Key Words:
Actual Behavior,
Behavior Factors,
Effectiveness of: educational/persuasive programs,
Effectiveness of: warning related litigation,
Existing/Past Behavior Patterns,
Overapplication of warnings,
Reading Measures,
Reading of: instructions,
Warnings: evaluating effects on behavior

324
McCarthy, R.L., Finnegan, J.P., Krumm-Scott, S. and McCarthy, G.E., "Product Information Presentation, User Behavior, and Safety," *Proceedings of the Human Factors Society - 28th Annual Meeting*, **Human Factors Society, Santa Monica, CA, 1984, 81-85.**

The authors review almost four hundred papers published in the area of product warning effectiveness and design. Of this literature, nearly 25% of the articles were of a qualitative editorial nature, providing no hard evidence of whether or not warnings are effective. A little over 10% of the papers evaluated the recognition or recall of warning messages forming the largest body of quantitative literature. Much smaller bodies of literature addressed labeling standards, legal requirements, or the effects of warnings on behavior. The researchers conclude the scientific evidence shows that warnings have no measurable impact on user behavior and safety.

Key Words:
Auditory,
Auditory Coding,
Auditory Noise,
Auditory Signal Strength,
Detection Intensity Level,
Emergency Vehicles,
Symbol Generation,
Traffic,
Traffic Settings

325
McClelland, I.L., "Audible Warning Signals for Police Vehicles," *Applied Ergonomics*, **11:3, September 1980, 165-170.**

Forty-two subjects were asked to detect emergency vehicle type signals of increasing intensity against a background of in-car noise, while subjects were simultaneously conducting a tracking task. The signals chosen by the Police Scientific Development branch were alternatives to the current signal. The signals were evaluated in the laboratory and then compared with the conventional emergency signals with respect to their ability to "get attention." The study found that a significant improvement over the conventional signal was achieved. The author recommends that any changes in audible warning signals be applied to appropriate vehicles.

Key Words:
Approaching Train,
Auditory,
Auditory Coding,
Railroad Settings,
Reaction Time,
Symbol Generation

326
McClelland, I.L., Simpson, C.T. and Starbuck, A., "An Audible Train Warning for Track Maintenance Personnel," *Applied Ergonomics*, 14:1, March 1983, 2-10.

This study investigated modifications of the audible signal provided by a portable device, used to warn British Rail track maintenance staff of approaching trains. The device was designed to emit a continuous tone when a train approached. If no trains were detected, the device emitted a series of "bleeps," signaling that it was safe to work. If no signal was emitted, maintenance persons could continue to work without the advantage of protection.

An experiment compared response times to the sudden disappearance of the bleeping signal for four different intervals between bleeps. A field study was also conducted to establish how operational conditions affected response times for the interval with the shortest response time in the laboratory. The authors recommended that the interval should be shortened from seven seconds, as specified at the time of the study, to two seconds, to facilitate quicker responses to the absence or cessation of the bleeping signal.

Key Words:
Design of: instructions,
Design of: labeling and safety signage systems

327
McFee, J.K., "Chapter 8: Visual Communication," in *Educational Media: Theory into Practice*, **Wiman, R.V. and Meierhenry, W.C. (Eds.), Charles E. Merrill Publishing Company, Columbus, 1969, 195-216.**

McFee notes that overly complex visual stimuli may lead to confusion on the part of some observers. It is also noted that viewers selectively extract information that is familiar, or valued, from messages or the environment in general.

To provide the opportunity for learning, McFee suggests that the ordering and varying of the information is critical and that the sender, the message, and the viewer are factors that must be understood by the designer. Furthermore, the author states that specific variables like culture, literacy, and individual response must be considered as they can influence the effectiveness of visual communications. To direct the observer's attention and to get a message across, the elements of information handling (similarity, proximity, closure and good form, and figure-ground relationships) are recommended. McFee concludes that a design that matches the message and the audience will be better comprehended than one that does not.

Key Words:
Loss Prevention
  Programs,
Warranties/Disclaimers

328
McGill, J., "Warranties: What They Are and How They Can Be Used in Risk Control," *Journal of Products Liability*, 2, 1978, 105-115.

The Uniform Commercial Code is discussed from a defense attorney's perspective. The following aspects of the code are covered: 1) warranty of title and infringement; 2) express warranties; 3) implied warranty of fitness for use; 4) implied warranty of merchantability; and 5) disclaimers. The Magnuson-Moss Act is covered briefly.

Key Words:
Consumer Labeling and
  Signage Systems,
Consumer Preferences,
Consumer Surveys,
Hazard/Alert,
Level of Detail,
Location,
Symbol Generation,
Symbol Usage

329
McGuinness, J., "Human Factors in Consumer Product Safety," *Proceedings of the Human Factors Society - 21st Annual Meeting*, Human Factors Society, Santa Monica, CA, 1977, 292-294.

Six hundred and twenty-one consumers were randomly surveyed in a study of consumer preferences conducted in the early stages of the design of a lawnmower safety warning label regarding the danger of contacting the moving blade while reaching beneath the mower. Over 84% of those surveyed believed that the presence of a warning label could reduce injuries. Almost half of the subjects thought the warning should be on the discharge chute, 33% thought it should be at the back of the mower, 6% felt it should be on the handle, and 16% thought it should be placed in more than one spot. The most preferred sign for indicating hazard was one that graphically showed severed fingers; the least preferred was the safety alert symbol (an exclamation point within a triangle).

Key Words:
Agreement with
  Symbol/Message,
Communication Theory,
Credibility of Source,
Design of:
  educational/persuasive
  programs,
Design of: labeling and
  safety signage systems,
Development Programs,
Effectiveness of:
  educational/persuasive
  programs,
Evaluation Difficulties,
Existing/Past Behavior
  Patterns,
Psychosocial Influences

330
McGuire, W.J., "The Communication-Persuasion Model and Health-Risk Labeling," in *Product Labeling and Health Risks*, Morris, L.A., Mazis, M.B. and Barofsky, I. (Eds.), Cold Spring Harbor Laboratory, Banbury Report 6, 1980, 99-122.

The author presents an input/output matrix which relates source, message, channel, receiver, and destination input factors to exposure, attention, reaction, comprehension, yielding, storage, retrieval, decision, behavior, and consolidation output factors. This model, used to organize the vast amount of communication-related literature, was reported in more detail in Lipstein and McGuire (1978). The present paper delineates several implications of the model: 1) output is a stochastic process involving a series of probabilistic steps; 2) communication impact can be measured at any response stage (proximal measure implication); 3) input variables have effects at each of the

Annotations (301-400)

Key Words (cont.):
Source,
Warning Process Models

different stages that may conflict (neglected mediator implication); 4) input variables tend to have inverse effects on different response stages - e.g., if they are positively correlated with one stage, they are likely to be negatively correlated with another stage (compensatory implication); 5) it can be inferred from the compensatory implication that intermediate input variable values are desirable (golden mean implication); and 6) optimal input variable values depend on situational factors (situational weighing implication).

McGuire then presents the following seven steps of his risk-labeling campaign design method: 1) reviewing realities (risk, effects of labeling, effectiveness of labeling, etc.); 2) examining ethics (questioning whether the campaign is consistent with the design team members' personal ethics); 3) surveying the socio-cultural situation surrounding risk behavior; 4) mapping the mental matrix (generating thoughts, feelings, and behavior surrounding any undesirable risky uses of the product); 5) brainstorming to develop campaign themes and targets; 6) constructing the persuasive communications, applying the input/output model; and 7) evaluating the campaign's effectiveness.

Key Words:
Communication Theory,
Effectiveness of:
  educational/persuasive
  programs,
Evaluation Difficulties,
Source

331
McGuire, W.J., "Attitudes and Opinions," *Annual Review of Psychology*, 17, 1966, 475-514.

The author summarizes research on selected attitude change factors. The factors (and illustrative issues) considered are: 1) source (intent to persuade, race versus belief similarity); 2) message (appeals based on fear, the size of the discrepancy, order effects); 3) channel (the resolution of opinion controversy in natural groups); 4) receiver (forced compliance, active versus passive participation, the effects of disconfirmation, personality correlates of persuasibility); and 5) destination (immunization against persuasion, interrelation among measures).

Key Words:
Evaluation Difficulties

332
McGuire, W.J., "Inducing Resistance to Persuasion: Some Contemporary Approaches," in *Advances in Experimental Social Psychology*, 1, Berkowitz, L. (Ed.), 1964, 191-229.

The investigation described in this paper addresses the pre-treatments which, when applied to the individual, make him less susceptible to persuasive messages than he would be prior to the pre-treatments. Resistance to persuasion is not necessarily "healthy" because there is a close psychological relationship between susceptibility to persuasion and the ability to learn. The discovery of pre-treatments that make the individual receptive to truth and resistant to false would be optimal. McGuire's discussion includes some potentially "unhealthy" pre-treatments such as enhancing the tendency to use perceptual distortion in the defense of preconceptions.

The paper reviews four approaches and variations of each to the issue of inducing resistance to persuasion. The four approaches presented are: The Behavioral Commitment Approach; Anchoring the Belief to Other Cognitions; Inducing Resistant Cognitive States; and Prior Training in Resisting Persuasive Attempts. The author's research, as well as some other relevant experiments, are also presented.

Key Words:
Advantages of Nonverbal Symbols,
Biohazard,
Caustic Materials,
Consumer Labeling and Signage Systems,
Hazard/Alert,
Hazardous Materials,
Poison

333
McIntyre, H., "What Next for Symbolic Hazard Labeling?" *Modern Packaging*, 46:5, May 1973, 30-33.

The author suggests a set of principles on which uniform symbolic labeling should be based in order to ensure a uniform system. Advantages and disadvantages of symbolic labels, especially as they apply to hazardous substances, are discussed.

Key Words:
Behavior Factors,
Feedback,
Incentives,
Warnings: evaluating effects on behavior,
Workers

334
McKelvey, R.K., Engen, T. and Peck, M.B., "Performance Efficiency and Injury Avoidance as a Function of Positive and Negative Incentives," *Journal of Safety Research*, 5:2, June 1973, 90-96.

The authors report a study focused on individuals' attentiveness to a red warning light and on their care in manipulating a power tool (drill press) under various incentive conditions. The subjects were divided into four groups of ten and were tested under four different incentive conditions. The different incentive conditions varied pay scales, as follows: 1) $1.00 for the preliminary session and $4.00 for the required two hours; 2) $1.00 for the preliminary session and a sum, as determined by performance, for the required two hours; 3) the same as condition #2 except that the press would not operate for five minutes after failure to perform the vigilance task with the warning light; and 4) the same as condition #3 except that the press would not operate for five minutes after failure to remove hands from the drill press.

The results indicated that work output, vigilance, and accident susceptibility were all significantly affected by varying the pattern of reinforcement. A balanced presentation of positive and negative incentives increased hazard awareness without

Annotations (301-400)

significantly affecting performance efficiency. Under these latter conditions, the participants also worked faster and more carefully than under other conditions.

Key Words:
Children,
Consumers,
Effectiveness of:
    educational/persuasive
    programs,
Newspapers,
Parents,
Radio/TV

335
McLoughlin, E., Vince, C.J., Lee, A.M. and Crawford, J.D., "Project Burn Prevention: Outcome and Implications," *American Journal of Public Health*, **72:3, March 1982, 241-247.**

Project Burn Prevention was implemented to assess a public education program's ability to increase burn hazard awareness and to reduce the incidence and severity of injuries due to burns. Media messages and school and community programs were utilized, and results suggest that the program did not meet its objectives. The media messages and the school campaign did not reduce burn incidence or severity. The community intervention program may have had a slight impact on injury reduction, but only temporarily. The authors speculate as to why the program failed and conclude that education for personal responsibility is insufficient. In order to successfully control burn injuries, it is recommended that, through legislation and education, product modification and environmental redesign be instituted.

Key Words:
Children,
Effectiveness of:
    educational/persuasive
    programs

336
McNeill, D.L. and Wilkie, W.L., "Public Policy and Consumer Information: Impact of the New Energy Labels," *Journal of Consumer Research*, **6, June 1979, 1-11.**

An experiment was designed and executed to evaluate the effects of providing energy information to consumers via labels. The subjects in the experiment performed a series of tasks where they used energy related information to a limited degree.

Key Words:
Abstractness,
Advantages of Nonverbal
    Symbols,
Consumers,
Hand Signals,
Industrial,
Ingress/Egress,
Prohibition,
Public Information,
Traffic

337
Mead, M. and Modley, R., "Communication Among All People, Everywhere," *Natural History*, **77, August/September 1968, 56-63.**

Universal graphic symbols, or "glyphs," are discussed. The authors recommend that these symbols be immediately understandable, perhaps by depicting the object's image. However, it is noted that such symbols may become outdated. Concept-based symbols, like a wavy line to represent water, are recommended. Arbitrary symbols, the authors caution, such as the question mark, should be avoided as they give no clue to their meanings.

Key Words:
User Modeling

338
Meister, D., "Development of Subjective Data for Performance Prediction," *Proceedings of the Human Factors Society - 32nd Annual Meeting*, Human Factors Society, Santa Monica, CA, 1988, 943-947.

The author notes that quantitative human performance data is often missing and that in such instances the use of subjective data is justifiable and necessary. Methods of obtaining subjective data are described. These include the paired comparisons procedure, rank and rating procedure, direct numerical estimation, indirect numerical estimation and the success likelihood index methodology (SLIM). The generation and formal application of subjective estimates by experts in the area of warnings might be useful when companies or corporations are making warning related decisions.

Key Words:
Adequacy of Warnings,
Design of: labeling and safety signage systems

339
Middendorf, L., "Chapter 20: Warnings in Automotive Systems," in *Automotive Engineering and Litigation*, 1, Peters, G.A. and Peters, B.J. (Eds.), Garland Publishing, Inc., New York, 1984, 575-594.

Middendorf presents a good general introduction to warnings along with some general criteria for warnings' design. She cites several examples from the automotive environment to illustrate points presented in her paper.

Key Words:
Loss Prevention Programs,
User Modeling

340
Millar, S.A., "Liability Prevention: Corporate Policies and Procedures," *Personnel Administrator*, February 1986, 47-56.

The author notes that a corporate liability prevention program seeks to insure that products are designed, manufactured and sold in a manner that reduces hazards to an acceptable level of corporate risk. Steps which a company can take in implementing a products liability prevention program are outlined. These procedures fall within the categories of product development and design, manufacturing, warnings and instructions, marketing, advertising, public relations and finally, post-sale monitoring.

We note that companies taking this approach not only reduce their liability risk but are likely to improve their products' image and ultimate performance. Another term for this approach might be "product assurance" and represents the direction of the state-of-the-art in manufacturing—although it is far from existing generally at this time.

Annotations (301-400)

Key Words:
Agencies

341
Miller, J.C. and Parasuraman, A., "Advising Consumers on Safer Product Use: The Information Role of the New Consumer Product Safety Commission," *1974 Combined Proceedings, New Marketing for Social and Economic Progress and Marketing's Contributions to the Firm and to the Society,* Curhan, R.C. (Ed.), American Marketing Association, Series No. 36, 1974, 372-376.

The authors emphasize that the impact of the new Consumer Product Safety Act on the design and performance of products cannot be ignored. It is suggested that marketers can help accomplish the Act's objective of reducing consumer injuries and deaths by providing assistance to the Consumer Product Safety Commission in educating consumers on safe product use. The CPSC is discussed in terms of its power to collect and distribute information. There are numerous opportunities available to marketers to supply input to the consumer education process. According to the authors, marketers and behavioral researchers possess skills that should be quite valuable in the tasks of pre-testing consumer product information and the post-evaluation of the effectiveness of messages.

Key Words:
Signal Words,
Signal Words/Hazard

342
Miller, J.M. and Lehto, M.R., "Comments on 29 CFR 1910.145," report submitted to Documents Department, Occupational Safety and Health Administration, June 1984.

The authors provide comments on three issues of the proposed modifications of 29 CFR 1910.145(f). With respect to the issue of the ability to read and understand, it is recommended that the standard allow the use of non-verbal symbols only when combined with verbal symbols. It is further recommended that emphasis be placed on setting criteria for symbol selection, instead of promulgating a non-verbal symbol standard.

Regarding the issue of viewing distance, it is suggested that the risk field concept be applied by requiring that accident prevention tags be visible at any point within the risk field. Also, the standard should propose a method by which the risk field can be specified for given applications of warning tags. With respect to the issue of "warning vs. caution," the authors find that there seems to be little evidence that individuals can distinguish between the level of hazard implied by the terms "warning" and "caution." Research is recommended, since it is not obvious that three gradations of hazard level are necessary for accident tags; adding an extra gradation might be harmful. It is recommended that if an extra gradation of hazard is desired, terms which directly denote the degree of hazard should be used. It is not recommended to add warning tags as an additional tag which is different from caution or danger tags.

343
Miller, R.E., Reisinger, K.S., Blatter, M.M. and Wucher, F., "Pediatric Counseling and Subsequent Use of Smoke Detectors," *American Journal of Public Health,* **72:4, April 1982, 392-393.**

Key Words:
Effectiveness of: educational/persuasive programs,
Formal Teaching/ Counseling/Education,
Parents,
Personal Presentations

Parents of healthy children were assigned to either an experimental or control group. The 120 parents in the experimental group participated in an education program concerning home fires and smoke detectors. The control group received no such treatment, only "routine" counseling on these subjects. Home visits were conducted between four and six weeks after parents visited their family pediatrician, who administered the program and gave counseling. Twenty-six of the fifty-five parents in the experimental group purchased smoke detectors after the program. (No parents in the control group purchased detectors after receiving only routine counseling.)

We point out that while "instructions" were not one of the factors of interest in this study, it was casually noted by the authors that only nineteen of the purchased detectors were installed correctly, which means that seven out of twenty-six, or more than 25%, apparently failed to follow the instructions despite participating in the education program, a finding of side interest to those of us interested in instruction design!

344
Milroy, R. and Poulton, E.C., "Labeling Graphs for Improved Reading Speed," *Ergonomics,* **21:1, 1978, 55-61.**

Key Words:
Reading Speed,
Visual Displays: miscellaneous

Three methods of labeling graphs were evaluated: 1) the direct labeling of lines; 2) a key on the graph field below the lines; and 3) a key located below the figure. The results indicate that figures could be read most quickly when the lines were directly labeled ($p < .01$).

345
Miyake, N. and Norman, D.A., "To Ask a Question, One Must Know Enough to Know What is Not Known," *Journal of Verbal Learning and Verbal Behavior,* **18, 1979, 357-364.**

Key Words:
Prior Knowledge

The authors present research suggesting that the interaction between user knowledge and material which is being learned influences the number and type of questions that will be asked. Sixty undergraduate students with two levels of background knowledge used learning material at two levels of difficulty in this experiment.

It was found that, for the easier material, novice learners asked more questions. For the harder material the trained learners asked more questions than novice learners. This, of course, implied that the trained learners had more knowledge than the novice learners and also implied that with too little knowledge, as in the situation where novice learners performed more difficult tasks, it may become impossible to ask relevant questions. Such results have obvious implications toward the design of instructions. Notably, a novice may not know enough to know where to look in an instruction manual for needed information As we reviewed this article, we were again reminded of the need to know well the characteristics of the cross sectional characteristics of users. Might some type of hierarchical structure for instruction manuals be suggested to accommodate users of different knowledge and experience levels?

Key Words:
Consumers,
Industrial,
Symbol Taxonomies,
Traffic

346
Modley, R., "The Challenge of Symbology," in *Symbology: The Use of Symbols in Visual Communications*, Whitney, E. (Ed.), Hastings House, New York, 1960, 17-30.

The author addresses the various challenges of symbology by first defining the term "symbol," and then reviewing the accomplishments and problems of symbol usage. Symbols for road signs and machine tool controls, professional symbols, and new symbol applications are also presented. The author then discusses a need for a science of symbology to bring some order to the field. He suggests gathering available information on symbols, classifying it, and cataloging it to create an organized collection of all the graphic symbols used in our society. Also proposed is a cooperative effort by leading designers to develop a limited series of pre-determined symbols for use in machine, highway, and packaging limited applications.

Key Words:
Conduct of Consumer/
User

347
Morgan, F.W. and Avrunin, D.I., "Consumer Conduct in Product Liability Litigation," *Journal of Consumer Research*, 9, June 1982, 47-55.

The authors discuss the legal doctrines of contributory negligence, assumption of risk, misuse, and comparative fault, all of which consider consumer behavior. The role of consumer research in determining how these legal doctrines should be interpreted in specific cases is also covered.

Key Words:
Design of: labeling and safety signage systems

348
Mori, M. and Abdel-Halim, M.H., "Road Sign Recognition and Non-Recognition," *Accident Analysis and Prevention*, 13, 1981, 101-115.

Driver recognition of road signs is obviously relevant to traffic safety. The author addresses the issue by measuring the time drivers spend reading road signs using eye-movement techniques and the recognition rate method.

Probabilistic models were then developed to characterize the various distributions of fixation durations. The parameters of these models were utilized to create a method for measuring the efficiency-level index of the road sign system.

Key Words:
Brochures/Flyers,
Consumers,
Effectiveness of:
  educational/persuasive programs,
Formal Teaching/
  Counseling/Education,
Medical Patients,
Patient Package Inserts (PPI),
Reading of: instructions,
Understanding of Instructions

349
Morris, L.A. and Halperin, J.A., "Effects of Written Drug Information on Patient Knowledge and Compliance: A Literature Review," *American Journal of Public Health*, 69:1, January 1979, 47-52.

The authors note that the failure to use prescription drugs appropriately is frequently reported in the literature and that non-compliance can frequently be traced to communication failures between the health care provider and the patient. In this paper, they review the impact of providing written prescription drug information sheets to help alleviate such problems. They were specifically concerned with the potential of using such information to increase the knowledge of patients as well as their compliance. They note that numerous surveys have been performed in the past pertaining to these issues as have certain more specialized studies. They place particular emphasis on evaluating drug information programs that studied patient populations rather than general surveys which may, in fact, not be addressing the patients who are taking drugs to control, cure, and prevent diseases. Existent studies appear to offer support for the conclusion that the provision of written information can improve patients' knowledge and compliance which antibiotic regimens. Such treatment is generally over a short time period.

For the situation where drugs are used over a long time period as exemplified by hypertensive patients, little evidence was found that written information, by itself, has been associated with improved compliance. The authors note that proper communication by itself does not guarantee that behavioral change will take place. They further note the need for interventions which go beyond the simple provision of written information. Among such programs are the provision of social support, described as efficient feedback tailored to the patients' specific needs.

350
Morris, L.A. and Kanouse, D.E., "Informing Patients About Drug Side Effects," *Journal of Behavioral Medicine,* **5:3, 1982, 363-373.**

Key Words:
Brochures/Flyers,
Effectiveness of:
    educational/persuasive programs,
Medical Patients,
Patient Package Inserts (PPI),
Psychosocial Influences

The authors report on a study in which 249 newly diagnosed hypertensive patients were provided a leaflet that described a particular drug and its possible side-effects. Of the 249 subjects, two-thirds received the leaflets, while one-third did not.

It was found that subjects receiving or not receiving the leaflet were equally likely to report symptoms of drug side effects. However, subjects who did receive the leaflet were more likely to attribute the experienced reactions to the drug, and this effect appeared to be present for symptoms which were not explicitly referred to on the leaflet as well as for those symptoms which were. The fact that subjects in both pools were equally likely to report symptoms was cited by the authors to support the theory that drug leaflets do not suggest or otherwise induce patients to report side-effects. This point was deemed important by the authors because other researchers have expressed the concern that forewarning patients about possible side-effects might cause them to report effects that were not actually present. On the other hand, the results did support the hypothesis that drug labeling increases the tendency of subjects to attribute side-effects to the specific drugs they are taking.

351
Morris, L.A. and Kanouse, D.E., "Consumer Reactions to the Tone of Written Drug Information," *American Journal of Hospital Pharmacy,* **38:5, May 1981, 667-671.**

Key Words:
Brochures/Flyers,
Comprehension of:
    warning labels,
Consumer Preferences,
Design of:
    educational/persuasive programs,
Design of: instructions,
Effectiveness of:
    educational/persuasive programs,
Level of Detail,
Medical Patients,
Memory of:
    symbol/message,
    warning labels,
Message Tone,
Organizing Information,

Four different patient package inserts (PPIs) describing flurazepam were tested via a questionnaire administered to 456 members of a college community. Each of the evaluated package inserts contained the same information but varied in terms of what was denoted as the tone of the information. Techniques that were used to vary the tone of the package inserts included: 1) ordering the information or varying the order of the information in the insert; 2) including statements endorsing the efficiency of the treatment in a reassuring version, but not doing so in a frank version; 3) using concrete terms to describe negative outcomes in the frank version, while using less concrete terms in the reassuring version; 4) using varied embellishments or explanations (e.g. negative outcomes were defined very carefully in the frank version).

Key Words (cont.):
Patient Package Inserts (PPI)
Recognition,
Sources of Bias,
Students

The two generated documents were evaluated in terms of five factors: the first factor described the clarity of the presented information, the second factor reflected the interest value of the information (the extent to which the information was lively or stimulating), the third factor denoted the level of reassurance, the fourth factor described the audience level, and the fifth factor was the length of the document. The frank version was rated significantly higher in clarity, interest value and length, while the reassuring versions scored significantly higher on the reassurance factor. Also evaluated during the course of this study was the degree to which certain critical knowledge items were communicated by the various versions. The more explicit information contained in the frank version resulted in significantly improved subject performance in answering some of the questions.

352
Morris, L.A. and Kanouse, D.E., "Consumer Reactions to Differing Amounts of Written Drug Information," *Drug Intelligence and Clinical Pharmacy,* **14, July/August 1980, 531-536.**

Key Words:
Amount of Information,
Consumers,
Information Overload,
Level of Detail,
Understanding of Instructions

A varying amount of information was provided on a package insert given to patients using antibiotics. The four levels of information on the leaflets were: 1) a short document that gave minimal details about the drug (about sixty half-page lines); 2) a short document plus explanations or rationale; 3) a short document plus explicit behavioral directions for following a regime; and 4) a short document with both types of supplemental information. The short document consisted of general information, warnings, side effects, and other information.

After reading a particular leaflet, presumably after their drug prescription was filled, the 325 subjects were first tested concerning their knowledge of the leaflets and then asked to evaluate each insert on a semantic differential scale and rate a list of purposes for providing the leaflets. Summary knowledge scores were not significantly different; depending on the question, some variation was noted for individual questions. Factor analysis of the semantic differential scores revealed factors describing: 1) perceived accuracy (65%); 2) stimulation value (20%); 3) understandability (9%); and 4) perceived length (5%). The fourth-level leaflet was judged to be significantly more accurate, and the first-level leaflet was judged to be significantly shorter. Factor analysis of purpose revealed that the full information leaflet was scored lowest on the factor dealing with the affording of good care while the leaflet providing behavioral instructions was scored highest on this factor.

Annotations (301-400)

Key Words:
Labels,
Medical Patients,
Parents,
Warnings: evaluating effects on behavior

353
Morris, L.A. and Klimberg, R., "A Survey of Aspirin Use and Reye's Syndrome Awareness Among Parents," *American Journal of Public Health*, 76:12, December 1986, 1422-1424.

The authors discuss a national telephone survey of 1,155 parents of children nineteen years of age and younger regarding their patterns of aspirin use during episodes of childhood flu and chicken pox. The survey was undertaken to obtain current national estimates of aspirin use for parents who had treated a recent episode of the flu or chicken pox.

About half of the parents were aware of the contraindication against aspirin use for young patients suffering from the flu or chicken pox. Twelve percent of the surveyed parents said they would give their children aspirin if they were to have the flu or chicken pox today. Three-fourths of these parents were unaware of the Reye's Syndrome aspirin contraindication. In summary, those parents who intended to administer aspirin were less likely to be aware of Reye's Syndrome, knew less about it, thought it was less dangerous, and, if aware, were less likely to have learned about it from their doctor.

Key Words:
Agencies,
Amount of Information,
Brochures/Flyers,
Buying Behavior,
Comprehension of: warning labels,
Consumer Labeling and Signage Systems,
Consumer Preferences,
Consumers,
Design of: educational/ persuasive programs,
Design of: instructions, labeling and safety signage systems,
Effectiveness of: educational/persuasive programs,
FDA,
Government Involvement,
Governmental Labeling and Signage Systems,
Industrial,
Influences of Warning Labels

354
Morris, L.A., Mazis, M.B. and Barofsky, I. (Eds.), "Product Labeling and Health Risks," Cold Spring Harbor Laboratory, Banbury Report 6, 1980.

This book is a compilation of papers presented at the sixth Banbury Conference in May 1980. Sessions at this conference addressed labeling as a communication device, labeling as a social policy, labeling of alcohol bottles with pregnancy warnings, and various labeling case studies. Specific papers within the report focus on the theories, research, and regulation pertinent to the labeling of consumer, industrial, and medical products. Many of the chapters conclude with a discussion among the conference participants about a particular aspect of labeling. The papers presented were:

Mazis, M.B., "An Overview of Product Labeling and Health Risks."
Murphy, R.D., "Consumer Responses to Cigarette Health Warnings."
Morris, L.A., "Estrogenic Drugs - Patient Package Inserts."
Ferrandino, D., Reich, A. and Ryer, F., "Labeling in the Workplace as Required by the Occupational Safety and Health Administration."
Staelin, R., "Appliance Performance Labeling and Point of Purchase Information: The Results of Three Experiments."

Key Words (cont.):
Introducing New Systems,
Labels, Level of Detail,
Medical Patients,
Memory of: warning labels,
Message/Tone/Voice,
OSHA,
Organizing Information,
Patient Package Inserts (PPI),
Perceived Risk,
Readability Measures,
Reading Measures,
Reading of: instructions, warning labels,
Review Papers, Smokers,
Sources of Bias,
Understanding of Instructions,
Warning Process Models,
Warnings: evaluating effects on behavior,
Workers

Key Words:
Agencies,
Amount of Information,
Brochures/Flyers,
Consumers,
Effectiveness of: educational/persuasive programs,
Familiarity with Product,
Level of Detail,
Memory of: symbol/message,
Patient Package Inserts (PPI),
Reading of: instructions,
Recall

Stokes, R.C., "Consumer Research on Food Label Information."
* Schwartz, S.P., "Consumer Attitudes toward Product Labeling."
* McGuire, W.J., "The Communication-Persuasion Model and Health-Risk Labeling."
* Olson, J.C., "An Information-Processing Approach to Health-Risk Labeling."
Ley, P., "Practical Methods of Improving Communication."
* Kanouse, D.E. and Hayes-Roth, B., "Cognitive Considerations in the Design of Product Warnings."
* Slovic, P., Fischhoff, B. and Lichtenstein, S., "Informing People about Risk."
Schultz, W.B., "Labels, Bans, and Consumer Preferences."
Walden, J., "From the Producer's Perspective."
Beales, H., "Benefits and Costs of Label Information Programs."
Barofsky, I., "The Psychosocial Consequences of Product Labels."
Rheinstein, P.H. and Baum, C.S., "Labeling Effectiveness and the Health Environment."
Cooper, R.M., "A Time to Warn and a Time to Ban."
Yesley, M., "Afterward: Policy Issues in Risk Labeling."

* Those papers for which annotations appear in this book are marked by an (*) asterisk.

355
Morris, L.A., Mazis, M.B. and Gordon, E., "A Survey of the Effects of Oral Contraceptive Patient Information," *The Journal of the American Medical Association*, **238:23, December 1977, 2504-2508.**

The authors discuss a nation-wide survey of 1,720 current and 949 former users of oral contraceptives. The focus was on evaluating the patient package insert provided with oral contraceptives. The authors gathered information regarding the proportion of women who received this information, the extent to which they read it, their resultant knowledge of oral contraceptives, and the behavioral changes spawned by the package insert.

Ninety-three percent of the women in the sample using oral contraceptives reported receiving the package insert. Of the users who received a copy, 97% reported that they read it. Only 1% said they did not read the insert because they thought it was not useful. Recall of information provided on the insert, not including the directions for use, varied from 27% to 53.6%. Readership was substantially higher for those younger than thirty years of age (38%) than for women thirty years of age and older (20%). Twelve percent of all users who had read the insert reported that it raised questions that caused them to contact their physicians. About 78% of the women read the information when they first started taking oral contraceptives, but less than 11% read the insert that accompanied subsequent prescription refills. It was also found that patients tended to prefer a longer information booklet over the short insert.

356
Morris, L.A., Myers, A. and Thilman, D.G., "Application of the Readability Concept to Patient-oriented Drug Information," *American Journal of Hospital Pharmacy,* **37, November 1980, 1504-1509.**

Key Words:
Consumer Preferences,
Consumers,
Design of: educational/persuasive programs,
Design of: instructions,
Level of Detail,
Patient Package Inserts (PPI),
Readability Measures,
Semantic Differential,
Students

The readability of four diazepam patient labeling documents was studied. A self-administered questionnaire was employed to evaluate four versions containing the same basic information but differing in vocabulary and complexity of sentence structure. Subjects for the study were students attending the University of Maryland and nearby areas. The 199 subjects evaluated had a mean age of 17.8 years. In the course of this study, each subject was asked to read one of four versions of the product information and then rate the information using a semantic-differential scale and estimate the reading level of the information. The responses on the questionnaire were then factor analyzed to extract five factors distinguishing the various versions of the package information.

The first factor described if the material was well written, the second described the accuracy of the insert, the third judged how interesting the insert was, while the fourth expressed a positive evaluation of the material. The fifth, and last, factor described the adult readability rating of the material. The four versions of the labeling information were also evaluated using thirteen readability formulas. The subjects rated the four versions roughly equivalently on accuracy and quality of writing. The easiest to read excerpt was rated lowest by the group on interest value, positive evaluation, and adult readability. For the adult readability factor, the most difficult to read version was rated highest. The readability formulas did rate the four versions equivalently in terms of relative rank. However, the study groups' own estimate of readability were variably higher or lower than those predicted by the readability formulas. For these reasons, the author concludes that patient labeling should be written for audience acceptance rather than for favorable scores on reading tests or readability formulas.

Key Words:
Agencies,
Brochures/Flyers,
Consumers,
Effectiveness of:
  educational/persuasive programs,
Elderly,
Medical Patients

357
Morris, L.A. and Olins, N.J., "Utility of Drug Leaflets for Elderly Consumers," *American Journal of Public Health,* **74:2, February 1984, 157-158.**

The authors report on a mail survey evaluation of the American Association of Retired Person's (AARP) Pharmacy Service drug leaflet program. Leaflets pertaining to anti-hypertensive and arthritis medicines were mailed to 2,400 elderly consumers in nine midwestern states. The leaflets provided information on uses, dosage, warnings, precautions and side effects, using minimal explanations.

Of the 2,400 questionnaires mailed out, 1,650 were returned. Although the overall response rate was 69%, the response rates varied depending on which of the two drugs was referred to in the leaflet. Of the respondents, 95% said they read it, three quarters of the respondents said they kept it, and slightly over half (56%) of those reading the leaflet said they discussed it with another person, usually with a family member. Only 6% of the respondents said the leaflet was not useful; 65% said it was very useful, and 29% rated it as slightly useful. Respondents taking anti-hypertensive medicine were more apt to keep the leaflet and report learning new information from it. Respondents who took tranquilizers were less likely to say the leaflet made them feel better about using the drug. The authors conclude that provision of the drug leaflets is likely to influence drug use in a logical fashion.

Key Words:
Accuracy,
Basic Associations,
Military

358
Moses, F.L., Maisano, R.E. and Bersh, P., " 'Natural' Associations Between Symbols and Military Information," *Proceedings of the Human Factors Society - 23rd Annual Meeting,* **Human Factors Society, Santa Monica, CA, 1979, 438-442.**

One group of military personnel rated concepts associated with symbols, while another group rated symbols associated with concepts. The two procedures did not define identical results since certain items with high associations in the first procedure had low associations in the second procedure.

Key Words:
Amount of Information,
Comprehension of:
  warning labels,
Consumer Labeling and Signage Systems,
Layout

359
Mrvos, R., Dean, B.S. and Krenzelok, E.P., "An Extensive Review of Commercial Labels...The Good, Bad and Ugly," *Veterinary and Human Toxicology,* **28:1, February 1986, 67-69.**

It is the opinion of the authors that, typically, consumers do not search for or read the precautionary statements accompanying

Key Words (cont.):
Organizing Information,
Print Size,
Reading of: instructions,
  warning labels,
Safety Information,
Simple Comprehension
  of: verbal symbols,
Stimulus Size,
Understanding of
  Instructions,
Warnings: evaluating
  effects on behavior

Key Words:
Buying Behavior,
Information Overload

a product before purchasing it. Instead, the authors believe that first aid and warning information is read only in the event of an exposure to a poisonous product. Since consumers tend to rely on this information when an exposure occurs, the authors sought to determine the extent to which first aid and precautionary information on the labels of consumer products are correct and adequate. A sample of 214 product labels were randomly selected from the homes of fifteen middle class families who had at least one child under five years of age. The sample consisted of 25 laundry products, 13 dishwashing products, 29 automobile products, 29 personal care products, 45 miscellaneous household products, and 43 over-the-counter drugs. Each label was evaluated according to the following criteria: the correctness and appropriateness of the medical advice and precautionary statements, the ease with which information could be located, the adequacy of the print size, and the comprehensibility of the information.

The researchers found that only 18.2% of the products displayed correct and appropriate precautions and first aid information. They also found that over half of these products were over-the-counter drugs. Other results include the following: incorrect first aid advice was found on 5.1% of the labels, only 9.8% of the labels were judged to have statements that were easily located and that had an adequate print size, and 9.8% of the labels were judged to have information that was too technical or confusing.

360
Muller, T.E., "Buyer Response to Variations in Product Information Load," *Journal of Applied Psychology*, **69:2, 1984, 300-306.**

Based on findings by Bettman (1979), the author postulates, that information load effects have been caused by the lack of subject control of information rate. It is suggested that in most realistic settings, the emphasis should be on consumer motivation to process information rather than on consumer ability.

A field study directed toward evaluating this hypothesis is described in which subjects were allowed to read whatever quantity of brand-choice information they desired about a food product. Signs were posted near the products with no experimenter present. The signs were in the form of nutritional information by brand in cue matrixes. Neither the number of listed brands nor the number of information cues significantly influenced buying behavior. The presence of the signs moderately increased the tendency of consumers to buy products with better nutritive values. The lack of influence of the information load variables may have been related to the small effect of the signs on behavior.

Key Words:
Adequacy of Warnings,
Duty/Failure to Warn,
Negligence and
 Warnings,
Product Literature,
Warranties/Disclaimers

361
Noel, D.W., "Products Defective Because of Inadequate Directions or Warnings," *Southwestern Law Journal*, **23:2, May 1969, 257-298.**

Criteria and case law pertaining to products defective because of inadequate directions or warnings are summarized in an exhaustive review. This article is of particular interest for its historical perspective.

Key Words:
Adequacy of Warnings,
Duty/Failure to Warn,
Negligence and Warnings

362
Noel, D.W., "Manufacturer's Negligence of Design or Directions for Use of a Product," in *Product Liability: Law, Practice, Science*, **Rheingold, P.D. and Birnbaum, S.L. (Eds.), Practising Law Institute, New York, 1975, 181-244.**

This chapter addresses the various legal issues involved in determining manufacturers' negligence in the design of a product or in the directions for the use of a product.

Key Words:
Adequacy of Warnings,
Duty/Failure to Warn,
Negligence and Warnings

363
Noel, D.W., "Statutory and Common Law Warnings," *The National Commission on Product Safety, Product Safety Law & Administration: Federal, State, and Common Law, Supplemental Studies*, **3, Government Printing Office, Washington, D.C., 1970, 215-220.**

The author summarizes statutory and common law related to warnings.

Key Words:
Maps,
Noise,
Recognition Time,
Visual Noise

364
Noyes, L., "The Positioning of Type on Maps: The Effect of Surrounding Material on Word Recognition Time," *Human Factors*, **22:3, 1980, 353-360.**

The author tested the effects of distracting material on visual searching for names on maps. The distractors consisted of other words which were printed vertically at pre-arranged distances from the searched-for name. Distractors close to the beginning of the searched-for name were particularly significant in prolonging word recognition time.

Annotations (301-400)

Key Words:
ANSI, Absolute Liability,
Adequacy of Warnings,
Advantages of Nonverbal
  Symbols,
Biohazard, CPSA,
Caustic Materials,
Chemicals, Color Coding,
Consensual Labeling and
  Signage Systems,
Consumer Labeling and
  Signage Systems,
Consumers, DOT,
Design Consistency,
Design of: labeling and
  safety signage systems,
Duty/Failure to Warn,
FDA, Foreseeability,
Governmental Labeling
  and Signage Systems,
Hazard Communication
  Rule,
Hazard Prevention/
  Analysis Models,
Hazard/Alert,
Hazardous Materials,
Industrial,
Influences of Warning
  Labels, Legibility,
Misuse, Motor Vehicle,
Negligence and
  Warnings, OSHA,
Organizing Information,
Poison, Signal Words,
Strict Liability and
  Warnings,
Symbol Generation,
Testing

365
O'Connor, C.J. and Lirtzman, S.I. (Eds.), *Handbook of Chemical Industry Labeling*, Noyes Publications, Park Ridge, NJ, 1984.

This handbook provides an extensive review of informative labeling associated with the chemical industry. Part I of the book considers labeling as a communication process and provides a review of factors which influence a label's effectiveness. A brief overview of testing methodologies and research findings in the area of hazard labeling is presented. Part II reviews methods used for classifying of physical/chemical attributes of materials and then translates these attributes into the appropriate messages and statements on a label.

Part III addresses product liability issues and government regulations applicable to chemical labeling. Chapters are devoted to the labeling requirements set forth by the Federal Insecticide, Fungicide, and Rodenticide Act, the Toxic Substances Control Act, the Resource Conservation and Recovery Act, the Federal Hazardous Substances Act, the Consumer Product Safety Act, the Hazardous Materials Transportation Regulatory Program, and the Occupational Safety and Health Act.

Part IV of the handbook is devoted to a review of industry standards and practices regarding informative labeling. This review includes labeling standards such as: the American National Standards Institute's "Guide to Precautionary Labeling of Hazardous Chemicals" (ANSI Z129.1), the National Fire Protection Association's "Identification System" (NFPA 704 Fire Hazards of Materials, 1980), the National Institute for Occupational Safety and Health's "An Identification System for Occupationally Hazardous Material, National Paint and Coating Association's Paint Industry Labeling Guide," and the American Society for Testing and Materials' Z535.2 proposal addressing environmental and facility safety signs.

Key Words:
Drivers,
Effectiveness of:
  educational/persuasive
  programs,
Formal Teaching/
  Counseling/Education

366
O'Neill, B., "Comments on 'An Evaluation of the National Safety Council's Defensive Driving Course in Various States'," *Accident Analysis & Prevention*, 6:3/4, December 1974, 299-301.

This paper is a brief discussion of the research by authors Planek, Schupack and Fowler that supported the introduction of defensive driving courses for average adult drivers. O'Neill concludes that the evidence advocating the advantages of such courses is weak and questions the validity and generality of the conclusions drawn by Planek, Schupack, and Fowler.

Annotations (301-400)

Key Words:
Discrepancy Between Self-Reports,
Existing/Past Behavior Patterns

367
Olshavsky, R.W. and Summers, J.O., "A Study of the Role of Beliefs and Intentions in Consistency Restoration," *Journal of Consumer Research*, **1, June 1974, 63-70.**

The participants in this study were 108 business students at Indiana University (81.5% male). All subjects were volunteers and smoked cigarettes. A questionnaire was used to collect data on the subjects' beliefs, behaviors, intentions, and knowledge regarding the effects of cigarette smoking. The questionnaire gave 103 statements about smoking. For each of the statements, respondents indicated the extent to which they endorsed the belief.

Beliefs related to cigarette smoking were found to be consistent with behavior; heavy smokers supported more beliefs than light smokers. Beliefs were found to be consistent with knowledge; the most knowledgeable subjects were least likely to endorse beliefs that denied evidence that smoking is a health threat. The relationship between intentions and behavior was not found to be consistent (i.e. persons' intended behavior often did not match their actual behavior). Several other findings are also mentioned in this paper.

Key Words:
Deep Processing,
Design of: labeling and safety signage systems,
Development Programs,
Prior Knowledge,
Understanding/ Perception Models

368
Olson, J.C., "An Information-Processing Approach to Health-Risk Labeling," in *Product Labeling and Health Risks*, **Morris, L.A., Mazis, M.B. and Barofsky, I. (Eds.), Cold Spring Harbor Laboratory, Banbury Report 6, 1980, 123-134.**

A general discussion of information processing issues relevant to product labeling is provided. Four assumptions are listed: 1) stimuli are mentally represented as cognitive symbols; 2) representations are stored as associative nets (cognitive structure); 3) activation processes triggered by memory cues are individually dependent; and 4) cognitive processes operate on representations. Other issues discussed are: levels of processing (deep semantic versus shallow processing); effects of knowledge on information processing activities; and the representation of health hazards in memory (abstract semantic versus concrete representation).

Key Words:
Color of Stimulus,
Contrast,
Drivers,
Legibility Distance,
Luminance

369
Olson, P.L. and Bernstein, A., "The Nighttime Legibility of Highway Signs as a Function of Their Luminance Characteristics," *Human Factors*, **21:2, 1979, 145-160.**

A four-phase investigation designed to develop predictive measures of legibility distance as a function of luminance, contrast,

Key Words (cont.):
Predictive User Response Equations,
Traffic,
Traffic Settings,
Viewing Distance,
Visual Acuity

Key Words:
Adequacy of Warnings,
Consumer Labeling and Signage Systems,
Duty/Failure to Warn,
Negligence and Warnings,
Problems in Design,
Product Literature

Key Words:
Behavior Factors,
Habituation,
Hazard,
Memory of: symbol/message,
Recall,
Workers

color, and drivers' visual characteristics was performed. The phases were: 1) a laboratory study; 2) a math model development; 3) a model validation; and, lastly, 4) a model application. Model predictions were within 10% of measured legibility distances, which would seem to suggest a well designed and executed investigation having significant applications relevance.

370
Orloff, D.I., "Potential Fire Hazards and the Role of Product Literature," *Journal of Products Liability*, **3, 1979, 29-41.**

The author reviews general legal issues, federal laws, and pending legislation relevant to fire hazards. The results of a study where product literature was obtained from manufacturers of carpets and rugs, home insulation, and wood-burning stoves and fireplaces showed the instructional and warnings literature to be less than satisfactory in many ways.

371
Orr, M. and Hughes, S.T., "Effectiveness of Product Safety Warnings Over Time, and the Generalization of Warning Signs," *Proceedings of the Human Factors Society - 32nd Annual Meeting*, **Human Factors Society, Santa Monica, CA, 1988, 897-900.**

This study addresses the potential for habituation to warning signs by subjects who are exposed to signs over a long period of time. It also examined the possible effect of a safety label on perceived risk.

An experiment was performed using sixty engineers from a defense contractor. Either a safety sign or no sign was placed on the computer terminal used by the subjects. Subjects were exposed to one of these conditions for periods ranging from 1-3 weeks. Following exposure the subjects were asked to identify safety hazards as part of a questionnaire ostensibly directed toward determining usage of the visual display unit. It was found that 70% of the subjects were able to remember the content of the computer displayed safety sign when asked by the experimenter; however, less than 25% of the subjects identified the message of the safety sign as a visual display unit (VDU) hazard when asked to identify hazards associated with the VDU. The authors felt that this indicated that the subjects had, over time, become habituated to the message. Another result in this experiment was that the presence of the safety sign on the terminal resulted in the subjects reporting more potential hazards associated with the VDU than in the case when no safety sign was present. As a result of this finding, the authors suggest that the mere presence of a safety label, of any kind, may increase user awareness of potential safety hazards and result in safer use of the product by the consumer.

372
Orwin, R.G., Schucker, R.E. and Stokes, R.C., "Evaluating the Life Cycle of a Product Warning: Saccharin and Diet Soft Drinks," *Evaluation Review*, **8:6, December 1984, 801-822.**

Using an auto-regressive moving average modeling approach, the authors evaluated the effect of the saccharin warning label on the sales of diet soft drinks. The results indicated that the label produced a small, yet statistically significant, reduction in sales, which had an onset shortly after the provision of the saccharin warning label and which has continued to remain apparent. The 95% confidence interval ranged from a maximum effect of 6.78% reduction in use of diet soft drinks containing saccharin, to a minimum of .88% decrease in the use of diet soft drinks. Notably, substantially higher effects were attributed to the impact of the media in general than for the warning labels. A 17.34% reduction in use was the inferred impact of the media coverage of saccharin issues.

Key Words:
Buying Behavior,
Consumers,
Effectiveness of:
 educational/persuasive programs,
FDA,
Labels,
Radio/TV,
Review Papers,
Warnings: evaluating effects on behavior

373
Osborn, M.R., "The Art of Creating Safety Symbols," *National Safety News*, **June 1974, 106-107.**

Osborn provides in this two page article a good, but very brief, introduction to safety symbols. He illustrates "... how an unlimited variety of symbol signs can be created simply by combining the basic elements of the message." His reason for providing such guidelines stems from his concern that the OSHA regulations (29 CFR 1910.145 Specifications for Accident Prevention Signs and Tags) only provide for pure symbols: poison, electricity, slow moving vehicles, radiation and biohazard. Reference is also made to OSHA's four classifications of safety signs (danger, caution, safety instruction and direction) as well as representative symbols from the Dreyfuss *Symbol Sourcebook* (1972).

Key Words:
Electrical Hazard,
Hazard/Alert,
Industrial,
Ingress/Egress,
Personal Protective Equipment,
Point of Operation Guarding,
Prohibition,
Routing,
Safety Information,
Slip/Fall,
Traffic

374
Otsubo, S.M., "A Behavioral Study of Warning Labels for Consumer Products: Perceived Danger and Use of Pictographs," *Proceedings of the Human Factors Society - 32nd Annual Meeting*, **Human Factors Society, Santa Monica, CA, 1988, 536-540.**

An experiment involving 131 undergraduate psychology students was performed in order to help determine what factors influence and how likely people are to comply with warning

Key Words:
Attention Measures,
Behavior Factors,
Belief in Danger,
Consumer Setting,
Filtering,
Hazard,
Influences of Warning Labels

Annotations (301-400)

Key Words (cont.):
Memory of: warning labels,
Perceived Risk,
Personal Protective Equipment,
Pictographs,
Prior Knowledge,
Reading Measures,
Reading of: warning labels,
Recall,
Saws,
Students,
Verbal vs. Nonverbal Symbol/Message,
Visual vs. Verbal Symbol/Message,
Warnings: evaluating effects on behavior

labels. This study placed subjects into eight different experimental conditions which corresponded to those defined by two levels of product danger (a circular saw corresponded to a high level of danger and a jigsaw corresponded to a low level of danger), and four levels (types) of a warning label (words only, pictograph only, words plus pictograph, and no warning). The warning labels were designed to convince people to wear gloves while using the tools. For the circular saw, 74% of the subjects noticed the warning, 52% said they read it, and 38% were observed to comply. On the other hand, for the jigsaw, 54% of the subjects noticed the warning, 25% read it, and 13% complied.

The results indicated that subjects were more likely to behave in accordance with the warning label when the product was perceived as being more dangerous. It was also true that the people who used the jigsaw perceived it to be easier to use, safer to use, felt less likely to be injured and felt more confident than when they were using the circular saw. Interestingly, the warning label factors, including the use of a pictograph, did not influence people's reading, complying, noticing, comprehending, or recalling the warning information.

People who read the warning were less likely to have had prior experience with the tool, while people who noticed the warning gave higher risk estimates than those who did not. Those subjects who complied with the warning tended to have less experience with tools or similar saws; they also had less confidence in using the saw and were more likely to have been personally injured using a similar tool. Interestingly, those who felt that a more severe injury would occur actually complied with the warning less than those who felt a less severe injury would occur. This effect is possibly correlated with the fact that gloves are likely to be effective for minor injuries rather than major injuries.

It was also found that people who had previously used a similar tool were less likely to be able to recall the danger and avoidance strategy listed on the warning label. Such results appear to support the theory that instructions on warning labels will be most effective for unknowledgeable subjects. We would suggest that in such circumstances the "warning label" is actually instructing or educating subjects rather than serving a true alerting or warning function.

Key Words:
Duty/Failure to Warn,
Effectiveness of: warning related litigation

375
Owles, D., "Pharmaceutical Manufacturers' Duty to Warn of Propensity to Harm," *Journal of Products Liability*, 3, 1979, 151-159.

This general paper considers: 1) the duty to warn; 2) the duty to warn users; 3) the purpose of warning; 4) the effectiveness of warnings; and 5) the jurisdiction of American courts.

Key Words:
Effectiveness of: educational/persuasive programs

376
Page, M.E. and Spicer, J., "Aids and Services for Disabled People—Getting the Message Across," *Applied Ergonomics*, 12, December 1981, 223-230.

Problems associated with getting information to administrators and from administrators to disabled people are discussed.

Key Words:
Contraceptives,
Drugs,
Duty/Failure to Warn

377
Palmateer, L.M., "Products Liability—Manufacturer of Oral Contraceptives Must Directly Warn Ultimate Consumers of Risks Inherent in the Use of Its Product," *Suffolk University Law Review*, 20:1, Spring 1986, 155-164.

According to the Massachusetts Supreme Court in MacDonald v. Ortho Pharmaceutical Corporation, the drug manufacturer must warn ultimate consumers directly: when a customer initiates the prescribing process to obtain a preventive drug; when a customer maintains infrequent contact with the prescribing physician; or when the customer directly receives the manufacturer's warning on labels and instructions booklets dispensed with the drug.

Key Words:
Adequacy of Warnings,
Duty/Failure to Warn,
Negligence and Warnings

378
Patterson, R.B., "Products Liability: The Manufacturer's Continuing Duty to Improve His Product or Warn of Defects After Sale," in *Product Liability: Law, Practice, Science*, 2nd Edition, Rheingold, P.D. and Birnbaum, S.L. (Eds.), Practising Law Institute, New York, 1975, 165-178.

Patterson discusses case law applicable to the theory of continuing duty to warn. This doctrine holds that manufacturers have a duty either to implement a post sale remedy or to provide a warning against product hazards which were unknown or not present at the time of manufacture or sale.

Key Words:
Children,
Effectiveness of:
   educational/persuasive
     programs

379

Pease, K. and Preston, B., "Road Safety Education for Young Children," *The British Journal of Educational Psychology*, 37:3, November 1967, 305-313.

This paper assesses the recent trend in road casualties among children. These researchers specifically evaluated the so-called "curb drill." This drill involves reciting the passage, "When you cross the road by day or night, beware of the dangers that loom in sight. Look to the left, and look to the right, then you'll never, never get run over." After reciting the passage and checking for traffic, children are expected to safely cross the street.

In this experimental setting, children seemed to regard the mere performance of the curb drill as sufficient to prevent dangers of the road! Young children were also found to have problems understanding directionality. Seventy participants (five- or six-year-old children from two state schools in Manchester) were put into either the experimental or the control group, depending on which school they attended. Twenty-one boys and twenty-one girls were in the treatment group, fourteen boys and fourteen girls were control subjects.

Key Words:
Behavior Factors,
Drivers,
Risk Taking,
Traffic,
Warnings: evaluating
    effects on behavior

380

Perchonok, K. and Hurst, P.M., "Effect of Lane-Closure Signals Upon Driver Decision Making and Traffic Flow," *Journal of Applied Psychology*, 52:5, 1968, 410-413.

This study operationalized variables related to the decision-making processes of drivers in merging situations. The model assumes that a gap of size g will be accepted if g is greater than G, the driver's threshold (the driver's smallest acceptable gap). The model implies that advance notice of the need for merging will be helpful to drivers. This implication was tested during a comparison of two lane closure notification signaling systems: conventional (a warning from a wooden panel with flashing lights, mounted on the rear of a truck); and, signal (an overhead sign located 1,200 ft. upstream of the truck). Traffic volumes under the two systems were equivalent.

When the signal system was used, the likelihood of a vehicle entering the observation area in the closed medial lane was less than for the conventional system. Therefore, early warning was effective in inducing drivers to leave the closed medial lane. It also resulted in a decrease in the slowing of subject vehicles and a shorter waiting time prior to leaving the closed lane. This signal system thus contributed to decreased confusion and an improvement in traffic flow.

Key Words:
Agreement with Symbol/Message,
Belief in Danger,
Consumers,
Credibility of Source,
Effectiveness of: educational/persuasive programs,
Emergency Warning Systems: general,
Newspapers,
Psychosocial Influences,
Radio/TV,
Source,
Warnings: evaluating effects on behavior

381
Perry, R.W., "Population Evacuation in Volcanic Eruptions, Floods, and Nuclear Power Plant Accidents: Some Elementary Comparisons," *Journal of Community Psychology,* **11, January 1983, 36-47.**

This study compares citizen evacuation responses to three different environmental threats: a river flood, a volcanic eruption, and the nuclear reactor accident at Three Mile Island, making it one of the first empirical studies to compare human responses to nuclear and non-nuclear threats. Citizen belief in real situational danger and warnings from officials were the most frequently cited reasons for leaving in all of the studied incidents. Most citizens who chose not to evacuate did not believe that any real danger existed. On the other hand, warnings given by the mass media were infrequently cited as important reasons for evacuation. Social network contacts were, however, relatively important in evacuation decision making in cases of natural disaster.

Key Words:
Duty/Failure to Warn

382
Peters, G.A., "Toward Effective Warnings for Automobiles: A Challenge to the Trial Bar," *Trial,* **19:11, 1983, 114-119.**

This article is directed toward trial lawyers and presents the warnings issue in relation to litigation. Arguments similar to those in Peters (1984) are discussed and specific automotive applications are presented.

Key Words:
Adequacy of Warnings,
Conduct of Consumer/User,
Duty/Failure to Warn,
Informed Choice,
Loss Prevention Programs

383
Peters, G.A., "Claims Handling and Safety Warnings," *National Underwriter,* **14, April 1984, 11, 18.**

Peters notes that product liability lawsuits frequently allege a failure to warn, and this often becomes the central issue of the case. He further notes that more warnings and safety related information has become available because of the more recent emphasis on communication guidelines for workplace hazards, the growth of workers' right-to-know legislation, and the effect of environmental entitlements relating to hazardous substances.

Peters concludes that successful warnings must communicate information that will give the prospective victim a fair opportunity to avoid personal harm. He notes that in so doing, properly designed warnings can actually strengthen the case for the defense counsel. Peters also questions the effectiveness of cross-cultural "standardized" symbols as a means for communicating with illiterate or non-native people. As an alternative, he suggests pictorials that outline the particular hazard and the necessary precautions. The article also describes six criteria for rating the process used to develop safety warnings and instructions.

Key Words:
Adequacy of Warnings,
Design of: labeling and safety signage systems,
Durability,
Duty/Failure to Warn,
Effectiveness of: warning related litigation,
Human Factors,
Point of Operation Guarding,
Safety Information,
Slip/Fall

384
Peters, G.A., "15 Cardinal Principles to Ensure Effectiveness of Warning System," *Occupational Health and Safety*, May 1984, 76-79.

The author suggests that there should be fifteen cardinal principles to ensure effective warning design. These are listed as: 1) readability; 2) understandability; 3) type; 4) practicality; 5) comprehensibility; 6) behavior modification; 7) compatibility; 8) reinforcement; 9) conspicuity; 10) durability; 11) reliability; 12) novelty; 13) effectiveness; 14) placement; and 15) danger signaling.

Key Words:
Advertising,
Caustic Materials,
Design of: labeling and safety signage systems,
Duty/Failure to Warn,
Electrical Hazard,
Human Factors,
Loss Prevention Programs,
Negligence and Warnings,
Patent Danger,
Personal Protective Equipment,
Point of Operation Guarding,
Product Literature,
Safety Information,
Strict Liability and Warnings,
Warranties/Disclaimers

385
Phelan, R. and Ross, K., "Product Warnings, Instructions, and Recalls," Practising Law Institute, 1983.

This book is comprised of a collection of warning related legal articles, many of which have been published elsewhere. They collectively address such topics as: the duty to warn for specific products; standards; warning label development; the post-sale duty to warn; product recalls; and human factors engineering.

Phelan and Ross were not only the editors, but also contributed several articles. Other authors who contributed are:

    Seltzer, R.A., "Substantive Law on Duty to Warn and Instruct."
    Birnbaum, S.L. and Wrubel, B., "State of the Art Evidence in Warning Cases: The Defense of Foreseeability."
    Phelan, R.J. and Chase, C., "Duty to Warn and Instruct in Specific Industries and with Specific Products."
    Dorris, A., "Concensus Standards for Precautionary Labels."
    Ross, K., "Creating the Warning Label System and Meeting the Duty to Instruct."
    Platt, W.E. and Williams, C.K., "Post-Sale Duty to Warn: The Genesis of an Expanded Cause of Action."
    Sussman, R.M., "Impact of Federal Regulation on Duty to Warn or Instruct."
    Kobayashi, J.M., "Admissibility Questions and Selected Evidentiary Developments Related to Products Liability Lawsuits (Emphasizing the Federal Rules of Evidence) For: Subsequent Remedial Measures Recall Letters and Notices."

Dimcoff, A.S., "Managing the Recall."
Bass, L., "Managing Product Recalls."
  Articles by Bass, L., "Product Recall Decision Making"; McCarthy, R.L., "Product Recall Decision Making: Valid Product Safety Indicators."
Dorris, A., "Human Factors Engineering and Product Safety."
  Articles by *Dorris, A.L. and Tabrizi, M.F., "An Empirical Investigation of Consumer Perception of Product Safety"; *Dorris, A.L. and Purswell, J.L., "Warnings and Human Behavior: Implications for the Design of Product Warnings"; Phelan, R.J. and Oliver, R., "Using Experts in Products Liability Cases."

The collection was prepared for distribution at the Product Warnings, Instructions and Recalls Program. The book is part of the Litigation and Administrative Practice Series (number 227) of the Practising Law Institute.

*The papers for which annotations appear in this book are marked by an (*) asterisk.

386
Phillips, R.J., "Why Is Lower Case Better?" *Applied Ergonomics*, 10:4, 1979, 211-214.

Key Words:
Case of Text,
Maps,
Search Time

A search task involving a map type display demonstrated that names set entirely in lower case take longer to find than names with a capitalized first letter.

387
Phillips, R.J. and Noyes, L., "A Comparison of Colour and Visual Texture as Codes for Use as Area Symbols on Thematic Maps," *Ergonomics*, 23:12, 1980, 1117-1128.

Key Words:
Color of Stimulus,
Information Coding,
Maps,
Search Time,
Symbol Taxonomies

The researchers state that information on maps can be divided into point, line, and area categories. Three experiments were performed in which 16 types of area symbols were encoded using color or texture. Symbols coded by color or a combination of color and texture were shown to be much easier to find than symbols coded by texture alone.

388
Phillips, R.J., Noyes, L. and Audley, R.J., "The Legibility of Type on Maps," *Ergonomics*, 20:6, 1977, 671-682.

Key Words:
Case of Text,
Maps,
Strokewidth,
Symbol Size,
Typeface/Font

The effects of typeface, weight, size, and case (lower vs. upper) were evaluated for four map reading tasks on the basis of type legibility. The principal recommendation was that names on maps should be in a typeface of normal weight in lower case with an initial capital letter.

Key Words:
Adequacy of Warnings,
Color Coding,
Design of: labeling and
 safety signage systems,
Durability,
Duty/Failure to Warn,
Human Factors,
Negligence and
 Warnings,
Signal Words,
Warranties/Disclaimers

389
Philo, H.M., "New Dimensions in the Tortious Failure to Warn," in *Safety Law, A Legal Reference for the Safety Professional*, Peters, G.A. (Ed.), American Society of Safety Engineers, Park Ridge, 1983, 95-99.

The author states that warning design requires the combined expertise of safety engineers, psychologists and human factors experts, semanticists, and graphic artists. A brief history of accident prevention signs is furnished. It is stated that warnings are not a substitute for good design, an inadequate warning is no warning at all, and that warnings are not disclaimers.

He also states that proper warnings can function as any or all of the following: to provide information enabling the potential user to make an informed choice as to whether or not the product's risks outweigh its benefits; to alert the potential buyer or user to hazard reduction procedures; to remind those already aware of a hazard; to provide information to help assure safe disposal of containers that held hazardous materials; to help minimize the extent of injury in case of product misuse; and to aid in recall campaigns. Several pro-plaintiff modifications of the law are proposed.

Finally, the following considerations in warning design are deemed necessary: 1) durability (the warning must last for the life of the product); 2) presence of a signal word that can communicate information about the character and gravity of the hazard; 3) color combination; 4) size of warning; 5) size of type; 6) message; 7) sign placement; and 8) sign illumination.

Key Words:
Patent Danger

390
Philo, H.M. and Rine, N.J., "The Danger Never Was Obvious," *Journal of Products Liability*, 1, 1978, 12-19.

As one of the nation's leading trial lawyers in the tort area, Philo criticizes the patent danger criteria, debates the assumption that safety is common sense, and defines a large number of terms.

Key Words:
Problems in Design

391
Pilditch, J., "Did You Read the Instructions Carefully?" *IEEE Transactions on Professional Communication*, 24:4, December 1981, 185-186.

This anecdotal article addresses the recognized fact that product instructions are often inappropriately written. The author notes that instruction manuals are often written by people with technical knowledge, but with no instruction writing knowledge. This may, in fact, hamper the writer's ability to

Annotations (301-400)

communicate necessary information to the nontechnical lay reader.

Key Words:
Legal Style

392
Pilfold, D., "Legal Style in Specifications," *IEEE Transactions on Professional Communication*, **30:3, September 1987, 168-172.**

The author provides recommendations for the use of legal style in writing engineering design specifications. Factors influencing the desirable level of formality in writing specifications are addressed. Recommendations are also made for engineering managers and communication teachers.

Key Words:
Drivers,
Effectiveness of: educational/persuasive programs,
Formal Teaching/ Counseling/Education

393
Planek, T.W., Schupack, S.A. and Fowler, R.C., "An Evaluation of the National Safety Council's Defensive Driving Course in Selected States," National Safety Council Research Department, October 1972, 1-107.

The impact of the National Safety Council's defensive driving course (DDC) was studied for a group of over eight thousand drivers from twenty-six states. These drivers self-reported their accident and violations for the previous year by completing a questionnaire prior to participating in the DDC. One year after the program, 72% of the studied graduates responded to a similar questionnaire. State records were also analyzed.

DDC graduates who completed the re-contact questionnaire reported significant reductions in both accidents and violations following completion of the course. These reductions were greater for males than for females. Drivers younger than 25 years old showed the least reduction. The data collected by the state on accidents and violations also indicated a decline after DDC. These latter reductions, however, were not significantly different from those of the comparison group who did not participate in the course.

Key Words:
Glance Legibility,
Motor Vehicle,
Prior Knowledge,
Reaction Time,
Traffic,
Traffic Settings,
Verbal vs. Nonverbal Symbol/Message,
Viewing Time

394
Plummer, R.W., Minarch, J.J. and King, L.E., "Evaluation of Driver Comprehension of Word versus Symbol Highway Signs," *Proceedings of the Human Factors Society - 18th Annual Meeting*, **Human Factors Society, Santa Monica, CA, 1974, 202-208.**

Twenty subjects evaluated the glance legibility of ten different versions of word and symbol traffic signs. The basic results were: 1) reaction times were lower for questions about word signs than for those about symbol signs; 2) glance legibility was higher for symbol signs; 3) reaction times for symbol signs were somewhat lower for subjects with knowledge of the symbols; and 4) reaction times were varied with different signs.

Key Words:
Emergency Vehicles, School Bus

395
Post, D.V., "Are Specifications of Signaling Systems for Emergency, School Bus, and Service Vehicles Adequate?" *Proceedings of the Human Factors Society - 23rd Annual Meeting*, Human Factors Society, Santa Monica, CA, 1979, 282-284.

The author critically reviews the specifications of signaling systems for emergency, school bus and service vehicles. He concludes that signaling systems on such vehicles are poorly specified. Lack of consistency, rigor, and meaningfulness are cited as deficiencies in both the legal specifications and the current signaling systems. It is recommended that a signaling scheme for special purpose vehicles be adopted, which would facilitate consistency and meaningfulness. Further research is suggested to determine the parameters which critically influence the conspicuity of signal lights.

Key Words:
Conveying Procedures, Development Cycle, Organizing Information

396
Post, T., Price, H. and Diffley, G., "A Guide for Selecting Formats and Media for Presenting Maintenance Information," Bio Technology, Inc., Falls Church, VA, NTIS No. AD A033921, November 1976.

This technical report describes work sponsored by the Navy Technical Information Presentation Project. This work was intended to guide the selection of the best media or formats for presenting maintenance information to Navy personnel. A five step procedure for selecting between media and formats was ultimately developed. These steps were to: 1) Gather source data describing the task and system; 2) Identify special maintenance actions. This includes standard.operating procedures and critical aspects of performance and maintenance; 3) Select formats for presenting the trouble shooting information. Here formats for describing procedures and hardware are distinguished. Procedural descriptions are broken down into two options: fully proceduralized format and partially proceduralized format. Hardware descriptions are also broken down into two options: simple block diagrams and schematics; 4) Select formats for presenting remove and replace actions. Formats considered include fully proceduralized, partially proceduralized and component description formats; 5) Establish technical manual support requirements. This includes access requirements, recording medium requirements and portrayal mode requirements.

In applying this five step selection procedure, emphasis is placed on matching technical manual formats to personnel equipment and work place characteristics, as well as bringing cost considerations into the technical manual selection process.

Key Words:
Basic Associations,
Information Coding,
Symbol Taxonomies

397
Poulton, E.C., "Colours for Sizes: A Recommended Ergonomic Colour Code," *Applied Ergonomics*, 6:4, December 1975, 231-235.

Common associations between size and color are investigated. Red was commonly associated with the largest size, and, to a lesser degree, white was associated with the smallest size. A recommended standard is proposed.

Key Words:
ANSI,
Consensual Labeling and Signage Systems,
Consumer Labeling and Signage Systems,
Governmental Labeling and Signage Systems,
ISO,
Industrial

398
Powderly, D., "Communicating with Standards," *ASTM Standardization News*, 4:12, December 1976, 22-23, 54.

The author discusses product information such as tags or statements on packages and describes some of the advantages of standardization. He also notes that the FTC, Congress, the Department of Commerce, and manufacturers are all interested parties who provide impetus for the development of standards. One difficulty cited by the author is that the ability of a standard to facilitate communication is inhibited when the precision of the standard or testing is not adequately understood.

Organizations involved in making specific standards and guidelines which are discussed in this article include: The National Bureau of Standards, the International Organization for Standardization, the American Society for Testing and Materials, and the American National Standards Institute.

Key Words:
Readability Measures

399
Powell, K.B., "Readability Formulas: Used or Abused?" *IEEE Transactions on Professional Communication*, 24:1, March 1981, 43-44.

This article provides a general introduction to readability formulas, their application, and some of their advantages and disadvantages. Powell concludes that readability formulas have several weaknesses, but these can be overcome when they are applied with appropriate knowledge and care. The use of readability formulas, however, cannot replace other evaluation methods used by writers; but they can provide a useful supplementary technique.

Key Words:
First Amendment

400
Powell, L.A., "Products Liability and the First Amendment: The Liability of Publishers for Failure to Warn," *Indiana Law Journal,* **59, 1983-1984, 503-526.**

This article discusses whether any conceivable circumstances exist in which a publisher owes a duty of care in the use of the printed word to prevent physical harm to readers. The author proposes a theory of liability based on the publisher's subjective intent that readers will rely upon the written material.

ANNOTATIONS 401-500

Key Words:
Drivers,
Effectiveness of:
 educational/persuasive
 programs,
Evaluation Difficulties,
Existing/Past Behavior
 Patterns,
Formal Teaching/
 Counseling/Education

401
Preusser, D.F., Ulmer, R.G. and Adams, J.R., "Driver Record Evaluation of a Drinking Driver Rehabilitation Program," *Journal of Safety Research*, 8:3, September 1976, 98-105.

The authors observe that, in recent years, efforts have been made to augment the traditional legal sanctions with therapeutic programs for drivers being convicted of drinking while driving charges. They note that few of these programs have been thoroughly evaluated with respect to their effect on the subsequent driving of program participants.

A program called the Nassau County Alcohol Safety Action Project Driver Rehabilitation Countermeasure ran from February 1971 through June 1973. The program's objective was to reduce the recidivism rate of drivers convicted of alcohol-related offenses. Random assignment of drivers to treatment and control groups was permitted by the legislation for the program. The experimental group of invited to attend the rehabilitation program consisted of 2,805 drivers. The control group consisted of 2,660 drivers. The results indicate that the program did not yield the desired reduction of repeat convictions for the offenders who participated. We add that these results agree with others who concluded that rehabilitating the drinking driver is an extremely difficult task.

Key Words:
Amount of Information,
Information Overload,
Prior Knowledge

402
Purswell, J.L., Krenek, R.F. and Dorris, A.L., "Warning Effectiveness: What Do We Need To Know?" *Proceedings of the Human Factors Society - 31st Annual Meeting*, 2, Human Factors Society, Santa Monica, CA, 1987, 1116-1120.

The authors describe four steps involved in the warning process. The first is perception, which may be impeded by: information overload, faulty risk assessment, and previous benign experiences with a product while disregarding the warning. The second step is comprehension which may depend on the meaningfulness of signal words, the reading comprehension level required, the meaningfulness of symbols and the meaningfulness of warnings as a function of the task being performed. The third step is memory, the extent to which warning information is stored in long-term memory and recalled when needed. The fourth is decision-making, the role safety-related information plays in risk assessment. The authors point out that further

Key Words:
Actual Behavior,
Behavior Factors,
Consumers,
Elderly,
Existing/Past Behavior
 Patterns,
Housewives,
Perceived Risk,
Prior Knowledge,
Reading Measures,
Reading of: instructions,
Reading of: warning
 labels,
Risk Coping Style,
Risk Taking,
Warning Process Models,
Warnings: evaluating
 effects on behavior

research is needed to better understand how each of these factors influences the effectiveness of warnings.

403
Purswell, J.L., Schlegel, R.E. and Kejriwal, S.K., "A Prediction Model for Consumer Behavior Regarding Product Safety," *Proceedings of the Human Factors Society - 30th Annual Meeting*, **Human Factors Society, Santa Monica, CA, 1986, 1202-1205.**

The authors' goal was to predict how safely subjects would use several different consumer products. Potential prediction variables included age, sex, familiarity with product, recency of product use, injury experience with a product, several more variables from the Zuckerman test, and risk-taking propensity as measured by a questionnaire. Example items on the questionnaire included the percentage of time individual subjects used seat belts, whether they would use life jackets when boating, and their reported tendency to cross a street against a light.

Having developed their prediction variables, fifty subjects from diverse backgrounds were observed using a chemical drain opener, electric carving knife, sabre saw, and router. The behavior of the subjects toward the products was categorized into five levels: 1) didn't look at either instructions or warnings, and used unsafely, 2) looked at instructions or warnings, but used unsafely, 3) didn't look at instructions or warnings but used safely, 4) looked at instructions only and used safely, and 5) looked at both warnings and instructions, and used safely. Levels 1 and 2 were considered unsafe, while levels 3, 4, and 5 were considered safe.

After subject behavior was observed, the questionnaires were administered to gather data regarding the prediction variables. Using discriminant analysis and data from the questionnaires, it was possible to distinguish at high levels of precision between the safe and unsafe groups. The discriminant function predicted the behavior of the subjects with the following accuracies: 68% for the electric knife, 73% for the sabre-saw, 79% for the drain-cleaner, and 86% for the router. Also, particular factors of the questionnaire varied in importance for the different products.

The researchers conclude that measures of risk-taking obtained from the questionnaires have significant value in predicting safe or unsafe behavior. They also note the value of discriminant analysis and the need for more research in this area. Considering the difficulties involved in observing actual product use behavior, we find these results particularly interesting.

Such an approach may also have application in assessing the likelihood that existing or alternate instructions or warnings would change the behavior of people who have been involved in accidents.

404
Pyrczak, F. and Roth, D.H., "The Readability of Directions on Non-Prescription Drugs," *Journal of the American Pharmaceutical Association*, NS 16:5, May 1976, 242-243, 267.

Key Words:
Biohazard,
Consumers,
Prior Knowledge,
Readability Measures,
Understanding of Instructions,
User Group

The statements of "warning" and "caution" found within the directions given for ten aspirin-type drugs were studied by the authors. The first directions sample included the following statement of warning: "Keep this and all medicines out of the reach of children. In case of accidental overdose, contact a physician immediately." The second sample included the following statement, or a variation of it: "If pain persists for more than 10 days or if redness is present, or in arthritic or rheumatic conditions affecting children under 12 years of age, consult a physician immediately."

The readability formula predicted that the first sample tested could be read with ease only by those who had comprehension skills at or above the eleventh or twelfth-grade level. The main source of difficulty for the first sample was associated with the use of five words requiring significant comprehension skills: accidental, overdose, contact, physician, and immediately. For the second sample the readability formula predicted that the directions could be read with ease only by those who had comprehension skills at or above the college level. The following words were identified as the main source of difficulty: persists, redness, arthritic, rheumatic, conditions, affecting, consult, physician, and immediately.

Using the Dale-Chall formula, a third sample of nine randomly selected, nationally advertised drugs was analyzed. A majority of the statements required comprehension skills at or above the college level. Only one of the statements was judged to require comprehension skills at the fourth-grade level or lower.

405
Ramsey, J.D., "An Ergonomic Model for Warning Assessment," in *Advances in Industrial Ergonomics and Safety*, 1, Mital, A. (Ed.), Taylor & Francis, London, 1989, 731-735.

Key Words:
Comprehension of: warning labels,
Design of: labeling and safety signage systems,
Hazard Prevention/ Analysis Models,
Warning Process Models

This paper is aimed at describing in a manner that is easily understood.the rules and principles for warning evaluation The author discusses a proposed sequence of four stages that a person exposed to a hazard must successfully go through in order to avoid an accident.

The first stage of the model involves perception of the hazard. In this stage the exposed person needs to encounter a warning that is both noticeable and readable. The second stage is the cognition of the hazard and implies that an effective warning must be comprehensible and practical. The third stage, decision to avoid the hazard, requires that the warning motivate a modification in behavior and provide justifiable behavior alternatives. The ability to avoid the hazard represents the fourth and final stage of the model; The author notes that it is important that the warning require only those behaviors that an exposed person is capable of performing, and claims that by analyzing these four stages and their components, the effectiveness of a warning can be systematically evaluated.

406
Ramsey, J.D. and Brinkley, W.A., "Enhanced Motorcycle Noticeability Through Daytime Use of Visual Signal Warning Devices," *Journal of Safety Research*, **9:2, June 1977, 77-84.**

Key Words:
Attention Measures,
Color of Stimulus,
Drivers,
Luminance,
Motorcycle,
Stimulus Size,
Traffic,
Traffic Settings

This investigation evaluated the use of several visual signal warning devices to enhance the noticeability of a motorcycle and rider to automobile drivers. The objective of the research was twofold: to determine if a visual warning device mounted on the front fender of a motorcycle would increase daytime noticeability; and to identify a commercially available visual signal warning device that would increase noticeability of the motorcycle in daylight. The experiment was comprised of three phases.

In phase one, the motorcycle and rider were located on a side street that ran perpendicular to traffic flow; the motorcycle appeared to be attempting to enter the flow of traffic. Once the traffic light stopped the flow of traffic, the automobile drivers were asked, "Did you see a motorcycle trying to enter the flow of traffic within the last two blocks?" If the response was "yes," the drivers were asked, "What attracted your attention to the motorcycle?" While the warning device was on, it was estimated that 31.8% of the passing drivers noticed the motorcycle. While the device was off, the estimated percentage was 29.3%. Phase two tested different visual signal warning devices and led to the conclusion that amber domes were more conspicuous during daylight hours than blue domes.

In the third phase, three different motorcycle and warning device configurations were tested: 1) the control condition in which the motorcycle had no warning device; 2) the test condition where a warning device was mounted on motorcycle's front fender; and 3) the test condition where a warning device was mounted on the front fender. Both of these warning devices improved the noticeability of the motorcycle. However, it was concluded that the size of these warning devices might interfere with projection of the headlight onto the driving surface during conditions of darkness or limited visibility.

407

Ream, D., "The Defense Can Win on Damages and Duty to Warn," *For the Defense,* **January 1988, 6-11.**

Key Words:
Duty/Failure to Warn,
Patent Danger

The author examines cases exemplifying the successful use of a number of defenses to failure to warn actions. These defenses include allegations that the danger was obvious, that the user was sophisticated and was already aware of the danger, that the inadequacy of the warning was not the cause of the plaintiff's injury, that the product was misused, that the warning was state-of-the-art at the time it was written, and that the defendant satisfied the duty to warn by adequately warning a learned intermediary.

408

Reder, L.M. and Anderson J.R., "Effects of Spacing and Embellishment on Memory for the Main Points of a Text," *Memory & Cognition,* **10:2, 1982, 97-102.**

Key Words:
Page Layout,
Summaries,
Understanding of Instructions

The authors note that past research has shown advantages of textbook summaries, rather than original prose, as a means of acquiring knowledge. They subsequently present three studies evaluating the advantage of summaries over the original text.

The results indicated that summaries may be better than the original text for at least two primary reasons. First, specific details in the original text may distract attention from the critical ideas that should be emphasized. Second, when reading summaries subjects tend to re-read the main points at spaced intervals, which may lead to higher retention levels.

409

Reisinger, K.S. and Williams, A.F., "Evaluation of Programs Designed to Increase the Protection of Infants in Cars," *Pediatrics,* **62:3, September 1978, 280-297.**

Key Words:
Brochures/Flyers,
Effectiveness of:
  educational/persuasive
  programs,
Parents,
Personal Presentations,
Seat Belt Nonusers

Within a hospital, three educational/persuasive programs were designed to increase the crash protection of infants in cars by increasing the use of infant carriers. The behavior of the women participating in the programs (all of whom were new mothers) was was then compared to that of women within a control group, whose members received no crash protection education.

The first program included literature and provided access to infant carriers that were convenient to purchase. The second program was like the first, but included discussion on infant crash protection. The third program included literature, plus the offer of a free infant carrier. A total of 1,200 babies were observed during the study; the three program groups, as well as the control group, had about three hundred subjects. The measured dependent variable in the study was the use of infant carriers fastened by a car seat belt to provide crash protection. Use of infant carriers was low in all of the evaluated groups; none of the educational/persuasive programs studied significantly affected the behavior of the women in the study.

Key Words:
Brochures/Flyers,
Drivers,
Effectiveness of:
    educational/persuasive programs,
Personal Presentations

410
Reisinger, K.S., Williams, A.F., Wells, J.K., John, C.E., Roberts, T.R. and Podgainy, H.J., "Effect of Pediatricians' Counseling on Infant Restraint Use," *Pediatrics,* **67:2, February 1981, 201-206.**

The subjects of Reisinger's study were 269 women who gave birth in Pittsburgh hospitals. During their postpartum stay and at their children's one and two month visits to the hospital, the experimental group participated in an educational, persuasive program designed to increase the use of infant restraints. During the course of the program, discussions, pamphlets, prescriptions for infant restraint, and demonstrations of how to use the restraint were provided by pediatricians. The control group was not provided with any of the educational or persuasive material.

When the infants arrived at the pediatrician's office for their one, two, four, and fifteen month visits, observations of how the infants traveled in the cars were recorded. The use of restraints anchored by car seat belts was higher for the experimental group than for the comparison group. The figures were higher by 23% at one month, 72% at two months, 9% at four months, and 12% at fifteen months.

Key Words:
Indexes/Quick
    References,
Organizing Information,
Summaries,
Titles

411
Reitman, P., "Streamlining Your Documentation Using Quick References," *IEEE Transactions on Professional Communication,* **31:2, June 1988, 75-83.**

The author notes the increasing prominence of short instructional reference guides that summarize essential information in a format which can be quickly accessed. By omitting impertinent and excess information, technical information can often be clarified. The author states that, for users of computer equipment, quick reference guides are much more likely to be consulted than in-depth documentation. Examples are given of information guides, quick procedure guides, posters and templates, all of which serve the function of providing quick access to information.

It is noted that many of the same principles used in the design of traditional documents are equally applicable to the design of quick references. Specific design suggestions noted in the paper include: 1) use white or blank space to separate units of information and allow easy discrimination between sections; 2) meet legibility requirements; 3) organize information logically . This is essential. Relevant approaches include: the organization of functional documents around actions; organization of information in accordance with common reader questions; temporal organization following the sequences in which information is likely to be requested; and spatial and directional orientations, such as exemplified by following a part as it is processed through a machine and describing the activity that takes place at each step.; 4) provide relevant information only Quick reference guides are not intended to be all-inclusive sources of information; 5) make the information physically accessible The information in a short booklet is more likely to be preferred than a long, folded card type of a format; and 6) use effective headings which contain actions or agents, which ask or answer questions.

Key Words:
Contraceptives,
Drugs,
Duty/Failure to Warn

412
Reskin, L.R., "New Duty to Warn for Birth Control Pill Manufacturers," *American Bar Association Journal,* **71, June 1985, 96.**

According to the Massachusetts Supreme Court, manufacturers of birth control pills must directly warn consumers of dangers inherent in the use of the pill. The reason for this decision is that women who take birth control pills are more involved in the decision-making process than are most other prescription drug users. Also, they usually see their doctor only once a year so they do not have frequent opportunity to ask questions.

Key Words:
Acceptability,
Frequency Estimates,
Severity Estimates

413
Rethans, A.J., "Consumer Perceptions of Hazards," in *PLP-80 Proceedings,* **1980, 25-29.**

The study described here was developed to: 1) determine consumers' subjective perceptions of product risks; 2) relate the subjective perceptions to objective measures of the risks; and 3) examine the relevance of a risk perception model.

Within the study, seventy-five subjects rated a set of consumer products on a series of seven point scales. The subject group was half male, half female, ranged in age from 20 to 52 years old, and 50% of the subjects had completed a university degree. The twenty-nine products chosen were intended to reflect the frequency range found in the CPSC data and to reflect the severity range of the NEISS data. Respondents were asked to rate the hazardousness of the products from a personal and from a societal perspective. They were also asked to rate the acceptability of the hazards presented by each product.

Among the most hazardous products considered from a societal perspective were fireworks, portable power saws, skateboards, power lawn mowers, and swimming pools. A high correlation ($r = 96$) was found between personal and societal hazard ratings. An inverse relationship between perceived risk and acceptability was identified; the rank correlation coefficient was -.62. Available objective data included the NEISS product severity ratings, NEISS frequency of injury data, and the product of the severity rating and the frequency measure, which was called a "total impact measure." The correlations between the subjective and the objective measures were 50% for severity, 72% for frequency, and 64% for total impact. These coefficients suggested that substantial discrepancies existed between the subjective perceptions and the best available data. The author provides data on the mean ratings of the risk characteristics of hazardous products. Also presented were the results of analysis in which perceived risk and acceptability of hazard were the dependent variables.

Key Words:
Acceptability,
Assumption of Risk,
Severity Estimates

414
Rethans, A.J. and Albaum, G.S., "Towards Determinants of Acceptable Risk: The Case of Product Risks," *Advances in Consumer Research*, **8, October 1980, 506-510.**

The authors discuss past research conducted by themselves and other authors which has shown, in numerous cases, that the acceptability of risk is determined by its voluntariness, the knowledge of the risk, the degree of risk control, the product's necessity, the foreseeability of risk, risk exposure, ease of risk reduction, user error, and the risk to children.

An experiment was performed to more precisely determine what factors determine consumers' subjective perceptions of product risk and to examine the relevance of an emerging model of risk acceptance in explaining judgements of the acceptability of product risk. Twenty-nine products which ran the spectrum of low to high injury severity and frequency were selected for the experiment. The acceptability associated with each of the twenty-nine products as well as the characteristics of the risks present during product use were rated by the subjects on a seven point scale. Twelve of the seven point scales used described risk characteristics (referred to earlier) which were shown in previous research to have some relationship to acceptability.

Numerous risk characteristics were found to be significantly related to acceptability. This relationship was analyzed further by performing stepwise regression analysis. During this analysis, five factors in particular were found to be strongly and significantly related to risk acceptability. These five factors were: 1) product necessity, with an $r = .68$; 2) user error, with an $r = .83$; 3) voluntariness, with an $r = .89$; 4) risk knowledge, with an $r = .91$; and 5) foreseeability, with an $r = .92$.

Based on the results of this analysis, the authors conclude that the Consumer Product Safety Commission should consider this or similar modeling approaches when making decisions as to what constitutes acceptable levels of risk for consumer products.

Key Words:
Familiarity with Product,
Memory of:
  symbol/message,
Visual vs. Verbal
  Symbol/Message

415
Rethans, A.J. and Hastak, M., "Representation of Product Hazards in Consumer Memory," *Advances in Consumer Research*, **9, October 1981, 487-491.**

This paper presents a unique study of how people represent product hazards in memory. The study focused upon twenty female staff members of a major Eastern university and a set of eight common consumer products. The procedure consisted of two stages, in the first, subjects were asked in a free call situation to verbalize all the hazard-related thoughts, sensations, feelings or images which were provoked by certain product-related hazard cues. In the second stage, the respondents were asked to elaborate on the pictures and/or mental images they reported upon in the early or first part of the interview. The elicited knowledge was coded into five categories which correspond to different ways of representing knowledge in memory. These categories were: 1) episodic knowledge; 2) personal episodic knowledge; 3) semantic; 4) personal semantic; and 5) affect.

Interestingly, the vast majority of hazard related thoughts were classified as being semantic; 69% of the thoughts falling into the general semantic category (i.e. knowledge void of personal reference); the remaining 25% were classified as personal semantic (i.e. thoughts with some degree of personal reference). Episodic responses accounted for 5% of the hazard thoughts; the remainder fell into the affect category. The episodic statements tended to be recalled in extensive detail compared to the semantic information. An additional finding was that the content of mental images appeared to be heavily influenced by

Annotations (401-500)

experiences in which the subject was either a participant or a witness.

Key Words:
Degradation/Noise,
Laboratory/Generic
   Settings,
Legibility,
Strokewidth,
Typeface/Font

416
Reynolds, L., "Chapter 10: The Legibility of Printed Scientific and Technical Information," in *Information Design: The Design and Evaluation of Signs and Printed Material*, Easterby, R.S. and Zwaga, H.J.G. (Eds.), John Wiley & Sons, New York, 1984, 187-209.

The author reports that letterpress and litho printing create printed images with different characteristics; letterpressing usually produces sharper images. Furthermore, it is stated that phototypesetting is a printing method free of the constraints imposed by the metal type body and that the effects of phototypesetting on legibility are not yet known.

It is noted that xerography and other office copying processes can significantly affect legibility due to a thickening-up or a thinning-down of the type image, the presence of random dots, or the introduction of a continuous grey tone on document copies. Also, computer printouts can pose reading difficulties. The author describes the process of reading and offers definitions and criteria for legibility. Eye movement studies, rate of work, and readers' preferences, as measures of the legibility of printed materials, are discussed. Legibility data for letters, numerals, and punctuation marks are presented, as are variations in character form and size. The spatial arrangement of the characters on the page is also discussed as it relates to legibility.

Key Words:
Degradation/Noise,
Laboratory/Generic
   Settings,
Strokewidth,
Typeface/Font

417
Reynolds, L., "Legibility Problems in Printed Scientific and Technical Information," *Journal of Audiovisual Media in Medicine*, 2, 1979, 67-70.

This report describes two investigations of legibility. The first study addressed the effects of office copying processes on legibility. Typeset text materials were degraded photographically under controlled conditions. The first three levels (1, 2, and 3) were "thinned-down." Level 4 was "normal," and levels 5, 6, and 7 were "thickened-up." Two groups of sixty-four subjects participated in the experiment.

The analysis revealed that the level of image quality had the greatest effect on legibility. The typeface, followed by the level of background noise, were the next most significant factors. Among the typefaces tested, Times and Univers were among the most suitable for material which is likely to be copied indiscriminately. Reynolds recommends that if thinning-down is likely to occur during copying, Baskerville should be avoided. If thickening-up is likely, she recommends avoiding Rockwell in favor of a typeface that has relatively thin strokes, open counters, and a generous set-width to x-height ratio.

Eighty subjects participated in the second study which investigated show-through. The conclusion was that paper opacity, single- or double-sidedness, and alignment or non-alignment were all statistically significant factors.

Key Words:
Visual Displays:
 miscellaneous

418
Reynolds, L., "Legibility Studies: Their Relevance to Present-Day Documentation Methods," *Journal of Documentation*, 35:4, December 1979, 307-340.

This paper discusses topics such as: trends in the production of information displays, the legibility of printed information, the relationships between form and content in printed material, the presentation of information in microform, and the presentation of information on cathode ray tube displays.

Key Words:
Effectiveness of: warning related litigation

419
Ricci, E.M., "The Nature and Function of Warnings in Products Liability," *Personal Injury Deskbook*, 1984, 867-874.

This article discusses the purposes of warnings. These include providing information about possible dangers, motivating the user to change behavior, and reminding the user at each use of the possible danger. The article also discusses the characteristics of effective warnings, including attracting attention, being in the right place at the right time, being explicit, making the danger obvious, and providing instructions on how to avoid the harm contemplated.

Key Words:
Association Rankings/
 Indexes,
Shape Coding,
Shape/Hazard,
Students,
Symbol Taxonomies

420
Riley, M.W., Cochran, D.J. and Ballard, J.L., "An Investigation of Preferred Shapes for Warning Labels," *Human Factors*, 24:6, 1982, 737-742.

Sixty-six college students made paired comparisons of nineteen different symbol shapes. A triangle on a point was judged to be the shape most associated with hazardousness. The four variants of equilateral triangles were rated within the top eight symbols. Other high-ranking symbols tended to have sharp angles, e.g., a square on a point, an octagon, a hexagon, and a pentagon.

Annotations (401-500)

Key Words:
Design of: labeling and safety signage systems,
Duty/Failure to Warn,
Testing

421
Riley, M.W., Cochran, D.J. and Ballard, J.L., "Designing and Evaluating Warning Labels," *IEEE Transactions on Professional Communication*, 25:3, September 1982, 127-130.

The authors provide a general introduction to why warning labels are necessary and describe characteristics that warning labels must meet in order to be effective. They also address the role of testing as a necessary requirement in the process of evaluating the effectiveness of particular warning labels. They describe, at an introductory level, how such testing should be performed and how results from such tests should be analyzed.

Key Words:
Advertising,
Caustic Materials,
Design of: labeling and safety signage systems,
Explosives,
Fire,
Loss Prevention Programs,
Poison,
Radiation

422
Riley, M.W., Cochran, D.J. and Deacy, J.E., "Warning Label Design," *Professional Safety*, October 1981, 44-46.

Safety considerations can conflict with sales, advertising, legal, material, and financial interests. Certain individuals may feel that warnings may be economically disadvantageous. The following general procedure for assembling data for label development is outlined: 1) obtain top management commitment to quality, reliability, and product safety; 2) apply fault tree analysis and failure modes and effects analysis; 3) test and evaluate a product under all foreseeable uses and keep detailed records; 4) evaluate the trade-off of product risk versus utility; 5) identify the product with its users; 6) evaluate and apply quality control; 7) decide on trade-offs between safety and production costs attributable to warning labels; 8) devise a feedback system; 9) maintain state-of-the-art technology; 10) keep a rein on sales pitches; 11) design a label which includes warnings that reasonably identify hazards that cannot be avoided by using safety devices; and 12) conduct and document effectiveness tests on the label.

We note that this last recommendation is not trivial; its results may have serious impact on the earlier recommendations. Even if the earlier recommendations are not followed, this procedure can answer the ultimate question; will the label be effective in eliciting the desired behavior?

Key Words:
ANSI,
Fire,
Personal Protective Equipment,
Prohibition

423
Roberts, J.H., "A Sign of the Times, Greater Use of Safety Symbols by Industry Predicted," *National Safety News*, June 1974, 104-105.

The author discusses the impact of ANSI Z35.1. He then makes a case for the increased use of symbols because of the standard.

Key Words:
Development Programs,
Traffic

424

Robertson, A., "A Road Sign for Warning of Close-Following: Form and Message Design," Crowthorne, Berkshire, Transport and Road Research Laboratory, TRRL Supplementary Report 324, 1977, 1-12.

One hundred randomly selected drivers viewed a film simulating the presence beside the road of six sign variants warning of the danger associated with following vehicles too closely. The subjects then completed questionnaires. Evaluation of the responses showed that two designs were generally acceptable, but no particular design appeared to be outstanding. These two designs were purely verbal, whereas the other messages were either purely symbolic or a combination of text and symbols.

Key Words:
Crosswalk,
Pedestrians

425

Robertson, H.D., "Pedestrian Signal Displays: An Evaluation of Word Message and Operation," *Transportation Research Record*, 629, 1977, 19-22.

The research reported in this paper was concerned with two problems. The first was that pedestrians complained about not having enough walk time to complete their crossing at street intersections. Pedestrians did not understand that a clearance interval was provided so that they could complete crossing the street before traffic resumed. The second problem focused on the effectiveness of the flashing signal as a warning to pedestrians that vehicles might be turning through the crosswalk.

The following experimental conditions were developed to investigate these problem areas: 1) comparison of steady DON'T WALK (DW) indication to the standard FLASHING DON'T WALK (FDW) indication; 2) replacement of DW message with a DON'T START (DS) message; and 3) comparison of STEADY WALK (W) to FLASHING WALK (FW). These three conditions were investigated in Buffalo, New York and Phoenix, Arizona. No behavioral differences were found between the indicators of condition #1. Except at one site in Phoenix, no behavioral differences occurred for condition #2. For condition #3. a number of differences were found in the behavioral data from Buffalo, but not from Phoenix. All differences favored the FW condition. Of particular interest in condition #3 was the finding that only 2.5% of the four hundred pedestrians surveyed understood the intended meaning of FW and steady W. Evidence suggested a need for instructions for increasing pedestrian awareness of turning vehicles. Pedestrians' observance of crossing signals varied slightly from intersection to intersection, but varied greatly from one city to the next.

The authors conclude that the DS message offers little or no improvement over the current DW message. They also note that pedestrians' observance of crossing signals varies from intersection to intersection and from city to city.

426
Robertson, L.S., "Chapter 5: Control Strategies: Educating and Persuading Individuals," in *Injuries: Causes, Control Strategies and Public Policy*, Insurance Institute for Highway Safety, Lexington, 1983, 91-115.

Key Words:
Design of:
  educational/persuasive programs,
Effectiveness of:
  educational/persuasive programs,
Evaluation Difficulties,
Review Papers

This is an excellent survey paper on the influence of education and persuasion in inducing behavioral change. Generally, pessimistic conclusions are drawn regarding driver education, drug and alcohol education, child pedestrian safety skills, information from physicians about child restraints, fire alarms, suicide, and mass media campaigns. More positive effects are attained by health department surveys, behavioral modification programs that continue to provide feedback, and experimental methods that alter perception.

427
Robertson, L.S. and Zador, P.L., "Driver Education and Fatal Crash Involvement of Teenaged Drivers," *American Journal of Public Health*, 68:10, October 1978, 959-965.

Key Words:
Drivers,
Effectiveness of:
  educational/persuasive programs,
Formal Teaching/
  Counseling/Education

From a data analysis, it is concluded that the differences among the states in fatal crash involvement rates per 10,000 licensed eighteen- and nineteen-year-old drivers were not significantly related to driver instructional education courses in high school or to delayed licensing. The study analyzed a total of 103 years of experience with providing driver education to sixteen and seventeen year old drivers in twenty-seven states.

428
Robertson, L.S., "The Great Seat Belt Campaign Flop," *Journal of Communication*, Autumn 1976, 41-45.

Key Words:
Discrepancy Between
  Self-Reports,
Effectiveness of:
  educational/persuasive programs,
Radio/TV,
Review Papers

This paper provides a general review of the effectiveness of seat belt safety campaigns. Some of its interesting points include: claimed seat belt use generally exceeds actual use; radio and television messages appear to have no influence on belt use; mandatory laws substantially increase seat belt use; and, even in cases of legislative or administrative directives, compliance rarely exceeds 80%. Compliance levels of public school immunization requirements are cited as evidence for the last point. This and other examples are provided as evidence of the difficulty encountered in persuading people to take precautions.

Key Words:
Behavior Factors,
Drivers,
Effectiveness of:
  educational/persuasive
  programs,
Seat Belt Nonusers,
Seat Belt Reminder

429

Robertson, L.S., "Safety Belt Use in Automobiles with Starter-Interlock and Buzzer-Light Reminder Systems," *American Journal of Public Health*, 65:12, December 1975, 1319-1325.

The author states that it cannot be assumed that the presence of interlock and buzzer-light systems is sufficient to induce vehicle occupants to use safety belts. A study evaluating this issue was conducted at 138 sites in Baltimore, Houston, Los Angeles, as well as suburbs of New York City, Richmond, and Washington, D.C. Use or non-use of safety belts by drivers was observed at each of these sites. The observers were unaware that buzzer-light and interlock systems were being compared.

It was found that 48% of the drivers of 1974 vehicles equipped with the interlock system were using lap and shoulder belts, while 11% were using lap belts only. Also, 21% of the drivers of 1973 vehicles equipped with the buzzer-light system were using lap and shoulder belts, while 21% were using lap belts only. The introduction of the interlock system was therefore shown to increase belt use in 1974 vehicles in urban areas. Although the law resulted in high compliance, it has since been abandoned in response to strong negative public reaction.

Key Words:
Auditory,
Behavior Factors,
Discrepancy Between
  Self-Reports,
Drivers,
Seat Belt Reminder

430

Robertson, L.S. and Haddon, W., "The Buzzer-Light Reminder System and Safety Belt Use," *American Journal of Public Health*, 64:8, August 1974, 814-815.

From May through early July, 1972, safety belt use or non-use by drivers was visually observed at 152 sites in four different states. Of the 2,864 vehicles equipped with the buzzer-light system, 18% of the drivers used belts. In the 2,795 vehicles without this system, belts were used by 16% of the drivers. The difference between these two figures was not found to be statistically significant. In previous studies, drivers responding to a questionnaire said the buzzer-light system was effective in increasing belt use, but this was not consistent with the documented figures of actual use.

Key Words:
Drivers,
Effectiveness of:
  educational/persuasive
  programs,
Radio/TV,
Seat Belt Nonusers

431

Robertson, L.S., Kelley, A.B., O'Neill, B., Wixom, C.W., Eiswirth, R.S. and Haddon, W., "A Controlled Study of the Effect of Television Messages on Safety Belt Use," *American Journal of Public Health*, 64:11, November 1974, 1071-1080.

The authors report on a study in which television campaigns were not found to affect the use of safety belts. This finding is

Annotations (401-500)

offered as evidence that approaches directed toward changing behavior are frequently inefficient and ineffective in reducing highway accidents and injuries.

Key Words:
Agreement with Symbol/Message,
Behavior Factors,
Conflicting Objectives,
Discrepancy Between Self-Reports,
Drivers

432
Robertson, L.S., O'Neill, B. and Wixom, C.W., "Factors Associated with Observed Safety Belt Use," *Journal of Health & Social Behavior,* **13, March 1972, 18-24.**

The authors note that it recently was shown that some people who report that they always use safety belts do not have the belts fastened when they are observed in their vehicles. Past research has identified several factors related to claimed use, one of these being formal education.

This study involved unobtrusive observations of driver safety belt use in three communities during October, 1970. Over 4,000 vehicle drivers were observed. Telephone interviews were also conducted to obtain ratings of lap and shoulder belts on a set of ten pairs of descriptive terms (the semantic differential technique was used). Of the more than 1,000 households identified as targets for the interview, 548 provided completed interviews.

The ratings were dependent on: 1) convenience and comfort of the belts; 2) the worth and safety of the belts; and 3) the degree of aesthetic appeal of the belts. Actual as opposed to claimed use of safety belts was determined to be quite low. Observed usage, from this or other studies, was not at or near the 40% estimate of the National Safety Council. The authors state that comfort and convenience are the elements most amenable to change, and that many current belt designs are neither comfortable nor convenient.

Key Words:
Consumers,
Control/Display Elements,
Design of: labeling and safety signage systems,
Development Programs,
Electrical Hazard,
Explosives,
FMC,
Fire,
Hazard/Alert,
Industrial,
Personal Protective Equipment,
Point of Operation Guarding,
Slip/Fall

433
Robinett, F. and Hughes, A., "Chapter 21: Visual Alerts to Machinery Hazards: A Design Case Study," in *Information Design: The Design and Evaluation of Signs and Printed Material,* **Easterby, R.S. and Zwaga, H.J.G. (Eds.), John Wiley & Sons, New York, 1984, 405-417.**

This chapter emphasizes that man's ability to communicate is severely limited by his dependence on language as a primary means of visual transmission of information. Even within a single language system, individual variances in intellect, literacy, and technical terminology create difficulties in the effective transmission of thought. The authors present the necessary characteristics of a visual message that will attract the immediate attention of a user in jeopardy. The criteria of the FMC hazard warning system and suggested formats for safety labels and signs are discussed. Recommendations for the selection and design of pictograms, as well as the use of color, are also presented. (Also see Rosenberg, 1981.)

Key Words:
Warning Process Models

434
Robinson, G.H., "Human Performance in Accident Causation: Toward Theories on Warning Systems and Hazard Appreciation," *Third International System Safety Conference*, Washington, D.C., 1977, 55-69.

Robinson proposes a unique information processing approach to the warnings issue utilizing models which, while previously available, had not been so specifically applied to warnings. He begins by noting the lack of human performance theory, models, and data applicable to accidents. Concepts from human performance are used to structure and explain the functions and limitations of warning systems and hazard appreciation by skilled operators. Particular emphasis is given to obvious hazards. He states that the function of a warning system is to call an operator's attention to some condition requiring or prohibiting a particular action.

Robinson notes that warnings vary from the abstract to the highly detailed, use different sensory channels, and usually contain little explicit information, relying instead on the listener's skill and experience. In a successful warning scenario, the operator's full attention is captured, and the appropriate response is performed within the required time. Two common failures in warning systems are the failure to capture the operator's attention and the failure of the operator to execute the proper response within the required time period.

An information processing view of the human mind is illustrated by following a warning light signal through the human information processing stages: 1) visual transducing; 2) attention (filtering out excessive information); 3) recognition (memory matching); 4) decision (searching the memory for an appropriate response); and 5) motor output. The assumption underlying this modeling approach is that information flows through a single channel during task performance. In this scheme, a warning can be thought of as a signal that causes attention to be redirected at the appropriate time. The role of short term memory is also discussed with the observation that it is difficult to include this aspect in the information diagram. Robinson notes that responses cannot be retained in short term memory indefinitely, and once gone, will need a specific cue to return. Appropriate warnings can, of course, act as such cues.

A new definition of the function of warnings based on this analysis is provided: "A warning signal captures the operator's attention, freeing up his central processor to use its decision and short-term memory capabilities to retrieve appropriate safety responses from long-term memory and subsequently produce the necessary responses." He concludes that even a highly skilled operator must be warned if the appropriate data is to be placed into memory at the appropriate time. Regarding hazard appreciation, Robinson states that humans must understand both the consequences of hazard exposure and the way that contact with hazard occurs. He feels that people may fail to correctly understand how contact with hazard occurs because accidents are rare events, learning occurs by experience, and causation involves multiple complicated interactions of events.

Key Words:
Communication Theory,
Human Factors,
Level of Detail,
Overapplication of warnings,
Warning Process Models

435
Robinson, G.H., "Toward a Methodology for the Design of Warnings," *Proceedings of the Human Factors Society - 30th Annual Meeting*, **Human Factors Society, Santa Monica, CA, 1986, 106-110.**

This paper provides a general introduction to the complexity of the warning issue by placing it into a "systems context." Several important issues are introduced, including the importance of having qualified personnel design the warning, the need to consider multiple objectives and perform testing, and the necessity of observing actual use of the product. The paper also introduces "communication" theory as an important means of conceptualizing the use of warnings and discusses methods of deciding whether to provide a warning. The paper concludes with a brief discussion of the role of motivation and physical design variables.

Key Words:
Design of: labeling and safety signage systems,
Electrical Hazard,
Point of Operation Guarding,
Slip/Fall

436
Rosenberg, S., "FMC's Systematic Approach to Product Safety Warning Labels," *Agricultural Engineering*, **62:10, October 1981, 22-24.**

The article provides a general nonacademic introduction to the FMC sign system. The system was developed in the mid-1970s in response to FMC's legal needs as well as their desire to improve communication with consumers and users. Devising a set of "goodness" criteria for labels was not the original intent; the initial objective was to provide a uniform format for labels. It is noted that the number of parties supporting this systemic approach is increasing.

Key Words:
Adequacy of Warnings,
Design of: labeling and safety signage systems,
Duty/Failure to Warn,
Marketing Defects,
Negligence and Warnings,
Patent Danger,
Strict Liability and Warnings

437
Ross, K., "Legal and Practical Considerations for the Creation of Warning Labels and Instruction Books," *Journal of Products Liability,* **4, 1981, 29-45.**

This paper provides a general, well-done and easy-to-read introduction to the legal principles and human factors information relevant to the warning issue. In particular, strict liability, the duty to warn, warning sufficiency, and post-sale duty to warn are covered. The author states that a marketing defect involves: 1) the failure to provide any warning of the risks or hazards involved with product use; 2) the failure to provide an adequate warning of the dangers, risks and hazards involved in product use; and 3) the failure to provide appropriate and adequate instructions and directions for use of the product.

The duty to warn exists when: 1) the product is dangerous; 2) the hazard is known or should be known by the manufacturer or supplier; 3) the danger is not obvious, known to, or readily discoverable by the user; and 4) the danger is not one which arises only when the product is put to some unforeseeable, unexpected use. The courts have said that an adequate warning identifies the gravity of the risk, describes the nature of the risk so that the user will understand it, provides the user with instructions that will allow him to avoid the hazard, and clearly communicates the risk to the exposed person. Finally, general guidelines for the design of warnings and instruction books are provided.

Key Words:
Amount of Information,
Information Overload,
Level of Detail,
Memory of: symbol/message,
Reading Measures,
Reading of: warning labels,
Recall,
Students

438
Rothstein, P.R., "Designing Warnings to be Read and Remembered," *Proceedings of the Human Factors Society - 29th Annual Meeting,* **Human Factors Society, Santa Monica, CA, 1985, 684-688.**

This study investigated the effects of message length, serial position, message format, and pre-questioning on the recall of several forms of information. The presented labels contained instructional information falling into three categories: that which defined the hazard; ways of avoiding hazards; and countermeasures. The labels themselves were presented either as lists or paragraphs of varying length. The considered products were party string, adhesive, fake snow, and play dough. The subjects were undergraduate students.

The results showed that increasing the length of the warnings by including more elements marginally increased the recall of product information over that of the control group, but it also increased the percentage of intrusions (answers which were

Annotations (401-500)

incorrect, but correct for another product used in the experiment). The most notable positive effect found was for the counter measure instructions that told how to avoid the hazard. Even this effect was small; the subjects exposed to two to three times as many instructions on the average recalled only one more item. It was also discovered that the list format resulted in slightly better recall of countermeasure information than did the paragraph format. Interestingly, no significant serial position effect was found; items were recalled equally poorly regardless of their position in the lists. A final result was that including questions about the material in the warning only moderately increased recall.

Key Words:
Asbestos,
Punitive Damages,
Strict Liability and Warnings

439
Roy, R.F., "Torts—Damages—Punitive Damages Recoverable in a Strict Products Liability-Failure to Warn Action Based on Exposure to Asbestos," *Rutgers Law Journal*, 18:4, Summer 1987, 979-993.

In Fischer v. Johns-Manville Corp., the New Jersey Supreme Court recognized for the first time the right of a plaintiff pursuing a strict liability claim to recover punitive damages. When deciding whether or not to award punitive damages, the court ordinarily focuses its inquiry on the conduct of the defendant. In contrast, strict products liability virtually ignores the conduct of the defendant. The author explores the conflict between these two rules and the future of punitive damage awards in products liability cases.

Key Words:
MUPLA (Model Uniform Product Liability Act),
Post-sale Warning

440
Royal, R.A., "Post Sale Warnings: A Review and Analysis Seeking Fair Compensation Under Uniform Law," *Drake Law Review*, 33, 1983-1984, 817-862.

This article concerns the post-sale duty to warn with reference to drug cases, product cases and treatise law. The author discusses federal and state legislation and the Model Uniform Product Liability Act. He considers such issues as when the post-sale duty to warn arises, who should be warned, determining who is a user or consumer, methods of communicating a warning, and what information the warning should contain.

Key Words:
Cartoons,
Illustrations

441
Rubens, P., "The Cartoon and Ethics: Their Role in Technical Information," *IEEE Transactions on Professional Communication*, 30:3, September 1987, 196-201.

The author addresses the need to visualize and perhaps operationalize those elements of a cartoon which might make it a useful communication medium in conveying technical information. In an interesting analytical way the author notes that the use of the cartoon as a viable sign system requires consideration of three aspects: 1) Leveling, which is the deletion of extraneous objects and details; 2) Sharpening or enhancing particular objects so that they stand out from the background; and 3) Assimilation, which refers to the use of exaggeration and other deforming techniques to increase the imaginative detail.

Practical guidelines regarding the use of cartoons and technical illustration provided by the author include: 1) The use of cartoons to promote audience identification with the message; 2) The need to consider cultural implications during the design of cartoons, since the correct interpretation of cartoon figures is very much dependent on the culture within which the viewer is imbedded; 3) The use of cartoons to support specific tasks. (In particular, cartoons may be well suited for presenting introductory or tutorial information.); 4) The use of cartoons to promote audience participation, which, again, seems to be a function well performed by cartoons.

442
Rubinsky, S. and Smith, N., "Safety Training by Accident Simulation," *Journal of Applied Psychology*, 57:1, 1973, 68-73.

Key Words:
Behavior Factors,
Feedback,
Kinesthetic/Tactile,
Students,
Warnings: evaluating effects on behavior

The authors hypothesized that accident simulation as a training approach can be effective in reducing the number of unsafe acts and can contribute to the retention of superior habit patterns for at least six months. To test this, three experiments were conducted using an accident simulating device involving an exploding bench grinding wheel.

In particular, the accident simulation training method was compared to training by written instructions and demonstrations. The accident simulator consisted of a bench grinder with two water jets attached. A spray of water, controlled by the experimenter, simulated the explosion of a grinding wheel. To compare the different types of safety training, subjects were assigned to one of four test groups: Group 1 received written instructions and a standard demonstration of the grinding task; Group 2 received written instructions as well as a demonstration of the water jets; Group 3 received the same training as Group 1, except that an accident was simulated during a trial run rather than during the standard demonstration; Group 4 received the same basic instructions as the previous groups, but they were also subjected to a demonstration of the water jets as well as experiencing the simulated accident while standing in front of the grinder. Three separate experiments were conducted with only minor variations in the procedure.

Subjects in the first experiment were thirty-two male, college sophomores enrolled in an introductory psychology course. In the second experiment, seventy-two students from an introductory psychology course participated in the experiment. In the final experiment, the subjects were 120 sophomores ranging in age from eighteen to twenty-two years old.

Results indicated that the control group, which experienced no simulated accidents, was significantly more prone to commit unsafe acts (i.e., stand directly in front of the grinding wheel). In addition, no significant difference existed between any of the simulated accident groups. We considered this a rare study for its time—to instruct through an accident simulation and compare to a written instruction approach. The idea still seems ripe for further exploration.

443

Ruzicka, M., "Liability Based on Warnings," *Product Liability Prevention Conference*, **IEEE Catalogue No. 79CH1512-3 R, 1979, 75-78.**

Key Words:
Duty/Failure to Warn,
Negligence and Warnings,
Strict Liability and Warnings,
Warranties/Disclaimers

Ruzicka provides a general introduction to the manufacturer's liability for having no warnings or insufficient warnings. He notes that the difference between suits brought on the grounds of negligence, breach of warranty, and strict liability is more conceptual than practical, and he comments on the difficulty such suits pose to manufacturers. General guidelines are given regarding who must be warned and how to warn. Also noted is the lack of rules with a general application in the area of warnings. The most prominent of these rules implies that a warning complying with federal and state labeling requirements is adequate. However, excellent warnings do not serve as a substitute for eliminating hazards.

444

Ryan, J.J., "Strict Liability and the Tortious Failure to Warn," *Northern Kentucky Law Review*, **11, 1984, 409-433.**

Key Words:
Jury Instructions,
Strict Liability and Warnings

The author advocates imposition of strict liability for failure to warn in order to provide a stimulus for the practice of engineering safer designs by product manufacturers. The author also encourages plaintiff's attorneys to request special jury instructions on this issue, which include the statement that "an inadequate warning is, in legal effect, no warning."

Key Words:
Hazard Prevention/
Analysis Models

445
Ryan, J.P., "Hazard Analysis Guidelines in Product Design," *Professional Safety*, March 1988, 17-19.

The author provides, at an introductory level, several guidelines for hazard analysis in product design. The need for hazard analysis, in all stages of the product development cycle, is cited. Also provided are several "critical factors" relating to the safe use of products which are suggested for consideration during product hazard analysis.

Key Words:
Adequacy of Warnings,
Conduct of Consumer/
 User,
Duty/Failure to Warn,
Marketing Defects,
Negligence and
 Warnings,
Patent Danger,
Strict Liability and
 Warnings

446
Sales, J.B., "The Duty to Warn and Instruct for Safe Use in Strict Tort Liability," *St. Mary's Law Journal*, 13, 1982, 521-586.

This well-done law review article addresses the following issues: 1) When does the duty to warn arise?; 2) What is the duty of product suppliers?; 3) What are the types of risk that mandate a warning? (These are suggested as being the potential for inherent or intrinsic danger or harm, foreseeability of danger from unintended use, unusual susceptibility of harm in use of a product and the unavoidably unsafe products); 4) To what extent is the foreseeability of the risk of harm an indication of a duty to warn?; 5) What is the basis for a marketing defect (such as, absence of any warning of the risk of harm or danger, inadequacy of existing warnings, or lack of directions or instructions for safe and effective use)?; 6) What are the general prerequisites of an adequate warning?; 7) What are the factors that establish adequacy (such as, conspicuousness, symbols versus words, communication of risk of harm, location of warning, clear and unambiguous warning, sufficiently broad and encompassing warning, or an undiluted warning)?; 8) The focus of the duty to warn deals with what?; and 9) What are the limitations on the duty to warn (e.g., open and obvious dangers; common knowledge of the general public; common knowledge within a user's trade or profession; and modification of the product)?

Key Words:
Writing Instruction
 Guidelines

447
Samet, M.G. and Geiselman, R.E., "Developing Guidelines for Summarizing Information," *Human Factors*, 23:6, December 1981, 727-736.

The validity and generalizability of previously developed guidelines for summarizing military intelligence messages were tested in the present study. The treatment group was given the following set of guidelines to use in developing the summaries: 1) prepare the intelligence summary in a conversational style; 2) provide an interpretation of the intelligence information, if that is possible; and 3) provide a dynamic portrayal of the particular enemy situation.

Analysis showed that raters judged the individual summaries, prepared with the aid of the guidelines, to be significantly better than those prepared without the guidelines. A general outline for describing message content was derived from the summaries that received the highest overall evaluations.

448
Samet, M.G., Geiselman, R.E. and Landee, B.M., "A Human Performance Evaluation of Graphic Symbol-Design Features," *Perceptual and Motor Skills*, **54, 1982, 1303-1310.**

Key Words:
Accuracy,
Control/Display Elements,
Development Programs,
Elemental Breakdowns,
Laboratory/Generic Settings,
Reaction Time,
Recognition Time,
Symbol Generation,
Symbol Taxonomies

It was assumed here that complex tasks can be decomposed according to basic perceptual-cognitive processes required for successful performance. The design features of iconicity, vector projection, and perimeter density were investigated by examining their influence on speed and accuracy of performance. Four behavioral processes (identification, search, comparison, and pattern recognition) were considered as being relevant to performance. The subjects were eight males and eight females, all non-military, between the ages of twenty and thirty.

The authors found that blocked iconic symbols did not facilitate human performance over conventional, non-iconic Army symbols. Of the eight analyses of reaction time, significant effects of type of symbols were evident in two of them; both showed performance was better for the conventional ones. When complexity was defined as the number of different lines and angles present in the symbol, iconic symbols were more complex than conventional ones. This provided an explanation for the better performance of the conventional symbol condition. The authors also reported that there was a trade off between the amount of appended information portrayed at a given time and the speed of basic symbol manipulation.

449
Scammon, D.L., "'Information Load' and Consumers," *The Journal of Consumer Research*, **4, 1977, 148-155.**

Key Words:
Amount of Information,
Consumers,
Information Overload,
Memory of: symbol/message,
Recall

Subjects were shown TV commercials which provided nutritional information about two brands of peanut butter. Nutritional information was provided on labels varying in the number of nutritional properties (four versus eight) and the nutritional information format (numerical versus adjectival ratings).

The results showed that nutritional data was understood better when it was presented in the adjectival format. Data on recall showed that items in four item lists were recalled better than the same items in eight item lists. Preference data, however, did not reflect the nutritional knowledge of subjects: even if one brand was perceived as being more nutritious it would not necessarily be the brand purchased. The researcher concludes that the recall data supports the theory that the presentation of too much information on multiple dimensions results in a division of information processing capacity.

450
Schneider, K.C., "Prevention of Accidental Poisoning Through Package and Label Design," *Journal of Consumer Research*, 4, September 1977, 67-74.

Key Words:
Behavior Factors,
Children,
Color Coding,
Consumer Setting,
Consumers,
Poison,
Signal Words,
Warnings: evaluating effects on behavior

Various label- and container-related factors were evaluated in an attempt to determine how the presence of information (and its size, if present) influence the behavior of children toward hazardous products. The factors considered were: 1) written label warnings (absent, small, large); 2) pictorial label warnings (absent, Mr. Yuk, skull and crossbones); 3) package color (red, white, black); 4) package shape (round, triangular, square); and 5) package fragrance (none, pleasant, antiseptic). Eighty-one subjects in the forty-two to sixty-six month age range were left alone in a room for three minutes with the container and other playthings; subject behavior was recorded via a hidden video camera. The experiment was designed as a 1/3 replicate of a factorial manipulation of the considered factors.

Only one significant effect was obtained: subjects were more attracted to containers with writing on them (e.g., DANGER—POISON) than containers without writing (19% versus 44.5%). Non-significant effects were: 1) pictorial warnings: absent (41%), Mr. Yuk (37%), skull & crossbones (30%); 2) package color: red (26%), white (48%), black (33%); 3) shape: round (30%), triangular (30%), square (48%); and 4) fragrance: none (30%), pleasant (33%), antiseptic (44%). Interestingly enough, there was a 67% attraction to the skull and crossbones symbol combined with the antiseptic fragrance, and a 56% attraction to the pleasant smell and the Mr. Yuk symbol. We note that these results are noteworthy for their non-intuitive nature, but the experiment was not large enough to allow statistical significance to be accurately accessed.

451
Schoff, G.H. and Robinson, P.A., *Writing and Designing Operator Manuals*, Wadsworth Inc., Belmont, CA, 1984.

Key Words:
Adequacy of Warnings,
Advantages of Nonverbal Symbols,
Amount of Information

This book is a concise and well done 158 page guide for creating operator manuals. The authors use a basic "how to" approach to

Annotations (401-500)

Key Words (cont.):
Cartoons,
Consumer Labeling and
 Signage Systems,
Conveying Action,
 Conditions, Procedures,
Describing Objects,
Design of: instructions,
Development Cycle,
Durability,
Duty/Failure to Warn,
FMC,
Hazard/Alert,
Illustrations,
Indexes/Quick
 References,
Industrial,
Instructions in Litigation,
Legal Style,
Legibility,
Organizing Information,
Page Layout,
Problems in Design,
Readability Measures,
Signal Words,
Tables and Flowcharts,
Titles,
Translation of
 Instructions,
Typeface/Font,
User Modeling,
Writing Instruction
 Guidelines,
Writing Instructions

assist writers, photographers, artists, engineers, technicians, and managers in the development of operator, owner, and user manuals. Examples of photography, drawings, charts, tables, and various writing techniques are provided. Major topics addressed in the book include:

1) project planning,
2) analyzing the manual user,
3) manual organization and writing strategies,
4) format, layout, and mechanics,
5) visual display of information,
6) strategies for safety warnings and instructions,
7) development of service as opposed to operator manuals,
8) manuals for international markets, and
9) managing and supervising manual production.

The authors themselves are associated with the Technical Communications and General Engineering departments at the University of Wisconsin which should be a good background from which to write such a book. They advise on the dust jacket that : "The book's valuable techniques and principles can be applied in creating manuals for virtually any product—be it household, automotive, chemical, recreational, or biomedical. Whether you produce instructions for assembly and operation or for troubleshooting, service, and repair, you'll find this an indispensable on-the-job reference and resource for learning how to: analyze user needs; plan large- and small-scale design strategies; write clear instructions; avoid ambiguous wording in developing safety messages; choose visuals and control design elements; format the manual; and coordinate the writing effort. Many examples and illustrations are included throughout. There's also a special chapter on writing for international markets."

We find that book should be among the collections of those practitioners who are writing either instruction or operator manuals.

Key Words:
Consumer Setting,
Contrast,
Design of: labeling and
 safety signage systems,
Ingress/Egress,
Luminance,
Visual Acuity

452
Schooley, L.C. and Reagan, J.A., "Visibility and Legibility of Exit Signs, Part 1: Analytical Predictions," *Journal of the Illuminating Engineering Society*, **October 1980, 24-28.**

This general review paper provides an analytical assessment of factors influencing the visibility and legibility of exit signs found in commercial buildings. Key among these factors discussed are: visual acuity, contrast, and threshold illumination.

Key Words:
Drivers,
Illumination Level,
Ingress/Egress,
Legibility Distance,
Luminance,
Visual Noise

453

Schooley, L.C. and Reagan, J.A., "Visibility and Legibility of Exit Signs, Part 2: Experimental Results," *Journal of the Illuminating Engineering Society*, **October 1980, 29-32.**

Four tests were conducted in an interior corridor 10 ft. wide, 12 ft. high, and 399 ft. long. Three men and two women, ranging in age from twenty-two to fifty-five, participated. All five of the subjects were licensed drivers who were required to wear corrective lenses.

The first test required each observer to determine the maximum distance at which an unlit electric sign, as well as an illuminated electric sign, were visible, distinguishable, and legible under clear conditions. In the second test, each subject was asked to determine the minimum foot-lamberts of internal illumination needed to make a standard electric exit sign legible under clear conditions. Test 3 was similar to Test 1, except that smoke was introduced into the corridor and the five observers walked through the testing site simultaneously, starting at a distance of 200 ft. from the signs. In Test 4, observers were positioned 75 ft. from the signs, and after a smoke candle was burned, viewed three exit signs.

From Test 1, the performance of all signs was virtually identical, all were visible at between 275 and 325 ft., all were distinguishable between 200 and 250 ft., and all were legible between 100 and 200 ft. Test 2 results indicated that increasing the brightness of the electric sign did not have a major effect on influencing legibility and could be harmful under certain conditions when thresholds were exceeded. The presence of moderately dense smoke in the corridor significantly affected the results just mentioned. In the clear corridor case, brightness was not identified as a significant factor. In the smoky corridor case, brightness is a significant factor. The authors' concluded that raising the brightness levels of electric signs increased visibility, but did not significantly affect legibility under smoke conditions, and, in the case of clear conditions, caused blurring.

Key Words:
State of the Art Defense

454

Schubert, J.C., "Uncertainty in the Courts—Should Manufacturers Be Held Liable for Failing to Warn of Scientifically Undiscoverable Hazards?" *Journal of Products Liability*, **7:1, 1984, 107-117.**

The majority of courts would not impose liability for failure to warn of scientifically undiscoverable hazards. A minority do, however, hold that a manufacturer can be held liable for failing to warn of a product hazard, even if the hazard was scientifically undiscoverable at the time of manufacture and sale. The authors examine both approaches in light of several recent cases.

455
Schucker, R.E., Stokes, R.C., Stewart, M.L. and Henderson, D.P., "The Impact of the Saccharin Warning Label on Sales of Diet Soft Drinks in Supermarkets," *Journal of Public Policy and Marketing*, 2, 1983, 46-56.

Key Words:
Agencies,
Buying Behavior,
Consumers,
Effectiveness of:
  educational/persuasive programs,
FDA,
Government Involvement,
Labels,
Newspapers,
Radio/TV

The authors evaluate the impact of the Saccharin Study and Labeling Act, passed by Congress in 1977, which required, among other things, that retail stores selling products containing saccharin prominently display saccharin notices and place conspicuous warning labels on products containing saccharin. The language of the warning label as specified in this act stated that: "Use of this product may be hazardous to your health. This product contains saccharin which has been determined to cause cancer in laboratory animals."

To evaluate the impact of the warning labels, the authors developed a model that specified soft drink sales as a dependent variable and the presence of a warning label, price of product, news reporting and diet drink advertising as independent variables. Also accounted for were seasonal trends of sales.

The results indicated that the warning label was associated with a reduction of sales of approximately 6%, and as such, was statistically significant. More detailed demographic analysis indicated that the label's impact was initially shown in better educated households; then it ultimately influenced the purchase behavior of households with young children. On the other hand, the warning label had no apparent moderating effect on the soft drink purchase habits of older consumers. News and media effects also had no apparent effect on diet soft drink sales. Similarly, advertising was not statistically significant. Seasonal effects and pricing were, on the other hand, quite significant in their impact. The authors conclude with a discussion of the public policy implications of these findings to public information programs in general.

456
Schumacher, G.M. and Waller, R., "Chapter 14: Testing Design Alternatives: A Comparison of Procedures," in *Designing Usable Texts*, **Duffy, T.M. and Waller, R. (Eds.), Academic Press Inc., Orlando, 1985.**

Key Words:
Organizing Information,
Task Analysis,
Testing Procedures,
User Modeling

The authors address the need for obtaining user feedback during the development of technical instructions. They note that there are numerous techniques for evaluating technical instructions. Desirable characteristics for these techniques include: prompt provision of results which are in a usable or applicable form; relevance to specific design-related questions which may come to bear; high reliability and validity of results; ease of use; and cost effectiveness.

The authors then review several techniques for evaluating a document's design. They divide these into two major categories. The first category emphasizes outcome measures. These measures include: 1) readability formulas, 2) performance tests based on document use, 3) structural analysis, and 4) user ratings from questionnaires based on usage trials. It is noted that readability formulas are probably most widely-used evaluation technique; however, the information provided by such analysis is usually too global to provide specific help in determining how to provide a well-designed document. Performance tests place emphasis on determining how well people remember, understand and use text; such measures are typically developed during some form of laboratory study and can quite often be obtained quickly, easily and inexpensively. The weak point of performance testing is that it provides little guidance as to how the text should be improved. Structural analysis has been directed toward describing the organization of text content by "mapping" the relationship of ideas presented in the text. Although structural analysis provides a formal description of how the information is presented, the author feels that the technique often provides little direct guidance as to how the structural properties influence comprehension and usability. User ratings provide probably the least formal of these outcome measure related procedures. Although user ratings have often been used by textbook publishers and others, the obtained ratings often are less reliable than those obtained by readability formulas and are often difficult to interpret.

The second major category of measures are termed process measures. Process oriented measures of text design include: 1) user edits of the text; 2) protocol analysis; 3) micro-eye movements; 4) macro-eye movements; and 5) macro-processing procedures. Process orientated measures have been a more recent development than the outcome oriented measures summarized above.

Among these approaches the evaluation of user edits is probably the simplest and easiest method to apply. This method consists of providing texts to potential users and having the individual work through the document page by page. In so doing, problems in the text can be identified. This approach, however, can be quite time consuming and data are often very difficult to summarize.

2) Protocol analysis involves having subjects think aloud as they attempt to understand the document which is being evaluated. This procedure, obviously, results in a massive amount of information from each subject which then must be analyzed to determine what difficulties or problems a user tends to have and/or what general processes users employ while trying to understand the text. Major drawbacks of this procedure are the vast amount of data generated and the difficulty in efficiently analyzing this information.

3) Micro and 4) macro eye movement procedures involve different methods of monitoring the eye movement patterns of people as they read the text. From such information, inferences can be made as to how the text is being used. Macro studies generally differ from the micro studies, in that, less precise measurements are taken such as at the sentence or paragraph level rather than at the word or character level. These eye movement related approaches do provide useful information but often are difficult to apply because of the need for specialized equipment. Methods for analyzing the data so generated are also quite labor intensive.

5) Macro processing procedures are concerned with determining how readers integrate information obtained from different parts of the text or from multiple sources of information. The Study Protocol Recorder is described as an approach falling into this category. This device provides a record over a period of up to several weeks of which pages in the text are consulted as well as how much time is spent consulting various pages. By analysis of page sequences, conclusions can be derived as to how information is integrated during the comprehension process. Such techniques could be highly useful when analyzing the comprehensibility of large documents.

The authors conclude that there are a wide variety of techniques available for the evaluation of technical material and that there has been a remarkable growth in the development of new process measures to aid document design since the mid-1970s. The newer process measures provide a method for helping designers make decisions during the earlier stages of document design on the basis of experimental information rather than tacit knowledge or assumptions. It has yet to be proved that such techniques can play a practical role in text design but if so their role could be quite important.

Key Words:
Behavior Factors,
Buying Behavior,
Perceived Risk

457

Schwartz, D.R, dePontbriand, R.J. and Laughery, K.R., "The Impact of Product Hazard Information on Consumer Buying Decisions: A Policy-Capturing Approach," *Proceedings of the Human Factors Society - 27th Annual Meeting*, **Human Factors Society, Santa Monica, CA, 1983, 955-957.**

Twenty-four male and female undergraduates rated their propensity to buy and use cleaning products. Information was furnished concerning: effectiveness (how much time is needed to clean an object when using the product); cost per cleaning application; and eye and skin hazards (the probability of a bee sting-like injury was supplied as odds). Multiple regression analysis revealed that effectiveness, cost, and hazard significantly contributed ($p<.001$) to the subjects' propensity to buy a given item (total R^2 of .875). The regression model indicated that subjects were willing to sacrifice economy and effectiveness for increased safety.

Key Words:
Search Time,
Visual Displays:
  miscellaneous,
Workload/Task

458

Schwartz, D.R., "The Impact of Task Characteristics on Display Format Effects," *Proceedings of the Human Factors Society - 32nd Annual Meeting*, **Human Factors Society, Santa Monica, CA, 1988, 352-356.**

The author reports on a study of how task and display format influenced the performance and perceived difficulty of the performance of subjects. The six stimulus formats were displayed on a Macintosh computer and were used for each of the four tasks. The tasks included: a scanning task, a pattern detection task, a multiple queue judgement task and an energy allocation task.

The scanning task corresponded to low complexity and no monitoring; pattern detection corresponded to low complexity with monitoring; multiple queue judgement corresponded to high complexity but no monitoring; and the energy allocation task corresponded to high complexity with monitoring. Interestingly, there did not appear to be any clear effects of format in the pattern detection, multiple queue judgement or energy allocation tasks. However, performance in the scanning task did vary significantly with the format dimensions. Scanning performance appeared to be predictable on the basis of stimulus format variables, as did self reports of scanning difficulty. It was also found that there was a low correlation between perceived difficulty ratings and actual performance. The authors conclude that these results indicate that undue consideration of the subjective impressions of users regarding best designs might lead to the adoption of inadequate or sub-optimal design criteria.

We note that such conclusions have clear implications toward studies of warning label effectiveness which have emphasized the perceived desirability of warning label designs as a primary criteria of "goodness."

459
Schwartz, S.P., "Consumer Attitudes Toward Product Labeling," in *Product Labeling and Health Risks*, Morris, L.A., Mazis, M.B. and Barofsky, I. (Eds.), Cold Spring Harbor Laboratory, Banbury Report 6, 1980, 89-96.

Key Words:
Consumer Preferences,
Government Involvement,
Reading of: warning labels

This article reviews several studies dealing with consumer attitudes and behavior in relation to product labels. Among such studies, 1) Thorelli et al. (1975) found that the average consumer in Indianapolis rated consumer protection methods in the following order of importance: preventing misleading advertising (3.7 rating score); product testing and reporting (3.0); consumer protection labeling (3.0); product information labeling (2.9); helping consumers with complaints (2.7); providing consumer education in schools (2.4); and establishing minimum quality standards (2.3).

2) Thorelli also asked respondents to indicate if there should be governmental involvement in the following seven areas: prevention of misleading advertising (47% agreed there should be); consumer complaints (45% agreed); minimum quality standards (42%); product testing (40%); information labeling (32%); consumer protection (28%); and consumer education (23%).

3) A Shell Oil Company study found that 66% of a representative sample of American thought that it is important that proof be established before a product is labeled a carcinogen; 21% thought it was somewhat important; 7% thought it wasn't very important. On the other hand, 56% of all respondents (66% of chemical workers) thought substances should be clearly labeled, and workers should be encouraged or even forced to be careful with these substances, while 29% disagreed (17% of chemical workers). Regarding carcinogen exposure, 64% of the sample (71% of chemical workers) thought the government should regulate involuntary exposure to carcinogens more strictly (18% and 15% disagreed). In another topic, 72% of the respondents (81% in the chemical industry) preferred making their own decisions regarding the use of carcinogenic products rather than having the government ban the product (23% and 16% thought the opposite). It was agreed by 72% of the respondents that carcinogens should not be allowed to be added to food or drugs; 17% thought the opposite.

The following results were obtained from studies of food labelling: 1) An FDA study (1975) showed that 70% of respondents looked at price; 41% at ingredients; 26% at additives; and 26% at nutritional information. Also, it was interesting that 25% were not willing to pay anything for nutritional data. 2) A later FDA study (1978) showed an increased emphasis on ingredients (50%). 3) Smith, et. al. (1979) revealed that 67% of shoppers thought ingredient information was very useful (65% in 1976); 63% thought nutritional information very useful (55% in 1976); and 90% thought dates and price very useful. 4) Woman's Day in 1980 indicated that 50% of the persons sampled sometimes considered nutritional information; 21% considered nutritional information a lot; 43% would occasionally put a product back on the shelf after noticing it contained unsatisfactory ingredients; 66% wanted more nutritional labeling even if it increased an item's cost; 43% were very concerned about pesticides (30% were fairly concerned); 35% were very concerned about nutritional labeling; 31% were concerned about additives; 31% were concerned about preservatives; 23% were concerned about artificial color; and 17% were concerned about the use of saccharin. In general, the older persons in the reviewed studies had less desire for labeling information.

Key Words:
Duty/Failure to Warn,
Point-of-sale Duty to Warn,
Post-sale Warning

460
Schwartz, V.E., "The Post-Sale Duty to Warn: Two Unfortunate Forks in the Road to a Reasonable Doctrine," *Defense Law Journal*, **33, 1984, 261-274.**

Traditionally, a manufacturer's duty to warn consumers about the hazards associated with its product has taken two distinct forms: a "point of sale" duty to warn about hazards discovered before the product is sold and a "post-sale" duty to warn about those discovered after. The author examines the post-sale duty which has historically only required a reasonable effort to alert customers. He argues that a more onerous post-sale duty would be undesirable in view of the practical difficulties and expense involved in contacting product users once the product leaves the manufacturer's control. He criticizes the recent judicial trend toward a more demanding post-sale duty.

Key Words:
Adequacy of Warnings,
Application Guidelines,
Communication Theory,
Conduct of Consumer/User

461
Schwartz, V.E. and Driver, R.W., "Warnings in the Workplace: The Need for a Synthesis of Law and Communication Theory," *Cincinnati Law Review*, **52, 1983, 38-83.**

The authors approach their topic by combining legal analysis and the principles of communication theory. The reasons why

Annotations (401-500)

Key Words (cont.):
Design of: labeling and safety signage systems,
Duty/Failure to Warn,
Human Factors,
Loss Prevention Programs,
Negligence and Warnings,
Overapplication of Warnings,
Strict Liability and Warnings

warnings are frequently a legal issue are summarized: 1) almost all products involve danger, particularly if misused; 2) in most cases a product can be used safely if adequate information is available; 3) warning information is inexpensive and does not reduce the utility of the product; 4) there is often a desire to compensate victims; 5) warnings are considered easy to litigate, since the warning issue is assumed to be less complex than other technical issues; and 6) an absence of scientific or technical guidelines allows adequacy to be decided by juries. Problems with this approach are: 1) legal rules regarding warnings are developed within an emotional case by case basis; 2) no distinction is made between a consumer warning and an industrial warning; 3) manufacturers have a problem with employer product modification; 4) contact with employees is through the employer, not the manufacturer (e.g., there is no manufacturer control over training); and 5) this approach encourages the use of encyclopedic or legalistic warnings that are not effective.

It is proposed that clear legal guidelines based on the principles of communication theory be used to determine when and to whom warnings should be directed and how warning effectiveness should be judged. Those parts of communication theory which might have application to warnings include: 1) the process (communication is a continuous, dynamic, and irreversible process); 2) the transmission (communications must overcome barriers to such transmissions); 3) media and channels; 4) the symbols used (verbal and non-verbal); 5) reception of transmitted information (reception is a function of semantics, receiver characteristics, perceptions, and environment); and 6) the meaning derived by the receiver (the same message may provide different meanings to different people).

Finally, applications of warnings to the workplace are evaluated. The major points in this evaluation are: 1) consumer and industrial products differ (industrial products are often more dangerous and complicated; normal industrial use includes service and repair; industrial users are well-trained and require more detailed product information; the employer is between the manufacturer and the user; and the influence of worker's compensation); 2) it is unlikely that warning labels can adequately transmit sufficiently detailed information; 3) training is necessary for many tasks; 4) since it is difficult for the manufacturer to supply training, the responsibility should be the employer's; 5) written warnings have a limited ability to draw attention to themselves; and 6) since certain types of information are difficult or impossible to communicate through written channels, warnings are not a substitute for training.

The conclusion is drawn that if manufacturers are held liable for accidents they could not reasonably be expected to prevent, the effect is the same as that of imposing strict liability on manufacturers. The authors' proposed solution is to force employers to communicate safety information through training and supervision. In other words, the manufacturer warns the employer, but it is the employer's responsibility to warn users. We suggest that this concept comes close in principle to the learned intermediary theory.

462
Sell, R.G., "What Does Safety Propaganda Do for Safety? A Review," *Applied Ergonomics*, **December 1977, 203-214.**

Key Words:
Actual Behavior,
Design of: labeling and safety signage systems,
Message Tone,
Review Papers,
Warnings: evaluating effects on behavior

In this paper the author reviews pre-1971 articles concerning the success of safety propaganda and safety training. He distinguishes between training and propaganda, stating that propaganda is an attempt to change the attitudes and/or the behavior of people who are not specifically in a learning situation and who do not expect, and may not even be aware of, the information and instructions being given. A distinction is made between general and specific propaganda, and it is stated that specific propaganda is more likely to be effective. The aims of propaganda are listed as: providing safety knowledge, changing worker attitudes, and ensuring safe behavior.

Sell notes that ergonomic considerations may be related to accidents, and that risk taking may be influenced by company philosophy, job design, and economic factors which may mask the effects of safety propaganda. Other factors which complicate the evaluation of propaganda programs are: 1) physiological effects of propaganda do not define expressed or actual behavior; 2) accident rates are subject to many factors, making the effects of propaganda hard to show; 3) errors and dangerous actions are a major concern; 4) propaganda may alter reporting activity; 5) there is a need for pre-testing; 6) there is a need for control groups; 7) there may be subject selection bias; and 8) there may be individual differences in susceptibility.

Literature documenting the effects of propaganda on behavior is reviewed and includes the following references: 1) Laner and Sell (1960). (reviewed earlier). 2) Belbin (1956). In an attempt to modify pedestrian crossing behavior by children, either slides, a talk by a police sergeant, cartoon slides, or a film plus a specific slide were given. Only the talk by the police sergeant affected behavior. Interestingly, there was no difference in recognition and recall of the given material between the children who crossed correctly and those who did not. 3) Kaestner (1960). Letters were sent out to traffic violators. Older drivers were not affected by letters, but younger drivers were susceptible to soft sell letters. 4) Chambers (1970). Thirty thousand leaflets describing the safe use of fireplace wood chip pans were sent to consumers. A significant drop in the number of fires was documented after the leaflets were distributed.

Literature documenting the effects of safety propaganda on attitudes is also reviewed and includes the following references: 1) Harper and Kalton (1966a). Two posters, one humorous and one serious were placed in a collier. The obtained results for recall and recognition were, respectively: a) both - recalled: 18.2%, recognized: 49%; b) neither - recalled: 52.3%, recognized 26.7%; c) humorous only - recalled: 18.3%, recognized 14.6%; d) serious only - recalled: 11.2%, recognized: 9.7%. Sixty-eight percent of the sample preferred the serious poster; 2) Harper (1966c). Some 65% of 1356 colliery workers thought training and supervision were more effective than propaganda, while 77% thought employees could do the most to prevent accidents. 3) Sheppard (1968). A drinking and driving propaganda campaign was evaluated in two surveys involving 2000 people. Sheppard found little effect on attitudes, but 80% of the subjects said they saw publicity concerning the campaign after it had started, and 60% claimed to have seen the publicity before the campaign had started. (We find the latter point of interest as it indicates the lack of reliability in either what subjects perceive or what they remember. It is also possible that such results evolve from poorly designated instruments.) 4) A fire research campaign was documented in which interviewers asked questions concerning homeowner fire knowledge, and in which the interviewers made comments concerning fire hazards. The result was that people with children were more inclined to ask questions after the campaign (58%) than before (45%). Although some increase in knowledge was noted, serious misconceptions remained, and the belief that fires break out quickly and trap people even if they behave sensibly rose by 20%. Similar results were obtained for two other campaigns.

Two studies of perception and comprehension were reviewed: 1) Ruckel and Folkman (1965). Perception of forest fire safety signs was studied as 1197 motorists driving by signs were questioned. For an experimental sign versus a standard sign, 15% versus 30% of subjects did not see any of the posted five signs, and 18% versus 44% of subjects were unable to recall any of the signs. 2) Winters (1963). Posters were shown to native South African workers. Only about half the subjects comprehended the posters because: a) symbols were not understood; b) depth and perspective were misinterpreted; c) behavior was not displayed according to native traditions; d) related scenes on a single poster were not connected; and e) captions did not help interpretation if the picture itself was not clear.

A final set of reviewed studies addressed the "message tone" of propaganda. These include: 1) Anon (1966). Posters were placed on the boarding steps of aircraft. The posters showed three levels of threat (low - a man holding the rail; medium - a man stumbling; or, high - a man sprawled at the bottom of the stairs). There were two levels of realism in that each of the above was illustrated with either a drawing or a photo. There were also two levels of specificity in that each of the above was presented with the words, "Safety first" or "Grasp the hand rail when boarding flights." The 2000 subject passengers entering the aircraft were observed. No effects due to realism or specificity were observed. A 6%, 13%, and 21% increase in grasping the railing was associated with the low, medium, and high threat. 2) Levanthal, et al. (1965). Students were given booklets which were either low or high fear arousing with a high or low specificity level of advice on tetanus shots. Eight of the nine subjects who chose to obtain shots were those who received high specific information on where to get shots. 3) Belbin (1965b). Posters were placed in a room where subjects sat for three minutes before identifying unsafe situations from 24 traffic photos. The presence of the safety posters increased identification of dangerous traffic situations. 4) Sheppard (1970). Drivers rated frightening posters as being more effective than non-frightening ones. 5) Wilkins and Sheppard (1970). A gruesome auto accident film was shown to subjects. Although the commentary explained why accidents occurred, only 1/3 of the subjects were able to remember these reasons. 6) Laner and Sell (1960). Some time after viewing the fire prevention commercial, "Nightmare," few subjects could recall the main message. 7) McKennel (1964). The horror sequences on lung cancer were studied. Subjects criticized posters that identified smokers with sheep, showed men smoking money, or that emphasized horror. They preferred posters that simply requested smokers to quit or to think before lighting up. A film stating that smoking causes lung cancer strengthened non-smokers' resolve to avoid smoking, but convinced many non-smokers that human lungs are strong and not easily damaged by smoking. 8) Beach (1966). Physiological measures, verbal responses and actual behavior as affected by a film on safety belts, with and without a horror sequence, were compared. Heart rate and stated intention to use belts were greater for subjects who viewed the film without the horror sequence, and actual installation of belts was slightly higher for those who viewed the low horror film. 9) Janis and Fesbach (1953). Low threat dental hygiene related information had a larger positive influence on teeth cleaning and dental visits by students than high threat information. 10) Berkowitz and Cottingham (1960). A high fear appeal for usage of safety belts was more convincing for subjects who rarely drive, prompting the theory that fear appeals are most effective for those to whom they are the least relevant. 11) Levanthal and Niles (1964). Various fear arousal messages regarding smoking were given to subjects attending a health fair. Smokers given the lowest fear arousal information were most likely to state that they would quit smoking. 12) McGuire

(1966). An interactive effect of concern and fear arousal on attitude change is suggested. At high levels of concern, low levels of fear arousal are more effective; at low levels of concern, high levels of fear arousal are more effective.

Sell then summarizes the use of and view toward propaganda by safety organizations, concluding that: 1) propaganda should be used as backup to training, not alone; 2) propaganda needs to be topical, noticeable, and frequently changed; and 3) horror posters only incite shock, not lasting effects. His final conclusions are: that posters should be specific, serve as back-up training, give a positive instruction, be placed close to the action, and emphasize non-safety aspects; they should not involve horror (which brings in defense mechanisms), not be negative (this can show an incorrect way of acting), or be general (almost all people think they behave safely).

Key Words:
Communication Theory

463
Shaw, M.E., "Communication Networks," in *Advances in Experimental Social Psychology*, 1, Berkowitz, L. (Ed.), 1964, 111-147.

This early but extensive general review paper discusses communication networks. The considered topics include: research methodologies, the effects of networks upon group process, explanatory concepts, independence and saturation in relation to other experimental variables. A summary with conclusions is provided.

Key Words:
Detection/Perception Measures,
Drivers,
Memory of: symbol/message,
Recall,
Recognition,
Traffic,
Traffic Settings,
Workload/Task

464
Shinar, D. and Drory, A., "Sign Registration in Daytime and Nighttime Driving," *Human Factors*, 25:1, 1983, 117-122.

The experimenters hypothesize that drivers will be more prone to notice signs containing information not easily obtained from the road, based on previous experiments which indicate that attentional-motivational factors rather than sensory-memory factors explain the low recall and recognition of road traffic signs. To test this hypothesis, an experiment was performed where drivers were stopped and asked to recall the last two road signs they had encountered; the two experimental signs were encountered two hundred meters away from the stopping point. Average sign recall and recognition was 4.5% and 8% during the day, and 16.5% and 20% during the night. Neither sign content nor roadway geometry significantly influenced recall or recognition. Since information is more difficult to acquire directly from the road at night, the researchers conclude that this data supports their hypothesis.

465

Key Words:
Readability Measures

Siegel, A.I., Federman, P.J. and Burkett, J.R., "Increasing and Evaluating the Readability of Air Force Written Materials," August, Brooks Air Force Base, Air Force Human Resources Laboratory, NTIS No. AD 786 820, 1974, 1-88.

This report describes, in a step-by-step fashion, how to apply techniques which have been used to evaluate the readability and comprehensibility of textual instructional materials. It also describes procedures for simplifying written materials and discusses experimental methods to determine the effectiveness of written material.

466

Key Words:
Organizing Information, Writing Instructions

Siegel, A.I., Lambert, J.V. and Burkett, J.R., "Techniques for Making Written Material More Readable/Comprehensible," August, Lowry Air Force Base, Air Force Human Resources Laboratory, NTIS No. AD 786 849, 1974, 1-24.

This report summarizes research directed toward enhancing both the readability and comprehensibility of Air Force training manuals, texts, and other written instructional materials by applying psycholinguistic and intellective concepts. The authors believe that the key to making written materials more understandable is to use materials that minimize the mental load needed to convey the information. Topics and recommendations aimed at increasing readability/comprehensibility include: 1) The use of morphemes. The authors' research indicates that readability may be increased more by reducing the number of morphemes per word than by reducing the number of letters per word; 2) Sentence voice - the authors state that their research indicates that the passive-negative voice should be avoided whenever possible; 3) Negativity problems - similar to the above recommendation, the authors suggest that negative words and morphemes be replaced, if possible, by positive phrases; 4) Self-embedding - The "center embedding" of a clause between the subject and the predicate of a sentence tends to confuse readers; and 5) Depth, complement, and branching - the authors suggest that breaking a long sentence into a number of shorter ones reduces sentence "depth" and increases readability.

In order to "help the reader's intelligence to work easily," the authors suggest that writers: 1) de-emphasize vocabulary diversity, 2) link up related thoughts for the reader, 3) aid readers in seeing generalizations, 4) eliminate unnecessary details presented in figures and diagrams, 5) repeat key facts, 6) organize material to facilitate the reader's goal(s), and

7) avoid abbreviations. The report concludes with a discussion of the various measures of readability.

Key Words:
Conveying Action,
Conveying Conditions,
Conveying Procedures,
Design of: instructions,
Prior Knowledge,
Problems in Design,
Task Analysis,
Understanding of Instructions,
Understanding/ Perception Models

467
Simon, H.A. and Hayes, J.R., "Chapter 14: Understanding Complex Task Instructions," in *Cognition and Instruction*, Klahr, D. (Ed.), Lawrence Erlbaum Associates, Hillsdale, NJ, 1976, 269-285.

Two generalizations are drawn from research addressing the causes of functional illiteracy: 1) as opposed to being a reading problem, functional illiteracy is primarily an understanding problem; and 2) following the instructions that an individual encounters in daily life is one of the most difficult tasks that people ordinarily face. It is stated that oral and written communication may affect understanding in different ways. Oral instructions may exceed the capacity limits of short-term memory. Differences due to voice stress and intonational cues, as compared to punctuation in written communication, are suspected to be minimal. It is speculated that problems may be poorly structured in that instructions may not contain enough information to allow a usable representation to be inferred from them, and that a poorly structured problem places excessive demands on the knowledge and resources of the solver's problem-solving skills. Irrelevance of information is distinguished from redundancy; according to the authors, redundancy may help the reader resolve ambiguities, while irrelevancy may make interpretation more difficult.

In analyzing these issues, the authors have developed and used a unique AI-based computer program that simulates human understanding of instructions. The UNDERSTAND program works in the following way. Input instructions are first analyzed syntactically; the analyzed text is then searched for sets of "objects" that need to be presented in the problem space; next a structure that permits objects and their relations to be represented is created; the text is searched for operators that change the relations among objects; and, finally, semantic memory is searched for possible semantic interpretations of the change operators.

Key Words:
Abstractness,
Accuracy,
Aircraft,
Aircraft Setting,
Control/Display Elements,
Pilots

468
Simonelli, N.M., "An Investigation of Pictorial and Symbolic Aircraft Displays for Landing," *Proceedings of the Human Factors Society - 22nd Annual Meeting*, Human Factors Society, Santa Monica, CA, 1978, 213-217.

Sixteen male flight instructors participated in this study which was designed to compare four different approach-to-landing displays. The flight experience of the subjects ranged from 285 to 1193 hours. Some pilots had prior experience in the simulator used in the study, and others had no previous experience. Overall, the best performance was achieved with a combination of both a pictorial approach "gate" symbology with a prospective runway and an electronic ILS-type display.

No reliable difference in lateral control performance were found to be attributable to the different displays, but the variability in performance tended to be less for displays with the perspective runway. For vertical control, those displays that contained the vertical deviation scale and pointer facilitated the best performance, regardless of the presence of the runway. Pictorial information was found to be beneficial in stabilizing lateral control, but the approach gates were not, by themselves, sufficient guidance cues for vertical control.

469
Simpson, C.A. and Williams, D.H., "Response Time Effects of Alerting Tone and Semantic Context for Synthesized Voice Cockpit Warnings," *Human Factors*, 22:3, 1980, 319-330.

Key Words:
Aircraft,
Aircraft Setting,
Auditory,
Auditory Coding,
Pilots,
Reaction Time,
Response Time,
Task Specific Context

The existing relevant studies are summarized. They show that: 1) combining auditory signals with visual displays can reduce response times significantly, and 2) voice warnings are an improvement over tones. It is then stated that the current assumption that voice warnings require an initial alerting tone is not supported by research.

An experiment was performed involving a simulated commercial jet transport flight and 4 airline pilots. Auditory warning messages using either semantic or key word contexts (the semantic context messages were .45 s longer on the average) preceded or not preceded by auditory tones .5 s before message initiation, were given to the pilots during their simulated flights. Mean system-response times (the times between message initiation and human response initiation) were 5.14 s for the key word context and 5.07 s for the semantic context. When the warning tone was present, the corresponding mean times were 5.75 s and 5.74 s. Although the presence of a tone actually increased system response time, pilots believed that the tone helped performance. The presence of extra semantic information in the messages was positively viewed by subjects and also reduced response time. Error analysis was not attempted because few errors were observed.

Annotations (401-500)

Key Words:
Risk Coping Style,
Warnings: evaluating
effects on behavior

470
Sims, J.H. and Baumann, D.D., "The Tornado Threat: Coping Styles of the North and South," *Science*, 176:4042, 30 June 1972, 1386-1392.

It is noted that in the southern portions of the United States, the number of deaths due to tornadoes is significantly higher than it is anywhere else in the nation. Interestingly, the casualty potential from tornadoes was found to be highest in an area running from Dallas through Topeka and Chicago, and ending in Detroit (Sadowski). The authors state that tornadoes are not more violent in the South. They also rule out possible differences in warning systems in various parts of the country. Until 1952, no community had the benefit of the nationwide tornado warning system, yet the South recorded the greatest frequency of tornado-caused deaths.

As a possible explanation of the discrepancy between Northern and Southern tornado deaths, the authors note that variations in socio-cultural groups have been related to internal versus external control. Data from this study indicated that Southerners may place more emphasis than Northerners on an external force (God) as a causal agent in their daily life. Based on this result, the authors concluded that Northerners are therefore likely to believe that they affect their own lives and can confront threats of tornadoes with their minds and technology. In conclusion, the authors state that a weak defense against a tornado strike is based on fatalism, passivity and a lack of trust resulting in inattentiveness to organized warning systems. On the other hand, it should be emphasized that the chance of a tornado striking is low, even after tornado warnings have been give. This may explain why a significant proportion of the population fails to heed these warnings in both the North and South; perhaps the prevalence of false alarms (i.e., a warning but no tornado) have led many people to ignore the warnings.

Key Words:
Basic Associations,
Cultural Factors,
Translation of
  Instructions,
Understanding of
  Instructions

471
Sinaiko, H.W., "Chapter 10: Verbal Factors in Human Engineering: Some Cultural and Psychological Data," in *Ethnic Variables in Human Factors Engineering*, Chapanis, A. (Ed.), Johns Hopkins University Press, Baltimore, 1975, 159-177.

This paper discusses the problems encountered when complex equipment designed for use in one country is transferred to another. The author notes that very little consideration is usually given to issues of speed of translation, handling unfamiliar terms, and accuracy of translating technical words. To improve the quality of translations, the following rules are suggested: 1) do not use long sentences; 2) do not use adverbs and prepositions that indicate degree; 3) do not use complex noun phrases; and 4) do not use abbreviations.

Studies reviewed in this paper indicated that the quality of translated material strongly influences performance. Translations by highly skilled bilinguals were superior to the best machine translations. However, whether a person is working in his native tongue or in a second language makes a significant difference. Comprehension scores for Vietnamese Air Force subjects were 66% for human translations, 57% for edited machine translations, and 41% for unedited machine translations. Illustrative figures in Western documents may present considerable difficulty for non-Western readers; and, people of different cultures use different conventions to portray and interpret three dimensions represented in two-dimensional space.

Key Words:
Understanding/
Perception Models

472
Singleton, W.T., "The Ergonomics of Information Presentation," *Applied Ergonomics*, December 1971, 213-220.

This paper addresses several general human information processing topics. Some of the topics included are: 1) The limits on information transmission: these limits are in the ranges of 5 to 10 bits/sec for key pressing, and 2 to 3 items/sec for auditory or visual processing. 2) Kidd's (1962) four-element error classification: a) failure to detect a signal (due to input overload, input underload, or to noisy conditions); b) incorrect identification of a signal (occurs when orientation cues are inadequate); c) incorrect weighting or incorrect action selection; and d) failure of the action (a wrong action at a right time, or a right action at a wrong time). 3) The limits on storage capacity for short-term memory (8 item or 30 bit limit). 4) The domination of auditory over visual interference. 5) Other points: Selective attention failure results in a narrowing of attention. Failure of perceptual organization results in reduction of size in data samples and action routines, or results in reduction in filtering efficiency. And, cumulative disruption results in a temporary opting out followed by restart.

Key Words:
Design of: labeling and safety signage systems,
Understanding/
Perception Models,
Visual Displays:
miscellaneous

473
Singleton, W.T., "General Theory of Presentation of Information," in *Displays and Controls*, Bernotat, R.K. and Gartner, K.P. (Eds.), Swets and Zeitlinger, N.V., Amsterdam, 1972, 75-81.

The author takes a general approach to display design, emphasizing the concepts of perception and sensation. The following eleven points are made: 1) sensation takes place over wide limits which should be easy to attain; 2) the problem is discrimination rather than intensity; 3) a visual signal can be defined by illumination, size, contrast, and available time; 4) visual noise is defined by glare and clutter; 5) an auditory signal is defined by amplitude, pitch and bandwidth, as is auditory noise; 6) sequential reduction of data is defined from sensation to attention to perception; 7) attention is defined by relevance; 8) the five basic perceptual systems are the basic orienting system, the visual system, the auditory system, the haptic system, and the taste-smell system; 9) learning to perceive involves differentiating the range of possible inputs, co-variation of inputs, isolation of external invariants, learning affordances, event invariance, and selective attention; 10) the levels of required information are objectives, strategies (alternatives and consequences) and tactics (the current state of the system); 11) the primary purpose of display design is to orient operators in time and space.

474
Sivak, M., Olson, P.L. and Pastalan, L.A., "Effect of Driver's Age on Nighttime Legibility of Highway Signs," *Human Factors*, 23:1, 1981, 59-64.

Young (18 to 24 years) and old (62 to 74 years) subjects either rode or drove in an automobile and watched for a small retro-reflective sign on the right side of the road. The two groups of subjects were matched on high-luminance visual acuity. Legibility distance for older subjects was lower than that of younger subjects for a wide range of signs under night viewing conditions.

Key Words:
Age,
Contrast Sensitivity,
Drivers,
Legibility Distance,
Traffic,
Traffic Settings

475
Sloan, G. and Eshelman, P., "The Development and Evaluation of Pictographic Symbols," *Proceedings of the Human Factors Society - 25th Annual Meeting*, Human Factors Society, Santa Monica, CA, 1981, 198-202.

It is stated that symbol development requires: 1) identification of situations that need warnings; 2) specification of an audience; 3) generation of the designs; 4) selection of the candidate designs; 5) determination of a best design; and 6) comparison to reasonable performance standards. Most studies have emphasized evaluation; the authors propose that the generation of symbols needs more study.

Their investigation consisted of four phases: 1) the development of symbol designs; 2) the ranking of designs by participants; 3) the analysis of negation signs; and 4) overall evaluation. In phase one, 34 warning symbols for oven and freezer related

Key Words:
Basic Associations,
Consumers,
Conveying Action,
Design of: labeling and safety signage systems,
Development Programs,
Production Method,
Prohibition,
Symbol Generation

problems were generated. In phase two, 32 subjects compared these designs in a sequence of pair-wise comparisons. In phase three, 32 different subjects rated various methods of conveying negation information. A solid cross (more like an "x") was rated as being most indicative of negation. Reaction times and error rates for the cross and slash variants were not significantly different. In phase four, 32 new subjects evaluated the 12 top-ranked designs from Phase two. These were the 5 designs inspired by user input, and the 9 randomly selected designs from symbols used by manufacturers. The best designs were without exception generated from this study, and the worst were without exception provided by manufacturers.

The conclusion of the researchers was that obtaining inputs from potential users during symbol development increases the chance of generating effective designs. We point out that the sample sizes involved in this study were small. Nevertheless, it still may point out that the state-of-the-art among manufacturers in providing what they consider to be good symbol information will be significantly improved as human factors methodologies are applied to target user populations.

Key Words:
Acceptability,
Belief in Danger,
Frequency Estimates,
Perceived Risk,
Sources of Bias

476
Slovic, P., "The Psychology of Protective Behavior," *Journal of Safety Research*, 10:2, Summer 1978, 58-68.

This article summarizes basic psychological research concerning the perceptions and responses to hazards. The first section discusses people's insurance buying decisions. Interesting points include: 1) a surprisingly small amount of research has been done on the subject; 2) residents of flood- and earthquake-prone areas tend to avoid buying insurance even if it is heavily subsidized by the government; 3) results from a farm type simulation indicate that people are more prone to insure against high probability, low cost events than against low probability, high cost events; this conclusion is supported by the popularity of low deductible insurance plans; 4) seat belt use also illustrates this tendency for people to neglect low-probability, high cost events; 5) repeated benign experience may explain this tendency; 6) this tendency may disappear if the users' perspective is changed from a single point in time to a longer period of time.

The second section addresses the perceived frequency of lethal events. The major points are: 1) the availability bias affects perceived frequency; 2) availability is affected by factors unrelated to likelihood, such as recency, vividness, and emotional salience; 3) these factors are influenced by the media; 4) biases in perceived relative frequency are assumed to be caused by the availability heuristic; 5) fault tree data may interact with availability related biases; 6) a discussion of low probability events may increase perceived likelihood; 7) entire segments can be left out of a fault tree without the omission being noted; 8) the perceived importance of a problem pathway can be reduced by increasing the number of branches in the fault tree.

The third section addresses risk acceptability. and its assessment. The two standard methods for assessing risk acceptability are the revealed preference method and the expressed preference method. The revealed preference method assumes that society has arrived at an optimal balance between risks and benefits. This allows risk acceptability to be calculated by examining the "risky" decisions society has made in the past. Such analysis has shown that the acceptable level of risk is higher when it is incurred voluntarily. Problems cited for the revealed preference method are: 1) the method assumes that past behavior is a valid indicator of present preferences; 2) strong assumptions are made about the rationality of human decision making; 3) the method may be unresponsive to risks that the marketplace responds to slowly; and 4) such risks and benefits are difficult to measure.

Studies of expressed preferences have shown that more risk is acceptable if it is controllable, familiar, or known, or if the effects are immediate rather than delayed. Less risk is acceptable if the likely results are catastrophic or dreadful. Criticisms of the risk acceptability measures generated by the expressed preference method are: 1) people may not really know what they want; 2) attitudes and opinions may be inconsistent; 3) people may not understand how their preferences translate into policy; 4) values may change rapidly; and 5) peoples' goals may be unobtainable.

477
Slovic, P., Fischhoff, B. and Lichtenstein, S., "Accident Probabilities and Seat Belt Usage: A Psychological Perspective," *Accident Analysis and Prevention***, 10:4, 1978, 281-285.**

Key Words:
Belief in Danger,
Perceived Risk,
Prior Knowledge

This review paper summarizes several of the authors' research findings and their implications to traffic safety. Much of the focus is on explaining why people often choose not to wear seat belts. They emphasize that the probability of death or injury on any given automobile trip is very low. This in itself is a logical reason for people not to voluntarily use seat belts. In addition, most people consider themselves to be better than average drivers. The knowledge that seat belts are not 100% effective and the tendency of drivers to consider vehicle risks as under their control are also presented as factors that may reduce support for "buckling up."

On the positive side, the authors cite evidence that when individuals believe that their personal likelihood of being in an accident is sufficiently high, they become likely to wear seat belts. The authors note that the probability of an auto accident becomes very high when time intervals of 20 or more years are considered. By framing a decision over such a time interval, favorable attitudes towards seat belts were created. There was no evidence, however, that these attitudes would influence behavior or that they would be maintained over time. Nevertheless, the influences of "framing" on safety-related choices appear to be important. Future work should focus on evaluating whether decision "framing" influences attitudes toward consumer products other than automobiles.

Key Words:
Frequency Estimates,
Sources of Bias

478
Slovic, P., Fischhoff, B. and Lichtenstein, S., "Facts and Fears: Understanding Perceived Risk," in *Societal Risk Assessment*, Schwing, R.C. and Albers, W.A. (Eds.), Plenum Press, New York, 1980, 181-216.

This paper summarizes many findings regarding subjective risk perceptions. The discussion considers judgmental biases and major determinants of perceived risk. It also provides several tentative conclusions regarding those factors influencing subjective risk.

Key Words:
Frequency Estimates,
Severity Estimates,
Sources of Bias

479
Slovic, P., Fischhoff, B. and Lichtenstein, S., "Informing People About Risk," in *Product Labeling and Health Risks*, Morris, L.A., Mazis, M.B. and Barofsky, I. (Eds.), Cold Spring Harbor Laboratory, Banbury Report 6, 1980, 165-180.

The researchers begin by noting that any effective program for informing people about risk must: 1) have empirical data defining what people know and want to know; 2) develop and test methods for expressing this information; and 3) consider the ethical, legal, and political issues raised by such programs. They note that providing information on labels is not a substitute for a carefully planned program that informs people about risk.

The authors then discuss some of the difficulties of informing people about risk. Some specific points they make are: 1) people find it hard to think quantitatively about risk; risk perceptions are often based upon the availability and representativeness heuristics; 2) perceptions of risk are frequently inaccurate. Estimates of risk developed by using the availability or representativeness heuristic are likely to be biased when the risks involve low probability events. Other misconceptions, such as belief in personal immunity from harm, may also bias people's subjective estimates of risk; 3) risk information may frighten and frustrate the public. People prefer not to worry about risks, but do desire risk information; 4) strong beliefs are hard to modify. Beliefs change slowly and are extraordinarily persistent in the face of contrary evidence; people tend to view evidence consistent with their beliefs as reliable, and new conflicting evidence as unreliable, erroneous, or unrepresentative.

The authors emphasize that people can be educated about risk. In general, people have a good basic understanding of it; the difficulty occurs when biased experiences have shaped a person's perceptions. During attempts to modify perception, presentation format is vitally important. Several studies have shown that framing can explain facets of risk acceptability.

Key Words:
Sources of Bias

480
Slovic, P., Fischhoff, B. and Lichtenstein, S., "Rating the Risks," *Environment*, **21:3, April 1979, 14-39.**

This article considers various attributes of human risk perception. The authors describe several judgmental biases commonly associated with the assessment of risk. Three sources of bias include: 1) the availability heuristic; 2) overconfidence; and 3) the desire for certainty. The availability heuristic refers to the tendency for people to judge an event as likely if instances of the event are easily recalled or imagined. Regarding overconfidence, the authors cite research supportive of the notion that people are often much more confident with their judgements than they should be.

The third source of bias, desire for certainty, refers to the longing of individuals to rid themselves of risk.

Next, the authors discuss the qualitative components of perceived risk. They present the results of a study in which several groups of people were asked to rate thirty activities and technologies according to the risk of death presented by each. Four different groups participated in the study: thirty college students; forty members of the League of Women Voters; twenty-five business and professional members of the "Active Club"; and fifteen persons selected for their expertise in risk assessment. In general, it was found that the experts' judgements of risk differed drastically from the judgements of the three lay groups. In order to discover the particular determinants of risk perception, the authors compared the ratings of perceived risk to estimates of annual death rates associated with each of the thirty activities. The results showed that the experts' mean judgements were extremely close to the calculated risks of all of the activities considered. For the lay groups, however, risk judgement showed only a moderate relationship to the annual frequencies of death. Further analysis revealed that lay people's judgements may be affected by qualitative aspects such as dread, the likelihood of a mishap being fatal, and the potential for catastrophic consequences. The authors conclude the paper by discussing implications of these findings to hazard management.

481

Key Words: Sources of Bias

Slovic, P., Fischhoff, B. and Lichtenstein, S., "Behavioral Decision Theory," *Annual Review of Psychology,* **28, 1977, 1-39.**

This paper provides an academic view of behavioral decision theory with sections on: experimental research; field studies; and decision aids and their applications.

482

Key Words: Belief in Danger, Perceived Risk

Slovic, P., Fischhoff, B., Lichtenstein, S., Corrigan, B. and Combs, B., "Preference for Insuring Against Probable Small Losses: Insurance Implications," *The Journal of Risk and Insurance,* **44:2, June 1977, 237-258.**

This paper discusses research on people's decisions to insure against possible losses. The authors note that almost all traditional thinking about insurance behavior has been within the utility theory framework. Utility theory does justify the rationality of buying insurance. However, the authors do question the descriptive adequacy of the utility theory. In particular, Kunreuther et al. (1977), found that between thirty to forty percent of subjects' insurance decisions were inconsistent with the predictions of utility theory.

The paper also discusses laboratory studies of insurance-buying decisions. One study of 109 subjects showed a strong preference for insuring against high-probability, low-loss events. Such behavior was irrational according to utility theory. The experiments described suggest two methods of changing people's views on hazard probability: 1) combine low and high probability hazards in one insurance package; and 2) compound the hazard over time. The authors further note that buying decisions are also often influenced by non-qualitative "social" factors. The opinions and statements of other people and the need to comply with social norms are especially important social factors.

Annotations (401-500)

Key Words:
Belief in Danger,
Perceived Risk,
Prior Knowledge

483
Slovic, P., Kunreuther, H. and White, G.F., "Decision Processes, Rationality, and Adjustment to Natural Hazards," in *Natural Hazards--Local, National, Global*, White, G.F. (Ed.), Oxford University Press, New York, 1974, 187-205.

The authors discuss the cognitive elements of decision making with uncertainty, particularly as they apply to decisions regarding natural hazards. The article gives an overview of the two leading theories of decision making: 1) expected utility; and 2) bounded rationality. The authors present research findings that support bounded rationality as a useful framework for understanding decision processes associated with natural hazards. Bounded rationality posits that decision makers try to avoid facing uncertainty directly, and they do not think in a probabalistic fashion. Furthermore, in bounded rationality, the decision maker's goal is to achieve a satisfactory outcome rather than a maximum which is postulated by expected utility theory. Several limitations of decision makers are cited as evidence of a bounded rationality framework rather than expected utility theory. These limitations include: 1) misperception of risks; 2) denial of uncertainty; 3) poor perception of randomness; 4) systematic biases in probability judgements; and 5) difficulty integrating information from multiple sources. The authors believe that bounded rationality can be used to improve a decision maker's assessment of natural hazards.

Key Words:
Conveying Procedures,
Instructions vs. Training,
Task Analysis,
User Modeling

484
Smillie, R.J., "Chapter 10: Design Strategies for Job Performance Aids," in *Designing Usable Text*, Duffy, T.M. and Waller, R. (Eds.), Academic Press Inc., Alexandria, 213-242, 1985, 341-375.

The author defines a job performance aid (JPA) as a set of step-by-step instructions supported by illustrations. He notes that a JPA will generally provide all of the information needed to perform a specific procedural step at the time that step is to be performed. In so doing, a JPA presents information which is task oriented. In other words, a JPA is always written for a specific task and leaves out all information extraneous to that particular task.

A JPA also focuses heavily on the particular user who will be using the information. As such, a JPA needs to be designed with a particular user in mind. The author recommends a systems approach to JPA development because of the need to fully integrate the JPA with both personnel and equipment requirements. One reason for providing a JPA, of course, is to reduce training or other personnel-related requirements.

The author provides an interesting set of rules for choosing the between JPAs or training. These rules, though not intended as absolute principles, appear to be quite useful when they are considered in the context of a particular task to be performed. They include:

1) Ease of communication. Put into training those tasks which are hard to communicate through words. Put into JPAs those tasks that would benefit from the inclusions of illustrations, tables, graphs, flow charts etc.

2) Criticality of the tasks. Put into training those tasks for which the consequences of error are serious. Put into JPAs those tasks which require verification of readings and tolerances.

3) Complexity of the task. Put into training those tasks with difficult adjustments and procedures that can only be achieved through practice. Put into JPAs those tasks that require long and complex behavioral sequences that are extremely costly to teach.

4) Time required to perform the task. Put into training those tasks with a required response rate which does not permit reference to a printed instruction. Put into JPAs those tasks that are long and require attention to detail.

5) Frequency of the task or similar task. Put into training those tasks that are easy to learn through experience. Put into JPAs those tasks that are rarely performed.

6) Psychomotor component of the task. Put into training those tasks that require extensive practise for acceptable performance. Put into JPAs those tasks in which reference to printed instructions are not disruptive to task performance.

7) Cognitive component of the task. Put into training those tasks that require evaluation of numerous existing conditions prior to making a decision. Put into JPAs those tasks in which binary fault trees can be developed into a decision aid.

8) Equipment complexity and accessibility. Put into training those tasks in which equipment is easily accessed. Put into JPAs those tasks that provide detailed procedures to properly access equipment.

9) Personnel constraints. Put into training those tasks that require a team effort. Put into JPAs one or two man tasks.

10) Consequences of improper task performance. Put into training those tasks in which an occasional error will not dam-

age equipment. Put into JPAs those tasks that require branching, such as a diagnostic decision aid that lists failure mode symptoms.

JPA Development

The author notes that behavioral task analysis can be a useful tool during JPA development. During behavioral task analysis, it is important to consider: the hardware interface, the criticality of each elemental task, the sensory cues employed by the user, the response that is required, the feedback used to indicate that the elemental task was completed correctly, the performance criteria (both time and accuracy) and references (that is, what source data was used to generate the task element). After completion of the behavioral task analysis the construction of the JPA begins and necessitates decisions regarding the layout and size of the text itself as well as factors such as type face borders, page numbering, indexing etc.

JPA Format

The author also notes the importance of design strategies and formats in the development of JPAs. For example, a JPA designed to present information that can be easily learned and recalled may differ significantly from one designed to describe the desired behavior in enough detail to permit proper assembly.

Related to this issue is whether or not a JPA format is directive or deductive. In a directive format all the information necessary to perform a task is included. On the other hand, in a deductive format the users are expected to have some knowledge by training and/or experience which they are expected to combine with the information in the JPA during the performance of a task. It is concluded by the author that directive formats are better for novice users, while deductive formats are better for experienced users. For the intermediate users more creativity is necessary since a combined format may be preferable. Several excellent examples describing such hybrid formats are provided. One of the more interesting approaches is to provide parallel information within the JPA. In this case, the JPA has one portion that is directed and a second portion that is deductive. An example along these lines would be where the directive portion is given by a decision tree, while the deductive portion is a functional flow diagram. In such a case, inexperienced users can use the directive portion while experienced users can use the deductive portion. On the other hand, intermediate users might use whatever part of the JPA that meets their information needs. The author also feels that inexperienced users can use such dual formats to gradually learn the deductive processes used by experienced users.

JPA Effectiveness and Acceptance

In the final section of this paper the author summarizes research on JPAs. Several studies are cited which show that JPAs can result in a reduction in training time and, ultimately, in performance times. Other studies have shown significant improvements in performance when JPAs were provided. It has also been found that JPAs have been well accepted by technicians as replacements for conventional technical manuals. As a concluding point, the author states JPA design strategies have to be centered around the user's acceptance, because even a well designed JPA is useless if the audience does not accept and use it. With respect to the critical issue of acceptability the author feels the level of detail is an essential determinant; both too much or too little detail can be counterproductive.

Key Words:
Duty/Failure to Warn,
Post-sale Warning,
Punitive Damages,
Unavoidably Unsafe Product

485
Smith, C.W., "Post-Sale Warnings: Products that Go 'Bump' in the Night," *Arizona State Law Journal*, **1984, 719-750.**

The author surveys post-sale duty to warn law and recommends adoption of the proposed Products Liability Act for several reasons: 1) it would bar recovery to a plaintiff who knows of the danger or misuses a product, 2) it would allow manufacturers to use the state-of-the-art defense while imposing a high standard of care on the technical, scientific and medical fields, 3) it would limit the claimant's right to bring an action under a 25 year statute of repose, and 4) it would allow punitive damages when the requisite state of mind is present but would remove determination of the financial amount from the jury.

Key Words:
Conveying Action,
Conveying Procedures,
Organizing Information,
Prior Knowledge,
Structured Text,
Summaries,
Task Analysis,
Titles,
Understanding/
  Perception Models,
User Modeling,
Writing Instructions

486
Smith, E.E. and Goodman, L., "Understanding Written Instructions: The Role of an Explanatory Schema," *Cognition and Instruction*, **1:4, 1984, 359-396.**

This article addresses the important issue of how individual steps in a sequence of instructions should be organized. The authors discuss two different methods of organization. The first method arranges the information in a set of linear steps which describes the process to be performed. The second arranges the steps in accordance with explanatory schema which organizes the material. Two forms of schema are detailed by the authors. The first breaks up the instructions in terms of the structure of the object which is being assembled. The second describes the object in terms of its functions.

The authors then develop means of hierarchically arranging the information within instructions into either functional or structural categories. The hierarchical instructions, in many cases, can be paraphrased as groups of linear steps which are performed in order to attain specific goals. These specific goals are described within the instructions as higher level headings in a fairly verbose manner. The authors feel that such hierarchically organized instructions should pose advantages in comprehension and ease of following.

In a series of three experiments involving the assembly of an electrical circuit, the authors develop several examples of such hierarchically organized instructions and compare them to the linear versions. It was found that subjects read and executed the hierarchically recognized instructions faster than the linear ones. This advantage was shown for both structurally and functionally organized versions of the hierarchical instructions. It was also found that subjects were better able to transfer the skills they learned in assembling a circuit to the assembly of another, different circuit when the original instructions were structurally or functionally organized.

It should be noted, however, that in this particular study the hierarchical instructions provided significantly more information than did the linear ones. Since the 36 subjects were students or secretaries, it is doubtful that they had any significant background regarding the assembly of electrical circuits and it may be, in fact, that the providing of this additional information, rather than the hierarchical structure, was responsible for their improved performance under the structural and functional conditions.

487
Smith, E.E. and Spoehr, K.T., "Basic Processes and Individual Differences in Understanding and Using Instructions," Bolt, Beranek, and Newman Inc., Cambridge, NTIS No. AD-A160 037, October 1985, 359-396.

Key Words:
Conveying Action,
Ordering of
  Conditions/Actions,
Prior Knowledge,
Structured Text,
Task Analysis,
Understanding/
  Perception Models,
User Modeling

The authors discuss the results of a project funded by the Office of Naval Research directed toward determining how people understand and use written instructions in operating a device or assembling an object. In the first experiment, subjects were asked to read and then execute single step instructions for operating a simple device. The information within the instructions was classified into three categories: antecedents, actions and consequences. Accordingly, instructions could be viewed as sequences of these more elemental components which could appear in arbitrary order. For example, an antecedent might be followed by an action, which is then followed by a consequence. It was found that, in general, an instruction was read faster if its elemental components were mentioned in the same order that they would be executed. The authors conclude that these results imply that the understanding of an instruction involves the instantiation of a step schema which is an abstract representation of an instructional step in terms of these three elemental components.

The second experiment used the same materials as the first experiment, but the subjects were asked only to memorize the material. In this situation there was little evidence suggesting that the order of the elemental components influenced the ability to memorize instructions.

In the third experiment the task was changed to an assembly task which required that a model helicopter be assembled by following a 72 step sequence. The information within each of the steps was further classified to include categories such as agent, action, object, and location. The number of elemental components in a single assembly step was also varied. It was found that these instructions were read faster when they contained fewer elemental components and when the elemental components were listed in the order of their execution. These effects were more pronounced for subjects with smaller working memory spans. The authors conclude that these results were again consistent with the idea that the understanding of the instruction involves schema instantiation.

In the fourth experiment, the research used a task in which a device was operated which was somewhat more complex than in the first experiment. The goal was to determine whether or not the subjects had learned a mental model of the device they were to operate. It was found that subjects who had a mental model were better able to remember the components of the device and were able to read the instructions more quickly and had better ability to reason about the device itself. Subjects, of course, were given the opportunity under specific experimental conditions to develop a mental model by presenting them with an elaborated story or scenario within which such a device would be used and for which purposes it was to be used.

We interpret the authors' results as supporting the feasibility of developing a true technology of instruction design—one that is based on a synthesis of cognitive psychology and artificial intelligence based techniques. The methodology described here is certainly worthy of further pursuit.

Annotations (401-500)

Key Words:
Contrast,
Drivers,
Subjective Ratings,
Traffic,
Traffic Settings,
Visual Noise

488
Smith, G. and Weir, R., "Laboratory Visibility Studies of Directional Symbols Used for Traffic Control Signals," *Ergonomics*, 21:4, 1978, 247-252.

Eight directional symbols suitable for traffic control are evaluated in three experiments. In experiment 1, the projected symbol image was blurred (defocused). Three distinct groups of symbols were revealed by the recognition data. In experiment 2, contrast was varied by introducing a veiling glare. Two distinct groups were revealed by the recognition data. In experiment 3, symbol preference was evaluated. Significant differences were found. The rank order of the symbols did not remain consistent for the three criteria considered.

Key Words:
Traffic

489
Smith, G.S., "Just How Many Accidents Are Caused by Bad Road Signs?" *Applied Ergonomics*, 7:3, September 1976, 157-158.

This short, anecdotal paper considers road signs used in London and their possible role in causing traffic accidents.

Key Words:
Case of Text,
Laboratory/Generic
  Settings,
Stimulus Size,
Symbol Size,
Viewing Distance,
Visual Angle

490
Smith, S.L., "Chapter 9: Letter Size and Legibility," in *Information Design: The Design and Evaluation of Signs and Printed Material*, Easterby, R.S. and Zwaga, H.J.G. (Eds.), John Wiley & Sons, New York, 1984, 171-186.

The following factors are discussed as they influence legibility: letter size, the letters used, the shape of the letter, the use of upper or lower case, and the height-to-width ratio. Design recommendations for acuity are summarized, ranging from about 10 to 30 minutes of arc. Results of the field study described here indicate that at the defined limit of normal acuity (5 minutes of arc), 38% of displayed letters could be read. The minimum label size specified by MIL-STD-1472B, 16 minutes of arc, achieved 98% legibility. To be read in dim light, letters had to be larger.

In terms of viewing distance, the author concludes that letters on equipment labels and in displays designed for close viewing should be relatively larger, in visual angle, than on signs to be read at a distance. Smith also concludes that visual angle alone captures the effects of distance and stimulus size. However, he adds, at viewing distances less than 2 meters, the required visual angles may be larger than at greater distances. Legibility is the first stage in the design of effective displays. Other factors such as the amount or the format of data, and the choice of words, may limit display use.

Key Words:
Accuracy,
Basic Associations,
Consumers,
Control/Display
 Elements,
Elemental Breakdowns,
Industrial
Population Stereotypes,
Traffic

491
Smith, S.L., "Exploring Compatibility with Words and Pictures," *Human Factors*, **23:3, 1981, 305-315.**

The author reports on a study of stimulus response (S/R) compatibility. In the study, 92 male engineers, 80 women and 55 human factors specialists responded to an 18 item questionnaire which displayed potentially ambiguous display-control relations, labels, and word usage. The items included: 1) knob turn; 2) quadrant labels; 3) left wing down; 4) numbered keys; 5) stove burners; 6) cross faucets; 7) a refrigerator door; 8) an auto transmission; 9) a digital counter; 10) pressure high; 11) a river bank; 12) highway lanes; 13) a locked box; 14) a door handle; 15) an adding machine; 16) a lever control; 17) lever faucets; and 18) "GREEN" written in red ink.

Certain items elicited strongly stereotypical responses. Other items elicited widely varying responses. Smith concludes that a taxonomy of S/R compatibility is needed if the concept of S/R compatibility is to attain predictive power.

Key Words:
Consumers,
Laboratory/Generic
 Settings,
Legibility Distance,
Stimulus Size,
Symbol Size,
Viewing Distance,
Visual Angle

492
Smith, S.L., "Letter Size and Legibility," *Human Factors*, **21:6, 1979, 661-670.**

(Author's abstract follows.)

The legibility of displayed letters depends upon their size, or more accurately, their subtended visual angle at any viewing distance. Current design standards recommend letter heights in the range from 0.003 to 0.007 rad (10 to 24 min of arc) for good viewing conditions, with 0.0015 rad (5 min) considered a lower limit based on normal visual acuity. A field study involving some 2000 measures for over 300 printed displays found a mean letter height of 0.0019 rad (7 min) at the limit of legibility, with over 90% legibility at 0.003 rad, and virtually 100% at 0.007 rad.

Key Words:
Error Detection,
Laboratory/Generic
 Settings,
Visual Displays:
 miscellaneous

493
Smith, S.L. and Goodwin, N.C., "Check-Reading as a Measure of Display Legibility," *Proceedings of the Human Factors Society - 17th Annual Meeting*, **Human Factors Society, Santa Monica, CA, 1973, 21-24.**

A technique for assessing display legibility is proposed that consists of placing random letter substitution errors into a text which is then displayed. The rate at which these errors can be detected is proposed as an index of display legibility. To test this theory, six conditions of progressively degraded text were displayed. The results showed that this index could be used to demarcate the degradation levels of the text.

494
Snyder, H.L. and Taylor, G.B., "The Sensitivity of Response Measures of Alphanumeric Legibility to Variations in Dot Matrix Display Parameters," *Human Factors*, **21:4, 1979, 457-471.**

Key Words:
Accuracy,
Data Processing Setting,
Detection Intensity Level,
Luminance,
Reaction Time,
Recognition Time,
Stimulus Size,
Symbol Size,
Viewing Distance,
Visual Displays:
 miscellaneous

This research evaluated the sensitivity of four measures of alpha-numeric legibility to some variations in the character size and dot luminance of a dot matrix display. The four measures of alpha-numeric legibility evaluated were recognition accuracy, response time, tachistoscopic recognition accuracy, and threshold visibility. The measures of legibility were evaluated by presenting alphanumeric characters in noncontextual form on a variable-parameter CRT display which was programmed and driven by a minicomputer to six subjects. The legibility measures were then related to display parameters.

Recognition accuracy (percent correct response) was found to be the most sensitive to the display parameters of character size and dot luminance. Character size, dot luminance, and viewing distance had consistent and significant effects at viewing distances of more than 1.52m. At lesser viewing distances, these parameters had little effect.

The results suggest that there is no major difference between the display requirements for computer-generated dot matrix type displays and those for conventional CRT displays.

495
Sperber, P., "The Strategy of Product Labeling for Loss Prevention," *Journal of Products Liability*, **1, 1978, 171-182.**

Key Words:
Conduct of Consumer/
 User,
Design of: labeling and
 safety signage systems,
Loss Prevention
 Programs,
Strict Liability and
 Warnings

Sperber states that the key to reducing the increasing cost of lawsuits is a strategically implemented labeling program. A labeling committee needs to be formed to consider issues such as: 1) analysis of each step of the manufacturing process to determine how a product might fail to meet performance specifications; 2) determination of the effects of vibration, shock, repeated loading, etc., on safety, durability, and reliability; 3) use of systems safety analysis, fault tree analysis, and failure modes and effects analysis; 4) determination of foreseeable uses without instructions; 5) consideration of misuse by other than the intended user; 6) 100% inspection and cautions for critical components; 7) consideration of how products in the field are affected by the committee's decisions; 8) study of the competition's labeling practices and standards; 9) placement, format, and content of labels; and 10) development of design alternatives to make the product safer.

He distinguishes between hazards associated with malfunctions and those associated with misuse. Several well-known legal decisions are also cited and the Restatement of Torts is briefly discussed. We point out that this author's strategy goes far beyond providing labeling and instruction. He really seems to be laying out the specifications for a product assurance program. This is not a negative editorial remark, but rather an observation of his apparent intent.

496
Sremec, B., "Instructions, Mechanical Ability and Performance," *Applied Ergonomics,* **3:2, 1972, 98-100.**

Key Words:
Behavior Factors,
Problems in Design,
Students

An experiment was performed where two groups of 15 students installed a window shade. The group using the manufacturer's instructions performed significantly worse than the group which used an improved version. The improved version contained 186 words and 5 schematic drawings, while the original contained 193 words and no drawings. It was concluded that the original instructions failed to attain their objective. We suggest that the absence of any schematics in the manufacturer's instructions played a significant negative role.

497
Staelin, R., "The Effects of Consumer Education on Consumer Product Safety Behavior," *Journal of Consumer Research,* **5, June 1978, 30-40.**

Key Words:
Actual Behavior,
Behavior Factors,
Design of:
  educational/persuasive programs,
Effectiveness of:
  educational/persuasive programs,
Prior Knowledge,
Students

The goal of the research reported in this paper is to develop a methodology for clearly defining the causal links between education and safety behavior. A series of structural equations which model the causality of an education program on behavior is postulated. The influence of an education program is then evaluated using the model.

The evaluated program consisted of eight 30 minute professionally developed instructional modules designed to teach basic safety-related operating principles of products. These modules were taught to 239 11th grade students by a female engineer. Priori and a priori behavior and knowledge of the students was measured using pen and pencil tests. Safety knowledge was measured on a 26 question multiple choice test concerning electricity, insulation, materials and fasteners, stability, heat, and flammability. Safety behavior was measured with an 11 question multiple choice test which asked for responses to the following situations: use of a three prong electric plug; the pouring or handling of volatile liquids; and the use of a power mower. Two types of response on the behavior test were elicited: 1) what one *would* do (actual); and 2) what one *should* do (normative). A separate analysis was performed on each response measure.

Results included: 1) a correlation of .3 to .6 between actual and normative behavior responses to the questions; 2) theoretical courses (physics, chemistry, shop, home economics, auto lab) were negatively related to prior safety knowledge; 3) practical courses (auto repair, TV repair, appliance repair) were positively related to prior safety knowledge; 4) males had greater prior safety knowledge than females; 5) prior safety knowledge was positively related to the actual behavior measure; 6) there was no correlation between prior safety knowledge and the normative behavior measure; 7) the education program did increase knowledge levels; 8) students with particularly high or low grades learned less than the average students; 9) females were more apt to behave safely and in a manner consistent with prior knowledge and also learned more from the program; 10) a change in knowledge was strongly correlated with a change in actual behavior but weakly correlated with normative behavior; and 11) the education program was negatively correlated with actual behavior, but it was positively correlated with normative behavior.

Staelin concludes that the program altered normative behavior significantly and increased knowledge. The program did not, however, increase actual safe behavior.

Key Words:
Design of:
educational/persuasive programs,
Prior Knowledge

498
Staelin, R. and Weinstein, A.G., "Correlates of Consumer Safety Behavior," in *Advances in Consumer Research, Association for Consumer Research 1973 Proceedings*, 1, Ward, S. and Wright, P. (Eds.), Association for Consumer Research, 1973, 87-100.

This paper reports work that was conducted as part of a project aimed at developing an educational consumer product safety program for high school students. The project attempted to empirically determine the relationship between safety behavior and the level of knowledge of safety principles. The primary source of date was a survey of sophomores in three Pittsburgh high schools.

Behavioral measures collected in the survey documenting purchasing decisions, use patterns and injury history. Knowledge measures were grouped as follows: safety related and product specific; safety related and theoretical; and non-safety related and theoretical. Subjects reported that performance, price, features, brand, durability, quality, safety, and retail outlet were factors considered prior to purchasing a product. In general, the subjects seemed relatively unconcerned with safety except when considering the purchase of a toy or a power tool.

Research by Newman and Staelin (1973) and also by Cox (1967) indicate four categories of information sources: technical, industry supplied, personal, and household. Educational level is very likely related to the use of the harder to understand technical materials. Industrial sources seem most often used by consumers with considerable practical safety knowledge, consumers who report safer use behavior, and consumers who say they can explain how consumer products operate. Household information was used most by subjects who showed better theoretical and practical safety knowledge, confidence in their ability to explain how products work, and poorer theoretical general knowledge. Thus, the use of all sources, except technical, is related to knowledge of safety principles and/or good safety behavior. As measured here, safe use behavior is positively related to specific and theoretical knowledge of safety principles and risk aversion. Theoretical knowledge of physics, mechanics, etc., was negatively related to safety behavior.

499
Starr, C., "Social Benefit versus Technological Risk," *Science*, **165, 19 September 1969, 1232-1238.**

Key Words: Acceptability

This article proposes the "revealed preference" approach to establishing a quantitative relationship between the benefits of technological development and the costs of accidental deaths arising from the use of such technology. Two assumptions are central to the validity of this approach: historical national accident data are adequate for revealing patterns of fatalities in the public use of technology; and historically revealed social preferences and costs are sufficiently enduring to allow their use for predictive purposes.

A study applying this approach revealed that: 1) the public is willing to accept voluntary risks one thousand times greater than involuntary risks; 2) the risk of death from disease is like a yardstick to assess the level of acceptability of other risks; 3) the acceptability of risk appears to be crudely proportional to the third power of the benefits; and 4) the social acceptability of risk is influenced by the public awareness of an activity's benefits.

Annotations (401-500)

Key Words:
Consumer Setting,
Location,
Luminance,
Reaction Time,
Task Specific Context,
Workload/Task

500
Stefl, M.E. and Persensky, J.J., "An Evaluation of a Range-Top Warning Light System," NBSIR 75-797, July 1975, 1-22.

An analysis of electric kitchen range-related accidents revealed a series of incidents in which range users were unaware that surface elements were "on." A proposed solution to the problem was to provide four warning lights that indicated which surface elements were on. In a laboratory study using human subjects, the effectiveness of the proposed lighting system was evaluated.

The backgrounds against which the lights were fitted and the intensity of the lights did not seem to influence the subjects' responses in a reaction time task. However, the position of the lights and the type of ancillary task being performed by the subject did influence the results of the reaction time task. The paper discusses the results of the study as they relate to product design, product safety, and the implications of the study for methodological development.

ANNOTATIONS 501-577

Key Words:
Auditory,
Auditory vs. Visual
 Messages,
Control/Display
 Elements,
Conveying Procedures,
Illustrations,
Prohibition,
Verbal vs. Nonverbal
 Symbol/Message

501
Stern, K.R., "An Evaluation of Written, Graphics, and Voice Messages in Proceduralized Instructions," *Proceedings of the Human Factors Society - 28th Annual Meeting*, **Human Factors Society, Santa Monica, CA, 1984, 314-318.**

Written messages, graphics, combined text and graphics, and digitized voice messages were evaluated in terms of their ability to communicate proceduralized instructions. The task was making cash withdrawals from an automated teller machine. As a primary means of communicating instructions, graphics was inferior to text, combined text and graphics, or voice. Voice, used as a supplement to visual error messages, did not provide a performance advantage. Subjects disliked voice messages, especially when used in public. The authors conclude that graphics messages should not be used alone to communicate proceduralized instructions.

Key Words:
Adequacy of Warnings,
Advertising,
Consumer Setting,
Design of: labeling and
 safety signage systems,
Governmental Labeling
 and Signage Systems,
Loss Prevention
 Programs,
Negligence and
 Warnings,
Strict Liability and
 Warnings

502
Stessin, L. (Ed.), *Product Liability Portfolio*, **Man & Manager, Inc., New York, 1977, 1-77.**

The chapters of this significant manual on product liability address several elements of a product liability program. The suggested program in this reading, while quite extensive, is summarized below. Although important elements of the program which are discussed or provided in this manual are limited in the extent to which they can be feasibly implemented, many fine points are provided, including:

1) Corporate statement of policy wherein marketing, general management, quality control, engineering, and field service are considered. A skeletal outline of a product safety policy is provided.

2) A chart of product safety responsibilities broken down into marketing, engineering, manufacturing, legal, and other coordinating services.

3) Guidelines for the product safety coordination committee which were to integrate safety knowledge in the fields of engineering, marketing, and manufacturing.

4) A job description for a product liability loss-control coordinator.

Annotations (501-577)

5) A product liability prevention plan consisting of specifications, sales materials, packaging and labeling, field service, record keeping, product control, liability insurance, product cost, and a practical example of this type of plan.

6) Rules for warning labels and instructions: warn against unpreventable hazards; warn against misuse or careless use; make the warning conspicuous, complete, durable, and legible; include any foreseeable danger including those that are remote; conform with standards; and keep the warning current.

7) A product liability prevention guide for sales and marketing personnel (consisting of a do's and don'ts list).

8) Product accident reporting (with illustrative forms).

9) The CPSC questionnaire that must be filed when reporting a suspected product hazard.

10) CPSC instructions to be followed after receiving a notice of defect from a manufacturer.

11) The CPSC form that demands information from manufacturers about a suspected product hazard.

12) A CPSC-approved news release to be circulated by a company announcing corrective action on a product hazard.

13) A CPSC approved news release to be circulated by a company announcing recall of a product.

14) Guidelines for avoiding a costly product recall (a matrix of companies, product, defect, and approved actions).

15) A questionnaire for subsidiaries and installations concerning familiarity with safety laws.

16) A flow chart for a recall campaign.

17) A checklist on advance recall policy.

18) A post-recall order checklist.

19) A product design review (preliminary design review, intermediate design review, and final design review).

20) A product design review checklist.

21) A product design review action report.

22) An insurance company product liability survey.

Key Words:
Instructions in Litigation

503
Strate, L. and Swerdlow, S., "The Maze of the Law: How Technical Writers Can Research and Understand Legal Matters," *IEEE Transactions on Professional Communication*, **30:3, September 1987, 136-148.**

The authors provide a tutorial paper describing the procedures for thoroughly researching legal thought, court opinions, case law and statutes on any selected legal topic. This tutorial is directed toward technical writers who may not have a legal background or direct access to legal counsel capable of explaining such topics.

Key Words:
Behavior Factors,
Location,
Memory of:
  symbol/message,
Reading Measures,
Reading of: warning
  labels,
Signal Words,
Students,
Underlining/
  Highlighting,
Warnings: evaluating
  effects on behavior

504
Strawbridge, J.A., "The Influence of Position, Highlighting, and Imbedding on Warning Effectiveness," *Proceedings of the Human Factors Society - 30th Annual Meeting*, **Human Factors Society, Santa Monica, CA, 1986, 716-720.**

This paper reports on a study which investigated how varying a product's warning position, highlighting and imbededness influenced effectiveness. The warning information told the subjects (195 undergraduate students) that the product they were using (a super-bonding glue) contained acid and must be shaken to avoid severe burns. A control condition was also used in which the directions simply told the subjects to shake the product.

Overall, 91% of the subjects noticed the warning, 77% read it, and 37% actually shook the product. This compared to 100%, 100%, and 33% under the control conditions, meaning that significantly more people read the warning directive when it was placed in the directions. More detailed analysis showed that when the warning message was not imbedded within the text, the behavior change was at its greatest (an average value of 47% vs. 27% when imbedded). Under certain non-imbedded conditions, the behavior reached values of up to 60%. The only significant effect due to highlighting was a significant increase in reading (83% vs. 71%). Only one significant effect was due to the position of the message; recall of the danger was better when the message was in the middle of the label.

Annotations (501-577)

Key Words:
Children,
Effectiveness of:
 educational/persuasive
 programs,
Formal Teaching/
 Counseling/Education,
Prior Knowledge

505
Stuart, R.B., "Teaching Facts About Drugs: Pushing or Preventing?" *Journal of Educational Psychology,* **66:2, 1974, 189-201.**

The author cites research showing that drug-related knowledge is associated with comparatively higher levels of drug use. Drug-related knowledge can, of course, be acquired in many ways. The question addressed in this study is "Does drug education reduce drug use?" To address this issue, more than 900 junior high school students were randomly assigned to either experimental drug education or control groups. The dependent measures consisted of self-reported knowledge of drugs, present or past use and sale of drugs, and attitudes believed to be related to drug use.

At pretest, seventh graders predictably had less information about drugs than the ninth grade subjects. Experimental subjects at both the seventh and the ninth grade levels had more drug knowledge than control subjects at similar levels. The experimental subjects also gained more knowledge than the control group. Classroom instruction was also shown to increase the level of students' knowledge about drugs. Relative to the control group, subjects in the experimental group reported a significant increase in their use of alcohol, marijuana, and LSD, while their worry about drugs decreased. Interestingly, neither the format nor the content of the education was shown to influence the results of the program. The author concluded that drug education may impede and exacerbate the use of drugs, and that the association between drug use and drug education may be a complex one.

Key Words:
Detection/Perception
 Measures,
Filtering,
Traffic,
Traffic Settings,
Workload/Task

506
Summula, H. and Näätänen, R., "Perception of Highway Traffic Signs and Motivation," *Journal of Safety Research,* **6:4, December 1974, 150-154.**

Nine subjects driving over a 257 kilometer route were asked to drive as safely as possible, to obey the traffic rules and signs, and to name every sign they saw along the route. Subject responses, including missed signs and traffic violations, were noted by the experimenter riding in the back seat of the car. The results were: 1) only 2.95% of the signs were missed; 2) signs were more likely to be missed in urban areas (8.95%); 3) only 2 of the 154 missed signs were danger or prohibitory signs; 4) the most frequently missed signs were either mandatory or informative signs; and 5) mandatory and informative signs tended to be found at intersections and other more difficult areas. The researchers conclude that the relative inefficiency of traffic signs found in earlier studies was caused by motivational factors.

507
Sumner, R. and Shippey, J., "The Use of Rumble Areas to Alert Drivers," Crowthorne, Berkshire, Transport and Road Research Laboratory, TRRL Lab Report 800, 1977, 1-29.

Key Words:
Auditory,
Behavior Factors,
Kinesthetic/Tactile,
Rumble Strips,
Symbol Generation

Rumble areas are patches of rough road designed to produce aural and tactile stimuli inside vehicles. Their objectives are to alert drivers and, if necessary, induce them to slow down. The authors utilized simulator experiments to find a suitable noise pattern for rumble areas. For the types of rumble areas tested there were no consistent effects on drivers' speeds. The authors note, however, that such rumble areas may still be effective in reducing accidents.

508
Szlichcinski, K.P., "Chapter 23: Factors Affecting the Comprehension of Pictographic Instructions," in *Information Design: The Design and Evaluation of Signs and Printed Material*, Easterby, R.S. and Zwaga, H.J.G. (Eds.), John Wiley & Sons, New York, 1984, 171-186.

Key Words:
Abstractness,
Accuracy,
Consumers,
Control/Display
  Elements,
Conveying Action,
Conveying Procedures,
Description/Modeling,
Design of: instructions,
Elemental Synthesis,
Illustrations,
Message Complexity,
Problems in Design,
Process Charts/
  Sequences,
Response Time

This chapter reports on experimental investigations conducted to identify factors that influence the comprehension of pictorial instructions. An experimental study of pictorial instructions evaluated the behavior of subjects who operated unfamiliar electro-mechanical equipment with the aid of the instructions. The number of errors and total time taken to successfully operate the equipment were measured and recorded. Twelve different styles of instruction presentation were selected and the effects on performance of several variables were assessed. The subjects were 465 men and 321 women, ranging in age from 10 to 90 years, who were visitors to the sales bureau of a local telephone office. They were classified, by occupation, into three categories: technical, 15%; semi-technical, 26%; and non-technical, 59%.

The author identified six factors and investigated their importance with respect to comprehension. The factors included: 1) the range from which controls should be depicted; 2) the view from which the equipment is depicted; 3) pictorial complexity; 4) different ways of representing actions; 5) syntax linking pictures into a sequence; and 6) graphic devices assisting visual search. Major causes of error were: problems locating the right control; misleading illustrations of hand positions; overlooking/ignoring arrows; failure to realize that controls to be operated were illustrated in starting position; not knowing in what sequence to read the pictures; and performing more than one operation per illustration. For the "best" sets of instructions, the success rates were about 98%. The set of instructions which resulted in the best performance was the one in which each stage of operation was shown by an overall view and an inset. The two worst sets were those which showed each stage of the operation in a detailed view only. The authors conclude that the most important factors were those associated with the way the apparatus itself was depicted.

509
Szlichcinski, K.P., "The Syntax of Pictorial Instructions," in *Processing of Visible Language*, 2, Plenum Press, New York, 1980, 113-124.

Key Words:
Abstractness,
Control/Display
    Elements,
Conveying Action,
Description/Modeling,
Design of: instructions,
Development Programs,
Elemental Breakdowns,
Elemental Synthesis,
Message Complexity,
Process Charts/
    Sequences,
Production Method,
Symbol Generation,
Verbal vs. Nonverbal
    Symbol/Message

The authors note that factors affecting the comprehensibility and communicative capabilities of pictorial materials have not received as much attention as those for verbal text. The author indicates that, in relation to the semantic organization of concepts of motion, representation of actions is of great interest. To this end, the objective of this study was to learn how actions should be represented and how pictorial elements may be combined to form a syntax of pictorial instructions. To achieve this objective, the production method was employed to discover the kinds of representations people use.

In this study, eighty volunteer subjects were asked to draw pictures to explain how to operate a set of controls (e.g., rotary switch, three-position rocker switch, push button, etc.). To represent action, seventy-seven subjects used arrows in some of their drawings. Although there were marked variations in the way subjects combined pictorial elements to convey an instruction, there were characteristics common to almost all of the instructions. A grammar which specified the mandatory, interchangeable, and optional elements of each subject's drawing was then developed. Syntactic functions and the nature and relative popularity of different forms were identified and assessed. Several findings emerged from the analysis of the different syntactic forms identified. Notably, it was found that the most widely used pictorial instruction syntax was comprised of an element representing the object and an element representing the action. This finding as well as the more detailed conclusions from this study have important implications for the design of instruction manuals that rely heavily upon illustrations to convey actions and states associated with objects.

Key Words:
Abstractness,
Accuracy,
Consumers,
Control/Display
  Elements,
Conveying Action,
Cultural Factors,
Design of: instructions,
Design of: labeling and
  safety signage systems,
Illustrations,
Prior Knowledge,
Problems in Design,
Process Charts/Sequences

510
Szlichcinski, K.P., "Telling People How Things Work," *Applied Ergonomics*, **10:1, 1979, 2-8.**

The author provides an explanation for the necessity of operating instructions and notes common problems associated with them. He than describes two studies aimed at evaluating the effectiveness of particular instructions. The author states that instructions are a necessary evil because financial constraints often prevent the development of completely self-explanatory equipment. A sample study of instructions for dialing international calls from England is presented. It was found that certain errors were much more common than others and were associated with subjects' failure to read instructions. Literature related to matching instructions to users is summarized, and the conclusion that diagrams can be useful is drawn.

A second study failed to reveal significant differences between instruction diagrams that showed controls in starting and finishing positions or between schematic diagrams and more conventional drawings. Many subjects (14%) had difficulty associating the individual diagrams with a sequence of steps. The author then identifies the users of diagrams, and provides evidence that the users may be a biased sample of the overall user group; specifically, foreign users of phones use instructions much more than natives do. The importance of calling attention to instructions by making them attractive and locating them appropriately is noted.

The author's final point is that ergonomists should start worrying about making sure the cognitive demands of products are within the capabilities of 95% of the user population. We note from this study how foreign users are more likely to rely on instruction. Does this mean, then, that the 95% includes all possible foreign users of a system such as a telephone? If so, we raise the feasibility question.

Key Words:
Consumer

511
Taylor, I.A., "Psychological Aspects of Visual Communications," in *Symbology: The Use of Symbols in Visual Communications*, **Whitney, E. (Ed.), 1960, Hastings House, New York, 123-138.**

This introductory paper examines the classic Gestalt psychological approach to describing aspects of visual communication.

Annotations (501-577)

Key Words:
Strict Liability and Warnings

512
Terry, N.P., "Stricter Products Liability," *Missouri Law Review*, 52:1, Winter 1987, 1-56.

In a failure to warn case, the plaintiff's task of demonstrating the existence of a marketing defect is two-fold. First, the product must be shown to be "unreasonably dangerous" when put to a reasonably anticipated use and without the user's knowledge of its characteristics. Second, it must be shown that the defendant did not provide an adequate warning. The author examines this and other facets of Missouri's product liability law.

Key Words:
Glance Legibility,
Legibility Distance,
Reaction Time,
Traffic,
Traffic Settings,
Workload/Task

513
Testin, F.J. and Dewar, R.E., "Divided Attention in a Reaction Time Index of Traffic Sign Perception," *Ergonomics*, 24:2, 1981, 111-124.

The validity of reaction time measures of traffic sign perception was evaluated by correlating reaction times with legibility distance. Reaction time measures were evaluated under single and dual task conditions. The dual task was a traffic sign task plus a cognitive loading task which consisted of either a detection, identification, or memory task.

It was found that reaction times measured during the dual task were not more strongly correlated with legibility distance than reaction times for the single task (traffic sign task only). Also, during the dual task condition with detection and identification tasks, reaction times were significantly longer than for the single task condition, but significantly shorter than during the dual task condition with the memory task. We question the validity of measuring the reliability of reaction time indexes by correlating them with legibility distance, since they measure different things.

Key Words:
Duty/Failure to Warn,
Immunizations,
Unavoidably Unsafe Product

514
Thomas, D.A., "Tort Law–Products Liability—Warning to Prescribing Physician Regarding Unavoidably Unsafe Drug Held Adequate Under Alabama Extended Manufacturers' Liability Doctrine," *Cumberland Law Review*, 15:2, 1985, 541-553.

As a general rule, the drug manufacturer's duty to warn extends to the person best able to make an informed decision regarding the use of a drug, the prescribing physician, or the pharmacist in the "learned intermediary" role. One exception to this rule is where mass immunization procedures are involved in which patients do not get the benefit of individualized medical attention.

515

Key Words:
Conveying Procedures,
Illustrations,
Organizing Information,
Problems in Design

Thomas, D.L., Johnson, R.C. and Dalezman, J.J., "Opinions of Air Force Maintenance Personnel About Conventional Technical Orders," Wright-Patterson Air Force Base, Advanced Systems Division, NTIS No. AD A058340, July 1978.

Two hundred forty-eight flight line and shop technicians assigned to maintain aircraft were administered a questionnaire to determine their opinions regarding the adequacy of Air Force technical orders as training and job performance aids. Numerous sources of dissatisfaction were isolated. Technical orders were frequently difficult to understand, did not allow for easy information access and did not provide necessary on-the-job information. Interestingly, technicians in the sample suggested that the technical orders should provide specific step-by-step job-related instructions supported by detailed illustrations. Such opinions were, perhaps, inspired by prior exposure to job performance aids which met such criteria.

516

Key Words:
Hazard Prevention/
Analysis Models

Thompson, D.A., "Fault Logic Analysis of Product Safety," *Proceedings of the Human Factors Society - 32nd Annual Meeting*, Human Factors Society, Santa Monica, CA, 1988, 527-531.

This paper provides a tutorial introduction to the use of fault trees in product safety analysis and their potential role in forensics. Selected applications are presented which refer to human reliability. Example situations included the operation of a freight elevator, the use of controls in a vehicle overturning accident, and a hot asphalt tar kettle analysis.

517

Key Words:
Drugs,
Duty/Failure to Warn,
FDA

Thompson, D.E., "The Drug Manufacturer's Duty to Warn—To Whom Does It Extend?" *Florida State University Law Review*, 13:1, Spring 1985, 135-157.

The author suggests that drug manufacturers should have a mandatory duty to warn the ultimate consumer in lieu of the current discretionary duty of the medical profession. The rationale behind this is that the manufacturer has tested the drugs for adverse effects in order to gain FDA approval.

Annotations (501-577)

Key Words:
Superseding Cause

518
Thompson, M.G., "Failure to Warn as a Superseding Cause in Pennsylvania Products Liability Actions," *Temple Law Quarterly*, 59:1, Spring 1986, 239-265.

The Van Buskirk v. Carey Canadian Mines decision made it virtually impossible for manufacturers in Pennsylvania to avoid liability by maintaining that an employer's failure to warn was a superseding cause of plaintiff's injury. The court emphasized that the manufacturer's duty to make a safe product is not delegable.

Key Words:
Accuracy,
Association Rankings/
 Indexes,
Drivers,
Glance Legibility,
Traffic,
Traffic Settings,
Training,
Verbal vs. Nonverbal
 Symbol/Message,
Viewing Time

519
Tierney, W.J. and King, L.E., "Traffic Signing–Symbols Versus Words," a paper presented at *The Sixth World Highway Conference of the International Road Federation*, Montreal, 4-10 October 1970, 1-40.

Symbol and word sign variants were flashed on a screen for time periods of 1/3, 1/6, 1/9, and 1/18 sec. The 208 subjects then attempted to match these briefly displayed images to items within an answer array. Subjects also indicated the meanings they attached to various signs and their preferences for specific sign variants. The results were: 1) many of the symbols were correctly interpreted by less than 50% of the subjects; 2) nondrivers performed much worse than drivers; 3) most pictographic symbols were correctly perceived over 65% of the time, a somewhat higher rate of perception than for legend signs; and 4) the glance legibility of symbol signs was progressively better than for legend signs as the display time was reduced.

Key Words:
Case of Text,
Contrast,
Degradation/Noise,
Illumination Level,
Justification of Text,
Legibility,
Line Spacing/Width,
Page Layout,
Separation Between
 Symbols,
Strokewidth,
Symbol Size,
Typeface/Font,
Viewing Distance

520
Tinker, M.A., "Legibility of Print," Iowa State University Press, Ames, IA, 1963, 1-329.

This classic text addresses the legibility of print within several types of written information. Topics examined here include: methodology; the legibility of letters and digits; kinds and size of type; the width of lines; the leading; the relationship of the leading to type size and line width; the spatial arrangements of the printed page; the color of print and background; printing surfaces; the cumulative effect of combining non-optimal typography arrangements; newspaper typography; and special printing situations and illumination for reading.

An annotated bibliography of articles on legibility published prior to 1963 is also included.

Key Words:
Consumer Preferences,
Reading of: warning
labels

521
Tokuhata, G.K., Colflesh, V., Smith, M., Ramaswamy, K. and Digon, E., "Consumer Behavior and Product Injuries," *Journal of Safety Research*, 8:3, September 1976, 116-125.

A survey of 4012 Pennsylvania households was performed to determine the incidence of injuries to consumers and the behavioral factors related to such injuries. Adequate data was obtained from 3807 households involving 11,453 individuals.

The survey results were: 1) 962 injuries were reported, defining an incidence rate of 84 injuries per 1000 persons; 2) households with injuries were significantly more likely to purchase reconditioned or blemished products and to repair or assemble products at home without outside assistance; 3) households with injuries were more likely to buy products at discount stores and less likely to buy at department stores; 4) in making product decisions, price, appearance, and quality were the top three factors, followed by safety for the accident group and usefulness for the no-accident group; 5) there were no significant differential effects due to advertising or interest in new products; 6) the accident-free group made significantly more joint buying decisions; 7) the accident group had significantly more antihistamines, depressants, diet pills, and hormones in the household (no difference was found for stimulants); 8) over 80% of the subjects from both households claimed that they always read instructions, with no differences observed between the two groups; 9) similar statistics for cautioning children and keeping poisons from children were present; 10) play habits between the groups differed in that children within the accident group tended to play more frequently with other children in the kitchen and in the workshop; 11) no differences were found with regard to children playing with parents outdoors as opposed to indoors, in garages, and in unfinished basements; 12) children in households reporting accidents were more likely not to have worn shoes than children in injury-free households, especially when the weather was cold; 13) there was a general tendency among both children and adults in families which reported injuries to use more plastic drinking containers and fewer glass containers than in the injury-free group; 14) households reporting accidents were more likely to contain cigarette or cigar smokers; 15) households reporting more accidents were more likely to contain beer drinkers (no difference was noted for drinkers of wine or hard liquor); and 16) households reporting accidents tended to be much more physically active.

Key Words:
Amount of Information

522
Tomlinson, G., "Thought for Food: A Study of Written Instructions," *Symbolic Interaction*, **9:2, 1986, 201-216.**

The author analyzes recipes from cookbooks in an attempt to determine how people interpret instructions. Preliminary conclusions are derived regarding the generic features of written instructions. Levels of incompleteness commonly found in instructions are also discussed.

Key Words:
Biohazard,
Consumer Labeling and Signage Systems,
Consumers,
Industrial,
Prohibition,
Safety Information

523
Torpy, T.F., "Graphic Symbols in an Occupational Health Service," *Journal of Occupational Medicine*, **17:12, December 1975, 756-759.**

This paper introduces a set of graphic symbols that represent various functions and facilities used in the Occupational Health Service.

Key Words:
Adequacy of Warnings,
Duty/Failure to Warn,
Effectiveness of: warning related litigation,
Negligence and Warnings,
Overapplication of Warnings,
Strict Liability and Warnings

524
Twerski, A.D., Weinstein, A.S., Donaher, W.A. and Piehler, H.R., "The Use and Abuse of Warnings in Products Liability: Design Defect Litigation Comes of Age," *Cornell Law Review*, **61:4, 1976, 495-540.**

The authors discuss at length whether or not design decisions are polycentric, noting that some individuals feel that failure to warn is a monocentric issue. The authors disagree, arguing that the warning issue is every bit as complex as the design issue. They provide a long discussion of the following points: 1) A decision on failure to warn grounds is frequently based on whether a product design must be modified to avoid liability; 2) Warnings are often ineffective at reducing risk to acceptable levels; 3) The warning issue is frequently polycentric; 4) In many cases, the warnings do not reduce risk and have only informational value; and 5) Failure to appreciate the complexity of the duty aspects of the warning issue may lead a court to impose some unnecessary and imprudent warnings on certain classes of products.

The following issues are also considered: 1) Sometimes a failure to warn case is really a design defect case. If a proper warning would result in the non-marketability of the product, then the true issue before the court is the acceptability of the basic design (McCormack v. Hankscraft, and Dudley Sports Co. v. Schmitt). 2) Warnings may not legally reduce the danger level. Section 402A allows a seller to assume that warnings will be read and heeded, except by children too young to appreciate the warning or by casual bystanders (Patten v. Logemann Brothers, and Phillips v. Kimwood Machine Co.). 3) The apparent inexpensiveness of warnings must be weighed against the cost of over-warning. 4) The costs of providing warnings are considered in Moran v. Faberge, Inc. 5) Some warnings do not reduce the inherent risk (Davis v. Wyeth Laboratories, Inc.) or affect the user's informed choice. 6) The duty aspect of warnings is the point at issue in West v. Broderick and Bascom Rope Company. 7) The role of the trial judge in warning cases should be to consider the interdependence of warnings and design. 8) There is a polycentrism in warning design and application. 9) The sophistication and consciousness of design choices is often overestimated (Garst v. General Motors Corp.); design is often not as systematically well defined as it is often thought to be, and there is a large emphasis on the competition rather than on objective analysis. 10) In the presentation of theoretical evidence, causation is often highly theoretical, and alternative design recommendations are often speculative and infeasible. 11) The design defect case is a litany of litigation problems, and there is the need for thoughtful intermediary, rather than polar, positions. 12) The dual existence of both private lawsuit and administrative law remedies has validity.

Key Words:
Description/Modeling,
Elemental Breakdowns,
Elemental Synthesis,
Symbol Taxonomies

525
Twyman, M., "A Schema for the Study of Graphic Language (Tutorial Paper)," in *Processing of Visible Language*, 1, Kolers, P.A., Wrolstad, M.E. and Bouma, H. (Eds.), Plenum Press, New York, 1979, 117-150.

The author attempts to encompass all graphic language with the schema presented here. The paper is written from the viewpoint of a practicing graphic designer. A matrix is used to illustrate a number of theoretical approaches to graphic language. This approach is particularly interesting as it outlines a number of ways of describing graphic forms of syntax. The author also briefly reviews legibility and related research and suggests a need for more research on the issues addressed in his paper.

Key Words:
Abstractness,
Conveying Action,
Conveying Procedures,
Decision Tables,
Describing Objects,
Description/Modeling,
Illustrations,
Multiple Referents,
Page Layout,
Process Charts/
  Sequences

526
Twyman, M., "Chapter 11: Using Pictorial Language: A Discussion of the Dimensions of the Problem," in *Designing Usable Texts*, Duffy, T.M. and Waller, R. (Eds.), Academic Press Inc., Orlando, 1985.

The author's stated goal is to draw attention to the diversity and complexity of pictorial language and to see it in the context of real communication problems. He begins the paper by noting that the traditional linguistic model does not accommodate pictures. As an alternative he presents a model devised to accommodate approaches to the language of linguistic scientists

Key Words (cont.):
Tables and Flowcharts,
Verbal vs. Nonverbal
Symbol/Message

and graphic designers. Within his model visual language is subdivided into graphic and nongraphic modes. Graphic modes are further divided into verbal, pictorial and schematic languages. Verbal languages include handwriting and printing while schematic languages include all purposeful graphic marks that are not words, numbers or pictures. Differences between categories are noted to be quite fuzzy or overlapping.

Two of the roles of pictorial language that become relevant in the development of instructions and warnings are those of description and narration. In playing these roles, it should be noted that pictographic language is often a difficult medium for making general rather than specific statements. However, its suitability for representing particular concepts often gives it distinct advantages over verbal language. In describing concepts it should be noted that pictures can vary between those which are observation based and those which are concept based. Concept based images often present advantages in communication over photographs because of their ability to help clarify any visual ambiguities. Images composed of discrete elements can be organized in a multitude of ways. Synoptic images can present single unified representations (of the world or other events) which are organized in a way to suggest a slice of the world that, although not conforming to reality, may convey much useful information. Other images consisting of discrete elements may conform to conventional patterns of reading verbal language (i.e. left to right and top to bottom) or may be extremely nonlinear. Elements within images may also be organized as lists, branching structures or matrices. Other common conventions include the cut-away, ghosted and exploded figures or those which are specific conventions developed in construction and engineering. Twyman presents Bertin's 1967 graphic variables (shape, scale, value, texture, color, location, and orientation) and adds time as an additional variable that can be illustrated graphically.

In practical applications of graphics techniques he notes the issues of reproduction of graphics and transmission of graphic images as being potentially problematic. In addition, there are potentially distinguishable cultural differences necessary in image-making and also in the interpretation of such images. Twyman also notes that pictorial language is by no means a natural language for many adults and mentions an educational program undertaken in England in the middle 1960s directed toward increasing students' graphical literacy. The results of such studies demonstrate that the correct understanding of pictures is something that cannot be taken for granted. He also notes that there is no direct way of providing feedback to the producer of graphic language. The feedback that can be obtained is almost always in verbal form, reducing the ease of directly applying such feedback.

Annotations (501-577)

Key Words:
Effectiveness of:
 educational/persuasive
 programs,
Formal Teaching/
 Counseling/Education,
Hazard/Alert,
Newspapers,
Parents,
Smokers

527
U.S. Department of Health, Education, and Welfare, "Adult Education," *Smoking and Health, A Report of the Surgeon General*, Government Printing Office, Washington, D.C., 1979, 21-1 - 21-32.

Topics included in this chapter are: health competency development and smoking education; accessibility to instruction; influence of adult role models; smoking education and cessation programs; laws and regulations; influence of school programs on parents; dissemination of smoking prevention methods and programs; and identification and replication of demonstration models.

Key Words:
Labels,
Psychosocial Influences,
Smokers

528
U.S. Department of Health, Education, and Welfare, "Behavioral Factors in the Establishment, Maintenance, and Cessation of Smoking," *Smoking and Health, A Report of the Surgeon General*, Government Printing Office, Washington, D.C., 1979, 16-1 - 16-23.

From the same report as the previous annotation, this chapter presents two explanatory models of smoking, the social learning model and the nicotine addiction model. A context for behavior research on smoking is also discussed.

Key Words:
ANSI,
Biohazard,
Hazard/Alert,
Industrial,
Ingress/Egress,
OSHA,
Point of Operation
 Guarding,
Routing,
Safety Information,
Traffic

529
U.S. Department of Health, Education, and Welfare, "Smoking in Children and Adolescents - Psychosocial Determinants and Prevention Strategies," *Smoking and Health, A Report of the Surgeon General*, Government Printing Office, Washington, D.C., 1979, 17-1 - 17-30.

The topics covered in this chapter are: current smoking patterns and beliefs; relevant conceptual models in developmental and social psychology; typical psychosocial influences on the smoking decision; critical evaluations of some current prevention programs; and recommendations for future research and prevention programs.

Key Words:
Children,
Design of:
 educational/persuasive
 programs,
Effectiveness of:
 educational/persuasive
 programs,
Psychosocial Influences,
Smokers

530
U.S. Department of Health, Education, and Welfare, "The Role of Educators," *Smoking and Health, A Report of the Surgeon General*, Government Printing Office, Washington, D.C., 1979, 23-1 - 23-45.

This chapter addresses U.S. school educational programs about smoking. Included are: the development and implementation of school policies on smoking; curriculum; the development of demonstration projects; identification of successful programs;

Annotations (501-577)

evaluation of educational programs designed to prevent smoking; dissemination and promotion of successful practices and products; and teacher education.

Key Words:
Children,
Formal Teaching/
  Counseling/Education,
Smokers

531
U.S. Department of Health, Education, and Welfare, "Youth Education," *Smoking and Health, A Report of the Surgeon General*, Government Printing Office Government Printing Office, Washington, D.C., 1979, 20-1 - 20-33.

Current approaches to smoking education including school and non-school programs are reviewed.

Key Words:
Psychosocial Influences,
Smokers

532
U.S. Department of Health, Education, and Welfare, "Psychosocial Influences on Cigarette Smoking," *Smoking and Health, A Report of the Surgeon General*, Government Printing Office, Washington, D.C., 1979, 18-1 - 18-31.

This paper discusses individual and social factors affecting the maintenance of and cessation of smoking. Included is a section on general psychosocial influences on smoking and recommendations for future research.

Key Words:
Consumer Preferences,
Influences of Warning
  Labels,
Level of Detail,
Memory of:
  symbol/message,
Recall,
Signal Words

533
Ursic, M., "The Impact of Safety Warnings on Perception and Memory," *Human Factors*, 26:6, December 1984, 677-682.

This study investigated the impact of safety warnings on the perception of product safety and effectiveness. The subjects were ninety-one undergraduate business students from the University of Florida. The products considered were bug killers and hair dryers.

During the experiment, each subject viewed display boards containing information on three hypothetical brands of each product. One of the brands had a safety warning. For the bug killers, the boards contained information on price, smell, ease of use, and safety. For hair dryers, information on price, amount of power, compactness, and safety was provided. Subjects also received written instructions telling them to examine the display boards and rate each brand's effectiveness and safety. One hour after exposure, subjects were asked to recall which brand had the warning and what the warning said. Brands with safety warnings were perceived as being significantly safer and more effective than brands without warnings. The use of a pictogram, the strength of a signal word, and the presence of capital letters all had no significant impact on the perceived effectiveness or safety of the products. Variations in the design of the warnings did not produce significant effects on memorability of the content of the warnings, nor did they impact the memorability of which brand had the warning.

Key Words:
CPSA,
Consumer Labeling and Signage Systems,
DOT,
Duty/Failure to Warn,
FDA,
Governmental Labeling and Signage Systems,
Industrial,
OSHA

534
Ursic, M., "Product Safety Warning: A Legal Review," *Journal of Public Policy & Marketing*, 4, 1986, 80-90.

The author provides a comprehensive overview of the statutory and common law requirements concerning safety warnings. The paper is directed toward a non-legal audience such as marketing experts or other business practitioners. Major federal agencies and departments empowered to make rules concerning warnings are briefly described including: the CPSC, FDA, FTC, OSRC, EPA and DOT, along with their enabling legislation. Common law legal issues including when to warn, how to warn and who to warn are also addressed. Selected studies falling into each of these categories are briefly summarized.

Key Words:
Accuracy,
Confusion Matrix,
Predictive User Response Equations,
Symbol Generation,
Symbol Taxonomies,
Viewing Distance

535
Van Nes, F.L. and Bouma, H., "On the Legibility of Segmented Numerals," *Human Factors*, 22:4, 1980, 463-474.

Numerals drawn from seven straight line segments are often used in computer displays. The researchers set out to determine the optimum seven-segment configurations for numerical digits. They cite three perceptual requirements for numerical digits (taken from Bouma and Leopold, 1969 and Bouma and Van Rens, 1971): visibility of each character and its individual parts; discriminability (the distinguishability of each character from other characters); and acceptability (each character's similarity to human internal concepts).

An experiment was then performed in which subjects identified digits at two different distances under two peripheral viewing conditions. The digits were displayed on either one or three indicator tubes with the luminance of the segments emitting green light at approximately 600cd/m^2. Digit height was 19mm and digit width was 11.5mm. The viewing distance was either 16m or 57cm, and the stimuli were presented at eccentricities of 0°, 7.5° or 30°. These conditions were fairly difficult, with average correct identifications of single digits being approximately 65%. For multiple digits, the hundreds digit was correctly identified 81% of the time, the tens 37%, and the units 53%.

Analysis of the derived confusion matrix showed that certain digits were more likely to be confused, and others were less likely to be correctly identified. These results are summarized by three rules: 1) the smaller the number of segments from which a digit is built up, the more easily it is recognized; 2) the larger the total number of segments in which two digits differ, the lower the probability that they will be confused; and 3) an incorrectly recognized digit is usually perceived as being a simpler digit. (We note that Rule 2 could also be phrased to state that the more segments that two digits have in common, the greater the likelihood that they will be confused.)

A simple function is defined that maps specific line segments to the number of digits distinguished by the line segment. This function was highly correlated with the number of confusions occurring within the sets of digits that had segments in common. This function and the acceptability data guided changes in the digits 6, 9, and 1. Important line segments were also accentuated by broadening or lengthening them slightly.

Key Words:
Industrial

536
Van Peski, R.F., "Hail!...The Mighty Safety Poster," *National Safety News***, May 1978, 90-92.**

The author gives a positive endorsement of safety posters based upon personal experience, personal observation, conversations with workers, and principles taught to the author by an unnamed psychologist. General opinions as to where to display posters, how many posters to use, how to select posters, and how long to leave them up are given.

Key Words:
Age,
Consumer Setting,
Elderly,
Line Spacing/Width,
Reading Speed,
Subjective Ratings,
Symbol Size,
Typeface/Font

537
Vanderplas, J.M. and Vanderplas, J.H., "Some Factors Affecting Legibility of Printed Materials for Older Adults," *Perceptual and Motor Skills***, 50:3, June 1980, 923-932.**

Twenty-eight older adults (mean age seventy-two) participated in two experiments designed to collect data on reading speed and acceptance ratings as a function of type size, type style, line width, and line spacing. The differences in performance found for the different styles and sizes of type were significant. The researchers note that for young adults, the most common recommendation of type size is at least 8 points, and that, except for Old English, which seems to degrade performance, the style of type is not significant to young adults.

In this experiment, older subjects preferred styles in sizes of at least 12 points and showed a preference for Roman styles, showing that research involving young adults could not be extended to an older population. Interactions between different line widths and spacing for different sizes of type of the same style were also found to be significant. This paper concludes with a discussion on the implications of these findings in terms of the design of printed materials for use by older adults.

Key Words:
ANSI,
Consensual Labeling and Signage Systems,
Consumer Labeling and Signage Systems,
FMC

538
Velotta, C., "Safety Labels: What to Put in Them, How to Write Them and Where to Place Them," *IEEE Transactions on Professional Communication,* **30:3, September 1987, 121-126.**

The author provides a general overview of current warning label standards developed by organizations such as ANSI, Westinghouse and FMC. These guidelines are provided in a brief and readable format. No attempt is made to consult academic literature regarding the demonstrated effectiveness of such guidelines or other scientific foundations.

Key Words:
Amount of Information,
Behavior Factors,
Cleaning Products/ Chemical Hazards,
Cleansers,
Consumers,
Expressed Value of Avoiding Damages,
Gender,
Influences of Warning Labels,
Personal Protective Equipment,
Risk Hazard Scales,
Warnings: evaluating effects on behavior

539
Viscusi, W.K. and Magat, W.A., *Learning About Risk: Consumer and Worker Responses to Hazard Information,* **Harvard University Press, Cambridge, 1987.**

This book expands upon the results of Viscusi, Magat and Huber (1986, see reference 540 below) by including detailed information regarding that study along with a discussion of information processing and decision making. The book includes chapters on information processing and individual decisions, cognitive considerations in presenting risk information, the design of a consumer information study, the effect of risk information on precautionary behavior, risk-dollar trade-offs, risk perceptions and consumer behavior, hazard warnings for workplace risk, and implications for economic behavior.

A study of the effects of hazard warnings on workers' risk perceptions, wage rates, and turnover behavior is also included. In this study, 335 chemical industry employees (engineers, technicians, chemists, mechanics, researchers, and supervisors) completed questionnaires designed to measure worker response to job hazard information. The first part of the questionnaire addressed the employee's perception of risk associated with the present working environment. It was found that the greater the perceived risk associated with one's job, the lower the probability of repeating one's initial job choice. Furthermore, the more dangerous a worker viewed his job to be, the more likely he was to express an intention to quit.

The second portion of the questionnaire was designed to assess workers' processing of risk information. Subjects were presented with a hazard warning label for a chemical that had not previously been used in the workplace and told that the chemical would soon be used in their daily job operations. One of four different chemical labels was introduced: sodium bicarbonate (CARB), lachrymator chloroacetophenone (LAC), asbestos (ASB), and TNT. After viewing the label subjects again assessed the risks associated with their jobs. The low risk chemical, CARB, led to a reduction in perceived risk. After exposure to the label for LAC, the second safest substance, risk perception increased dramatically. The asbestos label prompted workers to triple their assessed risk levels, but the TNT label generated the greatest risk assessment of the four labels. The authors compared the risk assessments before and after label presentation and concluded that the weight individuals place on their prior beliefs dominates the formation of workers' risk judgement unless hazard warnings convey information in a convincing manner

It was also found that the demand for wage increases was positively related to the change in risk. After workers saw the labels, demands for extra compensation ranged from $2,000 for LAC to over $5,000 for TNT. Regarding the intention to quit, the CARB label reduced the intent from 23% to zero, while the other three labels produced increases in the percentage of respondents reporting this intention. We consider this study to be significant and well-done and recommend that the reader also see Viscusi et al. (1986, annotated below).

540
Viscusi, W.K., Magat, W.A. and Huber, J., "Informational Regulation of Consumer Health Risks: An Empirical Evaluation of Hazard Warnings," *Rand Journal of Economics*, **17:3, Fall 1986, 351-365.**

Key Words:
Amount of Information,
Behavior Factors,
Cleaning Products/
  Chemical Hazards,
Cleansers,
Consumers,
Expressed Value of
  Avoiding Damages,
Gender,
Influences of Warning
  Labels,
Personal Protective
  Equipment,
Risk Hazard Scales,
Warnings: evaluating
  effects on behavior

The authors begin with the assumption that rational consumers undertake safety precautions only if the expected value of the safety gains exceeds the associated disutility of the precautionary actions. In order to assess the degree to which consumers make use of safety information provided on warning labels, the authors conducted a questionnaire study involving approximately four hundred consumers and two products. For each of the two products, a liquid bleach and a liquid drain opener, various warning label configurations were applied to the bottles containing the products. Subjects who were potential users or potentially exposed to the products were then given a questionnaire which was directed toward isolating the degree to which consumers would take precautions when using the products. Different labels were used on the products. The first type provided no hazard warning information. The others differed in the amount of risk informational content provided (as much as 78% of one label was devoted to conveying risk information).

Labeling experts designed ideal warning labels for each of the variants. Each consumer in the sample examined only one of the product labels before being interviewed. Note: the warning conditions for bleach corresponded to no warning, warnings currently used on Clorox bleach, warnings currently used on Bright bleach, and the test warning which had the highest amount of risk information. For the drain opener the three labels used were: no warning, the Drano warning, and a test label.

Results showed that for all the bleach labels, the test label was associated with the greatest self-reported propensity to take precautions. The incremental difference between the test label and no warning label was 23% for "do not mix with toilet bowl cleaner," 17% for "do not add to ammonia based cleaners," and 33% for "store in childproof location." The propensity to take the precaution when no warning was present was 17%, 69% and 43% for the three conditions respectively. Results for the drain opener product showed that the best results were associated with the Drano label, which corresponded to a 19% greater self-reported propensity to wear rubber gloves than when no warning was present and an 11% greater propensity for the precautionary action of storing the product in a childproof location. The self-reported propensity under the no warning label condition was 63% for "wear rubber gloves" and 57% for "store in childproof location." Note: the labels for all of the products were listed under imaginary product names.

A multivariate regression analysis was then undertaken in an attempt to establish what factors influenced the self-reported propensity for taking precautions. These results showed that other factors, in certain instances, were also significant influences on the self-reported propensity to follow the precautions. These included race, sex, income, education and having children under five years of age. Interestingly, the significance of particular variables varied with the specific hazard and the product in question. For example, males were unlikely to wear gloves while using the Drano drain cleaner but were not significantly less likely to follow the precautions for the other types of hazards. Further regression analysis also demonstrated that the proportion of the label which was devoted to conveying risk information was significantly correlated with the propensity to take precautions as was the amount of warning information devoted to the specific precautions considered. As might be expected, the influence of a message specifically recommending a particular precaution had a stronger influence than did the overall amount of warning information. We note that these findings suggest that over-warning may lead to less effective results than simple, more pointed warnings.

The study also includes an economic analysis of the consumer choices expressed in the questionnaire. Consumer choices indicated that for the bleach risk, precautions are desirable if the value of avoiding a chloramine gas poisoning is at least $37,900 and the child poisoning valuation is more than $32,000. Substantially lower critical valuations were obtained for the drain opener where a value of $5,200 was associated with avoiding hand burns and $6,500 for avoiding child poisoning. These results can be interpreted by assuming that those individuals who take precautions have health valuations above the critical amount and those who do not take precautions have health loss valuations below the critical amount. These monetary values inferred from the data for the drain opener product clearly implied non-optimal processing of the risk benefit information by the consumers.

The authors conclude that the evidence suggests that the diverse information contained on the labels was processed reliably. They also conclude that there is no clear-cut evidence of any distorting influence by the labels on other usage decisions. This conclusion was inferred from subject answers to other questions regarding how or for what purposes the products could be used safely. The authors also conclude that the consumers responded in a manner that was broadly consistent with the main predictions of an economic model of rational behavior. As such, labels will not lead all consumers to take precautions because, for some, the perceived costs associated with taking precautions are higher than the value of the perceived benefits of reduced risk.

We believe that this study is significant and well-done. The reader, however, must recognize that all results were based on questionnaires where consumers responded as to how they *thought* they would behave under various experimental conditions. It is quite possible that the "actual" behavior of the tested consumers differs significantly from the "self-reported propensity." It is only through a follow-up study of actual behavior that such issues can be resolved.

541
Voevodsky, J., "Evaluation of a Deceleration Warning Light for Reducing Rear-End Automobile Collisions," *Journal of Applied Psychology*, **59:3, 1974, 270-273.**

Key Words:
Behavior Factors,
Deceleration Warning Light,
Warnings: evaluating effects on behavior

This study assesses the effectiveness of a deceleration warning light as a means for preventing collisions under normal driving conditions. A total of 343 taxis operating with deceleration warning lights were compared to a control group of 160 taxis operating without the lights. Public information about the conditions was provided by limited news coverage. After the light-equipped taxis had traveled a total of 12.3 million miles, their rear-end collision rate was 3.51 collisions per million miles, a 60% reduction from the control group which had traveled 7.2 million miles and had a collision rate of 8.91 collisions per million miles.

There was no change in the rate of collisions in which the taxi driver ran into the rear end of a car in front of him. This latter finding supports the conclusion that the taxi drivers had not become more cautious as a result of driving a vehicle equipped with a safety device.

542
Waller, R., "Chapter 7: Text as Diagram: Using Typography to Improve Access and Understanding," in *The Technology of Text*, Jonassen, D.H. (Ed.), Educational Technology Publications, Inc., Englewood Cliffs, 1982, 137-166.

Key Words:
Illustrations,
Indexes/Quick References,
Legibility,
Organizing Information,
Page Layout,
Summaries,
Titles,
Verbal vs. Nonverbal Symbol/Message

The author notes that text and diagrams are usually considered opposites. He notes, however, that the layout of text can often take on aspects of graphic design. Many of the techniques used to display or summarize complex relationships in text are actually graphically oriented. These include methods of ordering and grouping text on the page. He notes that typography can serve as an access structure to the information embedded within any text. He distinguishes between global accessibility (which corresponds to the use of content lists, concept diagram, index, glossary, objectives and summary sections) and local accessibility (which is related to the use of headings and detailed methods of layout).

More specifically, Waller refers to typography as a technique for macro-punctuation. He describes four functions of punctuation that can be served at the text level by typography and layout: 1) Interpolation: footnotes, boxed items, marginalia and indentation; 2) Delineation: headings, bullets, title page, space, rules; 3) Serialization: headings, numerals, tabular format, regular spacing, patterning, regular styling, rules and arrows; and 4) Stylization: size variation, typeface variation, distinctive layout, background tint, colored paper, symbols and key words. Also provided in this article are numerous examples of these various techniques and their application.

Key Words:
Instructions in Litigation

543
Walter, C. and Marsteller, T.F., "Liability for the Dissemination of Defective Information," *IEEE Transactions on Professional Communication*, 30:3, September 1987, 164-167.

The authors provide a general introduction to liability for the dissemination of defective information, describing three cases where such liability is present: 1) where the information is inherently dangerous; 2) where the information could be made less dangerous by including precautionary information; and 3) where the information is dangerous because it is incorrect.

Legal grounds for recovery, including contract law and negligence, are introduced, as are defenses based on the theory of privity and First Amendment Rights. The authors emphasize that publishers, like authors, can be liable for the dissemination of defective information.

Key Words:
Buying Behavior,
Effectiveness of:
  educational/persuasive programs,
Radio/TV,
Review Papers,
Smokers

544
Warner, K.E., "The Effects of the Anti-Smoking Campaign on Cigarette Consumption," *American Journal of Public Health*, 67:7, July 1977, 645-650.

The purpose of this paper is to evaluate the effects of the anti-smoking campaign on annual U.S. per capita cigarette consumption. The anti-smoking campaign is referred to here as the collective, mostly uncoordinated, educational activities of a variety of organizations including the government, private voluntary agencies, and for-profit business firms.

To evaluate such effects, the authors compare current cigarette consumption to projections based upon cigarette consumption prior to enactment of the anti-smoking campaign. This comparison suggests that major events in the anti-smoking campaign, such as the surgeon general's report in 1964, caused immediate but transitory decreases of 4-5% in annual consumption. The cumulative effect of the campaign is estimated to be on the order of 20-30% as of 1975, supporting the theory that the sustained anti-smoking campaign has had a significant impact on the smoking behavior of Americans.

Key Words:
Adequacy of Warnings,
Duty/Failure to Warn,
Loss Prevention Programs,
Negligence and Warnings

545
Weinstein, A.S., Twerski, A.D., Piehler, H.R. and Donaher, W.A., "Chapter 5: Warnings and Disclaimers," in *Products Liability and the Reasonably Safe Product*, John Wiley & Sons, New York, 1978, 60-74.

This chapter discusses the role of warnings in litigation. The authors emphasize that there is an interplay between warnings

Key Words (cont.):
Overapplication of Warnings,
Warranties/Disclaimers

and product design; the sufficiency of providing a warning as a means of avoiding liability depends on whether design alternatives are present. Warnings are an inexpensive way to alleviate risks that cannot be removed from a product without increasing its cost or reducing its utility. They emphasize the need for selectivity when providing warnings and feel a warning should consider real and significant danger; making consumers account for trivia imposes real societal cost.

Several other points made by the authors include: 1) Warnings do not reduce inherent risk and only state that the product should never be used; problems can only be solved by design changes. 2) Some courts recognize that strict liability only applies to warning cases under negligence. 3) It is unclear whether liability can be disclaimed for consumer products, although it clearly can be for commercial clients; Section 402A states that liability cannot be disclaimed.

546
Weinstein, A.S., Twerski, A.D., Piehler, H.R. and Donaher, W.A., "Chapter 3: Product Defects–What Are They?" in *Products Liability and the Reasonably Safe Product*, John Wiley & Sons, New York, 1978, 28-42.

Key Words:
Adequacy of Warnings,
Duty/Failure to Warn,
Loss Prevention Programs,
Negligence and Warnings,
Strict Liability and Warnings

The paper begins with an explanation of the difference between design and production defects. The implications of negligence and strict liability are discussed in regard to both design and production defects. The concept of unreasonable danger is discussed in detail, as is the risk balancing test for reasonableness. The role of reasonable consumer expectations as criteria for performance standards is discussed, particularly in regard to useful product life. Finally, statutes of limitations are considered.

The following points are made about warnings and instructions: 1) products may give false impressions—the very opposite impressions given by the warning; 2) warnings may or may not shield from liability; 3) instructions tell the consumer how to use the product effectively; 4) warnings inform the consumer of the dangers of improper use and tell what, if any, precautions can be taken; and 5) warnings and instructions are frequently difficult to tell apart.

The paper then provides three criteria for evaluating the effectiveness of warnings. The first is that a warning must be in a form that could be expected to catch the attention of the reasonably prudent consumer in the conditions of its use. The second is that the warning's content must be comprehensible to average, reasonably prudent users and convey to them a fair indication of the nature and extent of danger (the degree of

Annotations (501-577)

intensity that would cause these users to exercise the caution commensurate with the potential danger is implicit). The third is that the warning must tell the consumer how to act to avoid the danger.

Key Words:
Consumer Preferences,
Message Tone

547
Weinstein, N.D., "Seeking Reassuring or Threatening Information About Environmental Cancer," *Journal of Behavioral Medicine*, 2:2, 1979, 125-139.

In a state with a high cancer rate, college students were given the chance to receive either a reassuring or a threatening informational message concerning cancer rates. Later, interviews were conducted with students who had not requested a message (N = 502). Lack of concern, as opposed to defensiveness, was indicated as the principal reason explaining why students did not seek information. Both information seekers and non-seekers tended to prefer the threatening message. However, the choice of message did depend on the students' beliefs concerning the seriousness of the threat of cancer. Respondents tended to choose the message which supported their personal view. The author proposed a model to help explain the data; this model stressed the ambiguity and the controversy surrounding many environmental and health warnings.

Key Words:
ANSI,
Advantages of Nonverbal Symbols,
Biohazard,
Color Coding,
Consensual Labeling and Signage Systems,
Consumer Labeling and Signage Systems,
Consumers,
Design Consistency,
Design of: labeling and safety signage systems,
Development Programs,
Duty/Failure to Warn,
Electrical Hazard,
Explosives,
FMC,
Governmental Labeling and Signage Systems,
Hazard/Alert,
ISO,
Industrial,
Negligence and Warnings

548
Westinghouse Electric Corporation, *Product Safety Label Handbook*, Westinghouse Printing Division, Trafford, PA, 1981.

This practical handbook for the engineer and product designer presents a large amount of warning information in a concise, well laid out form. Such an effort as this must be praised although there was little research to support many of the suggested guidelines. Nevertheless, it advanced the state-of-the-art by having brought this subset of materials together so well. We caution the reader that some of these guidelines may change as research progresses.

Among the information and guidelines in this handbook, we have selected fifteen areas to report on:

1) The reason for a safety label program is: to compensate for the fact that a wide variety of products make centralized label development impossible; to improve safety and ensure appropriate product use, installation, service, and maintenance; to meet or exceed current standards; to simplify the label design process; and to develop a unified label system with consistent labels.

Key Words (cont.):
Personal Protective
  Equipment,
Point of Operation
  Guarding,
Prohibition,
Radiation,
Signal Words,
Strict Liability and
  Warnings,
Symbol Generation

2) Labels and law issues seem to deal with negligence and strict liability, defect definition, duty to warn, whom to warn, adequacy of warning, and the post-sale duty to warn.

3) The book presents existing standards in matrix form where the x-axis identifies the categories of: NEMA, ANSI Z35.1 and Z535.4, SAE J115a, the ISO draft, and the Westinghouse handbook. These are cross referenced on the y-axis by the categories of: signal words, color system, color-signal word combinations, message panel, symbols and pictographs, label arrangement, and the classification procedure for hazards.

4) The seven elements in the anatomy of a label are suggested as being: the signal word, hazard alert symbol, color, symbols and pictographs, identification of a hazard, the result of ignoring a warning, and instructions on avoiding the hazard.

5) Sample labels (both good and bad examples) are given.

6) The following design hints are given: signal words and color should reflect a hazard's seriousness; overemphasis of the danger dilutes the warning's impact; careful label arrangement improves communication; operating symbols and information should not be included in warnings; warnings should be as descriptive as possible; label messages should be flush left and ragged right; sentences should begin with capital letters and continue with lower case type; centered type is hard to read; warnings should not be included with name plates or rating plates; and symbols and pictographs should be used whenever possible.

7) In identifying hazards, look at a product, think where it will be used, work in three dimensions, review installation, perform operation and maintenance procedures, coordinate safety labels with instruction literature, and consider product design changes.

8) To select a correct signal word, classify the hazard, assess its degree of potential injury or damage, and assess the likelihood of its occurrence.

9) To develop appropriate labels, consider who will read the label, decide if consumer age is important, think about consumers' education, training, and experience, visualize the context, consider users' dress and clothing, and compare anatomical differences.

10) When making label placement decisions, think chronologically, place labels close to hazards, check reading distance, check viewing angle, design the label for a specific area, think about light, and coordinate labels.

11) Writing a safety label requires use of active construction, concrete specific nouns, precise pure action verbs and strong auxiliary verbs. Do not use contractions or explicit modifiers. Eliminate non-essential words, write in headline style, organize the message, break lines logically, use parallel constructions and arrangements, use descriptive phrasing, and use special care in writing multiple hazard labels.

12) In selecting a symbol or pictograph, recognize symbols and their limitations, decide if symbols or pictographs will help, comply with standards, and consider new symbols or pictographs carefully.

13) To decide upon vertical and horizontal label formats, utilize graphic depiction of label components.

14) For making labels, step by step instructions are provided in a layout kit; the components of the layout kit also include example symbols.

15) In the selection of label materials, one must consider label components and material combinations, base materials, message and graphics, overlaminates, adhesives, backing material, fasteners, and label size versus reading distance tables.

549
Wheale, J.L., "Evaluation of an Experimental Central Warning System with a Synthesized Voice Component," *Aviation, Space, and Environmental Medicine,* **June 1983, 517-523.**

Key Words:
Aircraft,
Aircraft Setting,
Auditory,
Auditory Coding,
Auditory Noise,
Auditory vs. Visual Messages,
Behavior Factors,
Development Programs,
Pilots,
Reaction Time,
Warnings: as noise,
Workload/Task

Sixteen experienced commercial airline pilots were monitored during their use of an experimental central warning system. In the study, the pilots were initially familiarized with the warning system, took part in simulation training, and completed a practice flight. During the flying task, warning responses were evaluated. The focus was on comparing response times to audio warnings, synthesized voice messages, and panel legends. Audio warnings were found to elicit responses significantly faster than the voice messages or panel legends did. Responses to panel legends were also significantly slower at high levels of workload. However, both audio warnings and voice messages had a greater distracting effect on responses than the panel legends.

The authors note that the pilots had difficulty understanding the voice messages produced by the Votrax synthesizer. Results also indicated that the Votrax voice messages may have merely augmented the noise level of the flight deck; an attention-getting sound with a panel legend may be a good replacement.

The author concludes that responses to synthetic voice messages which can be understood on first presentation will be more positive than those presented by Votrax messages.

Key Words:
Association Rankings/ Indexes,
Basic Associations,
Control/Display Elements,
Elemental Breakdowns

550
Wheatley, E., "An Experiment on Coding Preferences for Display Symbols," *Ergonomics*, **20:5, 1977, 543-552.**

Forty-eight subjects, most of whom were female, made paired comparisons of objects that had arbitrary hostility values. Hostility or danger was shown by spikiness, higher numbers, and increased redness of the object. The resulting rank orders indicated that spikes and color were the most salient measures of hostility. Error analysis supported this conclusion.

Key Words:
Traffic

551
Whitaker, L.A. and Sommer, R., "Interference Between Pictorial Symbols and Arrows in Highway Guidance Signs," *Proceedings of the Human Factors Society - 28th Annual Meeting*, **Human Factors Society, Santa Monica, CA, 1984, 799-802.**

This paper was the basis for a subsequent article reviewed herein entitled, "Is the Airport Symbol Sufficient to Convey Route Information?" (See Whitaker, 1985)

Key Words:
Conveying Action,
Drivers,
Elemental Breakdowns,
Elemental Synthesis,
Public Information,
Response Time,
Routing

552
Whitaker, L.A., "Is the Airport Symbol Sufficient to Convey Route Information?" *Human Factors*, **27:2, April 1985, 229-233.**

Twenty young urban drivers were subjects in an experiment designed to test the directional information given by an airport symbol. The symbol, corresponding to the silhouette of an aircraft, appeared on highway route markers and was evaluated in conjunction with an arrow route marker and by itself. During testing, twelve observers had difficulty interpreting directional information from the "plane only" sign.

In the "plane + arrow" condition, response times to the tachistoscopically presented sign depended on the correspondence between the plane and the arrow. Response times were fastest when both symbols pointed in the same direction (i.e., concordantly). The mean response times to "the word AIRPORT + arrow" sign were close to those obtained for the concordant "plane + arrow" sign. Response times to the "plane-alone" signs varied as a function of the stimulus set; if the set of stimuli contained only "plane-alone" signs, the response times were the fastest of all signs. However, if other signs were mixed with the "plane-alone" sign in the stimulus set, the response times increased. It was concluded that subjects can derive directional information from the plane silhouette and that the best sign would contain the plane silhouette and the directional arrow pointing in the same direction.

Key Words:
Conveying Action,
Drivers,
Elemental Breakdowns,
Elemental Synthesis,
Population Stereotypes,
Students,
Traffic

553

Whitaker, L.A. and Stacey, S., "Response Times to Left and Right Directional Signs," *Human Factors*, **23:4, 1981, 447-452.**

In the first experiment twenty-eight students viewed sixty-four directional signs presented via a tachistoscope. The signs defined all possible combinations of the following variables: negation (do, do not); instruction (turn, keep, merge, exit); direction (left, right); and symbol type (word, arrow, word and arrow, integrated word and arrow). Subjects responded to the stimulus by saying the direction indicated by the sign. Significant results were: 1) negation increased auditory response time by 185 ms; 2) auditory response time was 142 ms longer for directional signs containing words alone than for arrows; and 3) negation increased auditory response time by 290 ms for word signs and by 150 ms for arrow signs.

The second experiment tested thirty students and was similar to the first except that subjects responded by moving their hand rather than by speaking. The merge instruction was also eliminated. The results were similar to those from the first experiment: 1) negation increased hand response time by 150 ms; 2) responses to word-only signs were 209 ms longer than for arrow-only; and 3) negation increased response time by 191 ms for word signs, and by 133 ms for arrow signs.

Other general results were: 1) response times for the word and arrow combination and the arrow alone were roughly equivalent; 2) the mean response time to the signs containing arrows was about 85 ms less when the response modality was hand instead of voice (no significance calculations were given for this particular result; in fact, the researcher said that no evidence was present for S/R compatibility); and 3) the longest response times and most errors were found for prohibitive directional signs.

Key Words:
Drivers,
Effectiveness of:
 educational/persuasive
 programs,
Existing/Past Behavior
 Patterns

554

Williams, A.F. and O'Neill, B., "On-The-Road Driving Records of Licensed Race Drivers," *Accident Analysis and Prevention*, **6, 1974, 263-270.**

The authors note the lack of evidence showing that advanced driver training reduces the chance of having accidents or violations. This issue was evaluated by analyzing the on-the-road

Key Words (cont.):
Formal Teaching/
 Counseling/Education

driving records of 477 national competition license holders (race car drivers) belonging to the Sports Car Club of America. Speeding, other moving violations, and non-moving violations comprised three violation categories. Accidents were also considered. The Sports Car Club of America National competition license holders had more crashes per driver and more violations of all three types when compared to the control group.

555
Witt, H. and Hoyos, C.G., "Advanced Information on the Road: A Simulator Study of the Effect of Road Markings," *Human Factors*, 18:6, December 1976, 521-532.

Key Words:
Behavior Factors

This study evaluated the influences of a sequence of stripes on the right edge of the pavement. The stripes were designed to indicate the radius of the curve ahead to the driver. The effects of these markings were analyzed using a driving simulator and twelve subjects. The driving tasks were on simulated roads of varying curvature with different placement of the stripes in the approach zone. Subjects drove more steadily, more precisely, and with a more suitable speed profile as a result of the advanced information provided by the stripes.

556
Wogalter, M.S., Desaulniers, D.R. and Brelsford, J.W., "Perceptions of Consumer Products: Hazardousness and Warning Expectations," *Proceedings of the Human Factors Society - 30th Annual Meeting*, Human Factors Society, Santa Monica, CA, 1986, 1197-1201.

Key Words:
Consumer Preferences,
Reading of: warning
 labels,
Workers

Seventy-two common household products that represented a wide range of danger were rated by 125 undergraduates on several dimensions. The products fell into three general categories, Electrical, Chemical, and Non-electrical Tools.

The ratings were developed by asking the subjects six questions: 1) If you saw a warning on this product would you read it? 2) How hazardous is the product? 3) How familiar is the product? 4) Do you think there should be a warning on this product? 5) Where would you expect to find a warning on this product (how far away)? 6) Do you think a warning that is visible when the product is in use would make the product less attractive? All answers were measured on 6 point scales; mean ratings were obtained for each of the seventy-two products.

From analysis of the correlations, the authors conclude that a product's perceived hazardousness is the primary determinant of willingness to read the warning (over 80% of the variance). They report that the more hazardous products tended to be least familiar (R=-.63). Negative correlations were found between the expected location of the warning and the location of the perceived hazard (R=-.81). The reported willingness to read a warning increased (R=-.89) as the expected distance between the hazard and warning decreased.

Key Words:
Consumer Preferences,
Laboratory/Generic Settings,
Level of Detail,
Redundancy

557
Wogalter, M.S., Desaulniers, D.R. and Godfrey, S.S., "Perceived Effectiveness of Environmental Warnings," *Proceedings of The Human Factors Society - 29th Annual Meeting*, Human Factors Society, Santa Monica, CA, 1985, 664-668.

Seventeen warnings were used in a study which encompassed a signal word (DANGER, WARNING, CAUTION), a hazard statement (SHALLOW WATER, HIGH VOLTAGE), a consequence statement (POSSIBLE HEAD INJURY, ELECTRICAL SHOCK), and an instruction statement (NO DIVING, DO NOT TOUCH).

The subjects in the study were 107 college undergraduates. The dependent measure was an effectiveness rating scored from 0 to 7. It was found that warnings of severe hazards were rated as more effective than those dealing with mild hazards. The elimination of either the hazard or the consequence statement was also perceived as increasing effectiveness in certain cases. In order for effectiveness to be perceived as being high, it seemed that each statement had to provide an incremental, nonredundant piece of information.

Key Words:
Behavior Factors,
Case of Text,
Location,
Reading of: warning labels,
Signal Words,
Students,
Warnings: evaluating effects on behavior

558
Wogalter, M.S., Fontenelle, G.A. and Laughery, K.R., "Behavioral Effectiveness of Warnings," *Proceedings of the Human Factors Society - 29th Annual Meeting*, Human Factors Society, Santa Monica, CA, 1985.

The authors conducted a two-stage experiment evaluating the influence of warning location and signal words on the use of gloves and masks in a chemistry lab task. The subjects were undergraduates performing basic chemistry demonstrations.

Of interest was the finding that using the signal word WARNING versus NOTE did not significantly affect behavior. The location of the warning did, however, have a large effect. Warnings placed at the beginning of the instructions had approximately twice as much effect on behavior as did warnings located at the end.

Key Words:
Color Coding,
Effectiveness of:
  educational/persuasive
  programs,
Print Size

559
Wogalter, M.S., Godfrey, S.S., Fontenelle, G.A., Desaulniers, D.R., Rothstein, P.R. and Laughery, K.R., "Effectiveness of Warnings," *Human Factors*, 29:5, October 1987, 599-612.

The authors conducted several experiments and found that: 1) a warning must be an appropriate size, color and design to attract attention; 2) the ideal warning clearly and concisely describes the hazard and gives instructions for avoiding it; and 3) the less time and effort required for compliance with a warning, the greater the impact it will have on behavior.

Key Words:
Cleaning Products/
  Chemical Hazards,
Cohort Behavior,
Cost of Compliance,
Personal Protective
  Equipment,
Warnings: evaluating
  effects on behavior

560
Wogalter, M.S., McKenna, N.A. and Allison, S.T., "Warning Compliance: Behavioral Effects of Cost and Consensus," *Proceedings of the Human Factors Society - 32nd Annual Meeting*, Human Factors Society, Santa Monica, CA, 1988, 901-904.

The authors examine the possible effects on warning-related behavior of two factors: 1) the cost of compliance; and 2) the behavior of cohorts. In both experiments, subjects from the University of Richmond were asked to perform a chemistry demonstration task. The instructions for the task contained a warning directing them to wear a safety mask and gloves.

In the first experiment, the cost of compliance was manipulated by locating the mask and gloves in either an accessible location (low cost) or a less accessible location (high cost). In the low cost conditions the gloves and mask were placed on the subject's work table. In the high cost conditions they were located in a different room. Under the low cost conditions the subjects complied with the warnings 73% of the time; only 17% of the subjects complied under the high cost conditions.

In the second experiment, a cohort performing the same task either did or did not comply with the warning. When the cohort complied with the warning, 100% of the experimental subjects complied. When the cohort did not comply with the warning, only 33% of the subjects complied. The authors conclude that both the cost of complying with a warning and the behavior of other cohorts can influence the effectiveness of warning labels.

Key Words:
Consumer Labeling and
  Signage Systems

561
Wolcott, R., *Informative Labeling*, National Consumer-Retailer Council, Inc., New York, 1941, 1-23.

This general document discusses the expected advantages of informative labeling, the process of building a label, and the

Annotations (501-577)

cooperation which is offered by the National Consumer-Retailer Council. Although much of the discussion is not supported by solid evidence, the document provides insight into the advantages of information labeling to consumers, retailers, and manufacturers.

Key Words:
Control/Display Elements,
Design of: labeling and safety signage systems,
Traffic

562
Woodson, W.E. and Conover, D.W., *Human Engineering Design Handbook: Information and Guidelines for the Design of Systems, Facilities, Equipment, and Products for Human Use*, McGraw-Hill, New York, 1981.

This very significant handbook provides an extensive collection of general human factors guidelines, including those related to the design of displays, labels, and signs.

Key Words:
Accuracy,
Active Processing,
Biohazard,
Memory of: symbol/message,
Reading Measures,
Reading of: warning labels,
Recall

563
Wright, P., "Concrete Action Plans in TV Messages to Increase Reading of Drug Warnings," *Journal of Consumer Research*, 6, December 1979, 256-269.

The author cites evidence that persuasive materials are more likely to elicit desired forms of behavior if concrete rich descriptions of the desired actions are given, or if people actively perform "action" planning. Both approaches increase the number of details remembered by the consumer. The impact of these two approaches on the reading of in-store drug warnings and the influence of TV ads are evaluated.

A complicated cover story about new TV shows was used to recruit the subjects, who then saw the TV shows and the experimental ads; afterwards, they received ten dollars plus coupons redeemable for antacids and other products at a specific store. Within the TV ads, several formats were tested. The variable "verbal action recommendations" sequence involved either a "concrete" ad, in which a person would be observed in a store reading the package label before buying, or a "general" ad, in which only reading the package warnings was emphasized. The variable "visual segment" sequence showed either a "package" sequence with a close-up view, front and back, allowing the warning to be seen, or a "shopper" sequence, which showed a woman picking up a package and reading its label while standing by the counter.

The elapsed time between when subjects viewed the TV show and when they arrived at the store to redeem their coupons was of interest. At the antacid display counter in the store, five (4 inch by 10 inch) warning signs were placed on the top shelf (5 feet off the ground). Each sign had the heading "ANTACID WARNING!!" Each cited the FDA as its informational source, urged that the sign be read before buying an antacid, and listed brands of antacids that were risky to certain groups.

As subjects redeemed their antacid coupons in the store, their behavior was unobtrusively observed. The behavior of shoppers in the store who were not exposed to the TV ads was also observed. A questionnaire that asked for information on the warning sign was completed by all persons buying or redeeming antacid coupons. The results were: 1) the subjects who went directly to the store (forty minutes or less after viewing the program) and who had been exposed to the "concrete-shopper" ad spent significantly more time examining the packages (about sixteen seconds compared to about six seconds for the regular shopper); the other TV ads had no significant effect; 2) subjects who went to the store more than forty minutes after viewing the program spent the same amount of time inspecting the package as the average shopper; 3) of the eighty-six regular antacid buyers, only nine (11%) spent time reading the warning sign; 4) in comparison to the regular antacid buyers, 37% of the subjects who viewed the "concrete-shopper" ad spent time reading the warning sign, which is a significant increase ($p<.001$); 5) inspection times for the different brands did not increase significantly when the warning sign was present, except that subjects who had seen the "concrete-shopper" ad and the stimulus message spent an average of 31.5 seconds examining the package; and 6) fewer than 10% of the shoppers could correctly identify one or more of the three at-risk groups mentioned in the package label. The questionnaire results showed no significant differences between the knowledge of sign and non-sign readers, nor did the individuals who had spent ten seconds or more examining the package (reading) know more than those who spent ten seconds or less.

In summary, some of the more interesting results of this study are: 1) the time elapsed after viewing the commercial did not affect sign reading, but did affect package reading when no sign was available; 2) there was a much lower frequency of sign reading among regular purchasers; 3) the knowledge level of regular purchasers about the product was generally low; and 4) TV commercials showing "concrete" action sequences increased the reading of drug messages.

Key Words:
Illustrations,
Task Analysis,
Writing Instruction
  Guidelines,
Writing Instructions

564
Wright, P., "Five Skills Technical Writers Need," *IEEE Transactions on Professional Communication*, 24:1, March 1981, 10-16.

This paper proposes that technical writers need to acquire five basic skills that go well beyond the common guidelines for "how to" write. The first skill, task analysis, includes finding, understanding, and reinterpreting information. Also required is the ability to know what perceptual processes should be considered and what assumptions readers may make. Language control is the second skill, and it incorporates such principles as avoiding jargon and complex sentences. The third skill, graphic and typographic presentation, includes the ability to provide illustrative materials as part of a coherent overall presentation. Interpretation of research findings is the fourth skill, and it emphasizes that the writer must communicate clearly and accurately with the reader. The fifth skill, management of a system for document production, refers to the ability to coordinate the activities necessary to produce the final written product.

Key Words:
Design of: instructions,
Problems in Design,
Writing Instructions

565
Wright, P., "'The Instructions Clearly State...' Can't People Read?" *Applied Ergonomics*, 12:3, 1981, 131-141.

At the beginning of this paper, Simon and Hayes (1976) are quoted as saying that following instructions is one of most difficult comprehension tasks people ordinarily encounter in daily life. Additional data are presented that show a significant reluctance to read and follow instructions. An example is cited in which several children failed to read a warning against eating too many mints and became sick. This example supports the need to consider who will be reading the instructions.

Several potential problems with instructions are cited. First, instructions may contain information which is factually wrong or designed for another version of the product. Errors in translation of instruction may compound the problems. A second potential problem is that the information may be incomprehensible in both the textual and illustrative portions. Finally, the information may be dependently structured under the assumption that a reader will sequentially move through a document. This latter problem can cause errors when readers skim through instructions looking for a specific fact without reading the entire text. Since the writer works from specifications given by the engineer, problems may arise if the design is changed after specifications are given. Also, unnecessary details that the customer does not want may be given in such specifications, and knowledge omitted by the engineer may not be common knowledge.

The author proposes that the development of adequate instructions requires: 1) the provision of adequate content (a model of the design process by Felker (1980), was cited); 2) a predesign analysis (what the consumer needs to know and how this can be most easily provided, which will likely require a questionnaire or survey); 3) adequate presentation (how the content should be presented, pictorially versus textually); and 4) an adequate structure that helps users find answers to specific questions; interestingly, people tend to avoid the use of indexes, and inappropriate headings can be counterproductive.

The author also notes that there is a common misconception that writing is an easy task. The author argues against this, pointing out that recommended do's and don'ts are difficult to apply because such guidelines have exceptions and are often overly long.

The author further notes that good technical writing often requires competence in several areas not traditionally associated with writing. These areas include: 1) cognitive task analysis evaluating perception, memory, language and decision making issues; 2) control over complex terminology, complex syntax, and problems with negative information; 3) control of graphic and typographic factors and use of the graphic triangle; 4) interpreting research findings using handbooks and checklists, and conducting experiments and surveys; 5) pilot testing of drafts using holistic approaches in which the editor reads the draft, interactive approaches where the instructions are used with the product present, and microapproaches which emphasize trouble spots; and 6) management of the production process.

The final conclusion is that a multidisciplinary approach to providing information should be taken, and the technical writer is more of a coordinator than a jack of all trades.

Key Words:
Design of: instructions,
Problems in Design,
Readability Measures,
Reading of: instructions,
Task Analysis,
Writing Instructions

566
Wright, P., "Usability: The Criterion for Designing Written Information," in *Processing of Visible Language*, 2, Kolers, P.A., Wrolstad, M.E., and Bouma, H. (Eds.), Plenum Press, New York, 1980, 183-205.

The author notes that an analysis of the concept of "usability" has both a research and a design component In designing usable written materials, many contextual factors not ordinarily addressed in research must be considered. These contextual factors are determined by the task which is being performed while reading the provided information; reading is done for a particular purpose in a specific task-related context. The reason for consulting written material, whether it be to complete a form or to answer questions verbally, must therefore be considered when analyzing usability.

To achieve usability, designers must learn about readers, decide how to present the text, and then test the adequacy of

Annotations (501-577)

the draft text. The author advocates the usability approach in most cases because it generates valid research, achieves practical relevance, and is applicable to a wide variety of written materials. She notes, however, that the analysis of usability is not reducible to procedural algorithms, such as readability formulas, process models, or psycholinguistic models.

567
Wright, P., "Writing To Be Understood: Why Use Sentences?" *Applied Ergonomics*, **December 1971, 207-209.**

Key Words:
Accuracy,
Decision Tables,
Description/Modeling,
Illustrations,
Logic Trees,
Message Complexity,
Response Time,
Task Specific Context,
Verbal vs. Nonverbal Symbol/Message,
Writing Instructions

A complicated example of prose is re-stated using a logical tree, a two dimensional table, and a list of short sentences. The list of short sentences is directly equivalent to simple rules. Studies are cited that show the prose version is more difficult to understand than the tree, list, or table alternatives. In a specific study comparing these four formats, the logical tree was shown to be particularly appropriate if the user was unsure as to which variables were important for the particular problem, since the error rate was the lowest, while the table was the best format if the user knew which variables were important. Both short sentences and tables were processed somewhat faster than logic trees under both conditions. Messages were remembered better when the list format was used.

A set of writing rules is given at the end of the paper: 1) when the information is available to be read as needed, use tables if the reader will know what to look up, use logical trees if the reader needs help finding the relevant part of the information, and use illustrations wherever possible to circumvent the need for technical jargon; 2) when the information must be remembered, use lists of simple sentences with appropriate subheadings; 3) whenever the information must be easily understood, avoid the use of prose written in bureaucratic style.

568
Wright, P., "Chapter 15: A User-Oriented Approach to the Design of Tables and Flowcharts," in *The Technology of Text*, **Jonassen, D.H. (Ed.), Educational Technology Publications, Inc., Englewood Cliffs, 1982, 317-340.**

Key Words:
Illustrations,
Tables and Flowcharts,
User Modeling,
Writing Instructions

This article evaluates some of the design choices available when presenting information in tables and flowcharts. The intent of the article is to provide some general principles to improve user friendliness, rather than to establish firm design guidelines. It is noted that people using a table usually have to do at least three things: 1) grasp the logical principles on which the information has been organized; 2) find the required information within the table; and 3) interpret the information once it has been found.

In comparing tables to flowcharts the author notes that flow charts usually provide explicit questions or alternatives which form the basis of the user's ultimate decisions, while most tables usually leave these questions for the user to formulate on the basis of information given in the row and column headings or from a pre-existing agenda of inquiry the user may have before the table is reviewed in detail.

Flowcharts, which help people process information in a particular sequence, may make things difficult for a reader who wants to use the information in some other way. In evaluating research studies of tables and flowcharts, the author indicates several general design principles as summarized below.

The author feels that redundancy is something which designers of tables and flowcharts frequently desire to eliminate for the purposes of saving space or paper. In certain cases, however, redundancy may actually make it easier for people to interpret the information so provided. Essential to the design of both flowcharts and tables is a need to help structure the decision process that people follow while using such materials. A well-designed decision structure uses the appropriate classification or categorization of items used in the database itself. A well-designed decision structure may help to prevent people making a series of decisions from slowing down and making errors. In any case, there is a need for the decision structure to be natural to the intended users. An appropriate decision structure can also help users minimize memory load while processing the information by eliminating their need to remember prior states. Facilitating comparisons with known values can also be helpful.

For the presentation of the information within tables, several guidelines are noted: 1) the rounding of numbers to just two or three figures; 2) the provision of row or column averages as appropriate; and 3) the arrangement of numbers and tables in some meaningful order. Functional grouping of material in tables has also been demonstrated to be useful as has avoiding the introduction of unnecessary gaps within tables.

The author further notes that typographic variation may be a valuable approach for creating perceptible groupings within tables. For flowcharts, variations in geometrical shapes may provide similar advantages. A major difficulty in obtaining acceptable forms of presentation is the influence of the available space within which the information must be contained. Failure to use what space is available will often result in legibility problems. The author concludes that designers need to be able to make explicit, as part of their predesign analysis, how readers proceed, on a step-by-step basis, from the cognitive beginning of formulating the question that motivates their

Annotations (501-577)

turning to the table or chart to ultimately arriving at an answer.

Key Words:
Perceived Risk,
Reading of: instructions,
Reading of: warning labels

569
Wright, P., Creighton, P. and Threlsall, S.M., "Some Factors Determining When Instructions Will Be Read," *Ergonomics*, 25:3, 1982, 225-237.

Fifty-two subjects were asked whether they would read the instructions that came with sixty different consumer products, thirty of which were electrical and thirty non-electrical. Electrical items were divided into three categories: those with complex operating instructions (e.g., video recorders and washing machines); those with simple operating instructions (e.g., hair dryers and vacuum cleaners); and those operated by a battery (e.g., digital watches and transistor radios). The non-electrical products were also divided into three categories: convenience foods; domestic tools (e.g., garden shears and vacuum flasks); and household potions (e.g., bleach and cough mixtures).

After listening to an introductory talk on how children became sick after ignoring a warning not to eat too many sweets, the subjects rated their propensity to read instructions on a six point scale developed in a pilot study. Subjects rated familiarity, safety, simplicity, cost, and frequency of use for each product on a five point scale. The results were: 1) 34% of the time subjects said they would read NONE of the instructions, and 53% of the time subjects said they would read ALL of the instructions; 2) the percentage was 25.9% NONE and 64.6% ALL for electrical products, compared to 41.5% NONE and 40.7% ALL for non-electrical products, a significant difference ($p<.001$); 3) for complex electrical products, the percentage was 76.6% ALL and 17.1% NONE, compared to 41.8% ALL and 47.9% NONE for non-electric tools; 4) both complexity ($R=.473$) and the frequency of use ($R=-.24$) were significantly correlated with propensity to read instructions; 5) no significant effects were found based on age; and 6) other dependent variables such as safety, familiarity, simplicity, and cost had fairly large simple correlations with the tendency to read instructions, but because there were intercorrelations, they were not significant.

Key Words:
Tables and Flowcharts

570
Wright, P. and Fox, K., "Explicit and Implicit Tabulation Formats," *Ergonomics*, 15:2, 1972, 175-187.

The researchers cite experimental evidence showing that use of a currency conversion table containing one long list of all pairs of conversions (explicit format) resulted in better performance than the use of a table containing two shorter lists where the results of searching each list were added together (implicit format). This advantage, however, tended to disappear after extensive practice.

To test the practical implications of such an effect, a second experiment was performed where subjects used the tables in a shopping task. The sixty-four subjects, most of whom were female, selected items from a shopping list and compared the prices on the labels with the conversions from the tables. The explicit table resulted in better initial performance, although the magnitude of the effect decreased with later shopping lists.

A third experiment was then performed using only implicit tables. One version of the table used a horizontal arrangement while the other table used a vertical arrangement. No significant performance differences were found. A fourth experiment showed that more subjects were able to use the explicit table correctly than could correctly use either the implicit table or the implicit table with instructions. A fifth experiment showed that when non-numeric data was given in the table, the explicit version was also more likely to be used correctly than the implicit version.

The researchers conclude that the advantage of the explicit version is due to the difficulty people have in combining information from more than one source. It is also stated that, since numerical tables frequently require synthesis of data, implicit formats should be avoided.

Key Words:
Accuracy,
Decision Tables,
Description/Modeling,
Logic Trees,
Message Complexity,
Response Time,
Verbal vs. Nonverbal Symbol/Message

571
Wright, P. and Reid, F., "Written Information: Some Alternatives to Prose for Expressing the Outcomes of Complex Contingencies," *Journal of Applied Psychology,* **57:2, 1973, 160-166.**

It had been previously stated that prose can sometimes be rewritten as a flow chart or a logic tree. This experiment studied how easily equivalent information can be used when presented as bureaucratic prose, logic trees, lists of short sentences, or decision tables. These presentation formats were compared under several different conditions of task complexity, distinguished as: 1) straightforward versus complicated problems; and 2) directly accessible text versus recall from memory.

Sixty-eight adult subjects, thirty-two males and thirty-six females, participated in the experiment. Logic trees were found to be the best format when the problems were difficult. For easier problems, non-prose formats were used more accurately than prose, but differences among the non-prose formats were not significant. When material was directly available, the decision table and the logic tree formats were most easily used. For easier problems, the decision table was much quicker to use. Logic trees appeared to be most useful when the problem's solution was imbedded in miscellaneous information, making it necessary to extract the relevant information. When the information was recalled from memory, sentential material appeared to be preferable. With respect to time measurements, error measurements, or both, all alternatives to the more bureaucratic type prose were found to yield considerable improvements.

Key Words:
Gender,
Perceived Risk

572
Young, S.L., Martin, E.G. and Wogalter, M.S., "Gender Differences in Consumer Product Hazard Perceptions," *Proceedings of INTERFACE '89 - The Sixth Symposium on Human Factors and Industrial Design in Consumer Products*, **Human Factors Society, Santa Monica, CA, 1989, 73-78.**

The authors describe a study directed toward determining the impact of gender on the perceived hazardousness of generic consumer products. In addition, this study examined the influence of the product's attributed masculinity/femininity on the product's perceived hazardousness. Twenty-five male and forty female undergraduates at the University of Richmond viewed a list of seventy-two generically-named consumer products and responded to five questions addressing product hazardousness, masculinity/femininity, frequency of use, confidence in use, and knowledge of someone being injured by the product.

The results indicated that masculine products were perceived as being more hazardous by both males and females. With regard to the confidence in use measure, males reported significantly greater confidence when using masculine products as opposed to feminine products. Likewise, females reported significantly greater confidence when using feminine products as opposed to masculine products.

The frequency of use measure showed that males reported using masculine products significantly more often than females. Similarly, females reported using feminine products more than males. The knowledge of severe injury measure indicated that both males and females had significantly more knowledge of severe injury for masculine products than for feminine products. The authors conclude that, in the design and display of warnings, consideration should be given to perceptual biases such as those illustrated in this study.

Key Words:
Hazard,
Pictographs,
Power/Electrical
  Generator,
Print Size,
Stimulus Size,
Verbal vs. Nonverbal
  Symbol/Message

573
Young, S.L. and Wogalter, M.S., "Memory of Instruction Manual Warnings: Effects of Pictorial Icons and Conspicuous Print," *Proceedings of the Human Factors Society - 32nd Annual Meeting*, Human Factors Society, Santa Monica, CA, 1988, 905-909.

In a study involving sixty-four undergraduate students from the University of Richmond, subjects were provided one of four instruction manuals for a gas-powered electric generator. Each manual contained eight different warning messages which were altered in two separate ways: 1) the verbal messages were printed with either very conspicuous letters, (large with color highlighting), or with plain lettering, (same as the other text); 2) icons related in a meaningful way to the warning message were either present or not present. Subjects were given the manuals to study for a four minute period after which they were tested on their memory of the content of the warnings in the particular manual.

It was found that warnings with conspicuous print and a relevant icon were more likely to be recalled than any of the other warning types. The authors conclude that conspicuous text and the presence of an icon increases the salience of the warnings and, therefore, enhances memory of their content.

Key Words:
Consumer Setting,
Underlining/
  Highlighting,
Warnings: evaluating
  effects on behavior

574
Zlotnik, M.A., "The Effects of Warning Message Highlighting on Novel Assembly Task Performance," *Proceedings of the Human Factors Society - 26th Annual Meeting*, Human Factors Society, Santa Monica, CA, 1982, 93-97.

Examples of NASA, DOD, FAA, UMTA, and NRC caution and warning highlighting configurations are given, followed by a summary of a 2 x 2 x 2 factorial experiment that considers the effect of warning message highlighting. The variables used are: 1) cross hatching (crossed versus non-crossed); 2) action emphasis (blocked versus non-blocked); and 3) dimensionality (2-D versus 3-D).

Two groups performed the same task of assembling several hobby kits, none of which originally had warnings or cautions in their assembly or use instructions. Instructions were provided to the subjects in notebooks, using a text-graphic presentation mode, wherein warnings were placed directly before each procedural step to which they applied. The control group received no warnings. Dependent variables used to assess subject performance consisted of task completion time, warning

Annotations (501-577)

message-related errors, warning message recall, and task performance time.

The results were: 1) none of the highlighting variables significantly influenced any of the dependent variables; 2) the subjects who received warnings imbedded within the instructions performed with fewer errors (p<.001) and were more likely to produce a functional model (p<.004) than subjects who received instructions without imbedded warnings; and 3) the subjects tended to complete the task more quickly when warnings were given.

We point out that many of the positive effects noted here probably occurred because the warnings added additional information at critical assembly points. The author did not provide sample warnings and did not elaborate on how the control group, which received no warnings, made errors which were the subject of the provided warnings.

Key Words:
Agreement with Symbol/Message,
Behavior Factors,
Feedback

575
Zohar, D., Cohen, A. and Azar, N., "Promoting Increased Use of Ear Protectors in Noise Through Information Feedback," *Human Factors*, 22:1, 1980, 69-79.

Feedback documenting temporary hearing loss was provided to selected workers in a noisy metal fabrication plant by conducting hearing tests. Over a period of five months, the workers receiving such feedback showed a steady increase in the use of ear plugs, up to a level of 85-90% use. A control group in another noisy section of the same plant, who received no feedback, used ear plugs at a level of less than 10%. The authors conclude that providing feedback is an effective means of increasing compliance with safety precautions.

Key Words:
Age,
Amount of Information,
Consumer Labeling and Signage Systems,
Conveying Conditions,
Conveying Procedures,
Elderly,
Labels,
Legibility,
Medical Patients,
Problems in Design,
Reading of: instructions,
Symbol Size

576
Zuccollo, G. and Liddell, H., "The Elderly and the Medication Label: Doing it Better," *Age and Ageing*, 14:6, 1985, 371-376.

A study of sixty elderly patients (average age of 79.2 years) was conducted to examine several factors thought to influence patient compliance with prescription drug labels. Each subject was asked to read the labels for their own medication (the sixty subjects had a total of 163 medications). They were then asked to interpret the directions and describe the purpose of each medication. In addition, they were asked to read the directions on five specimen labels which varied according to their typeface.

Key Words (cont.):
Typeface/Font,
Understanding of Instructions

Key Words:
Design of: labeling and safety signage systems,
Development Programs,
ISO,
Ingress/Egress,
Introducing New Systems,
Public Information

The results showed that 60% of the patients had difficulty reading their medication labels, and only 23% of the patients had a clear understanding of all the instructions, despite the fact that none of the patients were judged to be illiterate. It was determined that the purpose of only 27% of the medications was correctly interpreted by the test subjects; 18% of them were vaguely interpreted; and the purpose of 54% of the medications was unknown. Only 8% of the patients knew the purpose of all their medications.

It should be noted that the purpose of the medication was not stated on any of the labels examined. With regard to the typefaces, the authors found that 70% of the subjects rated the "Jumbo" typeface as the easiest typeface to read, 26% preferred the "Commodore" typeface, and 82% of the patients rated "Micro" type as the most difficult to read.

As a result of this study, the authors recommend that directions for use be made more clear and precise, that the currently prevalent "scriptwriter" typeface be replaced by a more preferred typeface such as "Jumbo" or "Commodore," and that the labels should provide some information regarding the purpose of the medication.

577
Zwaga, H.J.G. and Easterby, R.S., "Chapter 15: Developing Effective Symbols for Public Information," in *Information Design: The Design and Evaluation of Signs and Printed Material*, Easterby and Zwaga (Eds.), John Wiley & Sons, New York, 1984, 277-297.

The authors note that the use of graphic symbols in sign systems has increased in popularity during the last twenty years, and they stress the need for evaluating symbols prior to their implementation. Past failures to perform such evaluations have caused well-documented problems in the design, interpretation, and use of symbols.

This paper presents techniques for evaluating the proposed images for symbols. The focus is on describing the two-phase procedure advocated by the International Standards Organization (ISO). The first phase in the ISO procedure specifies the use of various tests to generate a standard image description. The second phase specifies the graphic design of symbols to conform to the standard image content and with empirical evaluation of the designs. The ISO recommends that once a symbol has been designed, it should be tested for legibility.

PART II

Topical Index

Primary Topics

COMMUNICATION THEORY 295
EDUCATIONAL/PERSUASIVE PROGRAMS 295
INFORMATION THEORY 296
INSTRUCTIONS 296
LABELING AND SAFETY SIGNAGE SYSTEMS 298
LITIGATION: WARNING RELATED 300
POSTERS 302
PRODUCT INFORMATION AND WARNINGS 302
RISK PERCEPTION 302
SYMBOL/MESSAGE DESCRIPTIONS 302
SYMBOL/MESSAGE DESIGN 304
SYMBOL/MESSAGE EVALUATION 305
VISUAL DISPLAYS 312
WARNING LABELS 312
WARNING SYSTEMS 313

Topical Index

COMMUNICATION THEORY
    Application of: *281, 330, 331, 435, 461, 463*

EDUCATIONAL/PERSUASIVE PROGRAMS

    Agencies involved in: *29, 34, 173, 234, 308, 321, 341, 354, 355, 357, 455*

    Design of: *9, 25, 29, 35, 61, 206, 207, 302, 330, 351, 354, 356, 426, 497, 498, 530*

    Effectiveness of
        General: *9, 34, 61, 106, 107, 148, 152, 153, 156, 160, 164, 166, 169, 172, 173, 186, 206, 207, 214, 224, 234, 238, 264, 265, 270, 271, 280, 281, 283, 284, 290, 297, 306, 308, 321, 324, 330, 331, 335, 336, 343, 349, 350, 351, 354, 355, 357, 366, 372, 376, 379, 381, 393, 401, 409, 410, 426, 427, 428, 429, 431, 455, 497, 505, 527, 530, 544, 554, 559*

        Existing Behavior Patterns,
            effects of: *148, 224, 247, 281, 284, 330, 401, 554*
        Feedback, effects of: *152, 160, 264, 265, 281*
        Incentives, effects of: *152, 281*
        Message Tone, effects of: *26, 156, 173, 238, 281, 283, 284, 290, 297, 308, 351, 547*
        Prior Knowledge, effects of: *183, 233, 247, 281, 283, 284, 402, 497, 498, 505*
        Psychosocial Influences on: *308, 330, 350, 381, 528, 530, 532*
        Source, effects of: *95, 281, 283, 284, 330, 331, 381*

    Evaluation, difficulties in: *25, 26, 35, 206, 207, 281, 283, 284, 330, 331, 332, 401, 426*

    Media Involved, effect of
        Brochures/Flyers: *107, 206, 207, 234, 271, 308, 321, 349, 350, 351, 354, 355, 357, 409, 410*

        Formal Teaching/
            Counseling/Education: *9, 148, 153, 172, 206, 207, 214, 265, 281, 284, 302, 306, 343, 349, 366, 393, 401, 427, 505, 527, 531, 554*

        Labels: *27, 29, 61, 164, 173, 180, 183, 247, 280, 281, 302, 308, 353, 354, 372, 455, 528, 576*

        Letters: *206, 207, 271*
        Newspapers: *335, 381, 455, 527*
        Patient Package Inserts (PPI):   *234, 308, 321, 349, 350, 351, 354, 355, 356*
        Personal Presentations: *61, 106, 107, 264, 271, 297, 343, 409, 410*
        Posted Feedback: *3, 264, 265, 281*
        Posters: *6, 11, 206, 207, 281, 283*
        Radio/TV: *29, 206, 207, 306, 308, 335, 372, 381, 428, 431, 455, 544*

Topical Index

EDUCATIONAL/PERSUASIVE PROGRAMS (cont.)

Review Papers: 2, 29, 61, 207, 281, 283, 284, 308, 354, 372, 426, 428, 462, 544

Targeted Population's Behavior
Children: 9, 25, 153, 156, 164, 306, 335, 336, 379, 505, 530, 531

Consumers: 29, 34, 35, 61, 95, 106, 107, 153, 173, 183, 233, 290, 306, 308, 321, 335, 349, 354, 355, 356, 357, 372, 381, 455

Drivers: 148, 152, 169, 172, 214, 238, 270, 366, 393, 401, 410, 427, 429, 431, 554

Elderly: 357, 576

Medical Patients: 234, 308, 349, 350, 351, 353, 354, 357, 576

Parents: 106, 107, 153, 271, 306, 335, 343, 353, 409, 527

Seat Belt Nonusers: 152, 409, 429, 431

Smokers: 9, 27, 103, 297, 354, 527, 528, 530, 531, 532, 544

Workers: 160, 302, 354

EFFECTIVENESS
see LABELING AND SAFETY SIGNAGE SYSTEMS; SYMBOL/MESSAGE EVALUATION

INFORMATION THEORY

Information Coding: 18, 41, 63, 69, 70, 71, 72, 147, 226, 227, 272, 281, 387, 397

Information Overload: 30, 31, 123, 225, 229, 230, 242, 281, 283, 284, 312, 352, 402, 438, 449

Models of the Warning Process: 112, 132, 279, 281, 282, 283, 284, 330, 354, 403, 405, 434, 435

Models of Understanding/Perception: 41, 119, 141, 142, 147, 196, 197, 235, 255, 272, 281, 283, 284, 304, 316, 318, 368, 467, 472, 473, 486, 487

INSTRUCTIONS
also see SYMBOL/MESSAGE EVALUATION; SYMBOL MESSAGE DESCRIPTIONS; SYMBOL/MESSAGE DESIGN

Design of
General: 18, 19, 24, 28, 30, 31, 32, 39, 43, 49, 67, 75, 78, 89, 93, 97, 115, 118, 119, 120, 181, 203, 204, 218, 223, 232, 242, 255, 260, 281, 283, 284, 327, 351, 354, 356, 451, 467, 508, 509, 510, 565, 566

INSTRUCTIONS (cont.)

Amount of Information to Provide:	*28, 30, 31, 123, 225, 229, 230, 242, 253, 281, 283, 284, 312, 321, 352, 354, 355, 402, 438, 449, 451, 522, 576*
Cartoons, use of:	*441, 451*
Comprehension *see* SYMBOL/MESSAGE EVALUATION	
Conveying Action:	*38, 55, 118, 232, 316, 451, 467, 486, 487, 526*
Conveying Conditions:	*38, 118, 232, 316, 451, 467, 576*
Conveying Procedures:	*18, 28, 38, 93, 111, 118, 194, 232, 252, 254, 316, 396, 451, 467, 484, 486, 501, 508, 515, 526, 576*
Describing Objects:	*18, 30, 451*
Development Cycle:	*18, 24, 79, 89, 120, 132, 218, 254, 257, 396, 451*
Illustrations	
abstraction of:	*43, 134, 219, 232, 269, 316, 441, 451, 510, 526*
integrating with text:	*38, 43, 68, 89, 93, 147, 203, 225, 314, 451, 501, 564, 568*
redundancy with text:	*38, 89, 225, 451, 526*
text as diagram:	*135, 451, 542*
types of:	*134, 135, 147, 441, 451, 526*
use of:	*19, 38, 43, 69, 70, 89, 93, 97, 134, 135, 147, 203, 204, 218, 219, 232, 254, 269, 441, 451, 501, 508, 515, 526, 567*
Indexes/Quick References:	*411, 451, 542*
Information Overload, effects of:	*30, 123, 229, 230, 242, 281, 283, 284, 312, 352, 449*
Legal Style:	*392, 451*
Message Modality, effects of:	*66, 69, 70, 71, 281*
Message/Tone/Voice, effects of:	*49, 242, 281, 283, 284, 290, 351, 354, 462, 547*
Ordering of Conditions/ Actions in Messages:	*18, 41, 49, 118, 316, 487*
Organizing Information Within:	*32, 75, 135, 198, 223, 351, 354, 396, 411, 451, 456, 466, 486, 515, 542*
Page Layout:	*68, 135, 408, 451, 520, 526, 542*
Prior Knowledge, role in design:	*18, 28, 31, 41, 55, 56, 57, 60, 208, 233, 242, 255, 281, 283, 284, 345, 368, 467, 486, 487*
Problems Found in Design:	*28, 67, 93, 97, 120, 203, 204, 208, 242, 273, 370, 391, 451, 467, 496, 508, 510, 515, 565, 566, 576*
Summaries, use of:	*267, 408, 411, 486, 542*
Structured Text:	*110, 223, 486, 487*
Tables and Flowcharts:	*30, 31, 32, 53, 134, 135, 223, 451, 526, 568, 570*
Task Analysis, application of:	*18, 38, 43, 67, 115, 232, 253, 255, 281, 456, 467, 484, 486, 487, 564, 566*
Titles, influence of:	*267, 411, 451, 486, 542*

Topical Index

INSTRUCTIONS (cont.)

Typography
see SYMBOL/MESSAGE EVALUATION

Underlining/Highlighting:	*135, 205, 267, 281, 574*
User Modeling:	*18, 41, 71, 119, 147, 235, 253, 267, 272, 304, 338, 340, 451, 456, 484, 486, 487, 568*
Writing: Readability Measures of:	*19, 85, 97, 137, 138, 260, 261, 273, 281, 354, 356, 399, 404, 451, 465, 566*
Writing, Rules for:	*19, 49, 67, 93, 118, 138, 203, 204, 242, 256, 451, 466, 486, 564, 565, 566, 567, 568*

Instructions vs. Training: *484*
Reading of: *30, 115, 182, 208, 224, 280, 281, 283, 284, 321, 324, 349, 354, 355, 359, 403, 566, 569, 576*
Testing Procedures: *456*
also see Writing: Readability Measures of:

Translation of: *19, 67, 281, 451, 471*
Understanding of: *18, 28, 38, 43, 49, 66, 67, 89, 97, 110, 119, 120, 137, 138, 208, 234, 252, 260, 261, 267, 349, 352, 354, 359, 404, 408, 467, 471, 576*

Writing Guidelines, teaching of: *77, 208, 447, 451, 564*

LABELING AND SAFETY SIGNAGE SYSTEMS
Design of: General
also see SYMBOL/MESSAGE DESIGN;
SYMBOL/MESSAGE EVALUATION

Advantages of Nonverbal Symbols:	*75, 130, 131, 159, 258, 281, 283, 284, 307, 333, 337, 365, 451, 548*
Color Coding, description of:	*1, 3, 75, 87, 281, 365, 389, 548*
Consistency in Design; need for:	*75, 87, 130, 131, 144, 145, 198, 200, 241, 281, 288, 365, 548*
General Approaches to Design:	*29, 32, 42, 50, 60, 73, 74, 75, 78, 90, 96, 130, 131, 144, 171, 200, 272, 281, 302, 303, 307, 318, 327, 330, 339, 348, 354, 365, 368, 384, 385, 389, 405, 421, 422, 433, 436, 437, 452, 461, 462, 473, 475, 495, 502, 510, 548, 562, 577*
Introducing New Systems, effects of:	*10, 29, 45, 131, 198, 241, 281, 297, 308, 354, 577*
Organizing Information Within:	*32, 75, 198, 354, 359, 365*
Risk Hazard Scales:	*198, 539, 540*
Signal Words, descriptions of:	*3, 47, 75, 87, 228, 281, 308, 342, 365, 389, 451, 548*

Symbols, descriptions of
see SYMBOL/MESSAGE DESCRIPTIONS

Task Analysis, application of:	*60, 90, 281*

298

LABELING AND SAFETY SIGNAGE SYSTEMS (cont.)

    Testing, role of: *365, 421*

Evaluation of: Experimental
also see SYMBOL/MESSAGE EVALUATION

Biohazard:	*83, 84, 85, 252, 277*
Cleansers:	*308, 539, 540*
Color Coding:	*46, 47, 83, 144, 180, 281, 286, 450, 559*
Electrical Hazard Signs:	*85, 143, 277*
Fire Safety Signs:	*84, 143, 252, 277, 288*
Hazard Signs, miscellaneous:	*143, 247, 277, 371, 374, 573*
Industrial Safety Signs:	*4, 10, 46, 47, 57, 83, 189, 276*
Ingress/Egress Signs:	*84, 251, 287, 288, 452, 453*
Layout:	*109, 359*
Mine Safety Signs:	*83*
Organization:	*109*
Personal Protective Equipment:	*374, 560*
Pictographs, influence of:	*277, 374, 573*
Print Size, effects of:	*103, 286, 359, 559, 573*
Public Information Signs:	*90, 145, 307, 552*
Radiation:	*252, 277*
Railroad Crossing Signs:	*82, 151, 228*
Routing Signs:	*37, 60, 90, 190, 199, 263, 552*
Shape Coding:	*46, 47, 81, 83, 144, 281, 420*
Signal Words:	*47, 281, 283, 284, 450, 504, 533, 558*
Slow Moving Vehicle Signs:	*17*
Smoking:	*27, 103, 164, 297, 308*
Swimming Pool:	*185, 187, 300*
Traffic Signs:	*12, 26, 45, 58, 99, 113, 114, 150, 151, 175, 190, 211, 221, 228, 231, 236, 258, 259, 314, 319, 322, 380, 394, 424, 464, 474, 489, 506, 513, 519, 553*

Existing Systems, descriptions of
Consensual

ANSI:	*10, 22, 24, 46, 47, 75, 237, 281, 365, 398, 423, 529, 538, 548*
FMC:	*3, 22, 75, 281, 433, 451, 538, 548*
ISO:	*46, 84, 145, 281, 398, 548, 577*
other:	*209, 281, 302, 365, 398, 538, 548*
Consumer:	*29, 61, 75, 84, 87, 143, 145, 198, 212, 213, 251, 281, 287, 288, 308, 329, 333, 354, 359, 365, 370, 398, 451, 523, 534, 538, 548, 561, 576*

Governmental

CPSA:	*154, 198, 308, 365, 534*
DOT:	*14, 365, 534*
FDA:	*29, 61, 91, 100, 161, 198, 212, 308, 354, 365, 372, 455, 517, 534*

Topical Index

LABELING AND SAFETY SIGNAGE SYSTEMS (cont.)

	OSHA:	*3, 42, 75, 83, 105, 117, 198, 209, 302, 354, 365, 529, 534*
	Smoking Education Act:	*27, 103, 157, 164, 297, 308*
	international:	*87, 241*
	other:	*61, 75, 173, 212, 213, 281, 354, 365, 398, 502, 534, 548*
	Industrial:	*1, 2, 3, 4, 10, 42, 46, 47, 57, 75, 83, 85, 105, 117, 183, 198, 237, 252, 302, 311, 354, 365, 373, 398, 451, 529, 534, 536, 548*
	Motor Vehicle:	*14, 45, 58, 82, 151, 228, 258, 259, 263, 319, 365, 394*

LITIGATION: WARNING RELATED

Absolute Liability:	*21, 92, 365*
Adequacy of Warnings:	*73, 96, 112, 125, 171, 201, 243, 283, 284, 339, 361, 362, 363, 365, 370, 378, 383, 384, 389, 437, 446, 451, 461, 502, 524, 545, 546*
Advertising:	*79, 220, 385, 422, 502*
Application Guidelines:	*24, 27, 73, 74, 96, 132, 171, 224, 281, 282, 283, 284, 323, 461*
Assumption of Risk:	*176, 414*
Bankruptcy:	*92*
Conduct of Consumer/User:	*189, 281, 347, 383, 446, 461, 495*
Consumer Expectation:	*48*
Contributory Negligence:	*176*
Defects: Marketing:	*281, 437, 446*
Disclosure Rule:	*154*
Durability:	*73, 125, 281, 384, 389, 451*
Duty/Failure to Warn:	*5, 16, 22, 23, 24, 52, 65, 78, 94, 98, 101, 104, 128, 140, 146, 168, 171, 178, 179, 188, 195, 201, 243, 250, 275, 281, 283, 284, 302, 309, 313, 320, 361, 362, 363, 365, 370, 375, 377, 378, 382, 383, 384, 385, 389, 407, 412, 421, 437, 443, 446, 451, 460, 461, 485, 514, 517, 524, 534, 545, 546, 548*
Effectiveness, analysis of:	*189, 224, 239, 279, 281, 282, 283, 284, 324, 375, 384, 419, 524*
Exclusionary Rule:	*11*
First Amendment:	*400*
Foreseeability:	*7, 101, 140, 365*
Hazard Communication Rule:	*65, 302, 365*
Human Factors, role of:	*33, 73, 74, 96, 124, 125, 243, 245, 281, 282, 283, 284, 384, 385, 389, 435, 461*
Individual Autonomy:	*149, 210*
Informed Choice:	*281, 283, 284, 293, 383*
Informed Consumer:	*149, 210*
Instructions:	*22, 24, 78, 120, 313, 451, 503, 543*

LITIGATION: WARNING RELATED (cont.)

Insurance:	310
Jury Instructions:	444
Learned Intermediary Rule:	16, 140, 146, 168, 179, 195, 320
Loss Prevention Programs:	24, 302, 328, 340, 383, 385, 422, 461, 495, 502, 545, 546
Marketplace Honesty Policy:	48
Misuse:	65, 101, 176, 365
MUPLA (Model Uniform Product Liability Act):	440
Negligence and Warnings:	5, 54, 128, 171, 176, 178, 245, 250, 281, 310, 361, 362, 363, 365, 370, 378, 385, 389, 437, 443, 446, 461, 502, 524, 545, 546, 548
Overapplication of warnings:	121, 123, 132, 224, 243, 245, 281, 283, 284, 323, 324, 435, 461, 524, 545
Patent Danger:	188, 281, 323, 385, 390, 407, 437, 446
Point-of-Sale Duty to Warn:	460
Post-Injury Warning:	8, 249
Post-Sale Warning (After Market Notification):	440, 460, 486
Preemption:	157, 161
Product Literature:	220, 250, 281, 283, 284, 361, 370, 385
Products	
Alcohol:	98
Asbestos:	439
Chemicals:	102, 158, 302, 320, 365
Cigarettes:	157
Contraceptives:	146, 168, 275, 377, 412
Drugs:	16, 52, 94, 146, 161, 168, 176, 179, 195, 275, 377, 412, 517
Food:	9
Immunizations:	140, 146, 168, 514
Polio Vaccine:	210
Smokeless Tobacco:	149
Swimming Pools:	186
Proximate Cause:	102, 315
Punitive Damages:	161, 439, 486
Sophisticated User Defense:	128, 158
State of the Art Defense:	127, 174, 176, 285, 454
Statute of Limitations:	98
Strict Liability and Warnings:	8, 52, 54, 104, 127, 128, 171, 174, 176, 178, 245, 249, 250, 281, 285, 320, 365, 385, 437, 439, 443, 444, 446, 461, 495, 502, 512, 524, 546, 548
Subsequent Remedial Measures:	8, 249
Superseding Cause:	518
Supremacy Clause:	91
Unavoidably Unsafe Product:	16, 140, 485, 514

Topical Index

LITIGATION: WARNING RELATED (cont.)

Warranties/Disclaimers:
24, 79, 176, 245, 281, 328, 361, 385, 389, 443, 545

POSTERS
also see LABELING AND SAFETY SIGNAGE SYSTEMS

Evaluation of
Posted Feedback: 3, 264, 265, 281
Posters: 6, 11, 206, 207, 281, 283

PRODUCT INFORMATION AND WARNINGS
Consumer Preferences for
Government Involvement: 61, 354, 455, 459
Level of Detail: 61, 281, 321, 329, 351, 352, 354, 355, 356, 557
Location: 61, 329
Redundancy: 557
Symbol Usage: 329
Types of Information: 61, 281, 295, 351, 354, 356, 459, 521, 547

Effects on Buying Behavior:
29, 61, 229, 230, 233, 281, 295, 308, 354, 360, 372, 455, 457, 544

Familiarity with Product:
108, 186, 233, 278, 295, 308, 355, 415

Information Overload:
29, 61, 123, 190, 229, 230, 281, 283, 284, 308, 312, 352, 360, 402, 449

RISK PERCEPTION
Acceptability: 76, 165, 166, 281, 295, 308, 413, 414, 476, 499
Biases: 108, 126, 139, 165, 167, 248, 278, 281, 283, 284, 294, 308, 317, 354, 379, 413, 476, 477, 478, 479, 480, 481, 530, 572

Expressed Value of
  Avoiding Damages: 539, 540

Frequency Estimates: 126, 139, 165, 167, 281, 294, 301, 413, 476, 478, 479

Influences of Warning Labels: 27, 247, 281, 283, 284, 297, 308, 354, 365, 374, 533, 539, 540

Severity Estimates: 126, 247, 281, 301, 308, 413, 414, 479
Sources of Bias: 86, 108, 165, 167, 248, 278, 281, 294, 295, 301, 308, 317, 351, 354, 476, 478, 479, 480, 481

SIGNS
see LABELING AND SAFETY SIGNAGE SYSTEMS

SYMBOL/MESSAGE DESCRIPTIONS
see LABELING AND SAFETY SIGNAGE SYSTEMS; WARNING SYSTEMS

Classified by Channel of Presentation
Auditory: 13, 66, 163, 175, 239, 244, 281, 325, 326, 430, 501, 507, 549
Kinesthetic/Tactile: 42, 175, 244, 281, 442, 507

SYMBOL/MESSAGE DESCRIPTIONS (cont.)

Olfactory:	*239, 281*
Temperature:	*239*
Visual:	*12, 15, 17, 20, 25, 26, 36, 37, 38, 40, 45, 46, 47, 55, 56, 57, 58, 59, 63, 64, 66, 75, 81, 82, 83, 84, 85, 99, 113, 114, 133, 143, 144, 150, 151, 175, 183, 184, 185, 187, 189, 190, 199, 211, 215, 216, 219, 221, 228, 231, 236, 247, 252, 258, 259, 262, 266, 272, 281, 287, 288, 290, 307, 334, 358, 365, 369, 371, 374, 380, 386, 387, 388, 394, 397, 403, 425, 429, 430, 432, 438, 442, 449, 450, 468, 475, 488, 490, 491, 492, 493, 494, 500, 501, 504, 506, 508, 509, 510, 513, 519, 533, 535, 537, 539, 540, 541, 550, 552, 553, 555, 556, 557, 558, 563*

Classified by Message

Airplanes:	*232, 549*
Biohazard:	*2, 10, 14, 57, 87, 117, 252, 277, 333, 365, 404, 523, 529, 548, 563*
Caustic Materials:	*2, 5, 14, 57, 85, 143, 144, 252, 277, 333, 365, 385, 422*
Control/Display Elements:	*4, 38, 40, 55, 56, 64, 130, 131, 141, 177, 192, 193, 202, 252, 433, 448, 468, 491, 501, 508, 509, 510, 550, 562*
Electrical:	*3, 57, 85, 87, 143, 252, 268, 277, 373, 385, 433, 436, 548*
Explosive:	*2, 5, 14, 57, 85, 117, 252, 277, 422, 433, 548*
Fire:	*2, 4, 5, 10, 14, 57, 84, 85, 87, 117, 143, 144, 209, 251, 252, 268, 277, 288, 422, 423, 433*
General Hazard/Alert:	*3, 10, 47, 57, 75, 85, 117, 143, 144, 251, 252, 296, 317, 329, 333, 365, 373, 433, 451, 527, 529, 548*
Hand Signals:	*133, 337*
Ingress/Egress:	*57, 84, 85, 87, 117, 251, 252, 268, 287, 288, 289, 337, 373, 452, 453, 529, 577*
Moving Vehicles:	*10, 85, 87, 117, 130, 131, 252*
Other/Miscellaneous:	*66, 75, 81, 83, 200, 262, 268, 269, 277, 282, 288, 311, 317, 329, 333, 337, 358, 365, 373, 385, 397, 420, 422, 433, 448, 471, 475, 491, 500, 501, 508, 509, 510, 511, 523, 548, 552, 562, 567, 571*
Personal Protective Equipment Requirements:	*57, 85, 117, 252, 277, 373, 385, 423, 433, 548*
Point of Operation Guarding:	*10, 87, 117, 142, 252, 373, 384, 385, 433, 436, 529, 548*
Poison:	*2, 5, 14, 85, 130, 131, 143, 144, 209, 252, 277, 296, 333, 365, 422, 450*

Topical Index

SYMBOL/MESSAGE DESCRIPTIONS (cont.)

Prohibition:	*46, 57, 75, 84, 85, 113, 117, 236, 288, 337, 373, 423, 475, 501, 523, 548*
Public Information:	*57, 62, 145, 159, 241, 251, 252, 268, 269, 288, 307, 337, 577*
Radiation:	*10, 14, 57, 87, 117, 130, 131, 209, 252, 277, 422, 548*
Routing:	*10, 37, 60, 84, 85, 87, 90, 130, 131, 241, 251, 252, 268, 373, 529, 552*
Safety Information(first aid):	*4, 10, 46, 47, 57, 85, 87, 117, 130, 131, 252, 268, 373, 384, 385, 523, 529*
Slip/Fall:	*4, 10, 42, 85, 87, 373, 384, 433, 436*
Traffic:	*12, 15, 17, 25, 26, 45, 58, 82, 113, 114, 129, 130, 131, 133, 150, 151, 163, 175, 221, 228, 231, 236, 252, 258, 259, 259, 269, 314, 322, 325, 337, 346, 369, 373, 380, 394, 406, 488, 489, 491, 513, 519, 529, 551, 553, 562*

Classified by User Population

Consumer:	*84, 113, 129, 130, 131, 143, 145, 192, 193, 239, 240, 251, 252, 287, 288, 337, 346, 365, 433, 450, 475, 491, 508, 511, 523, 548*
Industrial:	*13, 46, 47, 55, 56, 57, 75, 83, 85, 129, 130, 131, 252, 276, 287, 288, 311, 337, 346, 365, 373, 433, 491, 523, 536, 548*
Military:	*40, 64, 129, 262, 358*

SYMBOL/MESSAGE DESIGN
also see LABELING AND SAFETY SIGNAGE SYSTEMS;
INSTRUCTIONS

Consumer Surveys: use in design: *27, 143, 145, 314, 329*

Design Guidelines
see LABELING AND SAFETY SIGNAGE SYSTEMS;
INSTRUCTIONS;
SYMBOL/MESSAGE EVALUATION

Development Programs For: *43, 73, 75, 130, 131, 138, 200, 251, 268, 269, 272, 274, 281, 288, 330, 368, 424, 433, 448, 475, 509, 548, 549, 577*

Experimental Evaluation of Designs
see SYMBOL/MESSAGE EVALUATION

Hazard Prevention/Analysis Models: *73, 74, 75, 365, 405, 445, 516*

Pictographs, design of
also see SYMBOL/MESSAGE EVALUATION

Conveying Action, use in:	*55, 232, 236, 287, 316, 475, 508, 509, 526, 552, 553*
Describing Objects, use in:	*55, 232, 316, 526*

Topical Index

SYMBOL/MESSAGE DESIGN (cont.)

    Elemental Breakdowns: 75, 144, 177, 236, 262, 287, 316, 448, 491, 509, 525, 550, 552, 553
    Elemental Synthesis: 75, 177, 232, 316, 508, 509, 525, 552, 553
    Multiple Referents, effects of: 57, 130, 526
    Types of/examples:
        see SYMBOL/MESSAGE DESCRIPTIONS

Predictive User Response Equations: 36, 63, 72, 177, 281, 369, 535

Symbol Generation
    General: 45, 75, 130, 144, 163, 192, 232, 268, 272, 281, 288, 314, 325, 326, 329, 365, 448, 475, 507, 509, 535, 548
    Production Method: 45, 144, 192, 268, 288, 475, 509

Symbol Descriptions
    see SYMBOL/MESSAGE DESCRIPTIONS

Symbol Taxonomies: 75, 129, 130, 131, 144, 159, 177, 194, 196, 262, 281, 287, 316, 346, 387, 397, 420, 448, 525, 535

Task Analysis, use in design: 67, 74, 116, 217, 281, 284, 448
    Example Applications: 90, 116, 217, 274, 281

SYMBOL/MESSAGE EVALUATION

    All Studies Evaluating: 12, 13, 17, 27, 36, 37, 38, 40, 45, 46, 47, 55, 56, 57, 58, 59, 62, 64, 66, 75, 78, 81, 82, 83, 84, 85, 99, 103, 113, 114, 124, 133, 144, 150, 151, 163, 170, 175, 183, 184, 185, 187, 190, 192, 193, 199, 211, 215, 216, 221, 228, 231, 236, 239, 247, 252, 258, 259, 262, 266, 272, 274, 276, 277, 280, 281, 287, 288, 290, 291, 292, 297, 307, 308, 314, 317, 325, 326, 334, 338, 351, 352, 353, 356, 358, 359, 365, 369, 371, 374, 380, 386, 387, 388, 394, 397, 403, 404, 405, 406, 420, 425, 429, 430, 432, 438, 442, 448, 449, 450, 453, 457, 464, 468, 469, 474, 475, 488, 490, 491, 492, 493, 494, 496, 497, 500, 501, 504, 506, 507, 508, 509, 510, 513, 519, 533, 535, 537, 541, 549, 550, 552, 553, 556, 557, 558, 563, 567, 571, 575, 576

    Behavior Factors
        Actual Behavior: 25, 26, 156, 224, 276, 281, 284, 324, 403, 462, 497
        Agreement with, effects of: 27, 224, 276, 281, 283, 284, 330, 381, 432, 575
        Amount of Information, effects of: 29, 359, 539, 540
        Behavior of Cohorts, effects of: 560
        Belief in Danger, effects of: 189, 224, 281, 283, 284, 297, 374, 381, 476, 477, 482, 483
        Conflicting Objectives, effects of: 162, 183, 281, 283, 284, 432

Topical Index

SYMBOL/MESSAGE EVALUATION (cont.)

Cost of Compliance, effects of:	560
Credibility of Source, effects of:	95, 281, 283, 284, 295, 297, 330, 381
Discrepancy Between Self-Reports and Actual Behavior:	25, 44, 156, 281, 284, 367, 428, 430, 432
Existing/Past Behavior Patterns, effects of:	27, 148, 185, 187, 247, 276, 280, 281, 283, 284, 324, 367, 403
False Alarms, effects of:	125, 136, 281
Feedback, effects of:	152, 160, 264, 265, 281, 334, 442, 575
Gender, effects of:	185, 187, 539, 540, 572
Habituation over Time, effects of:	297, 308, 371
Incentives, effects of:	152, 281, 283, 284, 334
Message Tone, effects of:	156, 238, 281, 283, 284, 290, 351, 354, 462
Perceived Risk, effects of:	27, 108, 165, 182, 248, 276, 278, 281, 283, 284, 308, 354, 374, 403, 457, 476, 477, 482, 483, 569, 572
Prior Knowledge, effects of:	26, 27, 183, 185, 187, 281, 284, 295, 374, 403, 477, 483, 497, 498
Risk Compensation, effects of:	155, 281, 283, 284
Risk Coping Style, effects of:	281, 283, 295, 403, 470
Risk Taking, effects of:	27, 281, 283, 380, 403
Studies Evaluating:	25, 26, 156, 184, 185, 187, 189, 206, 207, 224, 276, 281, 283, 284, 290, 308, 319, 324, 334, 371, 374, 380, 403, 429, 430, 432, 442, 450, 457, 496, 497, 504, 507, 539, 540, 541, 549, 555, 558, 575
Warnings, effects of:	124, 136, 164, 184, 185, 187, 189, 276, 279, 280, 281, 283, 284, 308, 324, 334, 353, 354, 359, 372, 374, 380, 381, 403, 442, 450, 462, 470, 504, 539, 540, 541, 558, 560, 574

Comprehension Factors

Studies Evaluating Comprehension of Symbol/Message:	18, 28, 38, 40, 45, 46, 47, 55, 56, 57, 58, 62, 64, 66, 75, 81, 82, 83, 84, 85, 114, 138, 143, 144, 145, 150, 151, 173, 175, 193, 219, 236, 240, 247, 252, 258, 259, 262, 272, 277, 281, 287, 288, 307, 308, 314, 317, 352, 358, 359, 365, 394, 397, 404, 405, 420, 425, 448, 468, 469, 475, 491, 501, 508, 509, 510, 519, 550, 552, 553, 567, 571, 576
Context, effects of	
cultural:	57, 145, 281, 471, 510
definition of:	38, 141, 281
receiver specific factors	
age:	83, 84, 133, 143, 281, 288, 317, 576
population stereotypes:	18, 42, 45, 82, 144, 281, 287, 491, 553

SYMBOL/MESSAGE EVALUATION (cont.)

prior knowledge:	*18, 28, 45, 55, 56, 57, 83, 85, 114, 143, 193, 247, 281, 283, 284, 394, 404, 510*
training:	*55, 193, 247, 281, 519*
task specific:	*38, 115, 119, 175, 281, 469, 500, 567*

Measures of Comprehension
  accuracy

in performance:	*38, 151, 240, 258, 259, 281, 448, 468, 508, 510, 571*
in recall:	*57, 58, 84, 85, 143, 205, 267, 281, 288, 563, 567, 571*
in recognition/matching:	*45, 55, 56, 57, 58, 83, 84, 85, 133, 145, 173, 175, 193, 236, 252, 259, 262, 277, 281, 288, 358, 491, 519*
association rankings/indexes:	*46, 47, 83, 193, 262, 281, 420, 519, 550*
confusion matrix:	*40, 193, 226, 281*
fuzzy set membership:	*272*
reaction time:	*64, 150, 151, 190, 193, 281, 394, 448*
readability:	*97, 137, 138, 281, 322, 404*
response time:	*38, 240, 281, 469, 508, 552, 567, 571*
semantic differential:	*62, 114, 281, 307, 356*

Nonverbal Symbols
  basic associations

color/hazard:	*46, 47, 83, 144, 281*
shape/hazard:	*46, 47, 81, 83, 144, 281, 420*
other:	*62, 64, 236, 287, 358, 397, 471, 475, 491, 550*

  comprehension of

general:	*40, 45, 55, 56, 57, 58, 64, 75, 83, 84, 85, 277*

    specific nonverbal symbols

biohazard:	*2, 10, 14, 57, 87, 117, 252, 277, 333, 404, 523, 529, 548, 563*
caustic materials:	*2, 5, 14, 57, 85, 143, 144, 252, 277, 333, 385, 422*
control/display elements:	*4, 38, 40, 51, 55, 56, 64, 130, 131, 141, 177, 192, 193, 202, 252, 433, 448, 468, 491, 501, 508, 509, 510, 550, 562*
electrical:	*3, 57, 85, 87, 143, 252, 268, 277, 373, 385, 433, 436, 548*
explosive:	*2, 5, 14, 57, 85, 117, 252, 277, 422, 433, 548*
fire:	*2, 4, 5, 10, 14, 57, 84, 85, 87, 117, 143, 144, 209, 251, 252, 268, 277, 288, 422, 423, 433*
general hazard/alert:	*3, 10, 47, 57, 85, 117, 143, 144, 251, 252, 296, 317, 329, 333, 373, 433, 527, 529, 548*
hand signals:	*133, 337*
ingress/egress:	*57, 84, 85, 87, 117, 251, 252, 268, 287, 288, 289, 337, 373, 452, 453, 529, 577*

Topical Index

SYMBOL/MESSAGE EVALUATION (cont.)

	miscellaneous:	66, 81, 83, 200, 262, 268, 269, 282, 288, 311, 317, 329, 333, 337, 358, 373, 385, 397, 420, 422, 433, 448, 471, 475, 491, 500, 501, 508, 509, 510, 511, 523, 548, 552, 562, 567, 571
	moving vehicles:	10, 85, 87, 117, 130, 131, 252
	personal protective equip. requirements:	57, 85, 117, 252, 277, 373, 385, 423, 433, 548
	point of operation guarding	10, 87, 117, 142, 252, 277, 373, 384, 385, 433, 436, 529, 548
	poison:	2, 5, 14, 85, 130, 131, 143, 144, 209, 252, 277, 296, 333, 422, 450
	prohibition:	46, 57, 84, 85, 113, 117, 236, 288, 337, 373, 423, 475, 501, 523, 548
	public information:	57, 62, 145, 159, 241, 251, 252, 268, 269, 288, 307, 337, 577
	radiation:	10, 14, 57, 87, 117, 130, 131, 209, 252, 422, 548
	routing:	10, 37, 60, 84, 85, 87, 90, 130, 131, 241, 251, 252, 268, 373, 529, 552
	safety information (first aid):	4, 10, 46, 47, 57, 85, 87, 117, 130, 131, 252, 268, 359, 373, 384, 385, 523, 529
learning of (nonverbal symbols):		45, 57, 193, 281
pictographs, comprehension of		
	combining: *see* Nonverbal Syntax (below)	
	conveying action, use in:	55, 232, 236, 277, 287, 316, 475, 508, 509, 526, 552, 553
	describing objects, use in:	55, 232, 316, 526
	elemental breakdowns:	144, 177, 236, 262, 287, 316, 448, 491, 509, 525, 550, 552, 553
	also see Nonverbal Symbols (above)	
	elemental synthesis:	177, 232, 316, 508, 509, 525, 552, 553
	also see Nonverbal Syntax (below)	
	multiple referents, effects of:	57, 130, 526
simple comprehension factors		
	abstractness:	45, 55, 56, 57, 58, 66, 219, 232, 236, 281, 288, 307, 337, 468, 508, 509, 510, 526
	message complexity:	55, 56, 57, 58, 83, 85, 143, 232, 281, 508, 509
	slip/fall:	4, 10, 42, 85, 87, 373, 384, 433, 436
	traffic:	12, 17, 25, 26, 45, 58, 82, 113, 114, 130, 131, 150, 151, 175, 221, 231, 236, 252, 258, 259, 269, 322, 337, 373, 394, 488, 489, 491, 513, 519, 529, 551, 553, 562

SYMBOL/MESSAGE EVALUATION (cont.)

	targeted populations	
	children:	*25*
	consumers:	*57, 81, 84, 143, 144, 145*
	elderly:	*81, 143*
	housewives:	*143*
	industrial:	*55, 56, 57, 83, 85*
	military:	*40*
	motor vehicle:	*45, 55, 56, 58, 133, 150, 175*
Nonverbal Syntax		
	compared to verbal syntax:	*134, 232, 240, 281, 509, 526, 542, 567, 571*
	conveying action:	*134, 194, 232, 236, 281, 316, 486, 508, 509, 510, 526, 552, 553*
	decision tables:	*134, 281, 526, 567, 571*
	description/modeling of:	*134, 141, 177, 194, 269, 281, 316, 508, 509, 525, 526, 567, 571*
	logic trees:	*240, 281, 567, 571*
	process charts/sequences:	*110, 134, 194, 232, 240, 281, 316, 508, 509, 510, 526*
Verbal Symbols		
	auditory vs. visual:	*66, 226, 501, 549*
	readability: *see* INSTRUCTIONS	
	signal words/hazard:	*47, 281, 342*
	simple comprehension:	*85, 272, 281, 322, 359*
Verbal Syntax: *see* INSTRUCTIONS		
Verbal vs. Nonverbal Messages		
	redundancy, effects of:	*38*
	relative desirability	
	general:	*38, 69, 130, 147, 150, 221, 240, 258, 259, 281, 394, 501, 509, 519, 567, 571*
	as function of complexity:	*55, 56, 57, 58, 66, 281, 567, 571*
	as function of user group:	*56, 130, 131, 252, 281, 322, 404*

Memory Factors

All Studies Evaluating		
	Memory of Symbol/Message:	*25, 26, 57, 58, 111, 164, 173, 185, 187, 205, 221, 231, 233, 281, 292, 297, 308, 351, 355, 371, 415, 438, 449, 464, 504, 533, 563*
Active Processing, effects of:		*41, 205, 225, 231, 281, 289, 292, 563*
Capacity, effects of:		*221, 281*
Cueing, effects of:		*122*
Deep Processing, implications of:		*281, 368*
Information Overload:		*281, 283, 284, 438, 449*
Measurement of		
	forgetting rate:	*26, 281, 292*
	recall:	*25, 26, 57, 58, 111, 205, 221, 231, 281, 283, 284, 292, 297, 304, 355, 371, 374, 438, 449, 464, 533, 563*
	recognition:	*25, 26, 164, 173, 281, 297, 304, 351, 464*

SYMBOL/MESSAGE EVALUATION (cont.)

Redundancy, effects of:	*281, 292*
Summaries, effects of:	*408*
Visual vs. Verbal:	*69, 70, 225, 374, 415*

Noise Factors

Auditory:	*13, 281, 325, 549*
Effects of:	*13, 37, 222, 258, 281, 364*
False Alarms:	*281, 299*
Visual:	*12, 37, 222, 258, 281, 364*
Warnings as Noise:	*281, 549*

Perception Factors

All Studies Evaluating

Perception of Symbol/Message:	*12, 13, 15, 17, 20, 36, 37, 59, 72, 75, 82, 99, 103, 113, 114, 124, 133, 150, 151, 163, 164, 170, 183, 185, 187, 190, 199, 211, 215, 216, 228, 239, 258, 259, 266, 281, 287, 288, 291, 307, 314, 325, 326, 359, 365, 369, 374, 386, 387, 388, 394, 405, 406, 448, 453, 469, 474, 488, 490, 492, 493, 494, 500, 504, 506, 507, 513, 519, 535, 537, 549*

Abilities of User

contrast sensitivity:	*281, 474*
perceptual skills:	*246, 281, 298*
visual acuity:	*211, 228, 281, 369, 452*
Conspicuity, definition of:	*37, 281*

Conspicuity, effects and factors influencing

aesthetics:	*80, 266, 281*
age:	*281, 474, 537*
alcohol use, effects of:	*211*
attraction to: children:	*164, 281, 283, 284, 450*
auditory coding:	*13, 163, 325, 326, 469, 549*
auditory: signal strength:	*239, 325*
color of background:	*63, 72, 281*
color of stimulus:	*12, 17, 36, 63, 72, 151, 183, 281, 369, 387, 406*
contrast:	*199, 215, 281, 369, 452, 488*
location:	*164, 281, 283, 284, 500, 504, 558*
luminance:	*37, 99, 199, 211, 215, 281, 369, 406, 452, 453, 494, 500*

noise

auditory:	*13, 281, 325*
visual:	*12, 37, 190, 199, 222, 259, 281, 283, 284, 288, 298, 364, 453, 488*
personality factors:	*298*
probability/frequency of presentation:	*37, 136, 281, 283, 284, 291*
redundancy:	*12*

310

SYMBOL/MESSAGE EVALUATION (cont.)

stimulus size (i.e. letter size):	*37, 99, 103, 183, 199, 216, 228, 359, 406, 490, 492, 494, 573*
symbol legend:	*12, 199*
symbol shape:	*12, 228*
underlining/highlighting:	*205, 504, 574*
verbal vs. nonverbal symbols:	*150, 258, 259, 281, 283, 284, 298, 374, 394, 519, 573*
viewing time:	*258, 259, 394, 519*
visual angle:	*215, 281, 490, 492*
workload/task:	*246, 281, 283, 284, 291, 458, 464, 500, 506, 513, 549*
Filtering, evaluation of:	*124, 281, 284, 374, 506*
Filtering, factors influencing:	*124, 136, 182, 183, 239, 281, 283, 284, 374*
Information Overload, effects of:	*123, 190, 281, 283, 284, 312*
Legibility, factors influencing:	*103, 281, 305, 365, 416, 451, 520, 542, 576*
case of text:	*170, 216, 386, 388, 490, 520, 558*
contrast:	*83, 199, 215, 281, 369, 520*
degradation/noise:	*113, 281, 288, 416, 417, 520*
durability:	*83, 199, 281, 451*
illumination level:	*83, 99, 199, 281, 453, 520*
justification of text:	*59, 520*
line spacing/width:	*520, 537*
prohibitive slash:	*113, 281*
separation between symbols:	*15, 20, 520*
strokewidth:	*215, 281, 388, 416, 417, 520*
symbol size:	*99, 103, 216, 228, 281, 388, 490, 492, 494, 520, 537, 576*
typeface/font:	*203, 204, 215, 388, 416, 417, 451, 520, 537, 576*
viewing distance:	*99, 103, 281, 369, 490, 492, 494, 520, 535*
Measures of Perception	
accuracy:	*448, 494, 519, 535*
attention to:	*164, 281, 374, 406*
awakening:	*239*
confusion matrix:	*216, 226, 281, 535*
detection intensity level:	*325, 494*
detection/perception of:	*246, 281, 464, 506*
error detection:	*281, 493*
glance legibility:	*113, 114, 258, 259, 281, 307, 394, 513, 519*
legibility distance:	*82, 99, 151, 170, 211, 228, 281, 307, 369, 453, 474, 492, 513*
reaction time:	*13, 17, 163, 281, 298, 326, 394, 469, 494, 500, 513, 549*
reading speed:	*59, 344, 537*
recognition time:	*12, 72, 151, 364, 448, 494*
search time:	*36, 63, 72, 281, 386, 387, 458*
subjective ratings:	*199, 307, 488, 537*

311

Topical Index

SYMBOL/MESSAGE EVALUATION (cont.)

Setting
    aircraft: *202, 232, 291, 299, 468, 469, 549*
    consumer: *37, 80, 124, 182, 183, 239, 246, 266, 307, 374, 450, 452, 500, 502, 502, 537, 574*
    data processing: *20, 59, 494*
    industrial: *13, 83, 136, 216, 222*
    laboratory/generic: *36, 63, 72, 123, 170, 203, 204, 205, 226, 282, 416, 417, 448, 490, 492, 493, 557*
    maps: *364, 386, 387, 388*
    railroads: *82, 151, 326*
    traffic: *12, 15, 17, 99, 103, 113, 114, 133, 150, 163, 190, 199, 211, 215, 228, 258, 259, 298, 325, 369, 394, 406, 464, 474, 488, 506, 513, 519*

Populations
    Children: *25, 95, 164, 185, 187, 205, 317, 450*
    Consumers: *27, 29, 37, 57, 61, 84, 103, 143, 144, 145, 173, 183, 185, 187, 287, 288, 290, 292, 295, 297, 307, 308, 352, 355, 403, 404, 449, 455, 492, 508, 510, 539, 540*
    Drivers: *12, 15, 17, 26, 58, 82, 99, 116, 133, 150, 151, 163, 175, 190, 192, 199, 211, 215, 221, 228, 231, 258, 259, 314, 369, 380, 406, 429, 430, 432, 453, 464, 474, 488, 519, 552, 553*
    Elderly: *143, 288, 357, 403, 537, 576*
    Housewives: *143, 183, 252, 403*
    Military: *40, 64, 262, 358*
    Pedestrians: *314, 425*
    Pilots: *202, 291, 468, 469, 549*
    Students: *27, 45, 55, 56, 81, 111, 124, 182, 184, 185, 187, 216, 236, 239, 247, 251, 252, 277, 297, 351, 356, 374, 420, 438, 442, 496, 497, 504, 553, 558*
    Workers: *13, 46, 47, 57, 83, 85, 189, 240, 276, 334, 371, 556*

VISUAL DISPLAYS
Aircraft: *202, 468*
Automobile Controls: *192, 193*
Generic: *36, 51, 63, 72, 141, 202, 281, 344, 418, 458, 473, 493, 494*
Heavy Equipment Controls: *55, 56*
Radar Displays: *40, 64*

WARNING LABELS
also see LABELING AND SAFETY SIGNAGE SYSTEMS;
    PRODUCT INFORMATION AND WARNINGS;
    SYMBOL/MESSAGE DESIGN;
    SYMBOL/MESSAGE EVALUATION

WARNING LABELS (cont.)

Comprehension of:	*75, 81, 173, 281, 283, 284, 308, 351, 354, 359, 405*
Consumer Preferences:	*281, 329, 354, 533, 556, 557*
Level of Detail, effects of:	*123, 247, 281, 297, 308, 329, 435, 438, 533, 557*
Reading of	
Factors Influencing:	*44, 103, 124, 164, 182, 183, 184, 224, 281, 283, 284, 308, 354, 359, 374, 403, 438, 459, 504, 521, 556, 558, 563, 569*
Measures:	*124, 183, 185, 187, 281, 282, 283, 284, 324, 354, 374, 403, 438, 504, 563*
Memory of:	*111, 185, 187, 281, 283, 284, 297, 351, 354, 374*

WARNING SYSTEMS
also see LABELING AND SAFETY SIGNAGE SYSTEMS; SYMBOL/MESSAGE DESCRIPTIONS

Air Traffic Control:	*291*
Aircraft:	*291, 299, 469, 549*
All Terrain Vehicles (ATV):	*246, 247, 280, 308*
Approaching Train:	*326*
Auditory:	*13, 163, 239, 244, 325, 326, 469, 549*
Back-Up Signals:	*136*
Cleaning Products/Hazards:	*539, 540, 560*
Crosswalk:	*425*
Deceleration Warning Light:	*541*
Emergency: Fire:	*239*
Emergency: General:	*274, 381*
Emergency: Vehicles:	*163, 191, 325, 395*
Fall:	*42*
Hazardous Materials:	*14, 143, 183, 237, 302, 333, 365*
Motorcycle:	*406*
Personal Protective Equipment:	*374, 539, 540, 560*
Power (Electricity) Generator:	*573*
Roadside Radio Transmitter:	*88*
Rumble Strips:	*507*
Saws:	*374*
School Bus:	*395*
Seat Belt Reminder:	*116, 429, 430*
Slow Moving Vehicle:	*17*
Swimming Pool:	*185, 187, 300*

PART III

Author Index

Author Index

Author *	Ref.	Year
Abdel-Halim, M.H. *	348	1981
Adams, A.S.	12	1981
Adams, J.R. *	401	1976
Adams, S.K.	13	1976
Albaum, G.S. *	414	1980
Albers, W.A. (Ed.)	76	1980
Albers, W.A. (Ed.)	301	1980
Albers, W.A. (Ed.)	478	1980
Alff, T.R.	14	1974
Allen, B.P. *	156	1970
Allender, L. *	182	1983
Allison, S.T. *	560	1988
Anderson J.R.	408	1982
Anderton, P.J.	15	1982
Andreassi, J.L. *	40	1960
Ashman, A.	16	1984
Asper, O.	17	1972
Audley, R.J. *	388	1977
Avrunin, D.I. *	347	1982
Azar, N. *	575	1980
Babu, A.J.G. *	68	1988
Backlund, F. *	231	1970
Baggett, P.	18	1988
Bailey, R.W.	19	1982
Ballard, J.L. *	420	1982
Ballard, J.L. *	421	1982
Barbera, C. *	180	1987
Barnard, P.	20	1978
Barnard, P. *	316	1979
Barofsky, I. (Ed.)	242	1980
Barofsky, I. (Ed.)	330	1980
Barofsky, I. (Ed.)	354	1980
Barofsky, I. (Ed.)	368	1980
Barofsky, I. (Ed.)	459	1980
Barofsky, I. (Ed.)	479	1980
Barry, D.T.	21	1984-85
Bartlett, S. *	205	1980
Barwick, K.D. *	264	1978
Bass, L.	22	1986
Bates, P.	23	1984
Baumann, D.D. *	470	1972
Bedford, M.S.	24	1987
Belbin, E.	25	1956
Belbin, E.	26	1956
Beltramini, R.F.	27	1988
Berkowitz, L. (Ed.)	332	1964
Berkowitz, L. (Ed.)	463	1964
Berman, E.J. *	164	1989
Berning, C.K. *	230	1974
Bernotat, R.K. (Ed.)	473	1972
Bernstein, A. *	369	1979
Berry, E.	28	1982
Bersh, P. *	358	1979
Bettman, J.R.	29	1975
Bettman, J.R.	31	1980
Bettman, J.R.	32	1986
Bettman, J.R.	30	1977
Birnbaum, S.L. (Ed.)	378	1975
Black, J.B. *	41	1979
Blatter, M.M. *	343	1982
Bliss, W.D.	33	1979
Bloom, P.N.	34	1975
Bloom, P.N.	35	1979
Bloomfield, J.R.	36	1979
Boersema, T.	37	1984
Booher, H.R.	38	1975
Booher, H.R.	39	1978
Bouma, H. (Ed.)	316	1979
Bouma, H. (Ed.)	525	1979
Bouma, H. (Ed.)	566	1980
Bouma, H. *	535	1980
Bowen, H.M.	40	1960
Bower, G.H.	41	1979
Boydstun, L.E.	42	1978
Boyer, H.	43	1980
Bozinoff, L.	44	1981
Brainard, R.W.	45	1961
Branthwaite, A. *	205	1980
Brelsford, J.W. *	122	1988
Brelsford, J.W. *	278	1989
Brelsford, J.W. *	556	1986
Bresnahan, T.F.	46	1985
Bresnahan, T.F.	47	1975
Brinkley, W.A. *	406	1977
Britain, J.E.	48	1984
Broadbent, D.E.	49	1977
Bruce, M. *	170	1982
Bruening, E.B.	50	1972
Bryden, J.E. *	199	1977
Bryk, J. *	47	1975
Buck, J.R.	51	1983
Bukstein, Y.	52	1987
Burkett, J.R. *	465	1974
Burkett, J.R. *	466	1974
Burnhill, P.	53	1976
Burroughs, M. *	123	1977

* co-author   (Ed.) editor

Author Index

Author *	Ref.	Year
Bussain, J.A.	54	1987
Cahill, M.C.	55	1976
Cahill, M.C.	56	1975
Cahill, M.C. *	63	1979
Cairney, P.	57	1982
Cairney, P.	58	1982
Campbell, A.J.	59	1981
Campbell, R.J. *	45	1961
Canter, D.	60	1984
Capon, N.	61	1979
Caron, J.P.	62	1980
Carroll, L. *	77	1983
Carter, R.C.	63	1979
Carter, R.J.	64	1979
Centner, T.J.	65	1985
Chaffin, D.B. *	42	1978
Chaiken, S.	66	1976
Chapanis, A.	67	1965
Chapanis, A. (Ed.)	471	1975
Chawla, S. *	266	1972
Cheickna, S.	68	1988
Childers, T.L.	69	1986
Childers, T.L.	71	1985
Childers, T.L.	70	1984
Childers, T.L. *	225	1987
Christ, R.E.	72	1974
Christen, F.G. *	177	1982
Christensen, J.M.	73	1983
Christensen, J.M.	74	1980
Clark, D.R.	75	1988
Clark, W.C.	76	1980
Clarke, M.M.	77	1983
Clement, D.E.	78	1987
Clifton, P. *	131	1970
Close, D.B.	79	1987
Coates, F.D.	80	1973
Cochran, D.J.	81	1981
Cochran, D.J. *	420	1982
Cochran, D.J. *	421	1982
Cochran, D.J. *	422	1981
Cohen, A. *	575	1980
Cole, B.L.*	15	1982
Cole, B.L.	82	1981
Cole, B.L. *	228	1975
Colflesh, V. *	521	1976
Collins, B.L.	83	1983
Collins, B.L.	84	1982
Collins, B.L.	85	1982
Collins, B.L. *	288	1980
Collins, B.L. *	289	1983
Combs, B.	86	1979

Author *	Ref.	Year
Combs, B. *	166	1978
Combs, B. *	294	1978
Combs, B. *	482	1977
Comm. on Consumer Policy	87	1974
Connolley, D.	88	1979
Connolly, T. *	123	1977
Conover, D.W. *	562	1981
Conrads, J.A.	89	1987
Cook, T.R.	90	1980
Cooper, R.M.	91	1986
Cooter, R.D.	92	1985
Corrigan, B. *	482	1977
Coskuntuna, S.	93	1980
Cox, S.N.	94	1986
Craig, C.S.	95	1978
Crawford, J.D. *	335	1982
Crawshaw, C.M. *	217	1985
Creighton, P. *	569	1982
Cunitz, R.J.	96	1981
Curhan, R.C. (Ed.)	341	1974
Curran, T.E.	97	1977
D'Amico, D.	98	1987
Dahlstedt, S.	99	1977
Dalezman J.J.	515	1978
Dallas, H.	100	1943
Darden, T.M.	101	1987
Davé, N.	102	1988
Davis, R.M.	103	1989
Deacy, J.E. *	422	1981
Dean, B.S. *	359	1986
Dechert, C. *	256	1985
DeMarco, M.M.	104	1984-85
Dembroski, T.M. *	156	1970
Denkensohn, B.D. *	283	1988
Denny, D.	105	1984
dePontbriand, R.J. *	457	1983
Dershewitz, R.A.	106	1977
Dershewitz, R.A.	107	1979
Desaulniers, D.R.	108	1989
Desaulniers, D.R.	109	1987
Desaulniers, D.R.	110	1988
Desaulniers, D.R. *	559	1987
Desaulniers, D.R. *	557	1985
Desaulniers, D.R. *	556	1986
deTurck, M.A.	111	1988
deTurck, M.A. *	185	1988
deTurck, M.A. *	186	1988
deTurck, M.A. *	187	1988
Deutsch, S.	112	1980
DeVivo, E.C. *	21	1984-85
Dewar, R.E.*	62	1980

Author *	Ref.	Year
Dewar, R.E.	113	1976
Dewar, R.E.	114	1977
Dewar, R.E. *	150	1979
Dewar, R.E. *	151	1980
Dewar, R.E. *	307	1981
Dewar, R.E. *	513	1981
Diehl, W.	115	1981
Diffley, G. *	396	1976
Digon, E. *	521	1976
Dillon, J.	116	1975
Dionne, E.D.	117	1979
Dixon, P.	118	1982
Dixon, P.	119	1987
Dobrin, D.	120	1985
Dodds, T.	121	1985
Donaher, W.A. *	524	1976
Donaher, W.A. *	545	1978
Donaher, W.A. *	546	1978
Donner, K.A.	122	1988
Dorris, A.L.	123	1977
Dorris, A.L.	124	1977
Dorris, A.L.	125	1978
Dorris, A.L.	126	1978
Dorris, A.L. *	402	1987
Dossick, R.	127	1986
Douglass, E.I. *	81	1981
Downs, C.P.	128	1986
Dreyfuss, H.	129	1972
Dreyfuss, H.	130	1970
Dreyfuss, H.	131	1970
Driver, R.W.	132	1987
Driver, R.W. *	461	1983
Drory, A. *	464	1983
Drury, C.G. *	68	1988
Drury, C.G.	133	1979
Duchastel, P.C.	134	1979
Duchastel, P.C.	135	1982
Duchon, J.C	136	1986
Duffy, T.M.	137	1985
Duffy, T.M. (Ed.)	137	1985
Duffy, T.M.	138	1982
Duffy, T.M. (Ed.)	253	1985
Duffy, T.M. (Ed.)	456	1985
Duffy, T.M. (Ed.)	484	1985
Duffy, T.M. (Ed.)	526	1985
Dunn, J.G.	139	1976
Dupuy, R.K.	140	1985-86
Eagly, A.H. *	66	1976
Easterby, R.S. (Ed.)	60	1984
Easterby, R.S.	142	1970
Easterby, R.S.	141	1967

Author *	Ref.	Year
Easterby, R.S.	143	1981
Easterby, R.S.	144	1977
Easterby, R.S.	145	1976
Easterby, R.S. *	200	1984
Easterby, R.S. (Ed.)	200	1984
Easterby, R.S. (Ed.)	260	1984
Easterby, R.S. (Ed.)	416	1984
Easterby, R.S. (Ed.)	433	1984
Easterby, R.S. (Ed.)	490	1984
Easterby, R.S. (Ed.)	508	1984
Easterby, R.S. (Ed.)	577	1984
Eaton, J.T.	146	1986
Edell, J.A.	147	1983
Edwards, M.L.	148	1976
Ehrenfeucht, A. *	18	1988
Eiland, K. *	257	1986
Eiswirth, R.S. *	431	1974
Elkin, E.H. *	45	1961
Ellington, D.	149	1985
Ellis, N.C.	148	1976
Ells, J.G.	114	1977
Ells, J.G.	150	1979
Ells, J.G.	151	1980
Elman, D.	152	1978
Embry, D.D.	153	1978
Engen, T. *	334	1973
Enlow, M. *	100	1943
Epstein, J.M.	154	1986
Eshelman, P. *	475	1981
Evans, L.	155	1982
Evans, R.I.	156	1970
Ewell, T.A.	157	1987
Faulk, R.O.	158	1985
Federman, P.J. *	465	1974
Feinstein, R.A.	159	1971
Fellner, D.J	160	1984
Fern, F.H	161	1985
Fhaner, G.	162	1974
Fidell, S.	163	1978
Finnegan, J.P. *	323	1982
Finnegan, J.P. *	324	1984
Fischer, P.M.	164	1989
Fischhoff, B.	165	1977
Fischhoff, B.	166	1978
Fischhoff, B.	167	1978
Fischhoff, B. *	294	1978
Fischhoff, B. *	477	1978
Fischhoff, B. *	478	1980
Fischhoff, B. *	479	1980
Fischhoff, B. *	480	1979
Fischhoff, B. *	481	1977

Author Index

Author *	Ref.	Year	Author *	Ref.	Year
Fischhoff, B. *	482	1977	Gregory, R.L.	197	1970
Flannagan, B.P.	168	1986	Grove, M. *	271	1973
Fleischer, G.A.	169	1971	Hadden, S.G.	198	1986
Fliss, A.A. (Ed.)	283	1988	Haddon, W. *	430	1974
Foley, J. *	280	1989	Haddon, W. *	431	1974
Fontenelle, G.A. *	558	1985	Hahn, K.C.	199	1977
Fontenelle, G.A. *	559	1987	Hakiel, S.R. *	143	1981
Ford, G.T. *	35	1979	Hakiel, S.R. *	144	1977
Foster, J.J.	170	1982	Hakiel, S.R.	200	1984
Fowler, F.D.	171	1980	Hall, G.	201	1986
Fowler, R.C. *	393	1972	Halperin, J.A. *	349	1979
Fox, K. *	570	1972	Hane, M. *	162	1974
Franti, C.E. *	270	1975	Hart, S.G.	202	1980
Fuchs, C.	172	1980	Hartley, H. *	234	1986
Funkhouser, G.R.	173	1984	Hartley, J. *	53	1976
Funston, C.E.	174	1984	Hartley, J.	203	1978
Galer, I.A.R. *	116	1975	Hartley, J.	204	1981
Galer, M.	175	1980	Hartley, J.	205	1980
Gallagher, J.	176	1985	Haskins, J.B.	206	1969
Gartner, K.P. (Ed.)	473	1972	Haskins, J.B.	207	1970
Geiselman, R.E.	177	1982	Hastak, M. *	415	1981
Geiselman, R.E. *	447	1981	Hauke, R.N. *	254	1975
Geiselman, R.E. *	448	1982	Hayes, J.R. *	467	1976
Gershonowitz, A.	178	1987	Hayes-Roth, B. *	242	1980
Gilhooley, M.	179	1986	Heckler, S.E. *	69	1986
Gill, R.T.	180	1987	Heckler, S.E. *	71	1985
Gillan, D.J. *	110	1988	Heckler, S.E. *	225	1987
Gleason, J.P.	181	1984	Heimstra, N.W. *	317	1973
Godfrey, S.S.	182	1983	Heinzmann, A.T. *	265	1980
Godfrey, S.S.	183	1984	Helfeldt, J.P. *	208	1987
Godfrey, S.S.	184	1985	Henderson, D.P. *	455	1983
Godfrey, S.S. *	557	1985	Henk, W.A.	208	1987
Godfrey, S.S. *	559	1987	Henning, J.C.	209	1975
Goldhaber, G.M. *	111	1988	Hensely, D.R.	210	1988
Goldhaber, G.M.	185	1988	Hermann, P.W. *	295	1979
Goldhaber, G.M.	186	1988	Hicks, J.A.	211	1976
Goldhaber, G.M.	187	1988	Hicks, L.E.	212	1972
Golia, S.	188	1983-84	Hicks, L.E.	213	1974
Gomer, F.E.	189	1986	Hill, P.S.	214	1978
Goodman, L. *	485	1984	Hind, P.R.	215	1976
Goodwin, N.C. *	493	1973	Hodge, D.C.	216	1962
Gordon, D.A.	190	1981	Hodgkinson, G.P.	217	1985
Gordon, D.A. *	263	1973	Hodgkinson, R.	218	1982
Gordon, E. *	321	1978	Hoecker, D.G.	219	1982
Gordon, E. *	355	1977	Hoenig, M.	220	1982
Green, D.A.	191	1978	Hoffmann, E.R. *	215	1976
Green, P.	192	1979	Hoffman, E.R.	221	1980
Green, P.	193	1978	Hoffmann, E.R. *	322	1977
Green, T.R.G.	194	1982	Holahan, C.J.	222	1977
Gregory, D.R.	195	1984	Horn, R.E.	223	1982
Gregory, K.	196	1982	Horst, D.P.	224	1986

Author *	Ref.	Year	Author *	Ref.	Year
Houston, M.J. *	69	1986	Keating, F.J.	249	1984
Houston, M.J. *	71	1985	Keeton, W.P.	250	1970
Houston, M.J. *	70	1984	Kegerreis, R.J.	251	1977
Houston, M.J.	225	1987	Kejriwal, S.K. *	403	1986
Howard-Pitney, B. *	297	1988	Keller, A.D.	252	1972
Hoyos, C.G. *	555	1976	Kelley, A.B. *	431	1974
Hsu L.*	12	1981	Kendrick, J.S. *	103	1989
Huber, J. *	540	1986	Kern, R.P.	253	1985
Hughes, A. *	433	1984	Kern, R.P.	254	1975
Hughes, J. *	218	1982	Kieras, D.E.	255	1985
Hughes, S.T. *	371	1988	Kieras, D.E.	256	1985
Hull, A.J.	226	1976	Killebrew, T.J. *	152	1978
Hull, A.J.	227	1975	Killingsworth, M.J.	257	1986
Hurst, P.M. *	380	1968	King, L.E.	258	1975
Jacobs, R.J. *	82	1981	King, L.E.	259	1970
Jacobs, R.J.	228	1975	King, L.E. *	394	1974
Jacoby, J.	229	1977	King, L.E. *	519	1970
Jacoby, J.	230	1974	Klahr, D. (Ed.)	467	1976
Jamieson, B.D. *	214	1978	Klare, G.R.	260	1984
Jamieson, D.G. *	62	1980	Klare, G.R.	261	1974-75
Johansson, G.	231	1970	Klimberg, R. *	353	1986
John, C.E. *	411	1981	Knapp, B.G.	262	1984
Johnson, D.A.	232	1980	Knapp, B.G.	263	1973
Johnson, E.J.	233	1980	Kolers, P.A. (Ed.)	316	1979
Johnson, M. W.	234	1986	Kolers, P.A. (Ed.)	525	1979
Johnson, R.C. *	515	1978	Kolers, P.A. (Ed.)	566	1980
Johnson-Laird, P.N.	235	1980	Komaki, J.	264	1978
Johnston, A.W. *	228	1975	Komaki, J.	265	1980
Jonassen, D.H. (Ed.)	135	1982	Konz, S.	266	1972
Jonassen, D.H. (Ed.)	223	1982	Kozminsky, E.	267	1977
Jonassen, D.H. (Ed.)	542	1982	Krampen, M.	268	1969
Jonassen, D.H. (Ed.)	568	1982	Krampen, M.	269	1965
Jones, S.	236	1978	Kraus, J.F.	270	1975
Jones, W.H.	237	1978	Kravitz, H.	271	1973
Kabance, P. *	138	1982	Kreifeldt, J.C.	272	1986
Kaestner, N.	238	1967	Kreindler, R.J.	273	1978
Kahn, M.J.	239	1983	Krenek, R.F. *	402	1987
Kakkar, P. *	30	1977	Krenzelok, E.P. *	359	1986
Kammann, R.	240	1975	Kroemer, K.H.E.	274	1980
Kann, H.R.	241	1970	Krugman, D.M. *	164	1989
Kanouse, D.E.	242	1980	Krumm-Scott, S. *	224	1986
Kanouse, D.E. *	350	1982	Krumm-Scott, S. *	324	1984
Kanouse, D.E. *	351	1981	Kunreuther, H. *	483	1974
Kanouse, D.E. *	352	1980	Kurtz, J.	275	1986
Kantowitz, B.H. (Ed.)	51	1983	Laage, L.W. *	136	1986
Kantowitz, B.H.	243	1983	Lambert, J.V. *	466	1974
Kantowitz, B.H.	244	1983	Landee, B.M. *	177	1982
Kantowitz, B.H.	245	1983	Landee, B.M. *	448	1982
Karnes, E.W.	246	1988	Laner, S.	276	1960
Karnes, E.W.	247	1986	Lasater, T.M. *	156	1970
Kasper, R.G.	248	1980	Laughery, K.R. *	183	1984

* co-author   (Ed.) editor

Author Index

Author *	Ref.	Year
Laughery, K.R. *	182	1983
Laughery, K.R. *	184	1985
Laughery, K.R. *	457	1983
Laughery, K.R. *	559	1987
Laughery, K.R. *	558	1985
Laux, L.	277	1989
Laux, L.	278	1989
Lawrence, A.C.	279	1974
Lawson, L. *	265	1980
Layman, M. *	294	1978
Lee, A.M. *	335	1982
Lee, J.S. *	314	1979
Lehto, M.R.	280	1989
Lehto, M.R	281	1986
Lehto, M.R.	282	1984
Lehto, M.R.	283	1988
Lehto, M.R.	284	1988
Lehto, M.R. *	342	1984
Leibman, J.H.	285	1983-84
Leonard, S.D. *	246	1988
Leonard, S.D. *	247	1986
Leonard, S.D.	286	1986
Lerner, N.D. *	84	1982
Lerner, N.D. *	85	1982
Lerner, N.D.	287	1981
Lerner, N.D.	288	1980
Lerner, N.D.	289	1983
Leventhal, H.	290	1966
Lewis, M.F.	291	1973
Ley, P.	292	1979
Liccardo, S.A.	293	1978
Lichtenstein, S. *	166	1978
Lichtenstein, S. *	167	1978
Lichtenstein, S.	294	1978
Lichtenstein, S. *	477	1978
Lichtenstein, S. *	478	1980
Lichtenstein, S. *	479	1980
Lichtenstein, S. *	480	1979
Lichtenstein, S. *	481	1977
Lichtenstein, S. *	482	1977
Liddell, H. *	576	1985
Lirtzman, S.I. (Ed.)	366	1984
Locander, W.B.	295	1979
Loewenthal, A.	296	1980
Loken, B.	297	1988
Loo, R.	298	1978
Loomis, J.P.	299	1982
Loomis, L.L. *	202	1980
Lopes, L. *	234	1986
Loring, B.A.	300	1988
Lowrance, W.W.	301	1980
Lowry, G.G.	302	1985
Lowry, R.C. *	302	1985
Lozano, R.D.	303	1980
Luchsinger, V.P. *	273	1978
Lutz, R.J. *	61	1979
Lynch, J.G.	304	1982
MacDonald, W.A. *	221	1980
Macdonald-Ross, M.	305	1975
MacKay, A.M.	306	1982
Mackett-Stout, J.	307	1981
Macro Systems, Inc.	308	1987
Madden, M.S.	309	1987
Madden, M.S.	310	1984
Mader, D.A.	311	1983
Magat, W.A. *	539	1987
Magat, W.A. *	540	1986
Maisano, R.E. *	358	1979
Malfetta, J.L. *	153	1978
Malhotra, N.K.	312	1982
Manley, M.	313	1987
Manstead, A.S.R.	314	1979
Manta, J.G.	315	1984
Marcel, T.	316	1979
Marchetti, F.M. *	59	1981
Marras, W.S. *	274	1980
Marsteller, T.F. *	543	1987
Martin, E.G. *	572	1989
Martin, G.L.	317	1973
Mashour, M.	318	1977
Matthews, D. *	286	1986
Mauro, C. *	93	1980
May, K.A.	319	1973
Mayer, D.L. *	277	1989
Maynard, R.C.	320	1984-85
Mazis, M.B. (Ed.)	242	1980
Mazis, M.B.	321	1978
Mazis, M.B. (Ed.)	330	1980
Mazis, M.B. *	354	1980
Mazis, M.B. *	355	1977
Mazis, M.B. (Ed.)	368	1980
Mazis, M.B. (Ed.)	459	1980
Mazis, M.B. (Ed.)	479	1980
McCann, J.M. *	95	1978
McCarthy, G.E. *	224	1986
McCarthy, G.E. *	324	1984
McCarthy, J.V.	322	1977
McCarthy, R.L	323	1982
McCarthy, R.L. *	224	1986
McCarthy, R.L.	324	1984
McClelland, I.L.	325	1980
McClelland, I.L.	326	1983

Author Index

Author *	Ref.	Year
McFee, J.K.	327	1969
McGill, J.	328	1978
McGuinness, J.	329	1977
McGuire, W.J.	330	1980
McGuire, W.J.	331	1966
McGuire, W.J.	332	1964
McIntyre, H.	333	1973
McKelvey, R.K.	334	1973
McKenna, N.A. *	560	1988
McLoughlin, E.	335	1982
McNaught, E.D. *	199	1977
McNeill, D.L.	336	1979
Mead, M.	337	1968
Meierhenry, W.C. *	327	1970
Meister, D.	338	1988
Mewhort, D.J.K. *	59	1981
Middendorf, L.	339	1984
Mikulecky, L. *	115	1981
Millar, S.A.	340	1986
Miller, J.C.	341	1974
Miller, J.M. *	281	1986
Miller, J.M. *	283	1988
Miller, J.M. *	284	1988
Miller, J.M.	342	1984
Miller, R.E.	343	1982
Milloy, D.G. *	151	1980
Milroy, R.	344	1978
Minarch, J.J. *	394	1974
Mital, A. (Ed.)	405	1989
Mitch, W.E. *	234	1986
Mitchell, A.A. (Ed.)	44	1981
Miyake, N.	345	1979
Modley, R. *	337	1968
Modley, R.	346	1960
Monroe, K.E. (Ed.)	233	1980
Morgan, F.W.	347	1982
Mori, M.	348	1981
Morris, L.A. (Ed.)	242	1980
Morris, L.A. *	321	1978
Morris, L.A. (Ed.)	330	1980
Morris, L.A.	349	1979
Morris, L.A.	356	1980
Morris, L.A.	351	1981
Morris, L.A.	352	1980
Morris, L.A.	353	1986
Morris, L.A. (Ed.)	354	1980
Morris, L.A.	355	1977
Morris, L.A.	350	1982
Morris, L.A.	357	1984
Morris, L.A. (Ed.)	368	1980
Morris, L.A. (Ed.)	459	1980

Author *	Ref.	Year
Morris, L.A. (Ed.)	479	1980
Moses, F.L.	358	1979
Mrvos, R.	359	1986
Muller, T.E.	360	1984
Myers, A. *	356	1980
Näätänen, R. *	506	1974
Newbold, H.C. *	246	1988
Noel, D.W.	361	1969
Noel, D.W.	362	1975
Noel, D.W.	363	1970
Norman, D.A. *	345	1979
Noyes, L.	364	1980
Noyes, L. *	387	1980
Noyes, L. *	388	1977
O'Connor, C.J. (Ed.)	365	1984
O'Neill, B.	366	1974
O'Neill, B. *	431	1974
O'Neill, B. *	432	1972
O'Neill, B. *	554	1974
Olins, N.J. *	357	1984
Olshavsky, R.W.	367	1974
Olson, J.C.	368	1980
Olson, P.L.	369	1979
Olson, P.L. *	474	1981
Orlansky, J. *	40	1960
Orloff, D.I.	370	1979
Orr, M.	371	1988
Orwin, R.G.	372	1984
Osborn, M.R.	373	1974
Otsubo, S.M.	374	1988
Owles, D.	375	1979
Page, M.E.	376	1981
Palmateer, L.M.	377	1986
Parasuraman, A. *	341	1974
Park, C.W. *	31	1980
Pastalan, L.A. *	474	1981
Patterson, R.B.	378	1975
Payne, J.W. *	32	1986
Pease, K.	379	1967
Peck, M.B. *	334	1973
Perchonok, K.	380	1968
Persensky, J.J. *	500	1975
Perry, R.W.	381	1983
Peters, B.J. (Ed.)	339	1984
Peters, G.A. (Ed.)	73	1983
Peters, G.A. (Ed.)	339	1984
Peters, G.A.	382	1983
Peters, G.A.	383	1984
Peters, G.A.	384	1984
Peters, G.A. (Ed.)	389	1983
Peters, J.I. *	263	1973

* co-author   (Ed.) editor

Author Index

Author *	Ref.	Year	Author *	Ref.	Year
Pew, R.W. *	193	1978	Reisinger, K.S. *	343	1982
Phelan, R.	385	1983	Reisinger, K.S.	409	1978
Phillips, R.J.	386	1979	Reisinger, K.S.	410	1981
Phillips, R.J.	387	1980	Reitman, P.	411	1988
Phillips, R.J.	388	1977	Rennert, L. *	22	1986
Philo, H.M.	389	1983	Reskin, L.R.	412	1985
Philo, H.M.	390	1978	Rethans, A.J.	413	1980
Piehler, H.R. *	524	1976	Rethans, A.J.	414	1980
Piehler, H.R. *	545	1978	Rethans, A.J.	415	1981
Piehler, H.R. *	546	1978	Reynolds, L.	416	1984
Pierman, B.C. *	85	1982	Reynolds, L.	417	1979
Pietraszewski, P. *	133	1979	Reynolds, L.	418	1979
Pilditch, J.	391	1981	Rheingold, P.D. (Ed.)	362	1975
Pilfold, D.	392	1987	Rheingold, P.D. (Ed.)	378	1975
Planek, T.W.	393	1972	Ricci, E.M.	419	1984
Plummer, R.W.	394	1974	Richards, J.W. *	164	1989
Podgainy, H.J. *	411	1981	Riggins, R.S. *	270	1975
Porter, R.F. *	299	1982	Riley, M.W. *	81	1981
Post, D.V.	395	1979	Riley, M.W. *	296	1980
Post, T.	396	1976	Riley, M.W.	420	1982
Poulton, E.C. *	344	1978	Riley, M.W.	421	1982
Poulton, E.C.	397	1975	Riley, M.W.	422	1981
Powderly, D.	398	1976	Rine, N.J. *	390	1978
Powell, K.B.	399	1981	Roberts, J.H.	423	1974
Powell, L.A.	400	1983-84	Roberts, T.R. *	411	1981
Poydar, H.R. (Ed.)	43	1980	Robertson, A.	424	1977
Poydar, H.R. (Ed.)	74	1980	Robertson, H.D.	425	1977
Poydar, H.R. (Ed.)	90	1980	Robertson, L.S.	426	1983
Poydar, H.R. (Ed.)	93	1980	Robertson, L.S.	427	1978
Poydar, H.R. (Ed.)	171	1980	Robertson, L.S.	428	1976
Poydar, H.R. (Ed.)	232	1980	Robertson, L.S.	429	1975
Precht, T. *	180	1987	Robertson, L.S.	430	1974
Preston, B. *	379	1967	Robertson, L.S.	431	1974
Preusser, D.F.	401	1976	Robertson, L.S.	432	1972
Price, H. *	396	1976	Robinett, F	433	1984
Purswell, J.L. *	124	1977	Robinson, G.H.	434	1977
Purswell, J.L. *	125	1978	Robinson, G.H.	435	1986
Purswell, J.L.	402	1987	Robinson, J.N. *	224	1986
Purswell, J.L.	403	1986	Robinson, J.N. *	323	1982
Pyrczak, F.	404	1976	Robinson, P.A. *	451	1984
Rachwal, G. *	247	1986	Rosenberg, S.	436	1981
Ramaswamy, K. *	521	1976	Ross, K. *	385	1983
Ramsey, J.D.	405	1989	Ross, K.	437	1981
Ramsey, J.D.	406	1977	Roth, D.H. *	404	1976
Rao, K.V.N. *	272	1986	Rothman, K.J. *	306	1982
Read, S. *	166	1978	Rothstein, P.R. *	184	1985
Reagan, J.A. *	452	1980	Rothstein, P.R. *	438	1985
Reagan, J.A. *	453	1980	Rothstein, P.R. *	559	1987
Ream, D.	407	1988	Roy, R.F.	439	1987
Reder, L.M.	408	1982	Royal, R.A.	440	1983-84
Reid, F. *	571	1973	Rozelle, R.M. *	156	1970

Author Index

Author *	Ref.	Year	Author *	Ref.	Year
Rubens, P.	441	1987	Singleton, W.T.	473	1972
Rubinsky, S.	442	1973	Sivak, M.	474	1981
Rudisill, M.	110	1988	Sless, D. *	57	1982
Russo, J.E. *	233	1980	Sless, D. *	58	1982
Ruzicka, M.	443	1979	Sloan, G.	475	1981
Ryan, J.J.	444	1984	Slovic, P. *	86	1979
Ryan, J.P.	445	1988	Slovic, P. *	166	1978
Sadosky, T.L. *	123	1977	Slovic, P. *	167	1978
Sales, J.B.	446	1982	Slovic, P. *	294	1978
Samet, M.G.	447	1981	Slovic, P.	476	1978
Samet, M.G.	448	1982	Slovic, P.	477	1978
Sathaye, S. *	266	1972	Slovic, P.	479	1980
Scammon, D.L.	449	1977	Slovic, P.	480	1979
Schlegel, R.E. *	403	1986	Slovic, P.	481	1977
Schmidt, A. *	234	1986	Slovic, P.	482	1977
Schneider, K.C.	450	1977	Slovic, P.	483	1974
Schoff, G.H.	451	1984	Smillie, R.J.	484	1985
Schooley, L.C.	452	1980	Smith, C.W.	485	1984
Schooley, L.C.	453	1980	Smith, D.B. *	90	1980
Schubert, J.C.	454	1984	Smith, E.E.	486	1984
Schucker, R.E. *	372	1984	Smith, E.E.	487	1985
Schucker, R.E.	455	1983	Smith, G.	488	1978
Schumacher, G.M.	456	1985	Smith, G.S.	489	1976
Schupack, S.A. *	393	1972	Smith, M. *	521	1976
Schwartz, D.R	457	1983	Smith, N. *	442	1973
Schwartz, D.R.	458	1988	Smith, S.L.	490	1984
Schwartz, S.P.	459	1980	Smith, S.L.	491	1981
Schwartz, V.E.	460	1984	Smith, S.L.	492	1979
Schwartz, V.E.	461	1983	Smith, S.L.	493	1973
Schwing, R.C. (Ed.)	76	1980	Smith, V.L. *	182	1983
Schwing, R.C. (Ed.)	301	1980	Snyder, H.L.	494	1979
Schwing, R.C. (Ed.)	478	1980	Sommer, R. *	551	1984
Scott, L.R. *	264	1978	Sorkin, R.D. (Ed.)	51	1983
Sell, R.G. *	276	1960	Sorkin, R.D. *	243	1983
Sell, R.G.	462	1977	Sorkin, R.D. *	244	1983
Shah, P. *	266	1972	Sorkin, R.D. *	245	1983
Shaw, M.E.	463	1964	Speller, D.E. *	230	1974
Sherwood, J. *	234	1986	Sperber, P.	495	1978
Shinar, D.	464	1983	Spicer, J. *	376	1981
Shippey, J. *	507	1977	Spiegel, A.P. *	251	1977
Sichel, W.M. *	161	1985	Spoehr, K.T. *	487	1985
Siegel, A.I.	465	1974	Sremec, B.	496	1972
Siegel, A.I.	466	1974	Srull, T.K. *	304	1982
Simon, H.A.	467	1976	Stacey, S. *	553	1981
Simonelli, N.M.	468	1978	Staelin, R. *	32	1986
Simpson, C.A. *	326	1983	Staelin, R. *	147	1983
Simpson, C.A.	469	1980	Staelin, R.	497	1978
Sims, J.H.	470	1972	Staelin, R.	498	1973
Sinaiko, H.W.	471	1975	Starbuck, A. *	326	1983
Singer, R.P. *	290	1966	Starr, C.	499	1969
Singleton, W.T.	472	1971	Stearns, F.C. *	24	1987

* co-author   (Ed.) editor

Author Index

Author *	Ref.	Year	Author *	Ref.	Year
Stefl, M.E.	500	1975	U.S. Dept. HEW	528	1979
Stern, K.R.	501	1984	U.S. Dept. HEW	529	1979
Stessin, L. (Ed.)	502	1977	U.S. Dept. HEW	530	1979
Stewart, M.L. *	455	1983	U.S. Dept. HEW	531	1979
Sticht, T.G. *	254	1975	U.S. Dept. HEW	532	1979
Stobbe, T.J. *	42	1978	Ulmer, R.G. *	401	1976
Stokes, R.C. *	372	1984	Ursic, M.	533	1984
Stokes, R.C. *	455	1983	Ursic, M.	534	1986
Strate, L.	503	1987	Van Nes, F.L.	535	1980
Strawbridge, J.A.	504	1986	Van Peski, R.F.	536	1978
Stuart, R.B.	505	1974	Vanderplas, J.H. *	537	1980
Sulzer-Azaroff, B. *	160	1984	Vanderplas, J.M.	537	1980
Summers, J.O. *	367	1974	Velotta, C.	538	1987
Summula, H.	506	1974	Vince, C.J. *	335	1982
Sumner, R.	507	1977	Viscusi, W.K.	539	1987
Svenson, O. *	99	1977	Viscusi, W.K.	540	1986
Swerdlow, S. *	503	1987	Voevodsky, J.	541	1974
Syring, E.M. *	238	1967	Von Buseck, C.R. *	155	1982
Szlichcinski, C.	508	1984	Wackerman, J.P. *	181	1984
Szlichcinski, K.P.	509	1980	Waller, R. *	134	1979
Szlichcinski, K.P.	510	1979	Waller, R. (Ed.)	137	1985
Tabrizi, M.F. *	126	1978	Waller, R. (Ed.)	253	1985
Taylor, G.B. *	494	1979	Waller, R. *	305	1975
Taylor, I.A.	511	1960	Waller, R. *	456	1985
Taylor, R.K. *	323	1982	Waller, R. (Ed.)	456	1985
Terry, N.P.	512	1987	Waller, R. (Ed.)	484	1985
Testin, F.J.	513	1981	Waller, R. (Ed.)	526	1985
Thilman, D.G. *	356	1980	Waller, R.	542	1982
Thomas, D.A.	514	1985	Walter, C.	543	1987
Thomas D.L. *	515	1978	Ward, S. (Ed.) *	498	1973
Thompson, D.A.	516	1988	Warmoth, E.J. *	238	1967
Thompson, D.E.	517	1985	Warner, K.E.	544	1977
Thompson, M.G.	518	1986	Wasielewski, P. *	155	1982
Thompson, N.B. *	277	1989	Weinstein, A.G. *	498	1973
Threlsall, S.M. *	569	1982	Weinstein, A.S. *	524	1976
Tierney, W.J. *	259	1970	Weinstein, A.S.	545	1978
Tierney, W.J.	519	1970	Weinstein, A.S.	546	1978
Tinker, M.A.	520	1963	Weinstein, N.D.	547	1979
Tokuhata, G.K.	521	1976	Weir, R. *	488	1978
Tomlinson, G.	522	1986	Wells, J.K. *	411	1981
Torpy, T.F.	523	1975	Welty, D. *	254	1975
Tritt, B.H. *	215	1976	Westinghouse Corp.	548	1981
Truax, S. *	40	1960	Wheale, J.L.	549	1983
Trucks, L.B. *	13	1976	Wheatley, E.	550	1977
Turner, T.J. *	41	1979	Whitaker, L.A	551	1984
Twerski, A.D.	524	1976	Whitaker, L.A.	552	1985
Twerski, A.D. *	545	1978	Whitaker, L.A.	553	1981
Twyman, M.	525	1979	White, G.F. *	483	1974
Twerski, A.D. *	546	1978	White, G.F. (Ed.)	483	1974
Twyman, M.	526	1985	Whitney, E. (Ed.)	346	1960
U.S. Dept. HEW	527	1979	Whitney, E. (Ed.)	511	1960

Author *	Ref.	Year
Wiklund, M.E. *	300	1988
Wilcox, P. *	20	1978
Wilkie, W.L. *	336	1979
Williams, A.F. *	410	1978
Williams, A.F. *	411	1981
Williams, A.F.	554	1974
Williams, D. H. *	469	1980
Williamson, J.W.	106	1977
Wiman, R.V. (Ed.)	327	1970
Witt, H.	555	1976
Wixom, C.W. *	431	1974
Wixom, C.W. *	432	1972
Wogalter, M.S.	556	1986
Wogalter, M.S.	557	1985
Wogalter, M.S.	558	1985
Wogalter, M.S.	559	1987
Wogalter, M.S.	560	1988
Wogalter, M.S. *	572	1989
Wogalter, M.S. *	573	1988
Wolcott, R.	561	1941
Woodson, W.E.	562	1981
Wooller, J. *	319	1973
Wright, P. *	20	1978
Wright, P. (Ed.)	498	1973
Wright, P.	563	1979
Wright, P.	564	1981
Wright, P.	565	1981
Wright, P.	566	1980
Wright, P.	567	1971
Wright, P.	568	1982
Wright, P.	569	1982
Wright, P.	570	1972
Wright, P.	571	1973
Wrolstad, M.E. (Ed.)	316	1979
Wrolstad, M.E. (Ed.)	525	1979
Wrolstad, M.E. (Ed.)	566	1980
Wucher, F. *	343	1982
Young, M. *	53	1976
Young, S.L.	572	1989
Young, S.L.	573	1988
Zador, P.L.	427	1978
Zlotnik, M.A.	574	1982
Zohar, D.	575	1980
Zuccollo, G.	576	1985
Zwaga, H.J.G. *	37	1984
Zwaga, H.J.G. (Ed.)	60	1984
Zwaga, H.J.G. *	145	1976
Zwaga, H.J.G. (Ed.)	200	1984
Zwaga, H.J.G. (Ed.)	260	1984
Zwaga, H.J.G. (Ed.)	416	1984
Zwaga, H.J.G. (Ed.)	433	1984

Author *	Ref.	Year
Zwaga, H.J.G. (Ed.)	490	1984
Zwaga, H.J.G. (Ed.)	508	1984
Zwaga, H.J.G.	577	1984

* co-author   (Ed.) editor

PART IV

References by Year

References by Year

1940-1969 References

Wolcott, R., *Informative Labeling*, National Consumer-Retailer Council, Inc., New York, **1941**, 1-23. (Ref 561)

Dallas, H. and Enlow, M., "Read Your Labels," Institute for Consumer Education, Columbia, MO, **1943**, 1-31. (Ref 100)

Belbin, E., "The Effects of Propaganda on Recall, Recognition and Behaviour: I. The Relationship Between the Different Measures of Propaganda, Effectiveness," *British Journal of Psychology*, 47:3, August **1956**, 163-174. (Ref 025)

Belbin, E., "The Effects of Propaganda on Recall, Recognition and Behaviour: II. The Conditions Which Determine the Response to Propaganda," *British Journal of Psychology*, 47:4, **1956**, 259-270. (Ref 026)

Bowen, H.M., Andreassi, J.L., Truax, S. and Orlansky, J., "Optimum Symbols for Radar Displays," *Human Factors*, February **1960**, 28-33. (Ref 040)

Laner, S. and Sell, R.G., "An Experiment on the Effects of Specially Designed Safety Posters," *Journal of Occupational Psychology*, 34:3, July **1960**, 153-169. (Ref 276)

Modley, R., "The Challenge of Symbology," in *Symbology: The Use of Symbols in Visual Communications*, Whitney, E. (Ed.), Hastings House, New York, **1960**, 17-30. (Ref 346)

Taylor, I.A., "Psychological Aspects of Visual Communications," in *Symbology: The Use of Symbols in Visual Communications*, Whitney, E. (Ed.), Hastings House, New York, **1960**, 123-138. (Ref 511)

Brainard, R.W., Campbell, R.J. and Elkin, E.H., "Design and Interpretability of Road Signs," *Journal of Applied Psychology*, 45:2, **1961**, 130-136. (Ref 045)

Hodge, D.C., "Legibility of a Uniform-Strokewidth Alphabet: I. Relative Legibility of Upper and Lower Case Letters," *Journal of Engineering Psychology*, 1:1, January **1962**, 34-46. (Ref 216)

Tinker, M.A., "Legibility of Print," Iowa State University Press, Ames, IA, **1963**. (Ref 520)

McGuire, W.J., "Inducing Resistance to Persuasion: Some Contemporary Approaches," in *Advances in Experimental Social Psychology*, 1, Berkowitz, L. (Ed.), **1964**, 191-229. (Ref 332)

Shaw, M.E., "Communication Networks," in *Advances in Experimental Social Psychology*, 1, Berkowitz, L. (Ed.), **1964**, 111-147. (Ref 463)

Chapanis, A., "Words, Words, Words," *Human Factors*, 7, February **1965**, 1-17. (Ref 067)

References by Year

Krampen, M., "Signs and Symbols in Graphic Communication," *Design Quarterly*, 62, **1965**, 3-31. (Ref 269)

Leventhal, H. and Singer, R.P., "Affect Arousal and Positioning of Recommendations in Persuasive Communications," *Journal of Personality and Social Psychology*, 4:2, **1966**, 137-146. (Ref 290)

McGuire, W.J., "Attitudes and Opinions," *Annual Review of Psychology*, 17, **1966**, 475-514. (Ref 331)

Easterby, R.S., "Perceptual Organization in Static Displays for Man/Machine Systems," *Ergonomics*, 10:2, **1967**, 195-205. (Ref 141)

Kaestner, N., Warmoth, E.J. and Syring, E.M., "Oregon Study of Advisory Letters: The Effectiveness of Warning Letters in Driver Improvement," *Traffic Safety Research Review*, 11:3, September **1967**, 67-72. (Ref 238)

Pease, K. and Preston, B., "Road Safety Education for Young Children," *The British Journal of Educational Psychology*, 37:3, November **1967**, 305-313. (Ref 379)

Mead, M. and Modley, R., "Communication Among All People, Everywhere," *Natural History*, 77, August/September **1968**, 56-63. (Ref 337)

Perchonok, K. and Hurst, P.M., "Effects of Lane-Closure Signals Upon Driver Decision Making and Traffic Flow," *Journal of Applied Psychology*, 52:5, **1968**, 410-413. (Ref 380)

Haskins, J.B., "Effect of Safety Communication Campaigns: A Review of the Research Evidence," *Journal of Safety Research*, 1:2, June **1969**, 58-66. (Ref 206)

Krampen, M., "The Production Method in Sign Design Research," *Print*, November/December **1969**, 59-63. (Ref 268)

McFee, J.K., "Chapter 8: Visual Communication," in *Educational Media: Theory into Practice*, Wiman, R.V. and Meierhenry, W.C. (Eds.), Charles E. Merrill Publishing Company, Columbus, **1969**, 195-216. (Ref 327)

Noel, D.W., "Products Defective Because of Inadequate Directions or Warnings," *Southwestern Law Journal*, 23:2, May **1969**, 257-298. (Ref 361)

Starr, C., "Social Benefit versus Technological Risk," *Science*, 165, 19 September **1969**, 1232-1238. (Ref 499)

1970-1974 References

———, *National Commission on Product Safety: Final Report*, Government Printing Office, Washington, D.C., June **1970**, 63-79. (Ref 005)

Dreyfuss, H., "Visual Communication: A Study of Symbols," Society of Automotive Engineers, SAE 700103, **1970**, 1-7. (Ref 130)

Dreyfuss, H. and Clifton, P., "Visual Communication: A Study of Symbols," *Graphic Science*, April **1970**, 21-26. (Ref 131)

References by Year

Easterby, R.S., "The Perception of Symbols for Machine Displays," *Ergonomics*, 13:1, **1970**, 149-158. (Ref 142)

Evans, R.I., Rozelle, R.M., Lasater, T.M., Dembroski, T.M. and Allen, B.P., "Fear Arousal, Persuasion, and Actual vs Implied Behavioral Change: New Perspective Utilizing a Real-Life Dental Hygiene Program," *Journal of Personality and Social Psychology*, 16:2, **1970**, 220-227. (Ref 156)

Gregory, R.L., "On How Little Information Controls So Much Behaviour," *Ergonomics*, 13:1, **1970**, 25-35. (Ref 197)

Haskins, J.B., "Evaluative Research on the Effects of Mass Communication Safety Campaigns: A Methodological Critique," *Journal of Safety Research*, 2:2, June **1970**, 86-96. (Ref 207)

Johansson, G. and Backlund, F., "Drivers and Road Signs," *Ergonomics*, 13:6, **1970**, 749-759. (Ref 231)

Kann, H.R., "Symbololatry: ICAO's Information Symbols for Airports Heighten the Confusion of International Communications Creating a Modern Tower of Babble," *Industrial Design*, 17:8, October **1970**, 56-57. (Ref 241)

Keeton, W.P., "Products Liability—Inadequacy of Information," *Texas Law Review*, 48, **1970**, 398-415. (Ref 250)

King, L.E. and Tierney, W.J., "Glance Legibility—Symbol versus Word Highway Signs," *Proceedings of the Human Factors Society*, Human Factors Society, Santa Monica, CA, **1970**, 1-14. (Ref 259)

Noel, D.W., "Statutory and Common Law Warnings," *The National Commission on Product Safety, Product Safety Law & Administration: Federal, State, and Common Law, Supplemental Studies*, 3, Government Printing Office, Washington, D.C., **1970**, 215-220. (Ref 363)

Tierney, W.J. and King, L.E., "Traffic Signing—Symbols versus Words, Montreal," a paper presented at the Sixth World Highway Conference of the International Road Federation, October **1970**, 1-40. (Ref 519)

Feinstein, R.A., "Symbolically Speaking," *Bell Telephone Magazine*, 50:4, November/December **1971**, 10-14. (Ref 159)

Fleischer, G.A., "An Experiment in the Use of Broadcast Media in Highway Safety: Systematic Analysis of the Effect of Mass Media Communication in Highway Safety," National Highway Traffic Safety Administration, Washington, D.C., DOT HS-800 629, December **1971**, 1-131. (Ref 169)

Singleton, W.T., "The Ergonomics of Information Presentation," *Applied Ergonomics*, December **1971**, 213-220. (Ref 472)

Wright, P., "Writing To Be Understood: Why Use Sentences?" *Applied Ergonomics*, December **1971**, 207-209. (Ref 567)

Asper, O., "The Detectability of Two Slow Vehicle Warning Devices," *Journal of Safety Research*, 4:2, June **1972**, 85-89. (Ref 017)

Bruening, E.B., "Signs and Symbols for Safety," *National Safety News*, January **1972**, 59-63. (Ref 050)

References by Year

Dreyfuss, H., *Symbol Sourcebook*, McGraw-Hill, New York, **1972**. (Ref 129)

Dunn, J.G., "Subjective and Objective Risk Distribution," *Occupational Psychology*, 46, **1972**, 183-187. (Ref 139)

Hicks, L.E., *Coping with Packaging Laws*, AMACOM, New York, **1972**. (Ref 212)

Keller, A.D., "Evaluation of Graphic Symbols for Safety and Warning Signs," Master's Thesis, Department of Psychology, University of South Dakota, August **1972**. (Ref 252)

Konz, S., Chawla, S., Sathaye, S. and Shah, P., "Attractiveness and Legibility of Various Colours When Printed on Cardboard," *Ergonomics*, 15:2, **1972**, 189-194. (Ref 266)

Planek, T.W., Schupack, S.A. and Fowler, R.C., "An Evaluation of the National Safety Council's Defensive Driving Course in Selected States," National Safety Council Research Department, October **1972**. (Ref 393)

Robertson, L.S., O'Neill, B. and Wixom, C.W., "Factors Associated with Observed Safety Belt Use," *Journal of Health & Social Behavior*, 13, March **1972**, 18-24. (Ref 432)

Sims, J.H. and Baumann, D.D., "The Tornado Threat: Coping Styles of the North and South," *Science*, 176:4042, 30 June **1972**, 1386-1392. (Ref 470)

Singleton, W.T., "General Theory of Presentation of Information," in *Displays and Controls*, Bernotat, R.K. and Gartner, K.P. (Eds.), Swets and Zeitlinger, N.V., Amsterdam, **1972**, 75-81. (Ref 473)

Sremec, B., "Instructions, Mechanical Ability and Performance," *Applied Ergonomics*, 3:2, **1972**, 98-100. (Ref 496)

Wright, P. and Fox, K., "Explicit and Implicit Tabulation Formats," *Ergonomics*, 15:2, **1972**, 175-187. (Ref 570)

Coates, F.D., "Human Factors and the Consumer: The Aesthetic Factor," *Proceedings of the Human Factors Society - 17th Annual Meeting*, Human Factors Society, Santa Monica, CA, **1973**, 440-443. (Ref 080)

Knapp, B.G., Peters, J.I. and Gordon, D.A., "Human Factor Review of Traffic Control and Diversion Projects," Federal Highway Administration, Washington, D.C., FHWA-RD-74-22, July **1973**, 1-100. (Ref 263)

Kravitz, H. and Grove, M., "Prevention of Accidental Falls in Infancy by Counseling Mothers," *Illinois Medical Journal*, 144, December **1973**, 570-573. (Ref 271)

Lewis, M.F., "Frequency of Anti-Collision Observing Responses by Solo Pilots as a Function of Traffic Density, ATC Traffic Warnings, and Competing Behavior," *Aerospace Medicine*, 44:9, September **1973**, 1048-1050. (Ref 291)

Martin, G.L. and Heimstra, N.W., "The Perception of Hazard by Children," *Journal of Safety Research*, 5:4, December **1973**, 238-246. (Ref 317)

May, K.A. and Wooller, J., "A Review of Non-Regulatory Signs in Relation to Road Safety, Australian Government Printing Office, Canberra, Australia, September **1973**, 1-33. (Ref 319)

McIntyre, H., "What Next for Symbolic Hazard Labeling?" *Modern Packaging*, 46:5, May **1973**, 30-33. (Ref 333)

McKelvey, R.K., Engen, T. and Peck, M.B., "Performance Efficiency and Injury Avoidance as a Function of Positive and Negative Incentives," *Journal of Safety Research*, 5:2, June **1973**, 90-96. (Ref 334)

Rubinsky, S. and Smith, N., "Safety Training by Accident Simulation," *Journal of Applied Psychology*, 57:1, **1973**, 68-73. (Ref 442)

Smith, S.L. and Goodwin, N.C., "Check-Reading as a Measure of Display Legibility," *Proceedings of the Human Factors Society - 17th Annual Meeting*, Human Factors Society, Santa Monica, CA, **1973**, 21-24. (Ref 493)

Staelin, R. and Weinstein, A.G., "Correlates of Consumer Safety Behavior," in *Advances in Consumer Research, Association for Consumer Research 1973 Proceedings*, 1, Ward, S. and Wright, P. (Eds.), Association for Consumer Research, **1973**, 87-100. (Ref 498)

Wright, P. and Reid, F., "Written Information: Some Alternatives to Prose for Expressing the Outcomes of Complex Contingencies," *Journal of Applied Psychology*, 57:2, **1973**, 160-166. (Ref 571)

———, "Signs and Symbols: Trail-Blazing Through a Forest of Hazards," in *National Safety News*, June **1974**, 102-104. (Ref 009)

Alff, T.R., "Symbols for Materials Handling," *National Safety News*, July **1974**, 76-77. (Ref 014)

Christ, R.E., "Color Research for Visual Displays," *Proceedings of the Human Factors Society - 18th Annual Meeting*, Human Factors Society, Santa Monica, CA, **1974**, 542-546. (Ref 072)

Committee on Consumer Policy, "Compulsory Labeling of Packaged Consumer Products," Organization for Economic Cooperation and Development, Paris, France, **1974**, 5-42. (Ref 087)

Fhaner, G. and Hane, M., "Seat Belts: Relations between Beliefs, Attitude, and Use," *Journal of Applied Psychology*, 59:4, **1974**, 472-482. (Ref 162)

Hicks, L.E., "Product Labeling and the Law: An AMA Management Briefing," AMACOM, New York, **1974**. (Ref 213)

Jacoby, J., Speller, D.E. and Berning, C.K., "Brand Choice Behavior as a Function of Information Load: Replication and Extension," *Journal of Consumer Research*, 1, June **1974**, 33-42. (Ref 230)

Lawrence, A.C., "Human Error as a Cause of Accidents in Gold Mining," *Journal of Safety Research*, 6:2, June **1974**, 78-88. (Ref 279)

Miller, J.C. and Parasuraman, A., "Advising Consumers on Safer Product Use: The Information Role of the New Consumer Product Safety Commission," *1974 Combined Proceedings, New Marketing for Social and Economic Progress and Marketing's Contributions to the Firm and to the Society*, Curhan, R.C. (Ed.), American Marketing Association, Series No. 36, **1974**, 372-376. (Ref 341)

References by Year

O'Neill, B., "Comments on 'An Evaluation of the National Safety Council's Defensive Driving Course in Various States'," *Accident Analysis & Prevention*, 6:3/4, December **1974**, 299-301. (Ref 366)

Olshavsky, R.W. and Summers, J.O., "A Study of the Role of Beliefs and Intentions in Consistency Restoration," *Journal of Consumer Research*, 1, June **1974**, 63-70. (Ref 367)

Osborn, M.R., "The Art of Creating Safety Symbols," *National Safety News*, June **1974**, 106-107. (Ref 373)

Plummer, R.W., Minarch, J.J. and King, L.E., "Evaluation of Driver Comprehension of Word versus Symbol Highway Signs," *Proceedings of the Human Factors Society - 18th Annual Meeting*, Human Factors Society, Santa Monica, CA, **1974**, 202-208. (Ref 394)

Roberts, J.H., "A Sign of the Times, Greater Use of Safety Symbols by Industry Predicted," *National Safety News*, June **1974**, 104-105. (Ref 423)

Robertson, L.S. and Haddon, W., "The Buzzer-Light Reminder System and Safety Belt Use," *American Journal of Public Health*, 64:8, August **1974**, 814-815. (Ref 430)

Robertson, L.S., Kelley, A.B., O'Neill, B., Wixom, C.W., Eiswirth, R.S. and Haddon, W., "A Controlled Study of the Effect of Television Messages on Safety Belt Use," *American Journal of Public Health*, 64:11, November **1974**, 1071-1080. (Ref 431)

Siegel, A.I., Federman, P.J. and Burkett, J.R., "Increasing and Evaluating the Readability of Air Force Written Materials," Brooks Air Force Base, Air Force Human Resources Laboratory, NTIS No. AD 786 820, August **1974**, 1-88. (Ref 465)

Siegel, A.I., Lambert, J.V. and Burkett, J.R., "Techniques for Making Written Material More Readable/Comprehensible," Lowry Air Force Base, Air Force Human Resources Laboratory, NTIS No. AD 786 849, August **1974**, 1-24. (Ref 466)

Slovic, P., Kunreuther, H. and White, G.F., "Decision Processes, Rationality, and Adjustment to Natural Hazards," in *Natural Hazards-Local, National, Global*, White, G.F. (Ed.), Oxford University Press, New York, **1974**, 187-205. (Ref 483)

Stuart, R.B., "Teaching Facts About Drugs: Pushing or Preventing?" *Journal of Educational Psychology*, 66:2, **1974**, 189-201. (Ref 505)

Summula, H. and Näätänen, R., "Perception of Highway Traffic Signs and Motivation," *Journal of Safety Research*, 6:4, December **1974**, 150-154. (Ref 506)

Voevodsky, J., "Evaluation of a Deceleration Warning Light for Reducing Rear-End Automobile Collisions," *Journal of Applied Psychology*, 59:3, **1974**, 270-273. (Ref 541)

Williams, A.F. and O' Neill, B., "On-The-Road Driving Records of Licensed Race Drivers," *Accident Analysis and Prevention*, 6, **1974**, 263-270. (Ref 554)

Klare, G.R., "Assessing Readability," *Reading Research Quarterly*, 10:1, **1974-1975**, 62-102. (Ref 261)

1975-1979 References

Bettman, J.R., "Issues in Designing Consumer Information Environments," *Journal of Consumer Research*, 2, December **1975**, 169-177. (Ref 029)

Bloom, P.N., "How Will Consumer Education Affect Consumer Behavior?" *Proceedings of the Association for Consumer Research - 6th Annual Conference*, 3, **1975**, 208-212. (Ref 034)

Booher, H.R., "Relative Comprehensibility of Pictorial Information and Printed Words in Proceduralized Instructions," *Human Factors*, 17:3, **1975**, 266-277. (Ref 038)

Bresnahan, T.F. and Bryk, J., "The Hazard Association Values of Accident-Prevention Signs," *Professional Safety*, January **1975**, 17-25. (Ref 047)

Cahill, M.C., "Interpretability of Graphic Symbols as a Function of Context and Experience Factors," *Journal of Applied Psychology*, 60:3, **1975**, 376-380. (Ref 056)

Dillon, J. and Galer, I.A.R., "Car Starting Sequence and Seat Belt Reminders," *Applied Ergonomics*, 6:4, **1975**, 221-223. (Ref 116)

Henning, J.C., "Labeling Hazardous Materials Can Be Complex—A Practical Approach," *Professional Safety*, November **1975**, 36-40. (Ref 209)

Hull, A.J., "Nine Codes: A Comparative Evaluation of Human Performance with Some Numeric, Alpha and Alpha-Numeric Coding Systems," *Ergonomics*, 18:5, **1975**, 567-576. (Ref 227)

Jacobs, R.J., Johnston, A.W. and Cole, B.L., "The Visibility of Alphabetic and Symbolic Traffic Signs," *Australian Road Research*, 5:7, May **1975**, 68-86. (Ref 228)

Kammann, R., "The Comprehensibility of Printed Instructions and the Flowchart Alternative," *Human Factors*, 17:8, **1975**, 183-191. (Ref 240)

Kern, R.P., Sticht, T.G., Welty, D. and Hauke, R.N., "Guidebook for the Development of Army Training Literature," Human Resources Research Organization, Alexandria, NTIS No. AD AO33 935, November **1975**. (Ref 254)

King, L.E., "Recognition of Symbol and Word Traffic Signs," *Journal of Safety Research*, 7:2, June **1975**, 80-84. (Ref 258)

Kraus, J.F., Riggins, R.S. and Franti, C.E., "Some Epidemiologic Features of Motorcycle Collision Injuries: I. Introduction, Methods and Factors Associated with Incidence," *American Journal of Epidemiology*, 102:1, **1975**, 74-98. (Ref 270)

Macdonald-Ross, M. and Waller, R., "Criticism, Alternatives and Tests: A Conceptual Framework for Improving Typography," *Programmed Learning and Educational Technology*, 12:2, March **1975**, 75-83. (Ref 305)

Noel, D.W., "Manufacturer's Negligence of Design or Directions for Use of a Product," in *Product Liability: Law, Practice, Science*, Rheingold, P.D. and Birnbaum, S.L. (Eds.), Practising Law Institute, New York, **1975**, 181-244. (Ref 362)

References by Year

Patterson, R.B., "Products Liability: The Manufacturer's Continuing Duty to Improve His Product or Warn of Defects After Sale," in *Product Liability: Law, Practice, Science*, 2nd Edition, Rheingold, P.D. and Birnbaum, S.L. (Eds.), Practising Law Institute, New York, **1975**, 165-178. (Ref 378)

Poulton, E.C., "Colours for Sizes: A Recommended Ergonomic Colour Code," *Applied Ergonomics*, 6:4, December **1975**, 231-235. (Ref 397)

Robertson, L.S., "Safety Belt Use in Automobiles with Starter-Interlock and Buzzer-Light Reminder Systems," *American Journal of Public Health*, 65:12, December **1975**, 1319-1325. (Ref 429)

Sinaiko, H.W., "Chapter 10: Verbal Factors in Human Engineering: Some Cultural and Psychological Data," in *Ethnic Variables in Human Factors Engineering*, Chapanis, A. (Ed.), Johns Hopkins University Press, Baltimore, **1975**, 159-177. (Ref 471)

Stefl, M.E. and Persensky, J.J., "An Evaluation of a Range-Top Warning Light System," NBSIR 75-797, July **1975**, 1-22. (Ref 500)

Torpy, T.F., "Graphic Symbols in an Occupational Health Service," *Journal of Occupational Medicine*, 17:12, December **1975**, 756-759. (Ref 523)

———, "Color Coding Hazards (Compliance Procedure)," *National Safety News*, April **1976**, 54-58. (Ref 001)

Adams, S.K. and Trucks, L.B., "A Procedure for Evaluating Auditory Warning Signals," *Proceedings of the Human Factors Society - 20th Annual Meeting*, Human Factors Society, Santa Monica, CA, **1976**, 166-172. (Ref 013)

Burnhill, P., Hartley, J. and Young, M., "Tables in Text," *Applied Ergonomics*, 7:1, March **1976**, 13-18. (Ref 053)

Cahill, M.C., "Design Features of Graphic Symbols Varying in Interpretability," *Perceptual and Motor Skills*, 42:2, April **1976**, 647-653. (Ref 055)

Chaiken, S. and Eagly, A.H., "Communication Modality as a Determinant of Message Persuasiveness and Message Comprehensibility," *Journal of Personality and Social Psychology*, 34:4, **1976**, 605-614. (Ref 066)

Dewar, R.E., "The Slash Obscures the Symbol on Prohibitive Traffic Signs," *Human Factors*, 18:3, **1976**, 253-258. (Ref 113)

Edwards, M.L. and Ellis, N.C., "An Evaluation of the Texas Driver Improvement Training Program," *Human Factors*, 18:4, August **1976**, 327-334. (Ref 148)

Hicks, J.A., "An Evaluation of the Effect of Sign Brightness on the Sign-Reading Behavior of Alcohol-Impaired Drivers," *Human Factors*, 18:1, February **1976**, 45-52. (Ref 211)

Hind, P.R., Tritt, B.H. and Hoffmann, E.R., "Effects of Level of Illumination, Strokewidth, Visual Angle and Contrast on the Legibility of Numerals of Various Fonts," *Session 25: 8th Australian Road Research Board Proceedings*, Perth, Australia, **1976**, 46-55. (Ref 215)

Hull, A.J., "Reducing Sources of Human Error in Transmission of Alphanumeric Codes," *Applied Ergonomics*, 7:2, June **1976**, 75-78. (Ref 226)

Post, T., Price, H. and Diffley, G., "A Guide for Selecting Formats and Media for Presenting Maintenance Information," Bio Technology, Inc., Falls Church, NTIS No. AD A033921, November **1976**, 1-51. (Ref 396)

Powderly, D., "Communicating with Standards," *ASTM Standardization News*, 4:12, December **1976**, 22-23, 54. (Ref 398)

Preusser, D.F., Ulmer, R.G. and Adams, J.R., "Driver Record Evaluation of a Drinking Driver Rehabilitation Program," *Journal of Safety Research*, 8:3, September **1976**, 98-105. (Ref 401)

Pyrczak, F. and Roth, D.H., "The Readability of Directions on Non-Prescription Drugs," *Journal of the American Pharmaceutical Association*, NS 16:5, May **1976**, 242-243, 267. (Ref 404)

Robertson, L.S., "The Great Seat Belt Campaign Flop," *Journal of Communication*, Fall **1976**, 41-45. (Ref 428)

Simon, H.A. and Hayes, J.R., "Chapter 14: Understanding Complex Task Instructions," in *Cognition and Instruction*, Klahr, D. (Ed.), Lawrence Erlbaum Associates, Hillsdale, NJ, **1976**, 269-285. (Ref 467)

Smith, G.S., "Just How Many Accidents Are Caused by Bad Road Signs?" *Applied Ergonomics*, 7:3, September **1976**, 157-158. (Ref 489)

Tokuhata, G.K., Colflesh, V., Smith, M., Ramaswamy, K. and Digon, E., "Consumer Behavior and Product Injuries," *Journal of Safety Research*, 8:3, September **1976**, 116-125. (Ref 521)

Twerski, A.D., Weinstein, A.S., Donaher, W.A. and Piehler, H.R., "The Use and Abuse of Warnings in Products Liability: Design Defect Litigation Comes of Age," *Cornell Law Review*, 61:4, **1976**, 495-540. (Ref 524)

Witt, H. and Hoyos, C.G., "Advanced Information on the Road: A Simulator Study of the Effect of Road Markings," *Human Factors*, 18:6, December **1976**, 521-532. (Ref 555)

Bettman, J.R. and Kakkar, P., "Effects of Information Presentation Format on Consumer Information Acquisition Strategies," *Journal of Consumer Research*, 3, March **1977**, 233-240. (Ref 030)

Broadbent, D.E., "Language and Ergonomics," *Applied Ergonomics*, 8:1, March **1977**, 15-18. (Ref 049)

Curran, T.E., "Survey of Technical Manual Readability and Comprehensibility," Navy Personnel Research and Development Center, San Diego, NTIS No. AD AO42335, June **1977**. (Ref 097)

Dahlstedt, S. and Svenson, O., "Detection and Reading Distances of Retroreflective Road Signs During Night Driving," *Applied Ergonomics*, 8:1, March **1977**, 7-14. (Ref 099)

Dershewitz, R.A.and Williamson, J.W., "Prevention of Childhood Household Injuries: A Controlled Clinical Trial," *American Journal of Public Health*, 67:12, December **1977**, 1148-1153. (Ref 106)

References by Year

Dewar, R.E. and Ells, J.G., "The Semantic Differential as an Index of Traffic Sign Perception and Comprehension," *Human Factors*, 19:2, **1977**, 183-189. (Ref 114)

Dorris, A.L., Connolly, T., Sadosky, T.L. and Burroughs, M., "More Information or More Data?: Some Experimental Findings," *Proceedings of the Human Factors Society - 21st Annual Meeting*, Human Factors Society, Santa Monica, CA, **1977**, 25-28. (Ref 123)

Dorris, A.L. and Purswell, J.L., "Warnings and Human Behavior: Implications for the Design of Product Warnings," *Journal of Products Liability*, 1, **1977**, 255-263. (Ref 124)

Easterby, R.S. and Hakiel, S.R., "Safety Labelling of Consumer Products: Shape and Colour Code Stereotypes in the Design of Signs," University of Aston in Birmingham, AP Report No. 75, December **1977**. (Ref 144)

Easterby, R.S. and Zwaga, H.J.G., "Evaluation of Public Information Symbols, ISO Tests: 1975 Series," University of Aston in Birmingham, AP Report No. 60, December **1977**. (Ref 145)

Fischhoff, B., "Cognitive Liabilities and Product Liability," *Journal of Products Liability*, 1, **1977**, 207-219. (Ref 165)

Hahn, K.C., McNaught, E.D. and Bryden, J.E., "Nighttime Legibility of Guide Signs," New York State Department of Transportation, Albany, Research Report 50, August **1977**. (Ref 199)

Holahan, C.J., "Relationship Between Roadside Signs and Traffic Accidents: A Field Investigation," *Austin, Texas Council for Advanced Transportation Studies*, Austin, Research Report 54, November **1977**, 1-14. (Ref 222)

Jacoby, J., "Information Load and Decision Quality: Some Contested Issues," *Journal of Marketing Research*, 14, November **1977**, 569-573. (Ref 229)

Kegerreis, R.J. and Spiegel, A.P., "A Supplementary Emergency Signage System," *National Safety News*, November **1977**, 81-82. (Ref 251)

Kozminsky, E., "Altering Comprehension: The Effect of Biasing Titles on Text Comprehension," *Memory & Cognition*, 5:4, **1977**, 482-490. (Ref 267)

Mashour, M., "On Designing Signals and Their Meanings," *Ergonomics*, 20:6, **1977**, 659-664. (Ref 318)

McCarthy, J.V. and Hoffmann, E.R., "The Difficulty that Traffic Signs Present to Poor Readers," Department of Transport, Commonwealth of Australia, December **1977**, 1-201. (Ref 322)

McGuinness, J., "Human Factors in Consumer Product Safety," *Proceedings of the Human Factors Society - 21st Annual Meeting*, Human Factors Society, Santa Monica, CA, **1977**, 292-294. (Ref 329)

Morris, L.A., Mazis, M.B. and Gordon, E., "A Survey of the Effects of Oral Contraceptive Patient Information," *The Journal of the American Medical Association*, 238:23, December **1977**, 2504-2508. (Ref 355)

Phillips, R.J., Noyes, L. and Audley, R.J., "The Legibility of Type on Maps," *Ergonomics*, 20:6, **1977**, 671-682. (Ref 388)

References by Year

Ramsey, J.D. and Brinkley, W.A., "Enhanced Motorcycle Noticeability Through Daytime Use of Visual Signal Warning Devices," *Journal of Safety Research*, 9:2, June **1977**, 77-84. (Ref 406)

Robertson, A., "A Road Sign for Warning of Close-Following: Form and Message Design," Crowthorne, Berkshire, Transport and Road Research Laboratory, TRRL Supplementary Report 324, **1977**, 1-12. (Ref 424)

Robertson, H.D., "Pedestrian Signal Displays: An Evaluation of Word Message and Operation," *Transportation Research Record*, 629, **1977**, 19-22. (Ref 425)

Robinson, G.H., "Human Performance in Accident Causation: Toward Theories on Warning Systems and Hazard Appreciation," *Third International System Safety Conference*, Washington, D.C., **1977**, 55-69. (Ref 434)

Scammon, D.L., " 'Information Load' and Consumers," *The Journal of Consumer Research*, 4, **1977**, 148-155. (Ref 449)

Schneider, K.C., "Prevention of Accidental Poisoning Through Package and Label Design," *Journal of Consumer Research*, 4, September **1977**, 67-74. (Ref 450)

Sell, R.G., "What Does Safety Propaganda Do for Safety? A Review," *Applied Ergonomics*, December **1977**, 203-214. (Ref 462)

Slovic, P., Fischhoff, B. and Lichtenstein, S., "Behavioral Decision Theory," *Annual Review of Psychology*, 28, **1977**, 1-39. (Ref 481)

Slovic, P., Fischhoff, B., Lichtenstein, S., Corrigan, B. and Combs, B., "Preference for Insuring Against Probable Small Losses: Insurance Implications," *The Journal of Risk and Insurance*, 44:2, June **1977**, 237-258. (Ref 482)

Stessin, L. (Ed.), *Product Liability Portfolio*, Man & Manager, Inc., New York, **1977**, 1-77. (Ref 502)

Sumner, R. and Shippey, J., "The Use of Rumble Areas to Alert Drivers," Crowthorne, Berkshire, Transport and Road Research Laboratory, TRRL Lab Report 800, **1977**, 1-29. (Ref 507)

Warner, K.E., "The Effects of the Anti-Smoking Campaign on Cigarette Consumption," *American Journal of Public Health*, 67:7, July **1977**, 645-650. (Ref 544)

Wheatley, E., "An Experiment on Coding Preferences for Display Symbols," *Ergonomics*, 20:5, **1977**, 543-552. (Ref 550)

———, "Warning: Signs are Changing," *National Safety News*, March **1978**, 113-114. (Ref 010)

Barnard, P., Wright, P. and Wilcox, P., "The Effects of Spatial Constraints on the Legibility of Handwritten Alphanumeric Codes," *Ergonomics*, 21:1, **1978**, 73-78. (Ref 020)

Booher, H.R., "Job Performance Aids: Research and Technology State-of-the Art," Navy Personnel Research and Development Center, San Diego, NTIS No. AD AO57562, July **1978**, 1-86. (Ref 039)

References by Year

Boydstun, L.E., Stobbe, T.J. and Chaffin, D.B., "OSHA Standards: Human Factors Research Needs for Fall Hazard Warning Systems," *Proceedings of the Human Factors Society - 22nd Annual Meeting*, Human Factors Society, Santa Monica, CA, **1978**, 5-11. (Ref 042)

Craig, C.S. and McCann, J.M., "Assessing Communication Effects on Energy Conservation," *Journal of Consumer Research*, 5, September **1978**, 82-88. (Ref 095)

Dorris, A.L. and Purswell, J.L., "Human Factors in the Design of Effective Product Warnings," *Proceedings of the Human Factors Society - 22nd Annual Meeting*, Human Factors Society, Santa Monica, CA, **1978**, 343-346. (Ref 125)

Dorris, A.L. and Tabrizi, M.F., "An Empirical Investigation of Consumer Perception of Product Safety," *Journal of Products Liability*, 2, **1978**, 155-163. (Ref 126)

Elman, D. and Killebrew, T.J., "Incentives and Seat Belts: Changing a Resistant Behavior Through Extrinsic Motivation," *Journal of Applied Psychology*, 8:1, **1978**, 72-83. (Ref 152)

Embry, D.D. and Malfetta, J.L., "Reducing the Risk of Pedestrian Accidents to Preschoolers by Parent Training and Symbolic Modeling for Children: An Experimental Analysis in the Natural Environment," Research Report 2, **1978**, 1-78. (Ref 153)

Fidell, S., "Effectiveness of Audible Warning Signals for Emergency Vehicles," *Human Factors*, 20:1, **1978**, 19-26. (Ref 163)

Fischhoff, B., Slovic, P., Lichtenstein, S., Read, S. and Combs, B., "How Safe Is Safe Enough? A Psychometric Study of Attitudes Towards Technological Risks and Benefits," *Policy Sciences*, 9:2, April **1978**, 127-152. (Ref 166)

Fischhoff, B., Slovic, P. and Lichtenstein, S., "Fault Trees: Sensitivity of Estimated Failure Probabilities to Problem Representation," *Journal of Experimental Psychology: Human Perception and Performance*, 4:2, **1978**, 330-344. (Ref 157)

Green, D.A., "Emergency Vehicle Warning Systems and Identification," PND80019, N.S.W. Department of Public Works, New South Wales, May **1978**, 1-24. (Ref 191)

Green, P. and Pew, R.W., "Evaluating Pictographic Symbols: An Automotive Application," *Human Factors*, 20:1, **1978**, 103-114. (Ref 193)

Hartley, J., *Designing Instructional Text*, Nichols Publishing Company, New York, **1978**. (Ref 203)

Hill, P.S. and Jamieson, B.D., "Driving Offenders and the Defensive Driving Course—An Archival Study," *The Journal of Psychology*, 98, **1978**, 117-127. (Ref 214)

Jones, S., "Symbolic Representation of Abstract Concepts," *Ergonomics*, 21:7, **1978**, 573-577. (Ref 236)

Jones, W.H., "ANSI Standard: Simple, Direct, Flexible," *Occupational Health & Safety*, 47:2, March/April **1978**, 29-30. (Ref 237)

Komaki, J., Barwick, K.D. and Scott, L.R., "A Behavioral Approach to Occupational Safety: Pinpointing and Reinforcing Safe Performance in a Food Manufacturing Plant," *Journal of Applied Psychology*, 63:4, **1978**, 434-445. (Ref 264)

Kreindler, R.J. and Luchsinger, V.P., "How Readable Are Your Safety Publications?" *Professional Safety*, September **1978**, 40-42. (Ref 273)

Liccardo, S.A., "Consumer's Right to Know: A New Horizon in Drug Product Liability," *Journal of Products Liability*, 1, **1978**, 165-170. (Ref 293)

Lichtenstein, S., Slovic, P., Fischhoff, B., Layman, M. and Combs, B., "Judged Frequency of Lethal Events," *Journal of Experimental Psychology: Human Learning and Memory*, 4:6, November **1978**, 551-578. (Ref 294)

Loo, R., "Individual Differences and the Perception of Traffic Signs," *Human Factors*, 20:1, **1978**, 65-74. (Ref 298)

Mazis, M.B., Morris, L.A. and Gordon, E., "Patient Attitudes About Two Forms of Printed Oral Contraceptive Information," *Medical Care*, 16:12, December **1978**, 1045-1054. (Ref 321)

McGill, J., "Warranties: What They Are and How They Can Be Used in Risk Control," *Journal of Products Liability*, 2, **1978**, 105-115. (Ref 328)

Milroy, R. and Poulton, E.C., "Labeling Graphs for Improved Reading Speed," *Ergonomics*, 21:1, **1978**, 55-61. (Ref 344)

Philo, H.M. and Rine, N.J., "The Danger Never Was Obvious," *Journal of Products Liability*, 1, **1978**, 12-19. (Ref 390)

Reisinger, K.S. and Williams, A.F., "Evaluation of Programs Designed to Increase the Protection of Infants in Cars," *Pediatrics*, 62:3, September **1978**, 280-297. (Ref 409)

Robertson, L.S., and Zador, P.L., "Driver Education and Fatal Crash Involvement of Teenaged Drivers," *American Journal of Public Health*, 68:10, October **1978**, 959-965. (Ref 427)

Simonelli, N.M., "An Investigation of Pictorial and Symbolic Aircraft Displays for Landing," *Proceedings of the Human Factors Society - 22nd Annual Meeting*, Human Factors Society, Santa Monica, CA, **1978**, 213-217. (Ref 468)

Slovic, P., "The Psychology of Protective Behavior," *Journal of Safety Research*, 10:2, Summer **1978**, 58-68. (Ref 476)

Slovic, P., Fischhoff, B. and Lichtenstein, S., "Accident Probabilities and Seat Belt Usage: A Psychological Perspective," *Accident Analysis and Prevention*, 10:4, **1978**, 281-285. (Ref 477)

Smith, G. and Weir, R., "Laboratory Visibility Studies of Directional Symbols Used for Traffic Control Signals," *Ergonomics*, 21:4, **1978**, 247-252. (Ref 488)

Sperber, P., "The Strategy of Product Labeling for Loss Prevention," *Journal of Products Liability*, 1, **1978**, 171-182. (Ref 495)

Staelin, R., "The Effects of Consumer Education on Consumer Product Safety Behavior," *Journal of Consumer Research*, 5, June **1978**, 30-40. (Ref 497)

Thomas D.L., Johnson, R.C. and Dalezman J.J., "Opinions of Air Force Maintenance Personnel About Conventional Technical Orders," Wright-Patterson Air Force Base, Advanced Systems Division, NTIS No. AD A058340 July **1978**. (Ref 515)

References by Year

Van Peski, R.F., "Hail!...The Mighty Safety Poster," *National Safety News*, May **1978**, 90-92. (Ref 536)

Weinstein, A.S., Twerski, A.D., Piehler, H.R. and Donaher, W.A., "Chapter 5: Warnings and Disclaimers," in *Products Liability and the Reasonably Safe Product*, John Wiley & Sons, New York, **1978**, 60-74. (Ref 545)

Weinstein, A.S., Twerski, A.D., Piehler, H.R. and Donaher, W.A., "Chapter 3: Product Defects—What Are They?" in *Products Liability and the Reasonably Safe Product*, John Wiley & Sons, New York, **1978**, 28-42. (Ref 546)

Bliss, W.D., "Defective Product Design Role of Human Factors," *Lawyers Cooperative Publication*, 18 POF 2d, **1979**, 117-147. (Ref 033)

Bloom, P.N. and Ford, G.T., "Evaluation of Consumer Education Programs," *Journal of Consumer Research*, 6, December **1979**, 270-279. (Ref 035)

Bloomfield, J.R., "Visual Search with Embedded Targets: Color and Texture Differences," *Human Factors*, 21:3, **1979**, 317-330. (Ref 036)

Bower, G.H., Black, J.B. and Turner, T.J., "Scripts in Memory for Text," *Cognitive Psychology*, 11, **1979**, 177-220. (Ref 041)

Capon, N. and Lutz, R.J., "A Model and Methodology for the Development of Consumer Information Programs," *Journal of Marketing*, 43, January **1979**, 58-67. (Ref 061)

Carter, R.C. and Cahill, M.C., "Regression Models of Search Time for Color-Coded Information Displays," *Human Factors*, 21:3, **1979**, 293-302. (Ref 063)

Carter, R.J., "Standardization of Geometric Radar Symbology: Stereotyped Meanings and Paper-and-Pencil Testing," *Proceedings of the Human Factors Society - 23rd Annual Meeting*, Human Factors Society, Santa Monica, CA, **1979**, 443-447. (Ref 064)

Combs, B. and Slovic, P., "Newspaper Coverage of Causes of Death," *Journalism Quarterly*, Winter **1979**, 837-843, 849. (Ref 086)

Connolley, D., "AUDISAFE: A General Accident-Preventive Device," *Ergonomics*, 22:2, **1979**, 199-210. (Ref 088)

Dershewitz, R.A., "Will Mothers Use Free Household Safety Devices?" *American Journal of Diseases of Children*, 133, January **1979**, 61-64. (Ref 107)

Dionne, E.D., "Effective Safety Signs and Posters," *National Safety News*, October **1979**, 48-52. (Ref 117)

Drury, C.G. and Pietraszewski, P., "The Motorists' Perception of the Bicyclist's Hand Signals," *Ergonomics*, 22:9, **1979**, 1045-1057. (Ref 133)

Duchastel, P. and Waller, R., "Pictorial Illustration in Instructional Texts," in *The Technology of Text*, 19:11, Educational Technology Publications, Inc., Englewood Cliffs, **1979**, 20-25. (Ref 134)

Ells, J.G. and Dewar, R.E., "Rapid Comprehension of Verbal and Symbolic Traffic Sign Messages," *Human Factors*, 21:2, **1979**, 161-168. (Ref 150)

Green, P., "Development of Pictograph Symbols for Vehicle Controls and Displays," Society of Automotive Engineers, SAE 790383, **1979**, 1-31. (Ref 192)

Ley, P., "Memory for Medical Information," *British Journal of Social and Clinical Psychology*, 18:2, June **1979**, 245-255. (Ref 292)

Locander, W.B. and Hermann, P.W., "The Effect of Self-Confidence and Anxiety on Information Seeking in Consumer Risk Reduction," *Journal of Marketing Research*, 16, May **1979**, 268-274. (Ref 295)

Manstead, A.S.R. and Lee, J.S., "The Effectiveness of Two Types of Witness Appeal Sign," *Ergonomics*, 22:10, **1979**, 1125-1140. (Ref 314)

Marcel, T. and Barnard, P., "Paragraphs of Pictographs: The Use of Non-Verbal Instructions for Equipment," in *Processing of Visible Language*, 1, Kolers, P.A., Wrolstad, M.E. and Bouma, H. (Eds.), Plenum Press, New York, **1979**, 501-518. (Ref 316)

McNeill, D.L. and Wilkie, W.L., "Public Policy and Consumer Information: Impact of the New Energy Labels," *Journal of Consumer Research*, 6, June **1979**, 1-11. (Ref 336)

Miyake, N. and Norman, D.A., "To Ask a Question, One Must Know Enough to Know What Is Not Known," *Journal of Verbal Learning and Verbal Behavior*, 18, **1979**, 357-364. (Ref 345)

Morris, L.A. and Halperin, J.A., "Effects of Written Drug Information on Patient Knowledge and Compliance: A Literature Review," *American Journal of Public Health*, 69:1, January **1979**, 47-52. (Ref 349)

Moses, F.L., Maisano, R.E. and Bersh, P., " 'Natural' Associations Between Symbols and Military Information," *Proceedings of the Human Factors Society - 23rd Annual Meeting*, Human Factors Society, Santa Monica, CA, **1979**, 438-442. (Ref 358)

Olson, P.L. and Bernstein, A., "The Nighttime Legibility of Highway Signs as a Function of Their Luminance Characteristics," *Human Factors*, 21:2, **1979**, 145-160. (Ref 369)

Orloff, D.I., "Potential Fire Hazards and the Role of Product Literature," *Journal of Products Liability*, 3, **1979**, 29-41. (Ref 370)

Owles, D., "Pharmaceutical Manufacturers' Duty to Warn of Propensity to Harm," *Journal of Products Liability*, 3, **1979**, 151-159. (Ref 375)

Phillips, R.J., "Why Is Lower Case Better?" *Applied Ergonomics*, 10:4, **1979**, 211-214. (Ref 386)

Post, D.V., "Are Specifications of Signaling Systems for Emergency, School Bus, and Service Vehicles Adequate?" *Proceedings of the Human Factors Society - 23rd Annual Meeting*, Human Factors Society, Santa Monica, CA, **1979**, 282-284. (Ref 395)

Reynolds, L., "Legibility Problems in Printed Scientific and Technical Information," *Journal of Audiovisual Media in Medicine*, 2, **1979**, 67-70. (Ref 417)

References by Year

Reynolds, L., "Legibility Studies: Their Relevance to Present-Day Documentation Methods," *Journal of Documentation*, 35:4, December **1979**, 307-340. (Ref 418)

Ruzicka, M., "Liability Based on Warnings," *Product Liability Prevention Conference*, IEEE Catalogue No. 79CH1512-3 R, **1979**, 75-78. (Ref 443)

Slovic, P., Fischoff, B. and Lichtenstein, S., "Rating the Risks," *Environment*, 21:3, April **1979**, 14-39. (Ref 480)

Smith, S.L., "Letter Size and Legibility," *Human Factors*, 21:6, **1979**, 661-670. (Ref 492)

Snyder, H.L. and Taylor, G.B., "The Sensitivity of Response Measures of Alphanumeric Legibility to Variations in Dot Matrix Display Parameters," *Human Factors*, 21:4, **1979**, 457-471. (Ref 494)

Szlichcinski, K.P., "Telling People How Things Work," *Applied Ergonomics*, 10:1, **1979**, 2-8. (Ref 510)

Twyman, M., "A Schema for the Study of Graphic Language (Tutorial Paper)," in *Processing of Visible Language*, 1, Kolers, P.A., Wrolstad, M.E. and Bouma, H. (Eds.), Plenum Press, New York, **1979**, 117-150. (Ref 525)

U.S. Department of Health, Education, and Welfare, "Adult Education," *Smoking and Health, A Report of the Surgeon General*, Government Printing Office, Washington, D.C., **1979**, 21-1 - 21-32. (Ref 527)

U.S. Department of Health, Education, and Welfare, "Behavioral Factors in the Establishment, Maintenance, and Cessation of Smoking," *Smoking and Health, A Report of the Surgeon General*, Government Printing Office, Washington, D.C., **1979**, 16-1 - 16-23. (Ref 528)

U.S. Department of Health, Education, and Welfare, "Smoking in Children and Adolescents - Psychosocial Determinants and Prevention Strategies," *Smoking and Health, A Report of the Surgeon General*, Government Printing Office, Washington, D.C., **1979**, 17-1 - 17-30. (Ref 529)

U.S. Department of Health, Education, and Welfare, "The Role of Educators," *Smoking and Health, A Report of the Surgeon General*, Government Printing Office, Washington, D.C., **1979**, 23-1 - 23-45. (Ref 530)

U.S. Department of Health, Education, and Welfare, "Youth Education," *Smoking and Health, A Report of the Surgeon General*, Government Printing Office, Washington, D.C., **1979**, 20-1 - 20-33. (Ref 531)

U.S. Department of Health, Education, and Welfare, "Psychosocial Influences on Cigarette Smoking," *Smoking and Health, A Report of the Surgeon General*, Government Printing Office, Washington, D.C., **1979**, 18-1 - 18-31. (Ref 532)

Weinstein, N.D., "Seeking Reassuring or Threatening Information About Environmental Cancer," *Journal of Behavioral Medicine*, 2:2, **1979**, 125-139. (Ref 547)

Wright, P., "Concrete Action Plans in TV Messages to Increase Reading of Drug Warnings," *Journal of Consumer Research*, 6, December **1979**, 256-269. (Ref 563)

1980 References

Bettman, J.R. and Park, C.W., "Effects of Prior Knowledge and Experience and Phase of the Choice Process on Consumer Decision Processes: A Protocol Analysis," *Journal of Consumer Research*, 7, December **1980**, 234-248. (Ref 031)

Boyer, H., " 'Do-It-Yourself' IBM Products and the Role of the Technical Illustrator in Human Factors Testing," *Proceedings of the Symposium: Human Factors and Industrial Design in Consumer Products*, Poydar, H.R. (Ed.), Tufts University, Medford, **1980**, 342-351. (Ref 043)

Caron, J.P., Jamieson, D.G. and Dewar, R.E., "Evaluating Pictographs Using Semantic Differential and Classification Techniques," *Ergonomics*, 23:2, **1980**, 137-146. (Ref 062)

Christensen, J.M., "Human Factors in Hazard/Risk Evaluation," *Proceedings of the Symposium: Human Factors and Industrial Design in Consumer Products*, Poydar, H.R. (Ed.), Tufts University, Medford, **1980**, 442-477. (Ref 074)

Clark, W.C., "Witches, Floods, and Wonder Drugs: Historical Perspectives on Risk Management," in *Societal Risk Assessment*, Schwing, R.C. and Albers, W.A. (Eds.), Plenum Press, New York, **1980**, 287-318. (Ref 076)

Cook, T.R. and Smith, D.B., "Communications–Complex Problem Solving: Design and Development of a Signage System for the Columbus International Airport in Columbus, Ohio," *Proceedings of the Symposium: Human Factors and Industrial Design in Consumer Products*, Poydar, H.R. (Ed.), Tufts University, Medford, **1980**, 329-341. (Ref 090)

Coskuntuna, S. and Mauro, C., "Instruction Manuals: A Component of a Product's 'Teaching Package'," *Proceedings of the Symposium: Human Factors and Industrial Design in Consumer Products*, Poydar, H.R. (Ed.), Tufts University, Medford, **1980**, 300-313. (Ref 093)

Deutsch, S., "Product Design and Consumer Safety: An Informational Approach," in *CP News*, 5:2, Consumer Products Technical Group, The Human Factors Society, August **1980**, 3-4. (Ref 112)

Ells, J.G., Dewar, R.E. and Milloy, D.G., "An Evaluation of Six Configurations of the Railway Crossbuck Sign," *Ergonomics*, 23:4, **1980**, 359-367. (Ref 151)

Fowler, F.D., "Failure to Warn: A Product Design Problem," *Proceedings of the Symposium: Human Factors and Industrial Design in Consumer Products*, Poydar, H.R. (Ed.), Tufts University, Medford, **1980**, 241-250. (Ref 171)

Fuchs, C., "Wisconsin Driver Improvement Program: A Treatment-Control Evaluation," *Journal of Safety Research*, 12:3, Fall **1980**, 107-114. (Ref 172)

Galer, M., "An Ergonomics Approach to the Problem of High Vehicles Striking Low Bridges," *Applied Ergonomics*, 11:1, March **1980**, 43-46. (Ref 175)

Hart, S.G. and Loomis, L.L., "Evaluation of the Potential Format and Content of a Cockpit Display of Traffic Information," *Human Factors*, 22:5, **1980**, 591-604. (Ref 202)

References by Year

Hartley, J., Bartlett, S. and Branthwaite, A., "Underlining Can Make a Difference–Sometimes," *The Journal of Educational Research*, 73:4, March/April **1980**, 218-224. (Ref 205)

Hoffman, E.R. and MacDonald, W.A., "Short-Term Retention of Traffic Turn Restriction Signs," *Human Factors*, 22:2, **1980**, 241-251. (Ref 221)

Johnson, D.A., "The Design of Effective Safety Information Displays," *Proceedings of the Symposium: Human Factors and Industrial Design in Consumer Products*, Poydar, H.R. (Ed.), Tufts University, Medford, **1980**, 314-328. (Ref 232)

Johnson, E.J. and Russo, J.E., "Product Familiarity and Learning New Information," in *Advances in Consumer Research*, 8, Monroe, K.E. (Ed.), **1980**. (Ref 233)

Johnson-Laird, P.N., "Mental Models in Cognitive Science," *Cognitive Science*, 4, **1980**, 71-115. (Ref 235)

Kanouse, D.E. and Hayes-Roth, B., "Cognitive Considerations in the Design of Product Warnings," in *Product Labeling and Health Risks*, Morris, L.A., Mazis, M.B. and Barofsky, I. (Eds.), Cold Spring Harbor Laboratory, Banbury Report 6, **1980**, 147-163. (Ref 242)

Kasper, R.G., "Perceptions of Risk and Their Effects on Decision Making," in *Societal Risk Assessment*, Schwing, R.C. and Albers, W.A. (Eds.), Plenum Press, New York, **1980**, 71-84. (Ref 248)

Komaki, J., Heinzmann, A.T. and Lawson, L., "Effect of Training and Feedback: Component Analysis of a Behavioral Safety Program," *Journal of Applied Psychology*, 65:3, **1980**, 261-270. (Ref 265)

Kroemer, K.H.E. and Marras, W.S., "Ergonomics of Visual Emergency Signals," *Applied Ergonomics*, 11:3, September **1980**, 137-144. (Ref 274)

Lerner, N.D. and Collins, B.L., "The Assessment of Safety Symbol Understandability by Different Testing Methods," National Bureau of Standards, Washington, D.C., PB81-185647, August **1980**. (Ref 288)

Loewenthal, A. and Riley, M.W., "The Effectiveness of Warning Labels," *Proceedings of the Human Factors Society - 24th Annual Meeting*, Human Factors Society, Santa Monica, CA, **1980**, 389-391. (Ref 296)

Lowrance, W.W., "The Nature of Risk," in *Societal Risk Assessment*, Schwing, R.C. and Albers, W.A. (Eds.), Plenum Press, New York, **1980**, 5-17. (Ref 301)

Lozano, R.D., "The Visibility, Colour and Measuring Requirements of Road Signs," *Lighting Research & Technology*, 12:4, **1980**, 206-212. (Ref 303)

McClelland, I.L., "Audible Warning Signals for Police Vehicles," *Applied Ergonomics*, 11:3, September **1980**, 165-170. (Ref 325)

McGuire, W.J., "The Communication-Persuasion Model and Health-Risk Labeling," in *Product Labeling and Health Risks*, Morris, L.A., Mazis, M.B. and Barofsky, I. (Eds.), Cold Spring Harbor Lab, Banbury Report 6, **1980**, 99-122. (Ref 330)

Morris, L.A. and Kanouse, D.E., "Consumer Reactions to Differing Amounts of Written Drug Information," *Drug Intelligence and Clinical Pharmacy*, 14, July/August **1980**, 531-536. (Ref 352)

Morris, L.A., Mazis, M.B. and Barofsky, I. (Eds.), *Product Labeling and Health Risks,* Cold Spring Harbor Laboratory, Banbury Report 6, **1980.** (Ref 354)

Morris, L.A., Myers, A. and Thilman, D.G., "Application of the Readability Concept to Patient-Oriented Drug Information," *American Journal of Hospital Pharmacy,* 37, November **1980,** 1504-1509. (Ref 356)

Noyes, L., "The Positioning of Type on Maps: The Effect of Surrounding Material on Word Recognition Time," *Human Factors,* 22:3, **1980,** 353-360. (Ref 364)

Olson, J.C., "An Information-Processing Approach to Health-Risk Labeling," in *Product Labeling and Health Risks,* Morris, L.A., Mazis, M.B. and Barofsky, I. (Eds.), Cold Spring Harbor Laboratory, Banbury Report 6, **1980,** 123-134. (Ref 368)

Phillips, R.J. and Noyes, L., "A Comparison of Colour and Visual Texture as Codes for Use as Area Symbols on Thematic Maps," *Ergonomics,* 23:12, **1980,** 1117-1128. (Ref 387)

Rethans, A.J., "Consumer Perceptions of Hazards," in *PLP-80 Proceedings,* **1980,** 25-29. (Ref 413)

Rethans, A.J. and Albaum, G.S., "Towards Determinants of Acceptable Risk: The Case of Product Risks," *Advances in Consumer Research,* 8, October **1980,** 506-510. (Ref 414)

Schooley, L.C. and Reagan, J.A., "Visibility and Legibility of Exit Signs, Part 1: Analytical Predictions," *Journal of the Illuminating Engineering Society,* October **1980,** 24-28. (Ref 452)

Schooley, L.C. and Reagan, J.A., "Visibility and Legibility of Exit Signs, Part 2: Experimental Results," *Journal of the Illuminating Engineering Society,* October **1980,** 29-32. (Ref 453)

Schwartz, S.P., "Consumer Attitudes Toward Product Labeling," in *Product Labeling and Health Risks,* Morris, L.A., Mazis, M.B. and Barofsky, I. (Eds.), Cold Spring Harbor Laboratory, Banbury Report 6, **1980,** 89-96. (Ref 459)

Simpson, C.A. and Williams, D.H., "Response Time Effects of Alerting Tone and Semantic Context for Synthesized Voice Cockpit Warnings," *Human Factors,* 22:3, **1980,** 319-330. (Ref 469)

Slovic, P., Fischhoff, B. and Lichtenstein, S., "Facts and Fears: Understanding Perceived Risk," in *Societal Risk Assessment,* Schwing, R.C. and Albers, W.A. (Eds.), Plenum Press, New York, **1980,** 181-216. (Ref 478)

Slovic, P., Fischhoff, B. and Lichtenstein, S., "Informing People About Risk," in *Product Labeling and Health Risks,* Morris, L.A., Mazis, M.B. and Barofsky, I. (Eds.), Cold Spring Harbor Laboratory, Banbury Report 6, **1980,** 165-180. (Ref 479)

Szlichcinski, K.P., "The Syntax of Pictorial Instructions," in *Processing of Visible Language,* 2, Kolers, P.A., Wrolstad, M.E. and Bouma, H. (Eds.), Plenum Press, New York, **1980,** 113-124. (Ref 509)

Van Nes, F.L. and Bouma, H., "On the Legibility of Segmented Numerals," *Human Factors,* 22:4, **1980,** 463-474. (Ref 535)

References by Year

Vanderplas, J.M. and Vanderplas, J.H., "Some Factors Affecting Legibility of Printed Materials for Older Adults," *Perceptual and Motor Skills*, 50:3, June **1980**, 923-932. (Ref 537)

Wright, P., "Usability: The Criterion for Designing Written Information," in *Processing of Visible Language*, 2, Kolers, P.A., Wrolstad, M.E. and Bouma, H. (Eds.), Plenum Press, New York, **1980**, 183-205. (Ref 566)

Zohar, D., Cohen, A. and Azar, N., "Promoting Increased Use of Ear Protectors in Noise Through Information Feedback," *Human Factors*, 22:1, **1980**, 69-79. (Ref 575)

1981 References

———, "Messages for Men in Motion," *National Safety News*, May **1981**, 64-67. (Ref 004)

Adams, A.S. and Hsu L., "The Coding of Symbol Signs," *Hazard Prevention*, March/April **1981**, 5-7. (Ref 012)

Bozinoff, L., "A Script Theoretic Approach to Information Processing: An Energy Conservation Application," in *Advances in Consumer Research*, Mitchell, A.A. (Ed.), 9, **1981**, 481-486. (Ref 044)

Campbell, A.J., Marchetti, F.M. and Mewhort, D.J.K., "Reading Speed and Text Production: A Note on Right-Justification Techniques," *Ergonomics*, 24:8, **1981**, 633-640. (Ref 059)

Cochran, D.J., Riley, M.W. and Douglass, E.I., "An Investigation of Shapes for Warning Labels," *Proceedings of the Human Factors Society - 25th Annual Meeting*, Human Factors Society, Santa Monica, CA, **1981**, 395-399. (Ref 081)

Cole, B.L. and Jacobs, R.J., "A Comparison of Alternative Symbolic Warning Signs for Railway Level Crossings," *Australian Road Research*, 11:4, December **1981**, 37-45. (Ref 082)

Cunitz, R.J., "Psychologically Effective Warnings," *Hazard Prevention*, 17:3, May/June **1981**, 5-7. (Ref 096)

Diehl, W. and Mikulecky, L., "Making Written Information Fit Workers' Purposes," *IEEE Transactions on Professional Communication*, 24:1, March **1981**, 5-9. (Ref 115)

Easterby, R.S. and Hakiel, S.R., "Field Testing of Consumer Safety Signs: The Comprehension of Pictorially Presented Messages," *Applied Ergonomics*, 12:3, **1981**, 143-152. (Ref 143)

Gordon, D.A., "The Assessment of Guide Sign Informational Load," *Human Factors*, 23:4, **1981**, 453-466. (Ref 190)

Hartley, J., "Eighty Ways of Improving Instructional Text," *IEEE Transactions on Professional Communication*, 24:1, March **1981**, 17-27. (Ref 204)

References by Year

Lerner, N.D., "Experimental Evaluation of Exit Directional Indicators," *Proceedings of the Human Factors Society - 25th Annual Meeting*, Human Factors Society, Santa Monica, CA, **1981**, 193-197. (Ref 287)

Mackett-Stout, J. and Dewar, R., "Evaluation of Symbolic Public Information Signs," *Human Factors*, 23:2, **1981**, 139-151. (Ref 307)

Mori, M. and Abdel-Halim, M.H., "Road Sign Recognition and Non-Recognition," *Accident Analysis and Prevention*, 13, **1981**, 101-115. (Ref 348)

Morris, L.A. and Kanouse, D.E., "Consumer Reactions to the Tone of Written Drug Information," *American Journal of Hospital Pharmacy*, 38:5, May **1981**, 667-671. (Ref 351)

Page, M.E. and Spicer, J., "Aids and Services for Disabled People—Getting the Message Across," *Applied Ergonomics*, 12, December **1981**, 223-230. (Ref 376)

Pilditch, J., "Did You Read the Instructions Carefully?" *IEEE Transactions on Professional Communication*, 24:4, December **1981**, 185-186. (Ref 391)

Powell, K.B., "Readability Formulas: Used or Abused?" *IEEE Transactions on Professional Communication*, 24:1, March **1981**, 43-44. (Ref 399)

Reisinger, K.S., Williams, A.F., Wells, J.K., John, C.E., Roberts, T.R. and Podgainy, H.J., "Effect of Pediatricians' Counseling on Infant Restraint Use," *Pediatrics*, 67:2, February **1981**, 201-206. (Ref 410)

Rethans, A.J. and Hastak, M., "Representation of Product Hazards in Consumer Memory," *Advances in Consumer Research*, 9, October **1981**, 487-491. (Ref 415)

Riley, M.W., Cochran, D.J. and Deacy, J.E., "Warning Label Design," *Professional Safety*, October **1981**, 44-46. (Ref 422)

Rosenberg, S., "FMC's Systematic Approach to Product Safety Warning Labels," *Agricultural Engineering*, 62:10, October **1981**, 22-24. (Ref 436)

Ross, K., "Legal and Practical Considerations for the Creation of Warning Labels and Instruction Books," *Journal of Products Liability*, 4, **1981**, 29-45. (Ref 437)

Samet, M.G. and Geiselman, R.E., "Developing Guidelines for Summarizing Information," *Human Factors*, 23:6, December **1981**, 727-736. (Ref 447)

Sivak, M., Olson, P.L. and Pastalan, L.A., "Effect of Driver's Age on Nighttime Legibility of Highway Signs," *Human Factors*, 23:1, **1981**, 59-64. (Ref 474)

Sloan, G. and Eshelman, P., "The Development and Evaluation of Pictographic Symbols," *Proceedings of the Human Factors Society - 25th Annual Meeting*, Human Factors Society, Santa Monica, CA, **1981**, 198-202. (Ref 475)

Smith, S.L., "Exploring Compatibility with Words and Pictures," *Human Factors*, 23:3, **1981**, 305-315. (Ref 491)

Testin, F.J. and Dewar, R.E., "Divided Attention in a Reaction Time Index of Traffic Sign Perception," *Ergonomics*, 24:2, **1981**, 111-124. (Ref 513)

Westinghouse Electric Corporation, *Product Safety Label Handbook*, Westinghouse Printing Division, Trafford, PA, **1981**. (Ref 548)

References by Year

Whitaker, L.A. and Stacey, S., "Response Times to Left and Right Directional Signs," *Human Factors*, 23:4, **1981**, 447-452. (Ref 553)

Woodson, W.E. and Conover, D.W., *Human Engineering Design Handbook, Information and Guidelines for the Design of Systems, Facilities, Equipment, and Products for Human Use*, McGraw-Hill, New York, **1981**. (Ref 562)

Wright, P., "Five Skills Technical Writers Need," *IEEE Transactions on Professional Communication*, 24:1, March **1981**, 10-16. (Ref 564)

Wright, P., "'The Instructions Clearly State...' Can't People Read?" *Applied Ergonomics*, 12:3, **1981**, 131-141. (Ref 565)

1982 References

———, "How to Make Signs and Labels for Safety... A Guidepost," *National Safety News*, 125:3, March **1982**, 43-44. (Ref 002)

Anderton, P.J. and Cole, B.L., "Contour Separation and Sign Legibility," *Australian Road Research*, 12:2, June **1982**, 103-109. (Ref 015)

Bailey, R.W., "Chapter 19: Printed Instructions," in *Human Performance Engineering: A Guide for System Designers*, Prentice-Hall, Inc., Englewood Cliffs, **1982**, 403-445. (Ref 019)

Berry, E., "How to Get Users to Follow Procedures," *IEEE Transactions on Professional Communication*, 25:1, March **1982**, 22-25. (Ref 028)

Cairney, P. and Sless, D., "Communication Effectiveness of Symbolic Safety Signs with Different User Groups," *Applied Ergonomics*, 13:2, June **1982**, 91-97. (Ref 057)

Cairney, P.T. and Sless, D., "Evaluating the Understanding of Symbolic Roadside Information Signs," *Australian Road Research*, 12:2, June **1982**, 97-102. (Ref 058)

Collins, B.L. and Lerner, N.D., "Assessment of Fire-Safety Symbols," *Human Factors*, 24:1, **1982**, 75-84. (Ref 084)

Collins, B.L., Lerner, N.D. and Pierman, B.C., "Symbols for Industrial Safety," June National Bureau of Standards, Washington, D.C., NBSIR 82-2485, **1982**, 1-102. (Ref 085)

Dixon, P., "Plans and Written Directions for Complex Tasks," *Journal of Verbal Learning and Verbal Behavior*, 21, **1982**, 70-84. (Ref 118)

Duchastel, P.C., "Chapter 8: Textual Display Techniques," in *The Technology of Text*, Jonassen, D.H. (Ed.), Educational Technology Publications, Inc., Englewood Cliffs, **1982**, 167-191. (Ref 135)

Duffy, T.M. and Kabance, P., "Testing a Readable Writing Approach to Text Revision," *Journal of Educational Psychology*, 74:5, **1982**, 733-748. (Ref 138)

Evans, L., Wasielewski, P. and Von Buseck, C.R., "Compulsory Seat Belt Usage and Driver Risk-Taking Behavior," *Human Factors*, 24:1, February **1982**, 41-48. (Ref 155)

Foster, J.J. and Bruce, M., "Reading Upper and Lower Case on Viewdata," *Applied Ergonomics*, 13:2, June **1982**, 145-149. (Ref 170)

Geiselman, R.E., Landee, B.M. and Christen, F.G., "Perceptual Discriminability as a Basis for Selecting Graphic Symbols," *Human Factors*, 24:3, **1982**, 329-337. (Ref 177)

Green, T.R.G., "Pictures of Programs and Other Processes, or How to Do Things with Lines," *Behaviour and Information Technology*, 1:1, **1982**, 3-36. (Ref 194)

Gregory, K., "Determining the 'Consumer Object'," *Applied Ergonomics*, 13:1, March **1982**, 11-13. (Ref 196)

Hodgkinson, R. and Hughes, J., "Developing Wordless Instructions: A Case History," *IEEE Transactions on Professional Communication*, 25:2, June **1982**, 74-79. (Ref 218)

Hoecker, D.G., "Some Performance Correlates of Technical Illustration Level," *Proceedings of the Human Factors Society - 26th Annual Meeting*, Human Factors Society, Santa Monica, CA, **1982**, 88-92. (Ref 219)

Hoenig, M., "The Influence of Advertising in Products Liability Litigation," *Journal of Products Liability*, 5, **1982**, 321-340. (Ref 220)

Horn, R.E., "Chapter 16: Structured Writing and Text Design," in *The Technology of Text*, Jonassen, D.H. (Ed.), Educational Technology Publications, Inc., Englewood Cliffs, **1982**, 341-367. (Ref 223)

Loomis, J.P. and Porter, R.F., "The Performance of Warning Systems in Avoiding Controlled-Flight-Into-Terrain (CFIT) Accidents," *Aviation, Space, and Environmental Medicine*, 53:11, November **1982**, 1085-1090. (Ref 299)

Lynch, J.G. and Srull, T.K., "Memory and Attentional Factors in Consumer Choice: Concepts and Research Methods," *Journal of Consumer Research*, 9, June **1982**, 18-37. (Ref 304)

MacKay, A.M. and Rothman, K.J., "The Incidence and Severity of Burn Injuries Following Project Burn Prevention," *American Journal of Public Health*, 72:3, March **1982**, 248-252. (Ref 306)

Malhotra, N.K., "Information Load and Consumer Decision Making," *Journal of Consumer Research*, 8, March **1982**, 419-430. (Ref 312)

McCarthy, R.L, Robinson, J.N., Finnegan, J.P. and Taylor, R.K., "Warnings on Consumer Products: Objective Criteria for Their Use," *Proceedings of the Human Factors Society - 26th Annual Meeting*, Human Factors Society, Santa Monica, CA, **1982**, 98-102. (Ref 323)

McLoughlin, E., Vince, C.J., Lee, A.M. and Crawford, J.D., "Project Burn Prevention: Outcome and Implications," *American Journal of Public Health*, 72:3, March **1982**, 241-247. (Ref 335)

References by Year

Miller, R.E., Reisinger, K.S., Blatter, M.M. and Wucher, F., "Pediatric Counseling and Subsequent Use of Smoke Detectors," *American Journal of Public Health*, 72:4, April **1982**, 392-393. (Ref 343)

Morgan, F.W. and Avrunin, D.I., "Consumer Conduct in Product Liability Litigation," *Journal of Consumer Research*, 9, June **1982**, 47-55. (Ref 347)

Morris, L.A. and Kanouse, D.E., "Informing Patients About Drug Side Effects," *Journal of Behavioral Medicine*, 5:3, **1982**, 363-373. (Ref 350)

Reder, L.M. and Anderson J.R., "Effects of Spacing and Embellishment on Memory for the Main Points of a Text," *Memory & Cognition*, 10:2, **1982**, 97-102. (Ref 408)

Riley, M.W., Cochran, D.J. and Ballard, J.L., "An Investigation of Preferred Shapes for Warning Labels," *Human Factors*, 24:6, **1982**, 737-742. (Ref 420)

Riley, M.W., Cochran, D.J. and Ballard, J.L., "Designing and Evaluating Warning Labels," *IEEE Transactions on Professional Communication*, 25:3, September **1982**, 127-130. (Ref 421)

Sales, J.B., "The Duty to Warn and Instruct for Safe Use in Strict Tort Liability," *St. Mary's Law Journal*, 13, **1982**, 521-586. (Ref 446)

Samet, M.G., Geiselman, R.E. and Landee, B.M., "A Human Performance Evaluation of Graphic Symbol-Design Features," *Perceptual and Motor Skills*, 54, **1982**, 1303-1310. (Ref 448)

Waller, R., "Chapter 7: Text as Diagram: Using Typography to Improve Access and Understanding," in *The Technology of Text*, Jonassen, D.H. (Ed.), Educational Technology Publications, Inc., Englewood Cliffs, **1982**, 137-166. (Ref 542)

Wright, P., "Chapter 15: A User-Oriented Approach to the Design of Tables and Flowcharts," in *The Technology of Text*, Jonassen, D.H. (Ed.), Educational Technology Publications, Inc., Englewood Cliffs, **1982**, 317-340. (Ref 568)

Wright, P., Creighton, P. and Threlsall, S.M., "Some Factors Determining When Instructions Will Be Read," *Ergonomics*, 25:3, **1982**, 225-237. (Ref 569)

Zlotnik, M.A., "The Effects of Warning Message Highlighting on Novel Assembly Task Performance," *Proceedings of the Human Factors Society - 26th Annual Meeting*, Human Factors Society, Santa Monica, CA, **1982**, 93-97. (Ref 574)

1983 References

Buck, J.R., "Chapter 7: Visual Displays," in *Human Factors: Understanding People-System Relationships*, Kantowitz, B.H. and Sorkin, R.D. (Eds.), John Wiley & Sons, New York, **1983**, 195-231. (Ref 051)

Christensen, J.M., "Human Factors Considerations in Lawsuits," in *Safety Law: A Legal Reference for the Safety Professional*, Peters, G.A. (Ed.), American Society of Safety Engineers, Park Ridge, **1983**, 5-7. (Ref 073)

Clarke, M.M. and Carroll, L., "Human Factors Guidelines for Writers of User Manuals," *Proceedings of the Human Factors Society - 27th Annual Meeting*, Human Factors Society, Santa Monica, CA, **1983**, 496-500. (Ref 077)

Collins, B.L., "Evaluation of Mine-Safety Symbols," *Proceedings of the Human Factors Society - 27th Annual Meeting*, Human Factors Society, Santa Monica, CA, **1983**, 947-949. (Ref 083)

Edell, J.A. and Staelin, R., "The Information Processing of Pictures in Print Advertisements," *Journal of Consumer Research*, 10, June **1983**, 45-61. (Ref 147)

Godfrey, S.S., Allender, L., Laughery, K.R. and Smith, V.L., "Warning Messages: Will the Consumer Bother to Look?" *Proceedings of the Human Factors Society - 27th Annual Meeting*, Human Factors Society, Santa Monica, CA, **1983**, 950-954. (Ref 182)

Kahn, M.J., "Human Awakening and Subsequent Indentification of Fire-Related Cues," *Proceedings of the Human Factors Society - 27th Annual Meeting* Human Factors Society, Santa Monica, CA, **1983**, 806-810. (Ref 239)

Kantowitz, B.H. and Sorkin, R.D., "Chapter 7: Visual Displays," in *Human Factors: Understanding People-System Relationships*, Kantowitz, B.H. and Sorkin, R.D. (Eds.), John Wiley & Sons, Inc., New York, **1983**, 272-305. (Ref 243)

Kantowitz, B.H. and Sorkin, R.D., "Chapter 8: Auditory and Tactile Displays," in *Human Factors: Understanding People-System Relationships*, Kantowitz, B.H. and Sorkin, R.D. (Eds.), John Wiley & Sons, Inc., New York, **1983**, 232-271. (Ref 244)

Kantowitz, B.H. and Sorkin, R.D., "Chapter 20: Legal Aspects of Human Factors," in *Human Factors: Understanding People-System Relationships*, Kantowitz, B.H. and Sorkin, R.D. (Eds.), John Wiley & Sons, Inc., New York, **1983**, 629-644. (Ref 245)

Lerner, N.D. and Collins, B.L., "Symbol Sign Understandability When Visibility Is Poor," *Proceedings of the Human Factors Society - 27th Annual Meeting*, Human Factors Society, Santa Monica, CA, **1983**, 944-946. (Ref 289)

Mader, D.A., "Impact...With Pictographs," *National Safety News*, 128:1, July **1983**, 62-63. (Ref 311)

McClelland, I.L., Simpson, C.T. and Starbuck, A., "An Audible Train Warning for Track Maintenance Personnel," *Applied Ergonomics*, 14:1, March **1983**, 2-10. (Ref 326)

Perry, R.W., "Population Evacuation in Volcanic Eruptions, Floods, and Nuclear Power Plant Accidents: Some Elementary Comparisons," *Journal of Community Psychology*, 11, January **1983**, 36-47. (Ref 381)

Peters, G.A., "Toward Effective Warnings for Automobiles: A Challenge to the Trial Bar," *Trial*, 19:11, **1983**, 114-119. (Ref 382)

Phelan, R. and Ross, K., "Product Warnings, Instructions, and Recalls," Practising Law Institute, **1983**. (Ref 385)

References by Year

Philo, H.M., "New Dimensions in the Tortious Failure to Warn," in *Safety Law, A Legal Reference for the Safety Professional*, Peters, G.A. (Ed.), American Society of Safety Engineers, Park Ridge, **1983**, 95-99. (Ref 389)

Robertson, L.S., "Chapter 5: Control Strategies: Educating and Persuading Individuals," in *Injuries: Causes, Control Strategies and Public Policy*, Insurance Institute for Highway Safety, Lexington, **1983**, 91-115. (Ref 426)

Schucker, R.E., Stokes, R.C., Stewart, M.L. and Henderson, D.P., "The Impact of the Saccharin Warning Label on Sales of Diet Soft Drinks in Supermarkets," *Journal of Public Policy and Marketing*, 2, **1983**, 46-56. (Ref 455)

Schwartz, D.R, dePontbriand, R.J. and Laughery, K.R., "The Impact of Product Hazard Information on Consumer Buying Decisions: A Policy-Capturing Approach," *Proceedings of the Human Factors Society - 27th Annual Meeting*, Human Factors Society, Santa Monica, CA, **1983**, 955-957. (Ref 457)

Schwartz, V.E. and Driver, R.W., "Warnings in the Workplace: The Need for a Synthesis of Law and Communication Theory," *Cincinnati Law Review*, 52, **1983**, 38-83. (Ref 461)

Shinar, D. and Drory, A., "Sign Registration in Daytime and Nighttime Driving," *Human Factors*, 25:1, **1983**, 117-122. (Ref 464)

Wheale, J.L., "Evaluation of an Experimental Central Warning System with a Synthesized Voice Component," *Aviation, Space, and Environmental Medicine*, June **1983**, 517-523. (Ref 549)

Golia, S., "Products Liability—Manufacturers Not Liable for Failure to Warn Where the Danger is Obvious, Well-Known and Avoidable by the Exercise of Common Sense," *Seton Hall Law Review*, 14, **1983-1984**, 821-822. (Ref 188)

Leibman, J.H., "The Manufacturer's Responsibility to Warn Product Users of Unknowable Dangers," *American Business Law Journal*, 21, **1983-1984**, 403-438. (Ref 285)

Powell, L.A., "Products Liability and the First Amendment: The Liability of Publishers for Failure to Warn," *Indiana Law Journal*, 59, **1983-1984**, 503-526. (Ref 400)

Royal, R.A., "Post Sale Warnings: A Review and Analysis Seeking Fair Compensation Under Uniform Law," *Drake Law Review*, 33, **1983-1984**, 817-862. (Ref 440)

1984 References

———, "Products Liability—Problems of Proof," *Association of Trial Lawyers of America Law Reporter*, 27, April **1984**, 104-108. (Ref 008)

Ashman, A., "Manufacturer of Dangerous Drug Need Not Warn Consumer," *American Bar Association Journal*, 70, August **1984**, 145. (Ref 016)

Bates, P., "The Manufacturer's Liability for Failing to Warn of Defective Products," *Advocate's Quarterly*, 5, July **1984**, 253-256. (Ref 023)

References by Year

Boersema, T. and Zwaga, H.J.G., "Measuring the Conspicuity of Routing Signs in Public Environments," *Proceedings of the Human Factors Society - 28th Annual Meeting*, Human Factors Society, Santa Monica, CA, **1984**, 822-823. (Ref 037)

Britain, J.E., "Product Honesty is the Best Policy: A Comparison of Doctors' and Manufacturers' Duty to Disclose Drug Risks and the Importance of Consumer Expectations in Determining Product Defect," *Northwestern University Law Review*, 79:2, **1984**, 342-422. (Ref 048)

Canter, D., "Chapter 13: Way-finding and Signposting: Penance or Prosthesis?" in *Information Design: The Design and Evaluation of Signs and Printed Material*, Easterby, R.S. and Zwaga, H.J.G. (Eds.), John Wiley & Sons, New York, **1984**, 245-264. (Ref 060)

Childers, T.L. and Houston, M.J., "Conditions for a Picture-Superiority Effect on Consumer Memory," *Journal of Consumer Research*, 11, September **1984**, 643-654. (Ref 070)

Denny, D., "Labeling Standard May Re-define Health and Safety Responsibilities," *Occupational Health and Safety*, January **1984**, 30-32. (Ref 105)

Fellner, D.J. and Sulzer-Azaroff, B., "Increasing Industrial Safety Practices and Conditions Through Posted Feedback," *Journal of Safety Research*, 15:1, Spring **1984**, 7-21. (Ref 160)

Funkhouser, G.R., "An Empirical Study of Consumers' Sensitivity to the Wording of Affirmative Disclosure Messages," *Journal of Public Policy and Marketing*, 3, **1984**, 26-37. (Ref 173)

Funston, C.E., "The 'Failure to Warn' Defect in Strict Products Liability: A Paradigmatic Approach to 'State of the Art' Evidence and 'Scientific Knowability'," *Insurance Counsel Journal*, 51, January **1984**, 39-54. (Ref 174)

Gleason, J.P. and Wackerman, J.P., "Manual Dexterity–What Makes Instruction Manuals Usable," *IEEE Transactions on Professional Communication*, 27:2, June **1984**, 59-61. (Ref 181)

Godfrey, S.S. and Laughery, K.R., "The Biasing Effects of Product Familiarity on Consumers' Awareness of Hazard," *Proceedings of the Human Factors Society - 28th Annual Meeting*, Human Factors Society, Santa Monica, CA, **1984**, 483-486. (Ref 183)

Gregory, D.R., "Physician's Duty to Warn," *Legal Aspects of Medical Practice*, 12:4, April **1984**, 6-7. (Ref 195)

Hakiel, S.R. and Easterby, R.S., "Chapter 22: Issues in the Design of Safety Sign Systems," in *Information Design: The Design and Evaluation of Signs and Printed Material*, Easterby, R.S. and Zwaga, H.J.G. (Eds.), John Wiley & Sons, New York, **1984**, 419-448. (Ref 200)

Keating, F.J., "Evidence—Products Liability—Evidence of Manufacturer's Post-Injury Product Warning is Admissible in Strict Liability Action," *University of Detroit Law Review*, 62:1, Fall **1984**, 133-143. (Ref 249)

References by Year

Klare, G.R., "Chapter 25: Readability and Comprehension," in *Information Design: The Design and Evaluation of Signs and Printed Material*, Easterby, R.S. and Zwaga, H.J.G. (Eds.), John Wiley & Sons, New York, **1984**, 479-495. (Ref 260)

Knapp, B.G., "Scaling Military Symbols: A Comparison of Techniques to Derive Associative Meaning," *Proceedings of the Human Factors Society - 28th Annual Meeting*, Human Factors Society, Santa Monica, CA, **1984**, 309-313. (Ref 262)

Lehto, M.R., "Ergonomic Considerations in the Evaluation, Design, and Application of Product Warnings," September Seminar, University of Michigan, **1984**. (Ref 282)

Madden, M.S., "The 'Products' and 'Completed Operations' Exclusions and the Allegation of Failure to Warn," *Journal of Products Liability*, 7:3, **1984**, 205-13. (Ref 310)

Manta, J.G., "Proximate Causation in Failure to Warn Cases: The Plaintiff's Achilles Heel," *For the Defense*, 26, October **1984**, 10-14. (Ref 315)

McCarthy, R.L., Finnegan, J.P., Krumm-Scott, S. and McCarthy, G.E., "Product Information Presentation, User Behavior, and Safety," *Proceedings of the Human Factors Society - 28th Annual Meeting*, Human Factors Society, Santa Monica, CA, **1984**, 81-85. (Ref 324)

Middendorf, L., "Warnings in Automotive Systems," in *Automotive Engineering and Litigation*, 1, Peters, G.A. and Peters, B.J. (Eds.), Garland Publishing, Inc., New York, **1984**, 575-594. (Ref 339)

Miller, J.M. and Lehto, M.R., "Comments on 29 CFR 1910.145," report submitted to the Documents Department of OSHA, June **1984**. (Ref 342)

Morris, L.A. and Olins, N.J., "Utility of Drug Leaflets for Elderly Consumers," *American Journal of Public Health*, 74:2, February **1984**, 157-158. (Ref 357)

Muller, T.E., "Buyer Response to Variations in Product Information Load," *Journal of Applied Psychology*, 69:2, **1984**, 300-306. (Ref 360)

O'Connor, C.J. and Lirtzman, S.I. (Eds.), *Handbook of Chemical Industry Labeling*, Noyes Publications, Park Ridge, NJ, **1984**. (Ref 365)

Orwin, R.G., Schucker, R.E. and Stokes, R.C., "Evaluating the Life Cycle of a Product Warning: Saccharin and Diet Soft Drinks," *Evaluation Review*, 8:6, December **1984**, 801-822. (Ref 372)

Peters, G.A., "Claims Handling and Safety Warnings," *National Underwriter*, 14, April **1984**, 11, 18. (Ref 383)

Peters, G.A., "15 Cardinal Principles to Ensure Effectiveness of Warning System," *Occupational Health and Safety*, May **1984**, 76-79. (Ref 384)

Reynolds, L., "Chapter 10: The Legibility of Printed Scientific and Technical Information," in *Information Design: The Design and Evaluation of Signs and Printed Material*, Easterby, R.S. and Zwaga, H.J.G. (Eds.), John Wiley & Sons, New York, **1984**, 187-209. (Ref 416)

Ricci, E.M., "The Nature and Function of Warnings in Products Liability," *Personal Injury Deskbook*, **1984**, 867-874. (Ref 419)

Robinett, F. and Hughes, A., "Chapter 21: Visual Alerts to Machinery Hazards: A Design Case Study," in *Information Design: The Design and Evaluation of Signs and Printed Material*, Easterby, R.S. and Zwaga, H.J.G. (Eds.), John Wiley & Sons, New York, **1984**, 405-417. (Ref 433)

Ryan, J.J., "Strict Liability and the Tortious Failure to Warn," *Northern Kentucky Law Review*, 11, **1984**, 409-433. (Ref 444)

Schoff, G.H. and Robinson, P.A., *Writing and Designing Operator Manuals*, Wadsworth Inc., Belmont, CA, **1984**. (Ref 451)

Schubert, J.C., "Uncertainty in the Courts—Should Manufacturers Be Held Liable for Failing to Warn of Scientifically Undiscoverable Hazards?" *Journal of Products Liability*, 7:1, **1984**, 107-117. (Ref 454)

Schwartz, V.E., "The Post-Sale Duty to Warn: Two Unfortunate Forks in the Road to a Reasonable Doctrine," *Defense Law Journal*, 33, **1984**, 261-274. (Ref 460)

Smith, C.W., "Post-Sale Warnings: Products That Go 'Bump' in the Night," *Arizona State Law Journal*, **1984**, 719-750. (Ref 485)

Smith, E.E. and Goodman, L., "Understanding Written Instructions: The Role of an Explanatory Schema," *Cognition and Instruction*, 1:4, **1984**, 359-396. (Ref 486)

Smith, S.L., "Chapter 9: Letter Size and Legibility," in *Information Design: The Design and Evaluation of Signs and Printed Material*, Easterby, R.S. and Zwaga, H.J.G. (Eds.), John Wiley & Sons, New York, **1984**, 171-186. (Ref 490)

Stern, K.R., "An Evaluation of Written, Graphics, and Voice Messages in Proceduralized Instructions," *Proceedings of the Human Factors Society - 28th Annual Meeting*, Human Factors Society, Santa Monica, CA, **1984**, 314-318. (Ref 501)

Szlichcinski, K.P., "Chapter 23: Factors Affecting the Comprehension of Pictographic Instructions," in *Information Design: The Design and Evaluation of Signs and Printed Material*, Easterby, R.S. and Zwaga, H.J.G. (Eds.), John Wiley & Sons, New York, **1984**, 171-186. (Ref 508)

Ursic, M., "The Impact of Safety Warnings on Perception and Memory," *Human Factors*, 26:6, December **1984**, 677-682. (Ref 533)

Whitaker, L.A. and Sommer, R., "Interference Between Pictorial Symbols and Arrows in Highway Guidance Signs," *Proceedings of the Human Factors Society - 28th Annual Meeting*, Human Factors Society, Santa Monica, CA, **1984**, 799-802. (Ref 551)

Zwaga, H.J.G. and Easterby, R.S., "Chapter 15: Developing Effective Symbols For Public Information," in *Information Design: The Design and Evaluation of Signs and Printed Material*, Easterby, R.S. and Zwaga, H.J.G. (Eds.), John Wiley & Sons, New York, **1984**, 277-297. (Ref 577)

Barry, D.T. and DeVivo, E.C., "The Evolution of Warnings: The Liberal Trend Toward Absolute Product Liability," *The Forum*, 20, **1984-1985**, 38-58. (Ref 021)

DeMarco, M.M., "Products Liability—Strict Liability in Tort—Manufacturer's Duty to Warn Not Extinguished by User's Actual Knowledge of Danger," *Seton Hall Law Review*, 15, **1984-1985**, 714-716. (Ref 104)

References by Year

Maynard, R.C., "The Duty to Warn: Toxic Tort Litigation," *Cleveland State Law Review*, 33, **1984-1985**, 69-91. (Ref 320)

1985 References

———, "Making Warning Signs Effective," *Best's Safety Directory*, 25th Edition, **1985**, 1198-1199. (Ref 003)

Bresnahan, T.F., "The Hazard Association Value of Safety Signs," *Professional Safety*, 30:7, July **1985**, 26-31. (Ref 046)

Centner, T.J., "OSHA's Hazard Communication Rule and State Right to Know Laws," *Georgia State Bar Journal*, 21:4, May **1985**, 172-174. (Ref 065)

Childers, T.L., Houston, M.J. and Heckler, S.E., "Measurement of Individual Differences in Visual versus Verbal Information Processing," *Journal of Consumer Research*, 12, September **1985**, 125-134. (Ref 071)

Cooter, R.D., "Defective Warnings, Remote Causes, and Bankruptcy: Comment on Schwartz," *The Journal of Legal Studies*, 14:3, December **1985**, 737-750. (Ref 092)

Dobrin, D., "Do Not Grind Armadillo Armor in This Mill," *IEEE Transactions on Professional Communication*, 28:4, December **1985**, 30-37. (Ref 120)

Dodds, T., "On the Lighter Side," *Family Safety & Health*, 44:2, Summer **1985**, 11. (Ref 121)

Duffy, T.M., "Chapter 6: Readability Formulas: What's the Use?" in *Designing Usable Texts*, Duffy, T.M. and Waller, R. (Eds.), Academic Press, Inc., Orlando, **1985**, 113-140. (Ref 137)

Ellington, D., "The Smokeless Tobacco Industry's Failure to Warn," *Journal of Legal Medicine*, 6:4, December **1985**, 489-507. (Ref 149)

Faulk, R.O., "Product Liability and the Chemical Manufacture: Limitations on the Duty to Warn," *Oklahoma Law Review*, 38:2, Summer **1985**, 233-234. (Ref 158)

Fern, F.H. and Sichel, W.M., "Failure to Warn in Drug Cases: Are Punitive Damages Justifiable?" *For the Defense*, 27, June **1985**, 12-20. (Ref 161)

Gallagher, J., "Rise of the Phoenix—Feldman v. Lederle Laboratories: From the Remnants of State of the Art Evidence Comes a New Standard for Design Defect-Failure to Warn Cases," *The University of Toledo Law Review*, 16:4, Summer **1985**, 1053-1098. (Ref 176)

Godfrey, S.S., Rothstein, P.R. and Laughery, K.R., "Warnings: Do They Make a Difference?" *Proceedings of the Human Factors Society - 29th Annual Meeting*, Human Factors Society, Santa Monica, CA, **1985**, 69-673. (Ref 184)

Hodgkinson, G.P. and Crawshaw, C.M., "Hierarchical Task Analysis for Ergonomics Research," *Applied Ergonomics*, 16:4, December **1985**, 289-299. (Ref 217)

Kern, R.P., "Chapter 13: Modeling Users and Their Use of Technical Manuals," in *Designing Usable Texts*, Duffy, T.M. and Waller, R. (Eds.), Academic Press, Inc., Orlando, **1985**, 341-375. (Ref 253)

Kieras, D.E., "The Role of Prior Knowledge in Operating Equipment from Written Instructions," Report No. 19 (FR-85/ONR-19), University of Michigan, Ann Arbor, February **1985**. (Ref 255)

Kieras, D.E. and Dechert, C., "Rules for Comprehensible Technical Prose: A Survey of the Psycholinguistic Literature," Technical Report No. 21 (TR-85/ONR-21), June **1985**.(Ref 256)

Lowry, G.G. and Lowry, R.C., *Handbook of Hazard Communication and OSHA Requirements*, Lewis Publishers, Inc., Chelsea, MI, **1985**. (Ref 302)

Reskin, L.R., "New Duty to Warn for Birth Control Pill Manufacturers," *American Bar Association Journal*, 71, June **1985**, 96. (Ref 412)

Rothstein, P.R., "Designing Warnings to be Read and Remembered," *Proceedings of the Human Factors Society - 29th Annual Meeting*, Human Factors Society, Santa Monica, CA, **1985**, 684-688. (Ref 438)

Schumacher, G.M. and Waller, R., "Chapter 14: Testing Design Alternatives: A Comparison of Procedures," in *Designing Usable Texts*, Duffy, T.M. and Waller, R. (Eds.), Academic Press Inc., Orlando, **1985**. (Ref 456)

Smillie, R.J., "Chapter 10: Design Strategies for Job Performance Aids," in *Designing Usable Text*, Duffy, T.M. and Waller, R. (Eds.), Academic Press Inc., Alexandria, **1985**, 213-242. (Ref 484)

Smith, E.E. and Spoehr, K.T., "Basic Processes and Individual Differences in Understanding and Using Instructions," Bolt, Beranek, and Newman Inc., Cambridge, NTIS No. AD A160 037, October **1985**, 359-396. (Ref 487)

Thomas, D.A., "Tort Law–Products Liability—Warning to Prescribing Physician Regarding Unavoidably Unsafe Drug Held Adequate Under Alabama Extended Manufacturer' Liability Doctrine," *Cumberland Law Review*, 15:2, **1985**, 541-553. (Ref 514)

Thompson, D.E., "The Drug Manufacturer's Duty to Warn—To Whom Does it Extend?" *Florida State University Law Review*, 13:1, Spring **1985**, 135-157. (Ref 517)

Twyman, M., "Chapter 11: Using Pictorial Language: A Discussion of the Dimensions of the Problem," in *Designing Usable Texts*, Duffy, T.M. and Waller, R. (Eds.), Academic Press Inc., Orlando, **1985**. (Ref 526)

Whitaker, L.A., "Is the Airport Symbol Sufficient to Convey Route Information?" *Human Factors*, 27:2, April **1985**, 229-233. (Ref 552)

Wogalter, M.S., Desaulniers, D.R. and Godfrey, S.S., "Perceived Effectiveness of Environmental Warnings," *Proceedings of The Human Factors Society - 29th Annual Meeting*, Human Factors Society, Santa Monica, CA, **1985**, 664-668. (Ref 557)

References by Year

Wogalter, M.S., Fontenelle, G.A. and Laughery, K.R., "Behavioral Effectiveness of Warnings," *Proceedings of the Human Factors Society - 29th Annual Meeting*, Human Factors Society, Santa Monica, CA, **1985**. (Ref 558)

Zuccollo, G. and Liddell, H., "The Elderly and the Medication Label: Doing it Better," *Age and Ageing*, 14:6, **1985**, 371-376. (Ref 576)

Dupuy, R.K., "Torts—in Iowa, Warning of Forseeable Material Risk Must be Specific and is Not Encompassed by a General Description of Greater Peril, Must Extend to the Ultimate User of an Unavoidably Unsafe Product, and If Inadequate, Raises a Rebuttable Presumption of Causation in a Mass Utilization of 'Hardsell' Advertising Context," *Drake Law Review*, 34:4, **1985-1986**, 1091-1108. (Ref 140)

1986 References

———, "Posters, Bulletin Boards and Safety Displays," *National Safety and Health News*, 134:6, December **1986**, 35-42. (Ref 006)

———, "What Makes an Effective Safety Poster?" *National Safety and Health News*, 134:6, December **1986**, 32-34. (Ref 011)

Bass, L. and Rennert, L., "Chapter 10: Warnings," in *Products Liability: Design and Manufacturing Defects*, Shepard's/McGraw-Hill, Colorado Springs, **1986**, 190-222. (Ref 022)

Bettman, J.R., Payne, J.W. and Staelin, R., "Cognitive Considerations in Designing Effective Labels for Presenting Risk Information," *Journal of Public Policy & Marketing*, 5, **1986**, 1-28. (Ref 032)

Childers, T.L., Heckler, S.E. and Houston, M.J., "Memory for the Visual and Verbal Components of Print Advertisements," *Psychology & Marketing*, 3, Fall **1986**, 137-150. (Ref 069)

Cooper, R.M., "Drug Labeling and Products Liability: The Role of the Food and Drug Administration," *Food Drug and Cosmetics Law Journal*, 41, July **1986**, 41:3, 233-240. (Ref 091)

Cox, S.N., "The Drug Manufacturer's Duty to Warn and the Alabama Extended Manufacturer's Liability Doctrine," *Alabama Law Review*, 37:3, Spring **1986**, 681-698. (Ref 094)

Dossick, R., "The State of the Art Defense and Time Rule in Design and Warning Defect Strict Products Liability Cases," *Rutgers Law Review*, 38:3, Spring **1986**, 505-537. (Ref 127)

Downs, C.P., "Duty to Warn and the Sophisticated User Defense in Products Liability Cases," *University of Balitmore Law Review*, 15:2, Winter **1986**, 276-309. (Ref 128)

Duchon, J.C. and Laage, L.W., "The Consideration of Human Factors in the Design of a Backing-Up Warning System," *Proceedings of the Human Factors Society -*

30th Annual Meeting, Human Factors Society, Santa Monica, CA, **1986**, 261-264. (Ref 136)

Eaton, J.T., "The Manufacturer's Duty to Warn Consumers of Possible Side Effects of Prescription Drugs," *Illinois Bar Journal*, 74:8, April **1986**, 376-380. (Ref 146)

Epstein, J.M., "Failure to Warn," *Trial*, 22, April **1986**, 67-68. (Ref 154)

Flannagan, B.P., "Products Liability: The Continued Viability of the Learned Intermediary Rule as it Applies to Product Warnings for Prescription Drugs," *University of Richmond Law Review*, 20:2, Winter **1986**, 405-423. (Ref 168)

Gilhooley, M., "Learned Intermediaries, Prescription Drugs, and Patient Information," *Saint Louis University Law Journal; Health Law Symposium*, 30:3, **1986**, 633-702. (Ref 179)

Gomer, F.E., "Evaluating the Effectiveness of Warnings Under Prevailing Working Conditions," *Proceedings of the Human Factors Society - 30th Annual Meeting*, Human Factors Society, Santa Monica, CA, **1986**, 712-715. (Ref 189)

Hadden, S.G., *Read the Label*, Westview Press, Boulder, CO, **1986**. (Ref 198)

Hall, G., *The Failure to Warn Handbook*, Hanrow Press, Columbia, MD, **1986**. (Ref 201)

Horst, D.P., McCarthy, G.E., Robinson, J.N., McCarthy, R.L. and Krumm-Scott, S., "Safety Information Presentation: Factors Influencing the Potential for Changing Behavior," *Proceedings of the Human Factors Society - 30th Annual Meeting*, Human Factors Society, Santa Monica, CA, **1986**, 111-115. (Ref 224)

Johnson, M.W., Mitch, W.E., Sherwood, J., Lopes, L., Schmitd, A. and Hartley, H., "The Impact of a Drug Information Sheet on the Understanding and Attitude of Patients About Drugs," *Journal of the American Medical Association*, 256:19, November **1986**, 2722-2724. (Ref 234)

Karnes, E.W., Leonard, S.D. and Rachwal, G., "Effects of Benign Experiences on the Perception of Risk," *Proceedings of the Human Factors Society - 30th Annual Meeting*, Human Factors Society, Santa Monica, CA, **1986**, 121-125. (Ref 247)

Killingsworth, M.J. and Eiland, K., "Managing the Production of Technical Manuals: Recent Trends," *IEEE Transactions on Professional Communication*, 29:2, June **1986**, 23-26. (Ref 257)

Kreifeldt, J.C. and Rao, K.V.N., "Fuzzy Sets: An Application to Warnings and Instructions," *Proceedings of the Human Factors Society - 30th Annual Meeting*, Human Factors Society, Santa Monica, CA, **1986**, 1192-1196. (Ref 272)

Kurtz, J., "A Duty to Warn, a Right to Know: Odgers v. Ortho Pharmaceutical Corporation," *Detroit College of Law Review*, 1, **1986**, 163-181. (Ref 275)

Lehto, M.R. and Miller, J.M., *Warnings Volume I: Fundamentals, Design, and Evaluation Methodologies*, Fuller Technical Publications, Ann Arbor, **1986**. (Ref 281)

Leonard, S.D. and Matthews, D., "How Does the Population Interpret Warnings Signals?" *Proceedings of the Human Factors Society - 30th Annual Meeting*, 1, Human Factors Society, Santa Monica, CA, **1986**, 116-120. (Ref 286)

References by Year

Millar, S.A., "Liability Prevention: Corporate Policies and Procedures," *Personnel Administrator*, February **1986**, 47-56. (Ref 340)

Morris, L.A. and Klimberg, R., "A Survey of Aspirin Use and Reye's Syndrome Awareness Among Parents," *American Journal of Public Health*, 76:12, December **1986**, 1422-1424. (Ref 353)

Mrvos, R., Dean, B.S. and Krenzelok, E.P., "An Extensive Review of Commercial Labels...The Good, Bad and Ugly," *Veterinary and Human Toxicology*, 28:1, February **1986**, 67-69. (Ref 359)

Palmateer, L.M., "Products Liability—Manufacturer of Oral Contraceptives Must Directly Warn Ultimate Consumers of Risks Inherent in the Use of Its Product," *Suffolk University Law Review*, 20:1, Spring **1986**, 155-164. (Ref 377)

Purswell, J.L., Schlegel, R.E. and Kejriwal, S.K., "A Prediction Model for Consumer Behavior Regarding Product Safety," *Proceedings of the Human Factors Society - 30th Annual Meeting*, Human Factors Society, Santa Monica, CA, **1986**, 1202-1205. (Ref 403)

Robinson, G.H., "Toward a Methodology for the Design of Warnings," *Proceedings of the Human Factors Society - 30th Annual Meeting*, Human Factors Society, Santa Monica, CA, **1986**, 106-110. (Ref 435)

Strawbridge, J.A., "The Influence of Position, Highlighting, and Imbedding on Warning Effectiveness," *Proceedings of the Human Factors Society - 30th Annual Meeting*, Human Factors Society, Santa Monica, CA, **1986**, 716-720. (Ref 504)

Thompson, M.G., "Failure to Warn as a Superseding Cause in Pennsylvania Products Liability Actions," *Temple Law Quarterly*, 59:1, Spring **1986**, 239-265. (Ref 518)

Tomlinson, G., "Thought for Food: A Study of Written Instructions," *Symbolic Interaction*, 9:2, **1986**, 201-216. (Ref 522)

Ursic, M., "Product Safety Warning: A Legal Review," *Journal of Public Policy & Marketing*, 4, **1986**, 80-90. (Ref 534)

Viscusi, W.K., Magat, W.A. and Huber, J., "Informational Regulation of Consumer Health Risks: An Empirical Evaluation of Hazard Warnings," *Rand Journal of Economics*, 17:3, Fall **1986**, 351-365. (Ref 540)

Wogalter, M.S., Desaulniers, D.R. and Brelsford, J.W., "Perceptions of Consumer Products: Hazardousness and Warning Expectations," *Proceedings of the Human Factors Society - 30th Annual Meeting*, Human Factors Society, Santa Monica, CA, **1986**, 1197-1201. (Ref 556)

1987 References

———, "Products Liability: Deceptive Packaging," *Association of Trial Lawyers of America Law Reporter*, 30, February **1987**, 15-16. (Ref 007)

Bedford, M.S. and Stearns, F.C., "The Technical Writer's Responsibility for Safety," *IEEE Transactions on Professional Communication*, 30:3, September **1987**, 127-132. (Ref 024)

Bukstein, Y., "Drug Products Liability: Duty to Warn," *University of Pittsburgh Law Review*, 49:1, Fall **1987**, 283-306. (Ref 052)

Bussain, J.A., "Using Negligence Analysis to Win 'Strict Liability' Failure to Warn Cases," *For the Defense*, April **1987**, 6-8. (Ref 054)

Clement, D.E., "Human Factors, Instructions and Warnings, and Products Liability," *IEEE Transactions on Professional Communication*, 30:3, September **1987**, 149-155. (Ref 078)

Close, D.B., "The Risk Manager's Role in Preventing Product Liability Claims," *Risk Management*, May **1987**, 36-40. (Ref 079)

Conrads, J.A., " 'Illustruction': Increasing Safety and Reducing Liability Exposure," *IEEE Transactions on Professional Communication*, 30:3, September **1987**, 133-135. (Ref 089)

D'Amico, D., "A Spirited Call to Require Alcohol Manufacturers to Warn of the Dangerous Propensities of Their Products," *Nova Law Review*, 11:4, Summer **1987**, 1611-1629. (Ref 098)

Darden, T.M., "Products Liability in Minnesota: the Manufacturer's Duty to Warn of Forseeable Misuse," *William Mitchell Law Review*, 13:4, **1987**, 1011-1030. (Ref 101)

Desaulniers, D.R., "Layout, Organization, and the Effectiveness of Consumer Product Warnings," *Proceedings of the Human Factors Society - 31st Annual Meeting*, Human Factors Society, Santa Monica, CA, **1987**, 56-60. (Ref 109)

Dixon, P., "The Structure of Mental Plans for Following Directions," *Journal of Experimental Psychology: Learning, Memory, and Cognition*, 13:1, **1987**, 18-26. (Ref 119)

Driver, R.W., "A Communication Model for Determining the Appropriateness of On-Product Warnings," *IEEE Transactions on Professional Communication*, 30:3, September **1987**, 157-163. (Ref 132)

Ewell, T.A., "Preemption of Recovery in Cigarette Litigation: Can Manufacturers Be Sued for Failure to Warn Even Though They Have Complied with Federal Warning Requirements?" *Loyola of Los Angeles Law Review*, 20:3, April **1987**, 867-919. (Ref 157)

Gershonowitz, A., "The Strict Liability Duty to Warn," *Washington and Lee Law Review*, 44:1, Winter **1987**, 71-107. (Ref 178)

Gill, R.T., Barbera, C. and Precht, T., "A Comparative Evaluation of Warning Label Designs," *Proceedings of the Human Factors Society - 31st Annual Meeting*, 1, Human Factors Society, Santa Monica, CA, **1987**, 476-478. (Ref 180)

Henk, W.A. and Helfeldt, J.P., "How to Develop Independence in Following Written Directions," *Journal of Reading*, April **1987**, 602-607. (Ref 208)

References by Year

Houston, M.J., Childers, T.L. and Heckler, S.E., "Picture-Word Consistency and the Elaborative Processing of Advertisements," *Journal of Marketing Research*, 24, November **1987**, 359-369. (Ref 225)

Macro Systems, Inc., *Legislative Background Paper on the Issue of Alcohol Warning Labels*; Prepared for Office of Policy Analysis, National Institute of Alcohol Abuse and Alcoholism, January **1987**. (Ref 308)

Madden, M.S., "The Duty to Warn in Products Liability: Contours and Criticism," *West Virginia Law Review*, 89:2, Winter **1987**, 221-333. (Ref 309)

Manley, M., "Product Liability: You're More Exposed Than You Think," *Harvard Business Review*, September/October **1987**, 28-35. (Ref 313)

Pilfold, D., "Legal Style in Specifications," *IEEE Transactions on Professional Communication*, 30:3, September **1987**, 168-172. (Ref 392)

Purswell, J.L., Krenek, R.F. and Dorris, A.L., "Warning Effectiveness: What Do We Need to Know?" *Proceedings of the Human Factors Society - 31st Annual Meeting*, 2, Human Factors Society, Santa Monica, CA, **1987**, 1116-1120. (Ref 402)

Roy, R.F., "Torts—Damages—Punitive Damages Recoverable in a Strict Products Liability–Failure to Warn Action Based on Exposure to Asbestos," *Rutgers Law Journal*, 18:4, Summer **1987**, 979-993. (Ref 439)

Rubens, P., "The Cartoon and Ethics: Their Role in Technical Information," *IEEE Transactions on Professional Communication*, 30:3, September **1987**, 196-201. (Ref 441)

Strate, L. and Swerdlow, S., "The Maze of the Law: How Technical Writers Can Research and Understand Legal Matters," *IEEE Transactions on Professional Communication*, 30:3, September **1987**, 136-148. (Ref 503)

Terry, N.P., "Stricter Products Liability," *Missouri Law Review*, 52:1, Winter **1987**, 1-56. (Ref 512)

Velotta, C., "Safety Labels: What to Put in Them, How to Write Them and Where to Place Them," *IEEE Transactions on Professional Communication*, 30:3, September **1987**, 121-126. (Ref 538)

Viscusi, W.K. and Magat, W.A., *Learning About Risk, Consumer and Worker Responses to Hazard Information*, Harvard University Press, Cambridge, **1987**. (Ref 539)

Walter, C. and Marsteller, T.F., "Liability for the Dissemination of Defective Information," *IEEE Transactions on Professional Communication*, 30:3, September **1987**, 164-167. (Ref 543)

Wogalter, M.S., Godfrey, S.S., Fontenelle, G.A., Desaulniers, D.R., Rothstein, P.R. and Laughery, K.R., "Effectiveness of Warnings," *Human Factors*, 29:5, October **1987**, 599-612. (Ref 559)

1988 References

Baggett, P. and Ehrenfeucht, A., "Conceptualizing in Assembly Tasks," *Human Factors*, 30:3, June **1988**, 269-284. (Ref 018)

Beltramini, R.F., "Perceived Believability of Warning Label Information Presented in Cigarette Advertising," *Journal of Advertising*, 17:1, **1988**, 26-32. (Ref 027)

Cheickna, S., Drury, C.G. and Babu, A.J.G., "A Human Factors Design Investigation of a Computerized Layout System of Text-Graphic Technical Materials," *Human Factors*, 30:3, June **1988**, 347-358. (Ref 068)

Clark, D.R., "Model for the Analysis, Representation, and Synthesis of Hazard Warning Communication," Ph.D. Dissertation, Department of Industrial and Operations Engineering, University of Michigan, December **1988**. (Ref 075)

Davé, N., "Hazard Communication Standard Guidelines," *Professional Safety*, 33:1, January **1988**, 21-24. (Ref 102)

Desaulniers, D.R. and Gillan, D.J. and Rudisill, M., "The Effects of Format in Computer-Based Procedure Displays," *Proceedings of the Human Factors Society - 32nd Annual Meeting*, Human Factors Society, Santa Monica, CA, **1988**, 445-449. (Ref 110)

deTurck, M.A. and Goldhaber, G.M., "Consumers' Information Processing Objectives and Effects of Product Warnings," *Proceedings of the Human Factors Society - 32nd Annual Meeting*, Human Factors Society, Santa Monica, CA, **1988**, 445-449. (Ref 111)

Donner, K.A. and Brelsford, J.W., "Cuing Hazard Information for Consumer Products," *Proceedings of the Human Factors Society - 32nd Annual Meeting*, Human Factors Society, Santa Monica, CA, **1988**, 532-535. (Ref 122)

Goldhaber, G.M. and deTurck, M.A., "Effectiveness of Warning Signs: Familiarity Effects," Department of Communication, State University of New York, Buffalo, Report 14-260, **1988**. (Ref 185)

Goldhaber, G.M. and deTurck, M.A., "Effects of Consumers' Familiarity with a Product on Attention to and Compliance with Warnings," *Journal of Products Liability*, 11:1, **1988**, 29-37. (Ref 186)

Goldhaber, G.M. and deTurck, M.A., "Effectiveness of Warning Signs: Gender and Familiarity Effects," **1988**, Department of Communication, State University of New York, Buffalo, 14-260. (Ref 187)

Hensely, D.R., "Polio Vaccine Warnings—A Crippling Blow to Individual Autonomy," *Journal of Products Liability*, 11:1, **1988**, 39-54. (Ref 210)

Karnes, E.W., Leonard, D.S. and Newbold, H.C., "Safety Perceptions and Information Sources for ATVs," *Proceedings of the Human Factors Society - 32nd Annual Meeting*, Human Factors Society, Santa Monica, CA, **1988**, 938-942. (Ref 246)

References by Year

Lehto, M.R. and Miller, J.M., "The Effectiveness of Warning Labels," in *Personal Injury Review - 1988*, Denkensohn, B.D. and Fliss, A.A. (Eds.), Matthew Bender & Co., Inc., New York, **1988**, 468-524. (Ref 283)

Lehto, M.R. and Miller, J.M., "The Effectiveness of Warning Labels," *Journal of Products Liability*, 11, **1988**, 225-270. (Ref 284)

Loken, B. and Howard-Pitney, B., "Effectiveness of Cigarette Advertisements on Women: An Experimental Study," *Journal of Applied Psychology*, 73:3, **1988**, 378-382. (Ref 297)

Loring, B.A. and Wiklund, M.E., "Improving Swimming Pool Warning Signs," *Proceedings of the Human Factors Society - 32nd Annual Meeting*, Human Factors Society, Santa Monica, CA, **1988**, 910-914. (Ref 300)

Meister, D., "Development of Subjective Data for Performance Prediction," *Proceedings of the Human Factors Society - 32nd Annual Meeting*, Human Factors Society, Santa Monica, CA, **1988**, 943-947. (Ref 338)

Orr, M. and Hughes, S.T., "Effectiveness of Product Safety Warnings Over Time, and the Generalization of Warning Signs," *Proceedings of the Human Factors Society - 32nd Annual Meeting*, Human Factors Society, Santa Monica, CA, **1988**, 897-900. (Ref 371)

Otsubo, S.M., "A Behavioral Study of Warning Labels for Consumer Products: Perceived Danger and Use of Pictographs," *Proceedings of the Human Factors Society - 32nd Annual Meeting*, Human Factors Society, Santa Monica, CA, **1988**, 536-540. (Ref 374)

Ream, D., "The Defense Can Win on Damages and Duty to Warn," *For the Defense*, January **1988**, 6-11. (Ref 407)

Reitman, P., "Streamlining Your Documentation Using Quick References," *IEEE Transactions on Professional Communication*, 31:2, June **1988**, 75-83. (Ref 409)

Ryan, J.P., "Hazard Analysis Guidelines in Product Design," *Professional Safety*, March **1988**, 17-19. (Ref 445)

Schwartz, D.R., "The Impact of Task Characteristics on Display Format Effects," *Proceedings of the Human Factors Society - 32nd Annual Meeting*, Human Factors Society, Santa Monica, CA, **1988**, 352-356. (Ref 458)

Thompson, D.A., "Fault Logic Analysis of Product Safety," *Proceedings of the Human Factors Society - 32nd Annual Meeting*, Human Factors Society, Santa Monica, CA, **1988**, 527-531. (Ref 516)

Wogalter, M.S., McKenna, N.A. and Allison, S.T., "Warning Compliance: Behavioral Effects of Cost and Consensus," *Proceedings of the Human Factors Society - 32nd Annual Meeting*, Human Factors Society, Santa Monica, CA, **1988**, 901-904. (Ref 560)

Young, S.L. and Wogalter, M.S., "Memory of Instruction Manual Warnings: Effects of Pictorial Icons and Conspicuous Print," *Proceedings of the Human Factors Society - 32nd Annual Meeting*, Human Factors Society, Santa Monica, CA, **1988**, 905-909. (Ref 573)

1989 References

Davis, R.M. and Kendrick, J.S., "The Surgeon General's Warnings in Outdoor Cigarette Advertising: Are They Readable?" *The Journal of the American Medical Association*, 261:1, January **1989**, 90-94. (Ref 103)

Desaulniers, D.R., "Consumer Products Hazards: What Will We Think of Next?" *Proceedings of INTERFACE '89 - The Sixth Symposium on Human Factors and Industrial Design in Consumer Products*, Human Factors Society, Santa Monica, CA, **1989**, 115-120. (Ref 108)

Fischer, P.M., Richards, J.W., Berman, E.J. and Krugman, D.M., "Recall and Eye Tracking Study of Adolescents Viewing Tobacco Advertisements," *The Journal of the American Medical Association*, 251:1, January **1989**, 84-89. (Ref 164)

Laux, L., Mayer, D.L. and Thompson, N.B., "Usefulness of Symbols and Pictorials to Communicate Hazard Information," *Proceedings of INTERFACE '89 - The Sixth Symposium on Human Factors and Industrial Design in Consumer Products*, Human Factors Society, Santa Monica, CA, **1989**, 79-83. (Ref 277)

Laux, L. and Brelsford, J.W., "Locus of Control, Risk Perception, and Precautionary Behavior," *Proceedings of INTERFACE '89 - The Sixth Symposium on Human Factors and Industrial Design in Consumer Products*, Human Factors Society, Santa Monica, CA, **1989**, 121-124. (Ref 278)

Lehto, M.R. and Foley, J., "The Influence of Regulation, Training, and Product Information on Use of Helmets by ATV Operators: A Field Study," *Proceedings of INTERFACE '89 - The Sixth Symposium on Human Factors and Industrial Design in Consumer Products*, Human Factors Society, Santa Monica, CA, **1989**, 107-113. (Ref 280)

Ramsey, J.D., "An Ergonomic Model for Warning Assessment," in *Advances in Industrial Ergonomics and Safety*, 1, Mital, A. (Ed.), Taylor & Francis, London, **1989**, 731-735. (Ref 405)

Young, S.L., Martin, E.G. and Wogalter, M.S., "Gender Differences in Consumer Product Hazard Perceptions," *Proceedings of INTERFACE '89 - The Sixth Symposium on Human Factors and Industrial Design in Consumer Products*, Human Factors Society, Santa Monica, CA, **1989**, 73-78. (Ref 572)

PART V

Key Word Index

Key Word Index

A

Absolute Liability *21, 92, 365*
Abstractness:
    effects on comprehension *45, 55, 56, 57, 58, 66, 219, 232, 236, 281, 288, 307, 337, 468, 508, 509, 510, 526*
Acceptability:
    in risk perception *76, 165, 166, 281, 295, 308, 413, 414, 476, 499*
Accuracy:
    in performance *38, 151, 240, 258, 259, 281, 448, 468, 508, 510, 571*
    in recall *57, 58, 84, 85, 143, 205, 267, 281, 288, 563, 567, 571*
    in recognition/matching *45, 55, 56, 57, 58, 83, 84, 85, 133, 145, 173, 175, 193, 236, 252, 259, 262, 277, 281, 288, 358, 491, 519*
    measures of perception *448, 494, 519, 535*
Active Processing *41, 205, 225, 231, 281, 289, 292, 563*
Actual Behavior *25, 26, 156, 224, 276, 281, 284, 324, 403, 462, 497*
Adequacy of Warnings *73, 96, 112, 125, 171, 201, 243, 283, 284, 339, 361, 362, 363, 365, 370, 378, 383, 384, 389, 437, 446, 451, 461, 502, 524, 545, 546*
Advantages of Nonverbal Symbols *75, 130, 131, 159, 258, 281, 283, 284, 307, 333, 337, 365, 451, 548*
Advertising *79, 220, 385, 422, 502*
Aesthetics:
    effects on conspicuity *80, 266, 281*
Age:
    effects on comprehension *83, 84, 133, 143, 281, 288, 317, 576*
    effects on conspicuity, *281, 474, 537*
Agencies:
    involved in educational/persuasive programs *29, 34, 173, 234, 308, 321, 341, 354, 355, 357, 455*
Agreement with Symbol/Message *27, 224, 276, 281, 283, 284, 330, 381, 432, 575*

Air Traffic Control:
    warning systems *291*
Aircraft:
    description of symbol/message *232, 549*
    visual displays *202, 468*
    warning systems *291, 299, 469, 549*
Aircraft Setting:
    effects on perception *202, 232, 291, 299, 468, 469, 549*
Alcohol:
    effects on conspicuity *211*
    in litigation *98*
Amount of Information:
    effects on symbol/message *29, 359, 539, 540*
    needed in instructions *28, 30, 31, 123, 225, 229, 230, 242, 253, 281, 283, 284, 312, 321, 352, 354, 355, 402, 438, 449, 451, 522, 576*
ANSI *10, 22, 24, 46, 47, 75, 237, 281, 365, 398, 423, 529, 538, 548*
Application Guidelines *24, 27, 73, 74, 96, 132, 171, 224, 281, 282, 283, 284, 323, 461*
Approaching Train:
    warning systems *326*
Asbestos *439*
Association Rankings/Indexes *46, 47, 83, 193, 262, 281, 420, 519, 550*
Assumption of Risk *176, 414*
Attention Measures *164, 281, 374, 406*
ATV (All Terrain Vehicles):
    warning systems *246, 247, 280, 308*
Auditory:
    description of symbol/message *13, 66, 163, 175, 239, 244, 281, 325, 326, 430, 501, 507, 549*
    warning systems *13, 163, 239, 244, 325, 326, 469, 549*
Auditory Coding:
    effects on conspicuity *13, 163, 325, 326, 469, 549*
Auditory Noise:
    effects on conspicuity *13, 281, 325*
    effects on symbol/message *13, 281, 325, 549*

Key Word Index

Auditory Signal Strength:
    effects on conspicuity *239, 325*
Auditory vs. Visual Messages *66, 226, 501, 549*
Automobile Controls *192, 193*
Awakening *239*

B

Back-Up Signals *136*
Bankruptcy *92*
Basic Associations:
    miscellaneous symbol/hazard *62, 64, 236, 287, 358, 397, 471, 475, 491, 550*
Behavior Factors:
    in symbol/message evaluation *25, 26, 156, 184, 185, 187, 189, 206, 207, 224, 276, 281, 283, 284, 290, 308, 319, 324, 334, 371, 374, 380, 403, 429, 430, 432, 442, 450, 457, 496, 497, 504, 507, 539, 540, 541, 549, 555, 558, 575*
Belief in Danger *189, 224, 281, 283, 284, 297, 374, 381, 476, 477, 482, 483*
Biases:
    in risk perception *108, 126, 139, 165, 167, 248, 278, 281, 283, 284, 294, 308, 317, 354, 379, 413, 476, 477, 478, 479, 480, 481, 530, 572*
Biohazard:
    comprehension of symbol/message *2, 10, 14, 57, 87, 117, 252, 277, 333, 404, 523, 529, 548, 563*
    description of symbol/message *2, 10, 14, 57, 87, 117, 252, 277, 333, 365, 404, 523, 529, 548, 563*
    evaluation of labeling systems *83, 84, 85, 252, 277*
Brochures/Flyers:
    in educational/persuasive programs *107, 206, 207, 234, 271, 308, 321, 349, 350, 351, 354, 355, 357, 409, 410*
Buying Behavior *29, 61, 229, 230, 233, 281, 295, 308, 354, 360, 372, 455, 457, 544*

C

Cartoons:
    use in instructions *441, 451*

Case of Text:
    effects on legibility *170, 216, 386, 388, 490, 520, 558*
Caustic Materials
    comprehension of symbol/message *2, 5, 14, 57, 85, 143, 144, 252, 277, 333, 385, 422*
    description of symbol/message *2, 5, 14, 57, 85, 143, 144, 252, 277, 333, 365, 385, 422*
Chemicals:
    in litigation *102, 158, 302, 320, 365*
Children:
    attraction to symbol/message *164, 281, 283, 284, 450*
    comprehension of symbol/message *25*
    in educational/persuasive programs *9, 25, 153, 156, 164, 306, 335, 336, 379, 505, 530, 531*
    perception of symbol/message *25, 95, 164, 185, 187, 205, 317, 450*
Cigarettes:
    in litigation *157*
Cleaning Products/Hazards:
    warning systems *539, 540, 560*
Cleansers:
    evaluation of labeling systems *308, 539, 540*
Cohort Behavior *560*
Color Coding:
    evaluation of *46, 47, 83, 144, 180, 281, 286, 450, 559*
    in labeling and safety signage systems *1, 3, 75, 87, 281, 365, 389, 548*
Color of Background:
    effects on conspicuity *63, 72, 281*
Color of Stimulus:
    effects on conspicuity *12, 17, 36, 63, 72, 151, 183, 281, 369, 387, 406*
Color/Hazard:
    basic associations *46, 47, 83, 144, 281*
Communication Theory:
    application *281, 330, 331, 435, 461, 463*
Comprehension of:
    warning labels *75, 81, 173, 281, 283, 284, 308, 351, 354, 359, 405*
Conduct of Consumer/User:
    in litigation *189, 281, 347, 383, 446, 461, 495*

Key Word Index

Conflicting Objectives *162, 183, 281, 283, 284, 432*
Confusion Matrix:
    measures of comprehension *40, 193, 226, 281*
    measures of perception *216, 226, 281, 535*
Consensual Labeling and Safety Signage:
    miscellaneous *209, 281, 302, 365, 398, 538, 548*
Conspicuity, definition of *37, 281*
Consumer Expectation *48*
Consumer Labeling and Safety Signage:
    29, 61, 75, 84, 87, 143, 145, 198, 212, 213, 251, 281, 287, 288, 308, 329, 333, 354, 359, 365, 370, 398, 451, 523, 534, 538, 548, 561, 576
Consumer Preferences:
    for types of information *61, 281, 295, 351, 354, 356, 459, 521, 547*
    for warning labels *281, 329, 354, 533, 556, 557*
Consumer Setting *37, 80, 124, 182, 183, 239, 246, 266, 307, 374, 450, 452, 500, 502, 502, 537, 574*
Consumer Surveys:
    use in design *27, 143, 145, 314, 329*
Consumers:
    comprehension of symbol/message *57, 81, 84, 143, 144, 145*
    description of symbol/message *84, 113, 129, 130, 131, 143, 145, 192, 193, 239, 240, 251, 252, 287, 288, 337, 346, 365, 433, 450, 475, 491, 508, 511, 523, 548*
    in educational/persuasive programs *29, 34, 35, 61, 95, 106, 107, 153, 173, 183, 233, 290, 306, 308, 321, 335, 349, 354, 355, 356, 357, 372, 381, 455*
    perception of symbol/message *27, 29, 37, 57, 61, 84, 103, 143, 144, 145, 173, 183, 185, 187, 287, 288, 290, 292, 295, 297, 307, 308, 352, 355, 403, 404, 449, 455, 492, 508, 510, 539, 540*
Context, definition of *38, 141, 281*
Contraceptives:
    in litigation *146, 168, 275, 377, 412*
Contrast:
    effects on conspicuity *199, 215, 281, 369, 452, 488*
    effects on legibility *83, 199, 215, 281, 369, 520*
Contrast Sensitivity *281, 474*
Contributory Negligence *176*
Control/Display Elements:
    comprehension of symbol/message *4, 38, 40, 51, 55, 56, 64, 130, 131, 141, 177, 192, 193, 202, 252, 433, 448, 468, 491, 501, 508, 509, 510, 550, 562*
    description of symbol/message *4, 38, 40, 55, 56, 64, 130, 131, 141, 177, 192, 193, 202, 252, 433, 448, 468, 491, 501, 508, 509, 510, 550, 562*
Conveying Action:
    in instructions *38, 55, 118, 232, 316, 451, 467, 486, 487, 526*
    in nonverbal syntax *134, 194, 232, 236, 281, 316, 486, 508, 509, 510, 526, 552, 553*
    in pictographs *55, 232, 236, 277, 287, 316, 475, 508, 509, 526, 552, 553*
Conveying Conditions *38, 118, 232, 316, 451, 467, 576*
Conveying Procedures *18, 28, 38, 93, 111, 118, 194, 232, 252, 254, 316, 396, 451, 467, 484, 486, 501, 508, 515, 526, 576*
Cost of Compliance *560*
CPSA *154, 198, 308, 365, 534*
Credibility of Source *95, 281, 283, 284, 295, 297, 330, 381*
Crosswalk:
    warning systems *425*
Cueing:
    effects on memory *122*
Cultural Factors:
    effects on comprehension *57, 145, 281, 471, 510*

D

Data Processing Setting:
    effects on perception *20, 59, 494*
Deceleration Warning Light *541*
Decision Tables *134, 281, 526, 567, 571*
Deep Processing *281, 368*
Degradation/Noise:
    effects on legibility *113, 281, 288, 416, 417, 520*

Key Word Index

Describing Objects:
  in instructions *18, 30, 451*
  in pictographs *55, 232, 316, 526*
Description/Modeling *134, 141, 177, 194, 269, 281, 316, 508, 509, 525, 526, 567, 571*
Design Consistency:
  in labeling and safety signage systems *75, 87, 130, 131, 144, 145, 198, 200, 241, 281, 288, 365, 548*
Design of:
  educational/persuasive programs *9, 25, 29, 35, 61, 206, 207, 302, 330, 351, 354, 356, 426, 497, 498, 530*
  instructions *18, 19, 24, 28, 30, 31, 32, 39, 43, 49, 67, 75, 78, 89, 93, 97, 115, 118, 119, 120, 203, 204, 218, 223, 232, 242, 255, 260, 281, 283, 284, 327, 351, 354, 356, 451, 467, 508, 509, 510, 565, 566*
  labeling and safety signage systems *29, 32, 42, 50, 60, 73, 74, 75, 78, 90, 96, 130, 131, 144, 171, 200, 272, 281, 302, 303, 307, 318, 327, 330, 339, 348, 354, 365, 368, 384, 385, 389, 405, 421, 422, 433, 436, 437, 452, 461, 462, 473, 475, 495, 502, 510, 548, 562, 577*
Detection Intensity Level *325, 494*
Detection/Perception Measures *246, 281, 464, 506*
Development Cycle:
  in instructions *18, 24, 79, 89, 120, 132, 218, 254, 257, 396, 451*
Development Programs:
  symbol/message design *43, 73, 75, 130, 131, 138, 200, 251, 268, 269, 272, 274, 281, 288, 330, 368, 424, 433, 448, 475, 509, 548, 549, 577*
Disclosure Rule *154*
Discrepancy Between Self-Reports and Actual Behavior *25, 44, 156, 281, 284, 367, 428, 430, 432*
DOT *14, 365, 534*
Drivers:
  in educational/persuasive programs *148, 152, 169, 172, 214, 238, 270, 366, 393, 401, 410, 427, 429, 431, 554*
  perception of symbol/message *12, 15, 17, 26, 58, 82, 99, 116, 133, 150, 151, 163, 175, 190, 192, 199, 211, 215, 221, 228, 231, 258, 259, 314, 369, 380, 406, 429, 430, 432, 453, 464, 474, 488, 519, 552, 553*
Drugs:
  in litigation *16, 52, 94, 146, 161, 168, 176, 179, 195, 275, 377, 412, 517*
Durability:
  effects on legibility *83, 199, 281, 451*
  in litigation *73, 125, 281, 384, 389, 451*
Duty/Failure to Warn *5, 16, 22, 23, 24, 52, 65, 78, 94, 98, 101, 104, 128, 140, 146, 168, 171, 178, 179, 188, 195, 201, 243, 250, 275, 281, 283, 284, 302, 309, 313, 320, 361, 362, 363, 365, 370, 375, 377, 378, 382, 383, 384, 385, 389, 407, 412, 421, 437, 443, 446, 451, 460, 461, 485, 514, 517, 524, 534, 545, 546, 548*

E

EDUCATIONAL/PERSUASIVE PROGRAMS: *see* Topical Index
Effectiveness of:
  educational/persuasive programs *9, 34, 61, 106, 107, 148, 152, 153, 156, 160, 164, 166, 169, 172, 173, 186, 206, 207, 214, 224, 234, 238, 264, 265, 270, 271, 280, 281, 283, 284, 290, 297, 306, 308, 321, 324, 330, 331, 335, 336, 343, 349, 350, 351, 354, 355, 357, 366, 372, 376, 379, 381, 393, 401, 409, 410, 426, 427, 428, 429, 431, 455, 497, 505, 527, 530, 544, 554, 559*
  warning related litigation *189, 224, 239, 279, 281, 282, 283, 284, 324, 375, 384, 419, 524*
Elderly:
  comprehension of symbol/message *81, 143*
  in educational/persuasive programs *357, 576*
  perception of symbol/message *143, 288, 357, 403, 537, 576*
Electrical Hazard:
  comprehension of symbol/message *3, 57, 85, 87, 143, 252, 268, 277, 373, 385, 433, 436, 548*

description of symbol/message *3, 57, 85, 87, 143, 252, 268, 277, 373, 385, 433, 436, 548*
Elemental Breakdowns:
　in pictographs *75, 144, 177, 236, 262, 287, 316, 448, 491, 509, 525, 550, 552, 553*
Elemental Synthesis:
　in pictographs *75, 177, 232, 316, 508, 509, 525, 552, 553*
Emergency Vehicles:
　warning systems *163, 191, 325, 395*
Emergency Warning Systems: general *274, 381*
Error Detection *281, 493*
Evaluation Difficulties:
　in educational/persuasive programs *25, 26, 35, 206, 207, 281, 283, 284, 330, 331, 332, 401, 426*
Exclusionary Rule *8*
Existing/Past Behavior Patterns:
　effects on educational/persuasive programs *148, 224, 247, 281, 284, 330, 401, 554*
　effects on symbol/message *27, 148, 185, 187, 247, 276, 280, 281, 283, 284, 324, 367, 403*
Explosives:
　comprehension of symbol/message *2, 5, 14, 57, 85, 117, 252, 277, 422, 433, 548*
　description of symbol/message *2, 5, 14, 57, 85, 117, 252, 277, 422, 433, 548*
Expressed Value of Avoiding Damages *539, 540*

F

Fall:
　warning systems *42*
False Alarms:
　as function of noise *281, 299*
　effects on behavior *125, 136, 281*
Familiarity with Product:
　in product information and warnings *108, 186, 233, 278, 295, 308, 355, 415*
FDA *29, 61, 91, 100, 161, 198, 212, 308, 354, 365, 372, 455, 517, 534*

Feedback:
　effects on educational/persuasive programs *152, 160, 264, 265, 281*
　effects on symbol/message *152, 160, 264, 265, 281, 334, 442, 575*
Filtering:
　evaluation of *124, 281, 284, 374, 506*
　factors influencing *124, 136, 182, 183, 239, 281, 283, 284, 374*
Fire:
　comprehension of symbol/message *2, 4, 5, 10, 14, 57, 84, 85, 87, 117, 143, 144, 209, 251, 252, 268, 277, 288, 422, 423, 433*
　description of symbol/message *2, 4, 5, 10, 14, 57, 84, 85, 87, 117, 143, 144, 209, 251, 252, 268, 277, 288, 422, 423, 433*
　warning systems *239*
Fire Safety Signs, evaluation of *84, 143, 252, 277, 288*
First Amendment *400*
FMC *3, 22, 75, 281, 433, 451, 538, 548*
Food:
　in litigation *7*
Foreseeability *7, 101, 140, 365*
Forgetting Rate *26, 281, 292*
Formal Teaching/Counseling/Education:
　effects on educational/persuasive programs *9, 148, 153, 172, 206, 207, 214, 265, 281, 284, 302, 306, 343, 349, 366, 393, 401, 427, 505, 527, 531, 554*
Frequency Estimates *126, 139, 165, 167, 281, 294, 301, 413, 476, 478, 479*
Fuzzy Set Membership *272*

G

Gender:
　effects on behavior *185, 187, 539, 540, 572*
Glance Legibility *113, 114, 258, 259, 281, 307, 394, 513, 519*
Government Involvement:
　in product information and warnings *61, 354, 455, 459*

Key Word Index

Governmental Labeling and Signage Systems:
    miscellaneous *61, 75, 173, 212, 213, 281, 354, 365, 398, 502, 534, 548*

H

Habituation *297, 308, 371*
Hand Signals:
    comprehension of symbol/message *133, 337*
    description of symbol/message, *133, 337*
Hazard:
    labeling and safety signage systems *143, 247, 277, 371, 374, 573*
Hazard/Alert:
    comprehension of symbol/message *3, 10, 47, 57, 85, 117, 143, 144, 251, 252, 296, 317, 329, 333, 373, 433, 527, 529, 548*
    description of symbol/message *3, 10, 47, 57, 75, 85, 117, 143, 144, 251, 252, 296, 317, 329, 333, 365, 373, 433, 451, 527, 529, 548*
Hazard Communication Rule *65, 302, 365*
Hazard Prevention/Analysis Models *73, 74, 75, 365, 405, 445, 516*
Hazardous Materials:
    warning systems *14, 143, 183, 237, 302, 333, 365*
Heavy Equipment Controls:
    visual displays *55, 56*
Housewives:
    comprehension of symbol/message *143*
    perception of symbol/message *143, 183, 252, 403*
Human Factors:
    role in litigation *33, 73, 74, 96, 124, 125, 243, 245, 281, 282, 283, 284, 384, 385, 389, 435, 461*

I

Illumination Level:
    effects on legibility *83, 99, 199, 281, 453, 520*
Illustrations:
    abstraction of *43, 134, 219, 232, 269, 316, 441, 451, 510, 526*
    integrating with text *38, 43, 68, 89, 93, 147, 203, 225, 314, 451, 501, 564, 568*
    redundancy with text *38, 89, 225, 451, 526*
    text as diagram *135, 451, 542*
    types of *134, 135, 147, 441, 451, 526*
    use of *19, 38, 43, 69, 70, 89, 93, 97, 134, 135, 147, 203, 204, 218, 219, 232, 254, 269, 441, 451, 501, 508, 515, 526, 567*
Immunizations *140, 146, 168, 514*
Incentives:
    effects on behavior *152, 281, 283, 284, 334*
Indexes/Quick References *411, 451, 542*
Individual Autonomy *149, 210*
Industrial:
    comprehension of symbol/message *55, 56, 57, 83, 85*
    description of symbol/message *13, 46, 47, 55, 56, 57, 75, 83, 85, 129, 130, 131, 252, 276, 287, 288, 311, 337, 346, 365, 373, 433, 491, 523, 536, 548*
    labeling and safety signage systems *1, 2, 3, 4, 10, 42, 46, 47, 57, 75, 83, 85, 105, 117, 183, 198, 237, 252, 302, 311, 354, 365, 373, 398, 451, 529, 534, 536, 548*
Industrial Safety:
    evaluation of signage systems *4, 10, 46, 47, 57, 83, 189, 276*
Industrial Setting:
    effects on perception *13, 83, 136, 216, 222*
Influences of Warning Labels:
    in risk perception *27, 247, 281, 283, 284, 297, 308, 354, 365, 374, 533, 539, 540*
Information Coding *18, 41, 63, 69, 70, 71, 72, 147, 226, 227, 272, 281, 387, 397*
Information Overload:
    effects on memory *281, 283, 284, 438, 449*
    effects on perception *123, 190, 281, 283, 284, 312*
    in information theory *30, 31, 123, 225, 229, 230, 242, 281, 283, 284, 312, 352, 402, 438, 449*
    in instructions *30, 123, 229, 230, 242, 281, 283, 284, 312, 352, 449*

Key Word Index

in product information and warnings *29, 61, 123, 190, 229, 230, 281, 283, 284, 308, 312, 352, 360, 402, 449*
INFORMATION THEORY:
see Topical Index
Informed Choice *281, 283, 284, 293, 383*
Informed Consumer *149, 210*
Ingress/Egress:
comprehension of symbol message *57, 84, 85, 87, 117, 251, 252, 268, 287, 288, 289, 337, 373, 452, 453, 529, 577*
description of symbol/message *57, 84, 85, 87, 117, 251, 252, 268, 287, 288, 289, 337, 373, 452, 453, 529, 577*
evaluation of signage systems *84, 251, 287, 288, 452, 453*
INSTRUCTIONS: see Topical Index
Instructions in Litigation *22, 24, 78, 120, 313, 451, 503, 543*
Instructions vs. Training *484*
Insurance *310*
International Labeling and Signage Systems *87, 241*
Introducing New Systems:
effects of *10, 29, 45, 131, 198, 241, 281, 297, 308, 354, 577*
ISO *46, 84, 145, 281, 398, 548, 577*

J

Jury Instructions *444*
Justification of Text:
effects on legibility *59, 520*

K

Kinesthetic/Tactile:
description of symbol/message *42, 175, 244, 281, 442, 507*

L

LABELING AND SAFETY SIGNAGE SYSTEMS: see Topical Index
Labels:
effects on educational/persuasive programs *27, 29, 61, 164, 173, 180, 183, 247, 280, 281, 302, 308, 353, 354, 372, 455, 528, 576*

Laboratory/Generic Settings:
effects on perception *36, 63, 72, 123, 170, 203, 204, 205, 226, 282, 416, 417, 448, 490, 492, 493, 557*
Layout:
effects on labeling and safety signage systems *109, 359*
Learned Intermediary Rule *16, 140, 146, 168, 179, 195, 320*
Learning Nonverbal Symbols *45, 57, 193, 281*
Legal Style:
in instructions *392, 451*
Legibility Distance *82, 99, 151, 170, 211, 228, 281, 307, 369, 453, 474, 492, 513*
Legibility:
effects on perception *103, 281, 305, 365, 416, 451, 520, 542, 576*
Letters:
effects on educational/persuasive programs *206, 207, 271*
Level of Detail:
effects on warning labels *123, 247, 281, 297, 308, 329, 435, 438, 533, 557*
in product information and warnings *61, 281, 321, 329, 351, 352, 354, 355, 356, 557*
Line Spacing/Width:
effects on legibility *520, 537*
LITIGATION: WARNING RELATED:
see Topical Index
Location:
consumer preferences for *61, 329*
effects on conspicuity *164, 281, 283, 284, 500, 504, 558*
Logic Trees *240, 281, 567, 571*
Loss Prevention Programs *24, 302, 328, 340, 383, 385, 422, 461, 495, 502, 545, 546*
Luminance:
effects on conspicuity *37, 99, 199, 211, 215, 281, 369, 406, 452, 453, 494, 500*

M

Maps *364, 386, 387, 388*
Marketing Defects *281, 437, 446*
Marketplace Honesty Policy *48*
Medical Patients:

Key Word Index

in educational/persuasive programs *234, 308, 349, 350, 351, 353, 354, 357, 576*
Memory Capacity *221, 281*
Memory of:
    symbol/message *25, 26, 57, 58, 111, 164, 173, 185, 187, 205, 221, 231, 233, 281, 292, 297, 308, 351, 355, 371, 415, 438, 449, 464, 504, 533, 563*
    warning labels *111, 185, 187, 281, 283, 284, 297, 351, 354, 374*
Message Complexity:
    effects on comprehension *55, 56, 57, 58, 83, 85, 143, 232, 281, 508, 509*
    verbal vs. nonverbal messages *55, 56, 57, 58, 66, 281, 567, 571*
Message Modality *66, 69, 70, 71, 281*
Message Tone (Voice):
    effects on educational/persuasive programs *26, 156, 173, 238, 281, 283, 284, 290, 297, 308, 351, 547*
    effects on symbol/message *156, 238, 281, 283, 284, 290, 351, 354, 462*
    in instructions *49, 242, 281, 283, 284, 290, 351, 354, 462, 547*
Military:
    comprehension of symbol/message *40*
    description of symbol/message *40, 64, 129, 262, 358*
    perception of symbol/message *40, 64, 262, 358*
Mine Safety:
    evaluation of safety signage systems *83*
Misuse *65, 101, 176, 365*
Motor Vehicle:
    comprehension of symbol/message *45, 55, 56, 58, 133, 150, 175*
    labeling and safety signage systems *14, 45, 58, 82, 151, 228, 258, 259, 263, 319, 365, 394*
Motorcycle:
    warning systems *406*
Moving Vehicle:
    description/comprehension of symbol/message *10, 85, 87, 117, 130, 131, 252*
Multiple Referents:
    in pictograph design *57, 130, 526*
MUPLA (Model Uniform Product Liability Act) *440*

N

Negligence and Warnings *5, 54, 128, 171, 176, 178, 245, 250, 281, 310, 361, 362, 363, 365, 370, 378, 385, 389, 437, 443, 446, 461, 502, 524, 545, 546, 548*
Newspapers:
    effects on educational/persuasive programs *335, 381, 455, 527*
Noise:
    effects on symbol/message *13, 37, 222, 258, 281, 364*

O

Olfactory:
    description of symbol/message *239, 281*
Ordering of Conditions/Actions *18, 41, 49, 118, 316, 487*
Organizing Information:
    in instructions *32, 75, 135, 198, 223, 351, 354, 396, 411, 451, 456, 466, 486, 515, 542*
    in labeling and safety signage systems *32, 75, 109, 198, 354, 359, 365*
OSHA *3, 42, 75, 83, 105, 117, 198, 209, 302, 354, 365, 529, 534*
Overapplication of warnings *121, 123, 132, 224, 243, 245, 281, 283, 284, 323, 324, 435, 461, 524, 545*

P

Page Layout *68, 135, 408, 451, 520, 526, 542*
Parents:
    in educational/persuasive programs *106, 107, 153, 271, 306, 335, 343, 353, 409, 527*
Patent Danger *188, 281, 323, 385, 390, 407, 437, 446*
Patient Package Inserts (PPI):
    effects on educational/persuasive programs *234, 308, 321, 349, 350, 351, 354, 355, 356*
Pedestrians:
    perception of symbol/message *314, 425*

Key Word Index

Perceived Risk *27, 108, 165, 182, 248, 276, 278, 281, 283, 284, 308, 354, 374, 403, 457, 476, 477, 482, 483, 569, 572*
Perceptual Skills *246, 281, 298*
Personal Presentations:
    effects on educational/persuasive programs *61, 106, 107, 264, 271, 297, 343, 409, 410*
Personal Protective Equipment:
    description of symbol/message *57, 85, 117, 252, 277, 373, 385, 423, 433, 548*
    evaluation of safety signage systems *374, 560*
    requirements *57, 85, 117, 252, 277, 373, 385, 423, 433, 548*
    warning systems *374, 539, 540, 560*
Personality Factors:
    effects on perception *298*
Pictographs:
    effects on labeling and safety signage systems *277, 374, 573*
Pilots:
    perception of symbol/message *202, 291, 468, 469, 549*
Point of Operation Guarding:
    comprehension of symbol/message *10, 87, 117, 142, 252, 277, 373, 384, 385, 433, 436, 529, 548*
    description of symbol message *10, 87, 117, 142, 252, 373, 384, 385, 433, 436, 529, 548*
Point-of-sale Duty to Warn *460*
Poison:
    comprehension of symbol/message *2, 5, 14, 85, 130, 131, 143, 144, 209, 252, 277, 296, 333, 422, 450*
    description of symbol/message *2, 5, 14, 85, 130, 131, 143, 144, 209, 252, 277, 296, 333, 365, 422, 450*
Polio Vaccine *210*
Population Stereotypes *18, 42, 45, 82, 144, 281, 287, 491, 553*
Post-injury Warning *8, 249*
Post-sale Warning *440, 460, 486*
Posted Feedback:
    effects on educational/persuasive programs *3, 264, 265, 281*
    evaluation of *3, 264, 265, 281*
Posters:
    effects on educational/persuasive programs *6, 11, 206, 207, 281, 283*
    evaluation of, *6, 11, 206, 207, 281, 283*
Power/Electrical Generator:
    warning systems *573*
Predictive User Response Equations *36, 63, 72, 177, 281, 369, 535*
Preemption *157, 161*
Print Size *103, 286, 359, 559, 573*
Prior Knowledge:
    effects on comprehension *18, 28, 45, 55, 56, 57, 83, 85, 114, 143, 193, 247, 281, 283, 284, 394, 404, 510*
    effects on educational/persuasive programs *183, 233, 247, 281, 283, 284, 402, 497, 498, 505*
    effects on evaluation *26, 27, 183, 185, 187, 281, 284, 295, 374, 403, 477, 483, 497, 498*
    effects on instructions *18, 28, 31, 41, 55, 56, 57, 60, 208, 233, 242, 255, 281, 283, 284, 345, 368, 467, 486, 487*
Probability/Frequency of Presentation:
    effects on conspicuity *37, 136, 281, 283, 284, 291*
Problems in Design:
    of instructions *28, 67, 93, 97, 120, 203, 204, 208, 242, 273, 370, 391, 451, 467, 496, 508, 510, 515, 565, 566, 576*
Process Charts/Sequences *110, 134, 194, 232, 240, 281, 316, 508, 509, 510, 526*
PRODUCT INFORMATION AND WARNINGS: *see* Topical Index
Product Literature:
    in litigation *220, 250, 281, 283, 284, 361, 370, 385*
Production Method:
    in symbol/message design *45, 144, 192, 268, 288, 475, 509*
Prohibition:
    comprehension of symbol/message *46, 57, 84, 85, 113, 117, 236, 288, 337, 373, 423, 475, 501, 523, 548*
    description of symbol/message *46, 57, 75, 84, 85, 113, 117, 236, 288, 337, 373, 423, 475, 501, 523, 548*
Prohibitive Slash *113, 281*
Proximate Cause *102, 315*
Psychosocial Influences:
    effects on educational/persuasive programs *308, 330, 350, 381, 528, 530, 532*

Key Word Index

Public Information:
    comprehension of symbol/message
        57, 62, 145, 159, 241, 251, 252, 268, 269, 288, 307, 337, 577
    description of symbol/message *57, 62, 145, 159, 241, 251, 252, 268, 269, 288, 307, 337, 577*
    evaluation of labeling and safety signage systems *90, 145, 307, 552*
Punitive Damages *161, 439, 486*

R

Radar:
    visual displays *40, 64*
Radiation:
    comprehension of symbol/message *10, 14, 57, 87, 117, 130, 131, 209, 252, 422, 548*
    description of symbol/message *10, 14, 57, 87, 117, 130, 131, 209, 252, 277, 422, 548*
    evaluation of labeling and safety signage systems *252, 277*
Radio/TV:
    effects on educational/persuasive programs *29, 206, 207, 306, 308, 335, 372, 381, 428, 431, 455, 544*
Railroad Crossing:
    evaluation of safety signage systems *82, 151, 228*
Railroad Settings:
    effects on perception *82, 151, 326*
Reaction Time:
    measure of comprehension *64, 150, 151, 190, 193, 281, 394, 448*
    measure of perception *13, 17, 163, 281, 298, 326, 394, 469, 494, 500, 513, 549*
Readability Measures:
    as measure of comprehension *97, 137, 138, 281, 322, 404*
    in instructions *19, 85, 97, 137, 138, 260, 261, 273, 281, 354, 356, 399, 404, 451, 465, 566*
Reading Measures:
    applied to warning labels *124, 183, 185, 187, 281, 282, 283, 284, 324, 354, 374, 403, 438, 504, 563*
Reading of:
    instructions *30, 115, 182, 208, 224, 280, 281, 283, 284, 321, 324, 349, 354, 355, 359, 403, 566, 569, 576*
    warning labels *44, 103, 124, 164, 182, 183, 184, 224, 281, 283, 284, 308, 354, 359, 374, 403, 438, 459, 504, 521, 556, 558, 563, 569*
Reading Speed *59, 344, 537*
Recall, measurement of *25, 26, 57, 58, 111, 205, 221, 231, 281, 283, 284, 292, 297, 304, 355, 371, 374, 438, 449, 464, 533, 563*
Recognition, measurement of *25, 26, 164, 173, 281, 297, 304, 351, 464*
Recognition Time:
    measure of perception *12, 72, 151, 364, 448, 494*
Redundancy:
    consumer preferences for *557*
    effects on conspicuity *12*
    effects on comprehension *38*
    effects on memory *281, 292*
Response Time *38, 240, 281, 469, 508, 552, 567, 571*
Review Papers:
    effects on educational/persuasive programs *2, 29, 61, 207, 281, 283, 284, 308, 354, 372, 426, 428, 462, 544*
Risk Compensation *155, 281, 283, 284*
Risk Coping Style *281, 283, 295, 403, 470*
Risk Hazard Scales *198, 539, 540*
RISK PERCEPTION: see Topical Index
Risk Taking *27, 281, 283, 380, 403*
Roadside Radio Transmitter:
    warning systems *88*
Routing:
    comprehension of symbol/message *10, 37, 60, 84, 85, 87, 90, 130, 131, 241, 251, 252, 268, 373, 529, 552*
    description of symbol/message *7, 37, 60, 84, 85, 87, 90, 130, 131, 241, 251, 252, 268, 373, 529, 552*
    evaluation of safety signage systems *37, 60, 90, 190, 199, 263, 552*
Rumble Strips:
    warning systems *507*

S

Safety Information:
  comprehension of symbol/message *4, 10, 46, 47, 57, 85, 87, 117, 130, 131, 252, 268, 359, 373, 384, 385, 523, 529*
  description of symbol/message *4, 10, 46, 47, 57, 85, 87, 117, 130, 131, 252, 268, 373, 384, 385, 523, 529*
Saws:
  warning systems *374*
School Bus:
  warning systems *395*
Search Time *36, 63, 72, 281, 386, 387, 458*
Seat Belt Nonusers:
  in educational/persuasive programs *152, 409, 429, 431*
Seat Belt Reminder:
  warning systems *116, 429, 430*
Semantic Differential *62, 114, 281, 307, 356*
Separation Between Symbols:
  effects on legibility *15, 20, 520*
Severity Estimates *126, 247, 281, 301, 308, 413, 414, 479*
Shape Coding:
  in labeling and safety signage systems *46, 47, 81, 83, 144, 281, 420*
Shape/Hazard:
  basic associations *46, 47, 81, 83, 144, 281, 420*
Signal Words:
  evaluation of labeling and safety signage systems *47, 281, 283, 284, 450, 504, 533, 558*
  in labeling and safety signage systems *3, 47, 75, 87, 228, 281, 308, 342, 365, 389, 451, 548*
Signal Words/Hazard *47, 281, 342*
Simple Comprehension of:
  verbal symbols *85, 272, 281, 322, 359*
Slip/Fall:
  description of symbol/message *4, 10, 42, 85, 87, 373, 384, 433, 436*
Slow Moving Vehicle *17*
Smokeless Tobacco *149*
Smokers:
  in educational/persuasive programs *9, 27, 103, 297, 354, 527, 528, 530, 531, 532, 544*

Smoking Education Act *27, 103, 157, 164, 297, 308*
Smoking:
  evaluation of labeling systems *27, 103, 164, 297, 308*
Sophisticated User Defense *128, 158*
Source:
  effects on educational/persuasive programs *95, 281, 283, 284, 330, 331, 381*
Sources of Bias:
  in risk perception *86, 108, 165, 167, 248, 278, 281, 294, 295, 301, 308, 317, 351, 354, 476, 478, 479, 480, 481*
State of the Art Defense *127, 174, 176, 285, 454*
Statute of Limitations *98*
Stimulus Size:
  effects on conspicuity *37, 99, 103, 183, 199, 216, 228, 359, 406, 490, 492, 494, 573*
Strict Liability and Warnings *8, 52, 54, 104, 127, 128, 171, 174, 176, 178, 245, 249, 250, 281, 285, 320, 365, 385, 437, 439, 443, 444, 446, 461, 495, 502, 512, 524, 546, 548*
Strokewidth:
  effects on legibility *215, 281, 388, 416, 417, 520*
Structured Text *110, 223, 486, 487*
Students:
  perception of symbol/message *27, 45, 55, 56, 81, 111, 124, 182, 184, 185, 187, 216, 236, 239, 247, 251, 252, 277, 297, 351, 356, 374, 420, 438, 442, 496, 497, 504, 553, 558*
Subjective Ratings *199, 307, 488, 537*
Subsequent Remedial Measures *8, 249*
Summaries:
  effects on memory *408*
  in instructions *267, 408, 411, 486, 542*
Superseding Cause *518*
Supremacy Clause *91*
Swimming Pool:
  evaluation of safety signage systems *185, 187, 300*
  in litigation *186*
  warning systems *185, 187, 300*
Symbol Generation *45, 75, 130, 144, 163, 192, 232, 268, 272, 281, 288, 314,*

Key Word Index

325, 326, 329, 365, 448, 475, 507, 509, 535, 548

Symbol Legend:
   effects on conspicuity *12, 199*

Symbol Shape:
   effects on conspicuity *12, 228*

Symbol Size:
   effects on legibility *99, 103, 216, 228, 281, 388, 490, 492, 494, 520, 537, 576*

Symbol Taxonomies *75, 129, 130, 131, 144, 159, 177, 194, 196, 262, 281, 287, 316, 346, 387, 397, 420, 448, 525, 535*

Symbol Usage, consumer preferences for *329*

SYMBOL/MESSAGE DESCRIPTION:
   see Topical Index

SYMBOL/MESSAGE DESIGN:
   see Topical Index

SYMBOL/MESSAGE EVALUATION:
   see Topical Index

T

Tables and Flowcharts *30, 31, 32, 53, 134, 135, 223, 451, 526, 568, 570*

Task Analysis:
   example applications *90, 116, 217, 274, 281*
   in instructions *18, 38, 43, 67, 115, 232, 253, 255, 281, 456, 467, 484, 486, 487, 564, 566*
   in labeling and safety signage systems *60, 90, 281*
   in symbol/message design *67, 74, 116, 217, 281, 284, 448*

Task Specific Context *38, 115, 119, 175, 281, 469, 500, 567*

Temperature:
   description of symbol/message *239*

Testing:
   procedures *456*
   role in labeling and safety signage systems *365, 421*

Titles, effects of *267, 411, 451, 486, 542*

Traffic:
   comprehension of symbol/message *12, 17, 25, 26, 45, 58, 82, 113, 114, 130, 131, 150, 151, 175, 221, 231, 236, 252, 258, 259, 269, 322, 337, 373, 394, 488, 489, 491, 513, 519, 529, 551, 553, 562*
   description of symbol/message *12, 15, 17, 25, 26, 45, 58, 82, 113, 114, 129, 130, 131, 133, 150, 151, 163, 175, 221, 228, 231, 236, 252, 258, 259, 259, 269, 314, 322, 325, 337, 346, 369, 373, 380, 394, 406, 488, 489, 491, 513, 519, 529, 551, 553, 562*
   evaluation of safety signage systems *12, 26, 45, 58, 99, 113, 114, 150, 151, 175, 190, 211, 221, 228, 231, 236, 258, 259, 314, 319, 322, 380, 394, 424, 464, 474, 489, 506, 513, 519, 553*

Traffic Settings:
   effects on perception *12, 15, 17, 99, 103, 113, 114, 133, 150, 163, 190, 199, 211, 215, 228, 258, 259, 298, 325, 369, 394, 406, 464, 474, 488, 506, 513, 519*

Training:
   effects on comprehension *55, 193, 247, 281, 519*

Translation of Instructions *19, 67, 281, 451, 471*

Typeface/Font:
   effects on legibility *203, 204, 215, 388, 416, 417, 451, 520, 537, 576*

U

Unavoidably Unsafe Product *16, 140, 485, 514*

Underlining/Highlighting:
   in instructions *135, 205, 267, 281, 574*
   effects on conspicuity *205, 504, 574*

Understanding of Instructions *18, 28, 38, 43, 49, 66, 67, 89, 97, 110, 119, 120, 137, 138, 208, 234, 252, 260, 261, 267, 349, 352, 354, 359, 404, 408, 467, 471, 576*

Understanding/Perception Models:
   information theory *41, 119, 141, 142, 147, 196, 197, 235, 255, 272, 281, 283, 284, 304, 316, 318, 368, 467, 472, 473, 486, 487*

User Group:
   verbal vs. nonverbal messages *56, 130, 131, 252, 281, 322, 404*

User Modeling *18, 41, 71, 119, 147, 235, 253, 267, 272, 304, 338, 340, 451, 456, 484, 486, 487, 568*

V

Verbal vs Nonverbal Symbol/Message,
    comprehension of *38, 69, 130, 147, 150, 221, 240, 258, 259, 281, 394, 501, 509, 519, 567, 571*
    comprehension of syntax *134, 232, 240, 281, 509, 526, 542, 567, 571*
    perception of *150, 258, 259, 281, 283, 284, 298, 374, 394, 519, 573*

Viewing Distance:
    effects on legibility *99, 103, 281, 369, 490, 492, 494, 520, 535*

Viewing Time:
    effects on conspicuity *258, 259, 394, 519*

Visual Acuity *211, 228, 281, 369, 452*

Visual Angle:
    effects on conspicuity *215, 281, 490, 492*

Visual Displays:
    miscellaneous *36, 51, 63, 72, 141, 202, 281, 344, 418, 458, 473, 493, 494*

VISUAL DISPLAYS: *see* Topical Index

Visual Noise:
    effects on conspicuity *12, 37, 190, 199, 222, 259, 281, 283, 284, 288, 298, 364, 453, 488*
    in symbol/message *12, 37, 222, 258, 281, 364*

Visual vs. Verbal Symbol/Message:
    effects on memory *69, 70, 225, 374, 415*

W

WARNING LABELS: *see* Topical Index

Warning Process Models:
    information theory *112, 132, 279, 281, 282, 283, 284, 330, 354, 403, 405, 434, 435*

WARNING SYSTEMS: *see* Topical Index

Warnings:
    as noise *281, 549*
    evaluating effects on behavior *124, 136, 164, 184, 185, 187, 189, 276, 279, 280, 281, 283, 284, 308, 324, 334, 353, 354, 359, 372, 374, 380, 381, 403, 442, 450, 462, 470, 504, 539, 540, 541, 558, 560, 574*

Warranties/Disclaimers *24, 79, 176, 245, 281, 328, 361, 385, 389, 443, 545*

Workers:
    in educational/persuasive programs *160, 302, 354*
    perception of symbol/message *13, 46, 47, 57, 83, 85, 189, 240, 276, 334, 371, 556*

Workload/Task:
    effects on conspicuity *246, 281, 283, 284, 291, 458, 464, 500, 506, 513, 549*

Writing Instruction Guidelines, teaching of *77, 208, 447, 451, 564*

Writing Instructions, rules for *19, 49, 67, 93, 118, 138, 203, 204, 242, 256, 451, 466, 486, 564, 565, 566, 567, 568*

Appendix A

Appendix A

References From Proceedings of the Human Factors Society 33rd Annual Meeting, Denver, October 16-20, 1989

Shortly before this volume went to press, the authors attended the Human Factors Society's Annual Meeting in Denver. During this meeting, as in years past, a number of warnings-related papers were presented. The presenters were kind to recognize our contributions, and we would like to reciprocally recognize them for their recent contributions. The warnings issues were addressed within lecture sessions and panel discussions sponsored by three of the technical groups within the Human Factors Society: Consumer Products, Safety, and Forensics. We give credit to the following session organizers and session chairpersons who accepted warnings-related papers. They were: for the *Consumer Products Technical Group*: Jefferson M. Koonce; for the *Forensics Professional Technical Group* : Lorna K. Middendorf; and for the *Safety Technical Group*: David M. DeJoy. Notable session Chairs included: Daryl Jean Gardner-Bonneau, Valerie J. Gawron, Peter A. Hancock, Thomas H. Rockwell, Nicholas Simonelli, and Michael S. Wogalter. Listed below are the seventeen warnings and instructions papers presented at these sessions. Unfortunately, we could not include them in the integrated format of this volume.

Ayres, T.J., Gross, M.M., Wood, C.T., Horst, D.P., Beyer, R.R. and Robinson, J.N., "What Is a Warning and When Will It Work?" *Proceedings of the Human Factors Society - 33rd Annual Meeting*, Human Factors Society, Santa Monica, CA, 1989, 426-430.

Boersma, T. and Zwaga, H.J.G., "Selecting Comprehensible Warning Symbols for Swimming Pool Slides," *Proceedings of the Human Factors Society - 33rd Annual Meeting*, Human Factors Society, Santa Monica, CA, 1989, 994-997.

Brown, T.J., Salvador, A.P., O'Hearn, B.E. and Anderson, J.E., "Sentence Orientation and Semantic Processing Speed: Applicability to Label Design," *Proceedings of the Human Factors Society - 33rd Annual Meeting*, Human Factors Society, Santa Monica, CA, 1989, 470-473.

DeJoy, D.M., "Consumer Product Warnings: Review and Analysis of Effectiveness Research," *Proceedings of the Human Factors Society - 33rd Annual Meeting*, Human Factors Society, Santa Monica, CA, 1989, 936-939.

Gardner-Bonneau, D.J., Kabbara, F., Hwang, M., Bean, H., Gantt, M., Hartshorn, K., Howell, J. and Spence, R., "Cigarette Warnings: Recall of Content as a Function of Gender, Message Context, Smoking Habits and Time," *Proceedings of the Human Factors Society - 33rd Annual Meeting*, Human Factors Society, Santa Monica, CA, 1989, 928-930.

Goldhaber, G.M. and deTurck, M.A., "A Developmental Analysis of Warning Signs: The Case of Familiarity and Gender," *Proceedings of the Human Factors Society - 33rd Annual Meeting*, Human Factors Society, Santa Monica, CA, 1989, 1019-1023.

Haga, S., Watanabe, K. and Kusukami, K., "A New Warning System for Protected Level Crossings," *Proceedings of the Human Factors Society - 33rd Annual Meeting*, Human Factors Society, Santa Monica, CA, 1989, 975-978.

Appendix A

Harris, J.E. and Wiklund, M.E., "Consumer Acceptance of Threatening Warnings in the Residential Environment," *Proceedings of the Human Factors Society - 33rd Annual Meeting*, Human Factors Society, Santa Monica, CA, 1989, 989-993.

Laughery, K.R. and Stanush, J.A., "Effects of Warning Explicitness on Product Perceptions," *Proceedings of the Human Factors Society - 33rd Annual Meeting*, Human Factors Society, Santa Monica, CA, 1989, 431-435.

Leonard, D.C., Ponsi, K.A., Silver, N.C. and Wogalter, M.S., "Pest-Control Products: Reading Warnings and Purchasing Intentions," *Proceedings of the Human Factors Society - 33rd Annual Meeting*, Human Factors Society, Santa Monica, CA, 1989, 436-440.

Leonard, S.D., Hill, G.W. and Karnes, E.W., "Risk Perception and Use of Warnings," *Proceedings of the Human Factors Society - 33rd Annual Meeting*, Human Factors Society, Santa Monica, CA, 1989, 550-554.

Martin, E.G. and Wogalter, M.S., "Risk Perception and Precautionary Intent for Common Consumer Products," *Proceedings of the Human Factors Society - 33rd Annual Meeting*, Human Factors Society, Santa Monica, CA, 1989, 931-935.

Mayer, D.L. and Laux, L.F., "Recognizability and Effectiveness of Warning Symbols and Pictorials," *Proceedings of the Human Factors Society - 33rd Annual Meeting*, Human Factors Society, Santa Monica, CA, 1989, 984-988.

Silver, N.C. and Wogalter, M.S., "Broadening the Range of Signal Words," *Proceedings of the Human Factors Society - 33rd Annual Meeting*, Human Factors Society, Santa Monica, CA, 1989, 555-559.

Vaubel, K.P., Donner, K.A., Parker, S.L., Laux, L.F. and Laughery, K.R., "Public Knowledge and Understanding of Overhead Electrical Power Lines: A Second Look," *Proceedings of the Human Factors Society - 33rd Annual Meeting*, Human Factors Society, Santa Monica, CA, 1989, 560-563.

Zwaga, H.J.G., "Comprehensibility Estimates of Public Information Symbols: Their Validity and Use," *Proceedings of the Human Factors Society - 33rd Annual Meeting*, Human Factors Society, Santa Monica, CA, 1989, 979-983.

Zwahlen, H.T., Yu J., Xiong S., Li Q. and Rice, J.W., "Night Time Shape Recognition of Reflectorized Warning Plates as a Function of Full Reflectorization, Borders Only Reflectorization and Target Brightness," *Proceedings of the Human Factors Society - 33rd Annual Meeting*, Human Factors Society, Santa Monica, CA, 1989, 970-974.

Appendix B

Appendix B

Warnings: Volume 1: Fundamentals, Design, and Evaluation Methodologies

This volume was the first in a series, focusing on warning labels and other product- and situation-related characteristics intended to serve warning purposes. The development of the series was inspired by the increased importance of warning-related issues to both human factors and product design engineering, and by the limited degree to which these issues have been formally addressed within any discipline. During warnings related litigation, this lack of formal structuring has resulted in a large number of unsupported allegations by those who claimed expertise in the area. As a consequence, judicial decisions were and still are often based only on a "common sense" rationale resulting in some alarmingly inconsistent decisions. Subsequently, the warning precedence was established by both the engineering and legal professions with little underlying scientific foundation. In their defense, resource material, which reveals the level of complexity involved in the warnings issues had not previously been available.

Volume I was developed through a significant synthesis of different approaches used in human factors and safety engineering, along with the several new methodologies. Those methodologies structure general human factors problems in a way that provides the scientific foundation needed during the evaluation of either the effectiveness of warnings or the desirability of specific designs.

The approach we took in Volume I was conceptually simple. It consisted of breaking down the global "warnings issue" into smaller, well-defined, problems. Solutions to these smaller problems could then potentially be developed by applying existing knowledge or by performing a reasonable amount of research. To describe and organize these sub-problems, we relied heavily on established areas of psychology, including communications theory, sensory psychology, behavioral psychology, and human information processing. Ideas from the newer areas of artificial intelligence and knowledge engineering were also utilized to structure these problems.

CONTENTS

PREFACE	vii
LIST OF TABLES	xiii
LIST OF FIGURES	xvi
SECTION I. WARNINGS:THEIR COMPLEXITY AND RELATIONSHIP TO INFORMATION PROCESSING	1
Chapter 1. Important issues Related to Warnings	5
The Shortcomings of Common Sense	5
Contemporary Factions	6
Scope of Book	8
Chapter 2. Definitions of Modeling Techniques	12

Appendix

Definitions of the Term Warning	13
The Need for Appropriate Modeling	17
Describing the Structural Components	17
Describing the Procedural Components	26
Modeling the Procedural Components	30
Organizing the Structural and Procedural Components	41
Summary	45

SECTION II. THE EFFECTIVENESS OF WARNINGS 47

Chapter 3. Method for Evaluation of Effectiveness	49
The Need for Valid Measures	51
A Warning Tree Model	61
Chapter 4. The Effectiveness of Warnings in Eliciting Attention	58
The Exposure to Warnings	59
The Filtering of Warnings	61
Chapter 5. The Effectiveness of Warnings in Eliciting Comprehension	72
The Need for Active Processing	73
Agreement with Warning Messages	74
The Meaningfulness of Warning Messages	74
Conclusions	82
Chapter 6. The Effects of Warnings on Memory, Decisions and Responses	88
Eliciting Storage and Retrieval	189
Modifying Decisions	94
Modifying Actual Responses	98
Modifying the Adequacy of the Response	10

SECTION III. TYPES OF WARNINGS, THEIR APPLICATION AND DESIGN 109

Chapter 7. Classifying Warnings and Their Applications	112
Taxonomy #1: Warnings Types	113
Taxonomy #2: Warnings Scenarios	122
Summary	128
Chapter 8. Selecting Effective Applications of Warnings	132
The Legal Criteria	133
A Warning-Related Risk Assessment Taxonomy	136
Risk and Effectiveness Based Selection	141
Chapter 9. Guidelines for Warning Design	148
Standard Sources	149
Systems for Sign or Label Design	150
Conspicuity Related Design Guidelines	156
Life Cycle Considerations	166
Conclusions	166
Chapter 10. The Design Process	170
The Design Stages	171
Stage 1 - Specify the General Information Flow	172
Stage 2 - Isolate the Critical Information Transfers	177
Stage 3 - Describe the Critical Information Transfers	178

Appendix B

    Stage 4 - Evaluate the Critical Information Transfers 181
    Summary 190

SECTION IV. ADVANCED TOPICS 193

Chapter 11. A Knowledge Based Approach to Human Performance 196
    The Production System Model 197
    The General Warning Tree Information Processing Model 207
    Summary 224

Chapter 12. A Knowledge Based Approach to Task Analysis 228
    Modeling Tasks and the Flow of Information 230
    A General Knowledge Based Modeling Approach 231
    Modeling the Human, Product, and Environment 245
    Modeling the Task 255
    Modeling the Message 263
    Summary 264

REFERENCES 269

ADDENDUM REFERENCES 287